The Facts On File

DICTIONARY
of
EVOLUTIONARY
BIOLOGY

The Facts On File

DICTIONARY
of
EVOLUTIONARY
BIOLOGY

Edited by
Elizabeth Owen
Eve Daintith

Facts On File, Inc.

The Facts On File Dictionary of Evolutionary Biology

Facts On File, Inc.
132 West 31st Street
New York NY 10001

Library of Congress Cataloging-in-Publication Data

The Facts on File dictionary of evolutionary biology / edited by Elizabeth Owen, Eve Daintith.
        p. cm.
    Includes bibliographical references.
    ISBN 0-8160-4924-6
        1. Evolution (Biology)—Dictionaries. I. Title: Dictionary of evolutionary biology. II. Owen, Elizabeth, 1971- III. Daintith, Eve. IV. Facts on File, Inc.

QH360.2.F27 2004
576.8'03—dc22   2003061761

Facts On File books are available at special discounts when purchased in bulk quantities for businesses, associations, institutions, or sales promotions. Please call our Special Sales Department in New York at (212) 967-8800 or (800) 322-8755.

You can find Facts On File on the World Wide Web at
http://www.factsonfile.com

Compiled and typeset by Market House Books Ltd, Aylesbury, UK

Printed in the United States of America

    MP   10 9 8 7 6 5 4 3 2 1

This book is printed on acid-free paper

CONTENTS

PREFACE

This dictionary is one of a series covering the terminology and concepts used in important branches of science. *The Facts On File Dictionary of Evolutionary Biology* is planned as an additional source of information for students taking Advanced Placement (AP) Science courses in high schools. It will also be helpful to older students taking introductory college courses.

This volume covers the topics important for an understanding of evolutionary theory, including classification, paleontology, genetics, molecular biology, and some geology. The definitions are intended to be clear and informative and, where possible, we have provided helpful diagrams and examples. The book also has a selection of short biographical entries for people who have made important contributions to the field. There are appendixes showing the classification of animals and plants. We have also added a short list of useful webpages and an informative bibliography.

The book will be a helpful additional source of information for anyone studying the AP Biology course, especially the sections of the course covering Heredity and Evolution. However, we have not restricted the content to this syllabus. Evolutionary theory is an important, and sometimes controversial, area of modern science and we have tried to cover it in an interesting and informative way.

ACKNOWLEDGMENTS

Consultant editor

Robert Hine B.Sc.

A

A *See* adenine; genotypic effect.

ABC floral model In evolutionary development, a theory describing the HOMEOTIC GENES that bring about the arrangement of parts of a flower in whorls (circles) rather than along an axis. Working on *Arabidopsis* (a small annual plant of the Brassicaceae (mustard) family) it has been discovered that three classes of genes are involved, denoted A, B, and C. A genes alone are responsible for the outer whorl of leaflike sepals; A and B genes together regulate the development of the next whorl of petals; B and C genes control the development of the stamens; C genes alone determine the development of the inner whorl of carpels. What is most significant is that the gene *leafy* – a 'higher control' gene – regulates the ABC system showing that the flower parts are based on a leaf archetype or basic plan. *See also* recapitulation.

abiogenesis The development of living from nonliving matter, as in the ORIGIN OF LIFE.

absolute dating *See* dating techniques.

Acanthocephala *See* Rotifera.

Acasta rocks The oldest rocks known, dated at just over 4000 million years old, found in NW Canada. *See* Earth, age of.

acclimatization A method by which organisms adapt and survive temporary, but recurring, stressful environments in which prior exposure to a particular stress leads to the organism being better able to cope the next time it is encountered. The first exposure results in the expression of proteins, e.g. heat shock proteins, that help the organism cope and thereafter these proteins are only expressed when the stress is encountered. Expressing such proteins all the time would be a drain on resources so it is an advantage to be able to express them only when they are needed.

acentric Denoting a chromosome or fragment of a chromosome that lacks a centromere.

Acheulian tools Stone Age tools, especially hand axes. They have been excavated along with early hominid remains, for example, those of *Homo erectus* at Olduvai Gorge in East Africa and also with *Homo ergaster*. The use of these tools in human evolution is not thought to be as important as it once was as it has been discovered that chimpanzees have also used tools extensively. *See also* Oldowan industrial complex; Mousterian tools; Upper Paleolithic tools.

acoelomate An animal without a COELOM, i.e. there is no cavity between the digestive tract and the body wall. Examples are the PLATYHELMINTHES and the nemertines (ribbon worms).

acorn worm *See* Hemichordata.

acquired characteristic (acquired trait) A phenotypic change in the structure or function of an organ or system during the life of an organism, brought about by the use or disuse of that organ or system or by environmental influences. Most are the result of disease, injury, starvation, or senescence. Acquired characteristics are not genetically based and cannot be inherited.

1

For example, sportsmen may develop strong muscles, and plants growing near coasts show adaptations to the drying effects of sea air. *See also* Lamarckism.

acraniate Any chordate animal with a NOTOCHORD and lacking a brain and skull. Acraniates include the UROCHORDATA and the CEPHALOCHORDATA.

actinomorphy *See* radial symmetry.

actinopterygians *See* Osteichthyes.

active site *See* enzyme.

adapiformes *See* Primates; prosimians.

adaptation A property or trait (e.g. physiological, structural, or behavioral) that contributes to reproductive success or FITNESS. The genes favored by SELECTION are passed on to successive generations. Most organisms are not perfectly adapted because of developmental, genetic, and historical *constraints*, TRADE-OFFS between competing demands, and because it takes time for better adaptations to develop. Organisms that have become highly adapted to one environment are then often not so adaptable as less specialized organisms and are at a disadvantage in a changing environment (adaptation versus adaptability). *See* adaptive evolution; natural selection.

adaptationist program The investigation of the adaptive value of a character.

adaptive evolution Evolutionary change that is not random, but in which an organism becomes increasingly adapted to its environment. Adaptive evolution shows a strong correlation between reproductive success and heritable variation and is driven by natural selection. *Compare* neutral evolution.

adaptive landscape *See* adaptive topography.

adaptive logic A behavior in a population that favors an increase in the number of offspring produced. Even if such a behavior is only partly genetically determined, it will spread throughout the population. If circumstances change so that it no longer provides any survival or reproductive advantage, the behavior will continue to be exhibited. It will cease only if it becomes positively disadvantageous in the changed environment.

adaptive radiation The gradual formation through evolution of a number of different varieties or species from a common ancestor, each adapted to a different ECOLOGICAL NICHE. When a species develops a new characteristic, it may be able to inhabit a different niche. For example, when reptiles developed feathers and evolved into birds, they were able to inhabit an enormous new niche. There are, for example, over twice the number of bird species compared to those of mammals. There are also several million species of insects. A classic example of adaptive radiation is illustrated by the finches of the GALÁPAGOS ISLANDS investigated by Charles DARWIN (known as DARWIN'S FINCHES). There are 14 species. Darwin suggested that the finches inhabiting the northernmost islands were geographically isolated from those on the other islands and evolved independently. The common ancestor is thought to be a seed-eating ground finch, which evolved into two groups: ground finches and tree finches. The ground finches evolved into six modern seed-eating species and the tree finches evolved into eight modern species – one seed-eating and the other seven insect-eating.

adaptive topography (adaptive landscape; fitness surface) A graph of the mean fitness of a population against gene (or genotype) frequency. Peaks correspond to genotypic frequencies at which the average fitness is high; valleys correspond to genotypic frequencies at which the average fitness is low.

addition *See* gene mutation.

additive genetic effect *See* genotypic effect.

additive tree A phylogenetic tree in which the DISTANCE between any two points is the sum of the lengths of the branches along the path connecting two points. *See* phylogeny. *See also* neighbor joining.

sine found in AMP, ADP, and ATP. Adenine has a purine ring structure.

NH₂

Adenine

Adenosine

adenine Symbol: A. A nitrogenous base found in DNA and RNA. It is also a constituent of certain coenzymes, e.g. NAD and FAD, and when combined with the sugar ribose it forms the nucleoside adeno-

adenosine (adenine nucleoside) A nucleoside formed from adenine linked to D-ribose with a β-glycosidic bond. Adenosine triphosphate (ATP) is a nucleotide derived from adenosine.

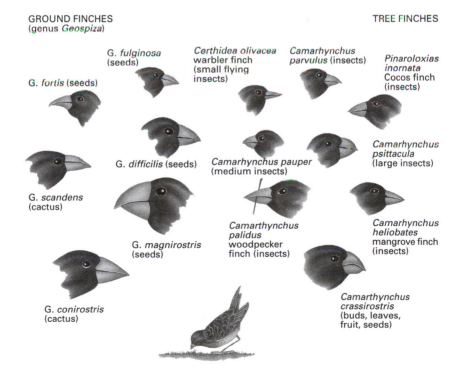

Adaptive radiation: illustrated by Darwin's finches

Aegyptopithecus *See* Primates.

aerobe An organism that can live and grow only in the presence of free oxygen, i.e. it respires aerobically. *See* respiration. *Compare* anaerobe.

aerobic respiration *See* respiration.

African Eve theory *See Australopithecus afarensis*; mitochondrial Eve; out of Africa theory.

agamospermy *See* apomixis.

Agassiz, Jean Louis Rodolphe (1807–73) Swiss–American biologist. His main work was on fish, publishing *Fishes of Brazil*, 1929, and following this with *History of the Freshwater Fishes of Central Europe* (1839–42), and an extensive pioneering work on fossil fishes, which eventually ran to five volumes: *Recherches sur les poissons fossiles* (1833–43; Researches on Fossil Fishes). These works established his reputation as the greatest ichthyologist of his day. Agassiz's best-known discovery, however, was that of the ICE AGES. Extensive field studies in the Swiss Alps, and later in America and Britain, led him to postulate glacier movements and the former advance and retreat of ice sheets; his findings were published in *Etudes sur les glaciers* (1840; Studies on Glaciers).

In 1847 he was appointed professor of zoology and geology at Harvard and his subsequent teachings emphasized the importance of first-hand investigation of natural phenomena, an approach that influenced academic study in America. His embryological work led to a recognition of the similarity between the developing stages of living animals and complete but more primitive species in the fossil record. Agassiz did not, however, share Darwin's view of a gradual evolution of species, but, like CUVIER, considered that there had been repeated separate creations and extinctions of species. His major work *Contributions to the Natural History of the United States* (4 vols., 1857–62) remained uncompleted at his death.

age *See* geological time scale.

Agnatha The superclass containing the earliest and most primitive vertebrates, characterized by the absence of jaws. The only living class is the CYCLOSTOMATA, which includes lampreys (e.g. *Petromyzon*) and hagfish (e.g. *Myxine*) – aquatic fishlike animals lacking the paired fins typical of true fishes. There are also several extinct Paleozoic groups (ostracoderms), whose members had a heavy armor of bony plates and scales. As these ancient Agnatha declined, the PLACODERMI, OSTEICHTHYES, and CHONDRICHTHYES attained greater importance. *Compare* Gnathostomata.

Agrobacterium A genus of soil bacteria, the species *A. tumefaciens* being the causative agent of crown gall, a type of tumor in plants. A segment of DNA (transferred DNA, T-DNA) from a plasmid in the bacterium is transferred into the host DNA and induces tumor formation. Since the plasmid is capable of independent replication in host cells of many dicotyledonous plants, it has been used as a cloning vector in GENETIC ENGINEERING. Once the desired segment of DNA, for example a gene, has been spliced into the T-DNA, the plasmid can be introduced into certain plant cultures and entire plants with the desired characteristic can be produced. Unfortunately, the bacterium does not infect monocotyledonous plants, which include important cereal crops. *See also* artificial selection; gene cloning.

AI *See* artificial insemination.

AIDS (acquired immune deficiency syndrome) A disease that destroys most of the immune system in humans by attacking the *helper T lymphocytes* (T cells). It is caused by a complex RETROVIRUS named HIV-1 (human immunodeficiency virus type 1). Initially after infection, there is a normal immune response, but the virus remains hidden in the helper T lymphocytes and progressively destroys them.

The virus consists of RNA genes (which code for its own proteins) inside a lipid coat. One of its proteins is an enzyme called REVERSE TRANSCRIPTASE. This reverses TRANSCRIPTION allowing a DNA copy of the RNA genes to be made. This copy is then spliced (*see* splicing) into the DNA of the helper T lymphocytes, so causing the latter to make thousands of new HIV viruses, and killing the helper cells in the process. The helper T lymphocytes stimulate other components of the immune system, e.g. the B lymphocytes to divide to produce antibody cells and the phagocytes (white blood cells) to engulf and destroy bacteria. Thus, affecting and destroying the helper T lymphocytes has extremely serious effects on the immune system.

Even worse for the patient, the viral genes code for a glycoprotein known as gp120 in the viral coat, which targets a molecule termed CD4 on the surface membrane of the helper T lymphocytes (also found on the membranes of B lymphocytes and phagocytes). gp120 binds with CD4 enabling the virus to become attached to its target cell and then to fuse with it and invade.

The success of HIV is, paradoxically, that it is poor at making exact copies of itself and there is a high MUTATION rate – a million times higher than that of its human host. This results in many mutants surviving by natural selection (although most will not), which means that one of the standard treatments with the drug AZT (azidothymidine) will prove to be less effective in time. The rate of its evolution could outstrip the race for a cure. HIV-2 is responsible for the illness in the heterosexual population. It has been suggested that the AIDS virus originated in African green monkeys, a result of a mutation that enabled it to thrive in humans. *See also* immune response.

air bladder   *See* swim bladder.

AL   *See* artificial life.

Albertus Magnus, St (1193–1280) German scholastic philosopher who also wrote extensively on physics and natural history. He believed that fossils were attempts by a life force (he called it *virtus for-*

mativa) to manufacture living organisms from rocks.

algae   A large mixed group of photosynthesizing organisms, now usually placed in the kingdom Protoctista, although there continues to be much controversy among taxonomists. They often resemble plants and are found mainly in marine or freshwater habitats, although some algae are terrestrial. Algae differ from plants in lacking any real differentiation of leaves, stems, and roots, and in not having an embryo stage in their life cycle. They can be unicellular (e.g. *Chlamydomonas*), colonial (e.g. *Volvox*), filamentous (e.g. *Spirogyra*), or thalloid (e.g. *Fucus*). All algae contain chlorophyll but this may be masked by various accessory pigments, these being one of the major characteristics used to divide the algae into their various phyla. Other characters used to classify the algae are the nature of storage products, the type of cell wall, the form and number of undulipodia (flagella), ultrastructural cell details, and reproductive processes. As they evolved, red and green algae obtained their chloroplasts by capturing a photosynthetic eubacterium. However, the yellow-green, brown, and golden-brown algae, and the diatoms obtained their chloroplasts later in the course of evolution from the green and red algae. The earliest The earliest fossils are dated at about 1700 mya, but they probably evolved much earlier, possibly 1000 mya (*see* Precambrian). *See also* Chlorophyta; Phaeophyta; Rhodophyta.

alignment   *See* sequence alignment.

allele (allelomorph)   One of the possible forms of a given gene. Different alleles of the same gene give rise to different effects on the PHENOTYPE. The alleles of a particular gene occupy the same positions (*loci*) on homologous chromosomes. A gene is said to be *homozygous* if the two loci have identical alleles and *heterozygous* when the alleles are different. When two different alleles are present, one (the *dominant* allele) usually masks the effect of the other (the *recessive* allele). For example, for the alleles determining the seed color of

Mendel's pea plants greenness is the dominant allele and yellowness is the recessive allele. The allele determining the normal form of the gene is usually dominant whereas mutant alleles are usually recessive. Thus most mutations only show in the phenotype when they are homozygous. In some cases one allele is not completely dominant or recessive with respect to another allele. Consequently an intermediate phenotype will be produced in the heterozygote. *See also* co-dominance; multiple allelism.

allelomorph *See* allele.

allometric relationship The relationship between the size of an organism and the size of any one of its parts. An example is the relationship between brain size and body size. The study of allometric relationships (*allometry*) is an important method for describing morphological evolution

Allopatric speciation

and can be applied to a single organism, organisms within a species, and organisms in different species.

allometry *See* allometric relationship.

allopatric speciation (geographical speciation) There are two forms of allopatric speciation: 1. *Dichopatric speciation*, in which the new species is formed by a geographically isolated subpopulation of the ancestral species. Geographical barriers include mountains, water (seas, lakes, rivers, streams), deserts, etc., and prevent gene flow between the isolated individuals

and the rest of the species, resulting in an isolated population or *incipient species*. A new species can arise in the isolated population by mutations, loss of genes, recombinations, or even new genes from other populations in the new area. The population may also be exposed to different selection pressures from the physical and biotic environment.
2. *Peripatric speciation (peripheral isolate speciation)*, in which a new species is formed by a small outlying FOUNDER POPULATION that becomes isolated from the main group. The majority of vertebrate species are believed to have evolved allopatrically.
See reinforcement; speciation. *Compare* parapatric speciation; sympatric speciation. *See also* cichlids.

allopatry Living in separate places. *Compare* sympatry.

allopolyploidy A type of polyploidy involving the combination of chromosomes from two or more different species (*see* polyploid). *Allopolyploids* usually arise from the doubling of chromosomes of a hybrid between species, the doubling often making the hybrid fertile. It provides a means by which new species can evolve quickly without a long period of geographical isolation. The properties of the hybrid, e.g. greater vigor and adaptability, are retained in the allopolyploid in subsequent generations and such organisms are often highly successful. The effect is rare in animals, but common in plants. Wild species of wheat began to be cultivated about 11 000 years ago. Modern wheat used for bread making (*Triticum aestivum*) is a *hexaploid* with 6 sets of 7 chromosomes. It is believed to have evolved from a sterile diploid hybrid with 14 chromosomes that doubled spontaneously to form a fertile TETRAPLOID (with 28 chromosomes) about 8000 years ago. Subsequently the tetraploid crossed again with a diploid species to form a fertile hexaploid with 42 chromosomes. *See also* colchicine; polyploidy. *Compare* autopolyploidy.

allospecies Populations of a species that

are geographically separated from each other.

allotetraploid (amphidiploid) An allopolyploid whose chromosomes are derived from two different species and which therefore has four times the haploid number of chromosomes. *See* allopolyploidy.

allozyme The variant of an ENZYME, expressed by a particular allele.

alternation of generations The occurrence of two, or occasionally more, generations during the life cycle of an organism. It is not found in animals, although some authorities use the term in describing the life cycles in certain parasites and hydrozoan coelenterates, such as *Obelia* (*see* Hydrazoa). It is very common in plants, being particularly clear in liverworts, mosses, and ferns where the generations are independent. Most commonly there is an alternation between sexual and asexual generations, which are usually very different from each other morphologically. In nearly all plants there is also an alternation between haploid and diploid stages. Generally the haploid plant produces gametes mitotically and is thus termed the *gametophyte*, while the diploid plant produces spores meiotically and is called the *sporophyte*, though many algae do not follow this rule. The gametes fuse to form a zygote, which develops into the sporophyte, and the spores germinate and produce the gametophyte, so forming a cycle. In bryophytes (liverworts and mosses) the haploid gametophyte is the dominant phase of the life cycle and the sporophyte is represented only by the capsule, seta, and foot. In vascular plants the diploid sporophyte has evolved to become the dominant phase and in the ferns, for example, the gametophyte is represented by a small prothallus. The concept of an alternation of generations can be extended to the flowering plants, in which the embryo sac and pollen represent the much reduced female and male gametophyte generations respectively. During evolution, the success of the sporophyte may be its possession of a diploid number of chromosomes coupled with its adaptation to life on land. The sporophyte generation of ferns and other TRACHEOPHYTES increased in size and developed vascular tissue enabling them to survive in drier conditions on land, but still required water for reproduction. This problem was solved by angiosperms and gymnosperms by the evolution of pollen and seeds (*see* Angiospermophyta; gymnosperm). Pollen grains do not need external water for fertilization and the seeds have a protective coat and stored food. The evolution of vascular tissue increased their success further. Another evolutionary trend is the development of HETEROSPORY. *See also* homospory.

alternative splicing *See* intron.

altruism Behavior by an animal that favors the survival of other animals of the same species at its own expense. The most common example is that of parents putting themselves at risk, and sometimes losing their lives, to protect and save their offspring. This has been shown to be genetically favorable to the altruist, increasing the chance that its genes will be passed on, particularly if the parent animal has exhausted, or nearly exhausted, its reproductive capacity. Similarly group altruism, in which genetically more distant group members are protected, will favor gene survival in the long term.

Reciprocal altruism occurs in small intimate groups when individual animals help one another as a 'favor' by, for example, mutually grooming one another when a particular body part is difficult to reach. It is difficult to see the evolutionary advantage when *cheating* occurs and the helpful behavior is not reciprocated. Vampire bats exhibit reciprocal altruistic behavior even though the individuals are not in a close kinship group. If a bat returns without successfully obtaining its animal blood, other group members will regurgitate blood for that individual. Bats that have received blood in this way have been observed to reciprocate this behavior. *See also* group selection; kin selection.

Alvarez theory The theory that the

MASS EXTINCTION at the end of the Cretaceous, including the complete extinction of the DINOSAURS, was caused by a large asteroid colliding with the Earth. It was suggested that an asteroid of 10 km diameter could throw up enough dust to darken the sky for several years. There is strong evidence for the theory: a high level of iridium in boundary rocks (*see* K–T event), a suitable impact crater (the Chicxulub (Yucatán) crater) of about 180 km diameter off the Yucatán coast of Mexico, and evidence from the fossil record showing a sudden and synchronous mass extinction. Interestingly, other reptiles – lizards, snakes, turtles, and crocodiles – survived. The theory is not universally accepted and there is no evidence that other mass extinctions were caused by asteroid impacts. The idea was put forward by the American physicist Luis Alvarez (1911–88) in 1980.

amber Fossilized resin from the trees of ancient forests in which numerous insects, spiders, plant parts, pollen, etc. are perfectly preserved. The sticky resin may have been produced by the trees to protect them against fungal or insect infestation, to prevent dessication, to attract pollinating insects, as protection for injuries caused by storm damage, or as a by-product of seasonal growth. The resin, with its trapped animals, collected on the surface of the soil and would have to have been quickly buried, thus preventing oxidation. Over millions of years and subjected to high temperature and pressure, terpenes slowly evaporated and polymerization processes occurred to convert the resin into amber. Major locations have been found in the Lebanon (Cretaceous); Sagreville, New Jersey, USA (Cretaceous); Baltic amber deposits around the Baltic peninsula and in Poland, Germany, Lithuania, Latvia, Estonia, Belorussia, the Netherlands, Sweden, and the UK from the Tertiary are the largest in the world; Dominican amber from the Dominican republic (Oligocene to Miocene), with a wealth of insects and spiders, and rarely, frogs, scorpions, and lizards. *Copal* is partially polymerized resin. It is found in many parts of the world and its name derived from the Spanish word *copalli*, meaning 'incense.' The largest deposits of copal are found in the Santander region of Columbia and are dated at about 1000 years old.

Amber has been used from earliest times to make jewelry and for ornamental purposes. The animals and plant parts preserved in amber provide a unique insight into the environment that existed when the resin was produced by the ancient forests. *See* fossil.

amblypods An extinct order of herbivorous Paleocene mammals that evolved to a very large size. The name means 'blunt footed.' Certain authorities divide the group up into three separate orders: the *pantodonts* (Pantodonta), the *uintatheres* (Dinocerata), and the *xenungulates* (Xenungulata). Fossil remains of Pantodonts have been discovered in Asia, North America, and more recently, in South America. The earliest were still quite small, e.g. *Archaeolambda* which had claws, probably lived in trees, and was omnivorous. *Titanoides* (weighing about 150 kg) was an enormous animal with saberlike upper canines, and large forelimbs with claws, probably to dig for food or to tear tough plant material. *Barylamda* (even bigger at about 650 kg) probably browsed. Its very heavy tail was possibly used to anchor it down as it grasped for leaves farther up a tree. *Coryphodon* (about 300 kg) was rhinolike, had huge tusklike canines for digging, possibly wallowed in water, and occurred all over the northern hemisphere in the Eocene. Pantodonts became extinct in the Oligocene.

The most advanced uintatheres (e.g. *Uintatherium*) probably weighed a massive 4500 kg. They had saberlike upper canines, huge jaws, and several blunt pairs of horns. They were rhinolike browsers. The earlier forms were smaller (about 300 kg) lacked horns, but the upper canines were large. Male (larger) and female (smaller) forms have been suggested for *Probathyopsis* of North America.

The xenungulates of the South American Paleocene are rare fossils (e.g. *Carodnia*). They were heavily built animals with large canines and crested cheek teeth, sim-

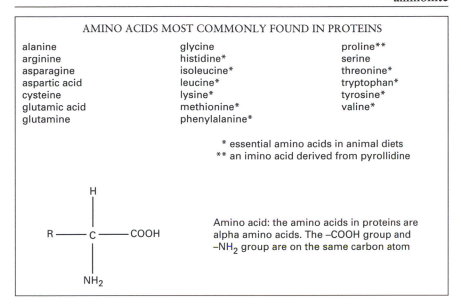

AMINO ACIDS MOST COMMONLY FOUND IN PROTEINS

alanine	glycine	proline**
arginine	histidine*	serine
asparagine	isoleucine*	threonine*
aspartic acid	leucine*	tryptophan*
cysteine	lysine*	tyrosine*
glutamic acid	methionine*	valine*
glutamine	phenylalanine*	

 * essential amino acids in animal diets
** an imino acid derived from pyrollidine

Amino acid: the amino acids in proteins are alpha amino acids. The –COOH group and –NH$_2$ group are on the same carbon atom

ilar to the uintatheres. It has been suggested that the common ancestors of uintatheres and xenungulates may have been related to *anagalids*, which are relatives of rodents and rabbits.

amino acids Derivatives of carboxylic acids containing both an acidic carboxylate group (–COOH) and a basic amino group (–NH$_2$). The simplest example is glycine (H$_2$NCH$_2$COOH). All are white, crystalline, soluble in water, and with the sole exception of glycine, all are optically active. Proteins are formed from chains of amino acids. In adult humans there are 20 amino acids, 10 of which can be synthesized by the body itself. Since these are not required in the diet they are known as *nonessential amino acids*. The remaining 10 cannot be synthesized by the body and have to be obtained in the diet. They are known as *essential amino acids*. Various other amino acids fulfill important roles in metabolic processes other than as constituents of proteins. For example, ornithine (H$_2$N(CH$_2$)$_3$CH(NH$_2$)COOH) and citrulline (H$_2$N.CO.NH.(CH$_2$)$_3$CH(NH$_2$)-COOH) are intermediates in the production of urea.

amitosis Nuclear division characterized by the absence of a nuclear spindle and leading to the production of daughter nuclei with unequal sets of chromosomes. The ordered process of division, duplication of chromosomes, dissolution of nuclear membrane, and production of a spindle as in MITOSIS is apparently absent. Cells produced amitotically inherit variable numbers of chromosomes. The chances of a daughter cell lacking essential genes are less than may be expected because many cells that characteristically divide amitotically are polyploid, e.g. the endosperm nucleus in angiosperms and the macronucleus of ciliates. *Compare* endomitosis.

ammonite (ammonoid) Fossil cephalopod mollusks with external coiled chambered shells related to present-day squids and nautiluses. They are one of the most important fossil groups used for dating the rocks of the Mesozoic because of their wide geographical distribution and also because they evolved rapidly over time. They resemble flattened gastropods, but possess *sutures* (wavy lines over the surface), *siphuncles*, which are tubes running through each chamber, and an *umbilicus*, which is a depression formed by the coiled shell. Examples include *Gastrioceras* (Carboniferous), *Ceratites* (Triassic), *Dactylioceras* (Jurassic), and *Hamites* (Cretaceous). They are not known after the Cretaceous period and probably became extinct during the Alvarez event. *See* Alvarez theory; Cephalopoda.

amnion *See* amniotes.

amniotes Reptiles, birds, and mammals, i.e. those vertebrates whose embryos always develop in an *amnion*. The amnion is a fluid-filled sac that surrounds and protects the embryo and is an evolutionary adaptation for reproducing on dry land. In contrast, *anamniotes* include fishes and amphibians, i.e. those vertebrates that rarely possess an amnion.

amniotic egg *See* cleidoic egg.

Amphibia The class of vertebrates that contains the most primitive terrestrial TETRAPODS – the frogs, toads, newts, and salamanders. They were the first group of vertebrates to become adapted to life on land resulting in the evolution of many changes in body structure. Amphibians have four PENTADACTYL LIMBS, a moist skin without scales, a pelvic girdle articulating with the sacrum, and a middle-ear apparatus for detecting airborne sounds, but no external ear. They are poikilothermic and the adults have lungs and live on land but their skin, also used in respiration, is thin and moist and body fluids are easily lost, therefore they are confined to damp places. In reproduction, fertilization is external and so they must return to the water to breed. The eggs are covered with jelly and the aquatic larvae have gills for respiration and undergo metamorphosis to the adult. The first amphibians probably lived mostly in water and were still quite fishlike. The oldest fossil amphibian *Icthyostega* from the Upper Devonian had a mixture of fish and amphibian characteristics, retaining a fish tail and a lateral line system. They were so numerous in the Carboniferous that this has often been termed the 'Age of Amphibians'. Their success continued into the Permian, but most amphibian groups became extinct during the Permo–Triassic

crisis. By the end of the Triassic, only the ancestors of present-day amphibia remained. Partial or complete neoteny occurs in some amphibians; for example *Ambystoma* (Mexican axolotl) is permanently aquatic, with larval gills retained in the adult and atrophied lungs. *See also* Anura; Ichthyosauria; geological time scale.

amphidiploid *See* allotetraploid.

amphimixis True sexual reproduction by fusion of gametes. *Compare* apomixis.

Amphioxus *See Branchiostoma.*

anaerobe An organism that can live and grow in the absence of free oxygen, i.e. it respires anaerobically. Anaerobes can be *facultative*, in that they usually respire aerobically but can switch to anaerobic respiration when free oxygen is in short supply, or *obligate*, in that they never respire aerobically and may even be poisoned by free oxygen. *See* respiration. *Compare* aerobe.

anaerobic respiration *See* respiration.

anagalids *See* amblypods; Rodentia.

anagenesis Evolutionary change occurring within a species, between speciation events. *Compare* cladogenesis. *See also* phylogenetic.

analogous Describing structures that are apparently similar (structurally or functionally) but have a different evolutionary origin, and thus a different embryological origin and structure. The wings of birds and insects and the legs of arthropods and mammals have a similar function, but are analogous not homologous. *Compare* homologous; orthologous; paralogous. *See also* convergent evolution.

anamniotes *See* amniotes.

anaphase The stage in MITOSIS or MEIOSIS when chromatids are pulled toward opposite poles of the nuclear spindle. In mitosis the chromatids moving toward the poles represent a single complete chromosome. During *anaphase I* of meiosis a pair of chromatids still connected at their centromere move to the spindle poles. During *anaphase II* the centromeres divide and single chromatids are drawn toward the poles.

Anapsida (anapsids)   *See* Reptilia.

ancestral homology   *See* homologous.

aneuploidy   The condition, resulting from NONDISJUNCTION of homologous chromosomes at MEIOSIS, in which one or more chromosomes are missing from or added to the normal somatic chromosome number. If both of a pair of homologous chromosomes are missing, *nullisomy* results. *Monosomy* and *trisomy* are the conditions in which one or three homologs occur respectively, instead of the normal two. *Polysomy*, which includes trisomy, is the condition in which one or more chromosomes are represented more than twice in the cell.

Angiospermophyta (angiosperms; Anthophyta; flowering plants)   An extremely important phylum of vascular seed plants, with almost 300 000 species, characterized by their flowers, which contain the male and female reproductive structures. They differ from conifers and other GYMNOSPERMS by having the ovule enclosed within an ovary, which after fertilization develops into a fruit. The female gametophyte is represented by the embryo sac, archegonia being absent. Angiosperms are divided into two major groups depending on the number of cotyledons, giving the MONOCOTYLEDONAE and DICOTYLEDONAE.

The Angiosperms originated in the late Jurassic, but did not flourish until the Cretaceous. Their ancestry remains obscure and BENNETTITALES, CAYTONIALES, CONIFEROPHYTA, and GNETOPHYTA have all been considered as possibilities. The enormous adaptive radiation in the middle of the Cretaceous coincided with a similar evolution (COEVOLUTION) of insects (*see* Insecta). The plentiful supplies of angiosperm fruits, seeds, and leaves was probably a major factor in the evolution of birds and mammals during this period. Once established, angiosperms were able to adapt to all types of climatic change and at the end of the Cretaceous, dominated the world's vegetation. No new forms evolved in the Cenozoic to displace the angiosperms and fossil representatives of most present-day families have been discovered. The ancient ancestors of the order Magnoliales are believed to have evolved into the Monocotyledonae and the Dicotyledonae. Fossil monocotyledons are more rare than dicotyledons, but grasses became widespread in the Miocene. In the Quaternary, modern angiosperm vegetation had become well established.

The dominant sporophyte generation contributed to a longer life cycle and there was an increased complexity in structure. The larger vascular elements have enabled a greater movement of fluids and an ability to grow larger (more mechanical support) and to survive in a dry environment. Pollen grains do not require water for fertilization, the seed habit protects the developing embryo, and dormancy helps survival in unfavorable conditions.

angiosperms   *See* Angiospermophyta.

animal   An organism that feeds on other organisms or on organic matter, is often motile, and reacts to stimuli quickly. Animal cells lack cell walls. There is no chlorophyll and growth is usually limited. Over a million species of present-day animals and those of past times (represented by fossils) have been identified. They range from the simplest forms to the highest INVERTEBRATES and vertebrates (*see* craniate). It is believed that life began in the seas and the earliest animal remains have been observed in the CAMBRIAN in rocks of marine origin. However, as many of these fossils represented highly differentiated animals, it is more likely that animals evolved even earlier in Precambrian times. Precambrian fossils are quite rare and a few disputed wormlike fossils have been discovered. Descendants of the early marine animals later evolved and adapted characteristics that enabled them to invade freshwater environments and then the land. Some groups have reinvaded the marine environment,

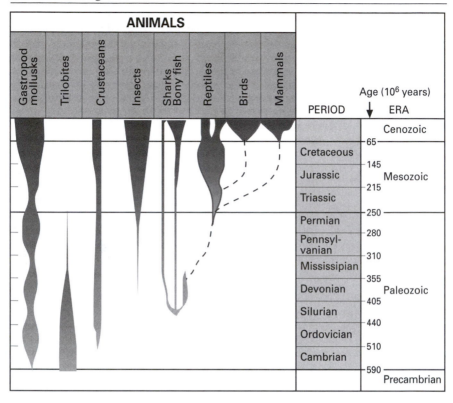

ANIMALS								PERIOD	Age (10⁶ years) ↓	ERA

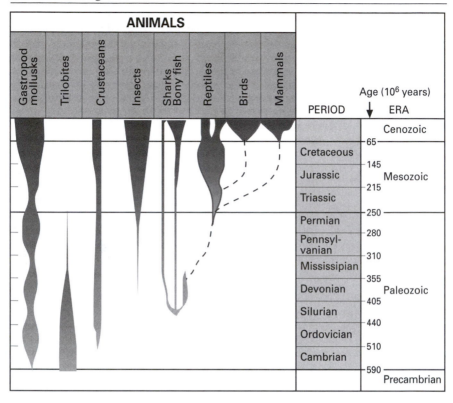

for example, the early sharks and bony fishes, the pleisiosaurs (ancient reptiles), and among the mammals, whales, sirenians, and seals. *Compare* plant.

animal breeding   *See* artificial selection.

anisogamy   The sexual fusion of non-identical gametes. Anisogamy grades from situations in which the gametes differ only in size to the extreme of *oogamy*, in which one gamete is a large immotile ovum and the other a small motile sperm. *Compare* isogamy.

ankylosaur   *See* dinosaur.

Annelida   A phylum of triploblastic bilaterally symmetrical metamerically segmented invertebrates, the segmented worms, including ragworms, earthworms, and the leeches. Segmentation (metamerism) probably evolved as an adaptation for burrowing. Annelids have a long soft cylindrical body covered by a thin cuticle and most have segmentally arranged chitinous bristles (chaetae), which assist in locomotion. Many are hermaphrodite. The gut runs from the mouth at the front to the posterior anus. There are well-developed blood and nervous systems and nephridia for excretion. The body wall contains layers of circular and longitudinal muscle and the body cavity is a COELOM isolating the gut from the body wall. These features, together with the metamerism, provide an efficient means of locomotion. The coelom provides a hydrostatic skeleton as it resists compression. Shortening of the body is accompanied by an increase in diameter. The phylum is divided into three classes (*see* Polychaeta; Oligochaeta; Hirudinea). Marine worms were as abundant in the seas of the Cambrian as they are today (*see* Burgess shale). Their soft bodies are not usually preserved as fossils and their exis-

DIFFERENCES BETWEEN PLANTS AND ANIMALS		
	Plants	*Animals*
Nutrition	by synthesis i.e. take in simple substances (carbon dioxide, water, minerals) and, using light energy, convert these into all the compounds needed for growth.	by breakdown i.e. take in complex substances (plant or animal tissues) and, by digestion, reduce these to simpler compounds that are absorbed into the body providing energy, or building blocks for growth; chlorophyll never present.
Support	by pressure exerted on rigid cellulose cell walls by water filled vacuole; additional strengthening tissues, e.g. lignin, are formed in older plants.	by various mechanisms, e.g. internal or external skeletons; cell walls not rigid, cellulose never present.
Sensitivity	response to stimuli slow, and generally only occuring if stimulus maintained over long period.	response to stimuli rapid and generally occurring immediately after the stimulus.
Mobility	land plants of necessity immobile as need to withdraw water and nutrients from the soil by roots; some aquatic microscopic plants possess flagella and are mobile.	organism able to move whole body from place to place

tence is represented by fossil traces, tubes, or burrows. Their burrowing habit means that annelids have probably played an important part in soil formation and marine sediments since Cambrian times. *See also* archiannelid.

annual ring   *See* dendrochronology.

anoxia   An absence or deficiency of oxygen.

antheridium   The male sex organ of algae, fungi, and non-seed-bearing plants. It may be unicellular or multicellular and produces (usually motile) male gametes. *Compare* archegonium.

Anthocerotae   (hornworts) A class of BRYOPHYTA, in some classifications placed in a separate phylum Anthocerophyta, consisting of a flattened green thallus (GA-

METOPHYTE) in which the foot of a horn-shaped SPOROPHYTE is embedded. They differ from other bryophytes in that each chloroplast contains a pyrenoid (a protein structure packed with starch), which is a feature associated with protoctists rather than plants. Also, the sporophyte grows continuously from a meristem between the sporangium and foot. Spore dispersal, as in mosses, is aided by elaters, but there are no protonemata (resembling algal filaments). Sexual reproduction resembles the other bryophytes and asexual reproduction also occurs by means of gemma. Hornworts are believed to have evolved independently of mosses and liverworts, their origin remaining obscure.

Anthophyta   *See* Angiospermophyta.

Anthozoa   A class of cnidarians, the sea anemones and CORALS, in which the polyp

is the only form and the medusa is absent. The solitary sea anemone has numerous feathery tentacles. Corals are colonial, with the polyp contained in a gelatinous matrix (the soft corals), a horny skeleton (the horny corals), or a skeleton of calcium carbonate (the stony or true corals). Accumulations of these corals in warm shallow seas form coral reefs, atolls, and islands. Fossil relics of anthozoans have been discovered from Cambrian to recent times.

anthropoids A suborder (Anthropoidea) of the PRIMATES comprising three superfamilies: Tarsidae (the TARSIERS); Platyrrhini (or Ceboidea) (also known as platyrrhines), consisting of New World Monkeys, marmosets, and Goeldi's monkey; and Catarrhini (also known as catarrhines), consisting of Old World Monkeys and baboons, gibbons, great apes, and humans. *See also* prosimians.

anthropology The study of humans, including their origin (evolution), physical characteristics, social behavior, religious beliefs, and cultural institutions.

antibiotic resistance A heritable trait in microorganisms, especially disease-causing bacteria, that enables them to survive in the presence of an antibiotic. Once acquired, the resistance will be strongly selected for and the bacterial population will rapidly evolve to become resistant to a particular antibiotic. The widespread use of antibiotics in humans and animals over the last 50 years has exerted a massive selection pressure on bacteria, resulting in an alarming increase in antibiotic-resistant bacteria – the so-called 'superbugs'.

anticodon A nucleotide triplet on transfer RNA that is complementary to and bonds with the corresponding codon of messenger RNA in the ribosomes. *See* transfer RNA.

anti-Darwinian theory *See* creationism; orthogenesis; saltationism.

antisense DNA *See* noncoding strand.

ants *See* Hymenoptera.

aortic arches Six pairs of blood vessels present in all vertebrate embryos, which link the ventral aorta leaving the heart with the dorsal aorta. The early embryos of fish, amphibia, reptiles, birds, and mammals resemble one another closely, but as the embryos develop, there are changes. Arches one and two soon disappear and in adult fish arches three to six lead to the gills. Adult tetrapods lose arch five, arch three becomes the carotid arch supplying the head, arch four becomes the systemic arch supplying the body, and arch six becomes the pulmonary arch supplying the lungs. *See also* Haeckel; recapitulation.

Apatosaurus *See* dinosaurs.

apes *See* anthropoids; Primates.

Apicomplexa A phylum of spore-forming protoctists that are parasites of animals, e.g. the malaria parasite (*Plasmodium*). Apicomplexans are known for having an 'apical complex' visible at one end of the cell, consisting of fibrils, vacuoles, and organelles. They reproduce sexually, have complex life cycles (often involving several hosts) and can proliferate by a series of cell division (schizogony). They were formerly classified as SPOROZOANS.

apogamy In pteridophytes, the development of the sporophyte directly from a cell of the gametophyte, so fusion of gametes is bypassed. It frequently occurs in gametophytes that have been produced aposporously and are thus diploid. The term also describes the development of an unfertilized female gamete into the sporophyte, a phenomenon described as PARTHENOGENESIS. *See* apospory; apomixis.

apomixis (agamospermy) A modified form of reproduction by plants in which seeds are formed without fusion of gametes. It is comparable to the conditions of APOGAMY and APOSPORY, which are seen in many pteridophytes. Apomixis includes the process whereby a diploid cell of the nucellus develops into an embryo giving a diploid seed with a genetic constitution identical to the parent. Another form of apomixes in which seeds develop from unfertilized gametes can also be termed PARTHENOGENESIS. Seeds produced in this way may be either haploid or diploid depending on whether or not the megaspore mother cell undergoes meiosis. Often, in the process termed *pseudogamy*, entry of the male gamete is required to stimulate the development of the female gamete, even though nuclear fusion does not occur. Such cases of apomixis are difficult to distinguish from true sexual reproduction. *Compare* amphimixis.

apomorphy A derived CHARACTER STATE. *Compare* plesiomorphy.

aposematic coloration *See* warning coloration.

apospory The development of the gametophyte directly from the cell of a sporophyte, thus bypassing meiosis and spore production. Gametophytes produced in this manner are thus diploid instead of haploid. If such gametophytes produce fertile gametes the resulting sporophyte is then tetraploid, and large polyploid series may subsequently be developed. Apospory is found in some bryophytes and pteridophytes. *See also* apogamy; apomixis.

appendix (vermiform appendix) *See* vestigial character.

apses *See* temporal fossae.

Arabidopsis A small annual plant of the family Brassicaceae, which certain authorities have described as the 'Drosophila' of plant genetics. Its genome has been fully sequenced. *See* ABC floral model.

Arachnida The class of the ARTHROPODA that contains the mostly terrestrial and carnivorous scorpions and spiders, which typically have spinnerets on the abdomen for web spinning, and the parasitic ticks and mites. The body is divided into two parts, the anterior cephalothorax (*pro-*

soma), and the posterior abdomen (*opisthosoma*), and there are four pairs of walking legs. There are no antennae and the eyes are simple. The cephalothorax bears prehensile chelicerae and leglike, usually sensory, pedipalps, as well as the legs. Respiration is carried out by lung books and/or tracheae and excretion is by coxal glands and Malpighian tubules.

The evolution of arachnids continues to be controversial. Scorpions have been part of the fossil record since Silurian times, whip scorpions, spiders, and harvestmen (daddy longlegs) evolved in the Carboniferous, and mites and ticks evolved in the Oligocene. The earliest scorpions were probably aquatic and later evolved adaptations to life on land. Certain authorities believe that spiders and scorpions exhibit CONVERGENT EVOLUTION, i.e. certain adaptations, such as malpighian tubules, and lung books, evolved independently in each group. *See also* Chelicerata.

Archaea (archaebacteria) One of the three cellular kingdoms (or DOMAINS) in certain classifications – the other two are EUKARYA and BACTERIA. (In the Five Kingdoms classification scheme, it is a subkingdom of the BACTERIA.) They are bacteria-like organisms and can be distinguished from Bacteria on the basis of biochemical differences in the nature of their lipid constituents, and their gene expression machinery. Included in the Archaea are the methanogic (methane-producing), thermophilic (heat-loving), and halophilic (salt-loving) species and therefore many live in harsh environments, such as hot springs, salt flats, or sea vents, thought to resemble the early earth environment. However, they are not restricted to such extreme lifestyles, and are widespread in more congenial settings.

The three kingdoms were identified by sequence analysis of rRNA genes and the resulting phylogeny implies that the division between the kingdoms is ancient – at least 3500 million years old. Because RNA is considered to evolve very slowly, these differences are thought to be important in this classification. Recent analysis of entire genomes has produced some data that is not consistent with there being three kingdoms but it is not known whether the inconsistencies are due to gene transfer between the kingdoms or a more complex phylogeny. It is currently accepted that there are three cellular kingdoms. *See also* Cyanobacteria.

Archaean *See* Precambrian.

archaebacteria *See* Archaea.

Archaeopteryx One of two primitive fossil birds (intermediate between AR- CHOSAURS and modern birds, AVES) discovered preserved in two slabs of limestone in the Upper Jurassic in Solnhöfen in southern Germany in 1861. The fossil has both reptilian and bird characteristics. Its teeth and long pointed tail are reptilian characteristics, whilst its feathers, wings, large brain, and large eyes are bird characteristics. This type of fossil is often termed a 'missing link' or transitional fossil, bridging the gap in evolution between reptiles and birds. *See also* Aves.

archaic *Homo sapiens* *See* Homo sapiens.

Archean *See* Precambrian.

archegonium The female sex organ of bryophytes, pteridophytes, most gymnosperms, and some red and brown algae. It is a multicellular, flask-shaped structure with a narrow neck and a swollen base (venter) that contains the female gamete. *Compare* antheridium.

archenteron The earliest gut cavity of most animal embryos. It is produced by an infolding of part of the outer surface of a blastula to form an internal cavity that is in continuity with the outside via the blastopore.

archeology The study of the past of humans by the scientific analysis and observation of material remains and cultural artefacts.

Archeozoic *See* Precambrian.

archetype The original form or body plan (*bauplan*) from which a group of organisms develops.

archiannelid Any of various small marine annelid worms most of which are scavengers with a protrusible tongue for conveying food to the mouth. They are regarded as remnants of ancestral annelids, and some authorities place them in a separate class, Archiannelida. *See also* Annelida.

archosaurs (Archosauria, thecodonts) Often termed the 'Ruling Reptiles', this group contains the PTEROSAURIA (flying reptiles), the DINOSAURS, ancient members of the present-day crocodilians, and the birds. They were formerly known as thecodonts. The archosaurs are a superorder of DIAPSID reptiles that evolved from the COTYLOSAURS in the Late Pennsylvanian and diverged from the superorder Lepidosauria later in the Mesozoic. The latter is represented by the Rhyncocephalia and the Squamata. *See also* Reptilia; mass extinction.

Arctogea *See* zoogeography.

Ardipithecus ramidus The oldest AUS- TRALOPITHECINE. 'Ardi' means 'ground' or 'floor' in the Afar language; 'rami' is the Afar word for 'root'. The first fossils were discovered by Tim White *et al.* in 1993 in the Afar Depression in Ethiopia. Other fossils have been found in the Middle Awash valley of Ethiopia and are dated 5.2–5.8 million years old. The dentition appears to have apelike and hominid features: the canine teeth resemble those of hominids, while the molars are more apelike. Details of the cranium (e.g. a forwardly placed foramen magnum) and the position of the big toe (not opposable) indicate bipedalism, a hominid characteristic.

area cladogram *See* cladistics.

Aristotle Ancient Greek philosopher and zoologist (384–322 BC). He was the first zoologist to record his observations and also wrote on philosophy, politics, and many other subjects. He postulated an evolutionary development from 'lower' to 'higher' forms that he believed were overseen by a supreme 'guiding intelligence'.

Arthropoda   The largest phylum in the animal kingdom and the only invertebrate phylum with aquatic, terrestrial, and aerial members. Arthropods are bilaterally symmetrical segmented animals with a characteristic tough chitinous protective exoskeleton flexible only at the joints; growth is by ecdysis. Each segment typically bears a pair of jointed appendages, which are modified for different functions. The phylum includes the crustaceans, insects, centipedes, millipedes, and spiders. Some authorities divide the arthropods into three separate phyla, the CHELICERATA, MANDIBULATA, and CRUSTACEA.

In the Arthropoda the coelom is reduced and the body cavity is a hemocoel. There is a ventral nerve cord with a pair of cerebral ganglia and paired segmental ganglia. Arthropods evolved either from a polychaete annelid or an ancestor of the polychaetes. The earliest arthropods had segmented bodies, each with a pair of legs. During their evolution the segments have segregated into three distinct regions: head, thorax, and abdomen. The numbers of segments has also reduced. More segments have been incorporated into the head (CEPHALIZATION) and nervous tissue and sensory organs have concentrated in or near the head region. Some legs have been specialized for walking, and other functions.

The Arthropoda evolved in the Cambrian, represented by TRILOBITES (an extinct group), aquatic crustaceans, and king crabs. Scorpions appeared in the Silurian and winged insects evolved in the Carboniferous. Most of the insect orders had evolved by the end of the Paleozoic era, with a vast number of species. There was another great period of evolution of insects in the Cretaceous (COEVOLUTION with flowering plants). *See also* Annelida; Arachnida; Chilopoda; Diplopoda; Insecta; Onychophora.

articular   A small bone of the lower jaw

in bony fish (Osteichthyes), amphibians, and reptiles that forms a hinge joint with the quadrate bone of the upper jaw. The articular is derived in the course of evolution from the ossification of MECKEL'S CARTILAGE.

artificial insemination (AI)   A method of artificially inserting semen (spermatozoa) from male animals into the reproductive tract of female animals. It is widely used in animal breeding, especially of farm animals, such as cattle, sheep, etc. Males with beneficial characteristics are enabled by this method to fertilize large numbers of females without the need for mating or transporting male animals over distances. The collected semen can be refrigerated and stored for long periods in *sperm banks*. A single male animal can inseminate many thousands of female animals. Artificial insemination is also used in human reproduction to help infertile couples to have children. The identification of *sperm donors* in some countries is protected, but in others, children have been allowed to trace their biological fathers. *See also* eugenics.

artificial Life (AL)   A research computer program in which virtual living things are created (simulated) and evolving systems are generated and tracked. Such programs could be used to find out useful things about evolution on Earth or to discover abstract properties that could be applied to many other models.

artificial selection   Intervention by humans to alter a population deliberately. It was originally carried out by selective breeding (most of today's agricultural crops and animals are the result of selective breeding). Breeders select individuals with desired characteristics and allow them to interbreed. They prevent individuals lacking these characteristics from breeding. New breeds or varieties can be developed for special purposes after many generations. *Inbreeding* involves crossing two closely related individuals, which has its risks as harmful or lethal ALLELES may result and lead to *inbreeding depression*.

Outbreeding in which individuals from different varieties are crossed produce HYBRIDS in which harmful alleles can be masked by healthy ones, resulting in hybrid vigor. Artificial selection can now be achieved by directly altering the genome using recombinant DNA technology. *See also* artificial insemination; cloning; eugenics. *Compare* natural selection.

Artiodactyla The order of mammals that contains the even-toed ungulates, in which the weight of the body is supported on the third and fourth digits only. These large herbivorous mammals include sheep, goats, deer, domestic cattle, antelopes, pigs, hippopotamuses, camels, and giraffes, which are adapted to diverse environments. The cud-chewing cloven-hoofed camels and *ruminants* have three or four chambers in the stomach; food being regurgitated from the first and chewed while the animal is resting before being swallowed again for complete digestion.

The earliest artiodactyl is *Diacodexis* from the early Eocene, which resembled a modern muntjac and was the size of a rabbit. Artiodactyls became more widespread as the perissodactyls declined later in the Miocene. They were highly adapted to the savanna, especially that of the North American Pliocene, when deer were very abundant and other modern groups evolved. Pigs, camels, and cattle gradually rose to prominence and at the present day, there are 79 artiodactyl genera compared to 6 perissodactyl genera. *Compare* Perissodactyla.

Ascomycota (ascomycetes) A large phylum of FUNGI characterized by a distinctive reproductive structure, the ascus, in which usually eight spores are formed. The phylum includes blue and green molds, morels, and truffles. Parasites include ergot of rye and powdery mildews. It also contains the yeasts: *Saccharomyces* used in fermentation processes; *Penicillium* a source of antibiotics; and *Candida albicans* a parasite of humans.

asexual reproduction The formation of new individuals from a single parent without the production of gametes or special reproductive structures. It occurs in many plants, usually by vegetative propagation or spore formation; in unicellular organisms usually by fission; and in multicellular invertebrates by fission, budding, fragmentation, etc.

assortative mating Reproduction of animals in which the males and females appear not to pair at random but tend to select partners of a similar phenotype.

asteroid *See* Alvarez theory; origin of life.

Asteroidea The class of ECHINODERMATA that contains the starfish (e.g. *Asterias*), which are often found just below the low-tide mark. A starfish typically has five arms radiating from a central disk, which contains the main organs and has a mouth on the ventral surface. Chalky plates in the skin form a skeletal test. Suckered tube feet on the underside of the arms are used for locomotion and holding prey. The BIPINNARIA larva is a form of dipleurula. Starfish fossils have been found since Cambrian times.

atavism Resemblance to a distant ancestor rather than a parent.

Atlantic period A period between about 5000 and 3000 BC, which encompasses most of the warmest postglacial times and was characterized by oceanic climatic conditions in northwest Europe. It was preceded by the BOREAL PERIOD and followed by the sub-Boreal period.

atomistic Describing inheritance in which the entities controlling it are relatively distinct, permanent, and capable of independent action. An example is Mendelian inheritance. *See* Mendel's laws.

auricularia *See* dipleurula; Holothuroidea.

Aurignacian *See* Cro-Magnon man.

Australasian Describing one of the six

main zoogeographical areas, composed of Australia and the islands of its continental shelf, Tasmania, New Guinea, and New Zealand. Marsupial (pouched) and monotreme (egg-laying) mammals are particularly characteristic, but many other unique vertebrates and invertebrates are also found. Most of the ancestors of the present-day fauna were probably present before the breakup of PANGEA (225 mya) and Australia has had no land connection since GONDWANA started to break up 135 mya. The marsupials (*see* Metatheria) evolved very striking convergent similarities to the placental mammals, occupying the same niches that were filled by the latter elsewhere. *See* continental drift; zoogeography. *See also* Wallace's line.

australopithecines Extinct early hominids whose fossils show features intermediate between those of apes and humans (*compare Homo*). Originally australopithecines were grouped within a single genus *Australopithecus* (southern ape), but subsequent discoveries show that there are five genera. *Ardipithecus* is the oldest. The other genera are *Australopithecus* and *Paranthropus* (formerly also included in the genus *Australopithecus*), and the more recently discovered *Kenyanthropus* and *Orrorin*.

Australopithecus species include the so-called *gracile australopithecines*. They have moderately sized teeth and jaws and light bones, indicating that they were more slightly built. They include *A. anamensis*, *A. afarensis*, *A. Africanus*, *A. garhi*, and *A. bahrelghazali*. The latter (a mandible discovered in 1995 by Michel Brunet at Bahr el Ghazal in Chad) shows that the australopithecines were more widespread than once thought as all the other fossils had been found only in East and South Africa. *A. bahrelghazali* was first identified as *A. afarensis*, but the mandible has a more modern form.

Paranthropus species include *P. eithiopicus*, *P. boisei*, and *P. robustus*, also described as the *robust australopithecines* because they have a large skeleton with long arms, a massive cranium with a bony ridge (the *sagittal crest*) running along the top, large jaws and molars, and pronounced cheek bones. Their huge teeth were adapted to eating tough siliceous grasses.

Ardipithecus is believed to have been bipedal, feeding on fruit and leaves. It closely resembles *A. amanensis* (3.9–4.1 million years old). *A. afarensis* (the famous 'Lucy') is 3.1 million years old. *A. afarensis* and *A. amanensis* are believed to have been knuckle walkers, because of the arrangement of their wrist bones. *A. afarensis* is now thought to be the ancestor of the later australopithecines and also of the *Homo* line (*see* human evolution). The larger robust australopithecines lived contemporaneously with *A. africanus* for over a million years before dying out.

The rarity of early hominid fossils causes much controversy and new discoveries continue. In 1999, another australopithecine, *Kenyanthropus platyops* (flat-faced Kenya man) was discovered at Lake Turkana, Kenya, dated 3.5–3.2 million years old. Some authorities suggest that *Homo rudolfensis* should be assigned to this genus. In 2001, an even older australopithecine was found in the Lukeino formation, Kenya. It was named *Orrorin tugenensis* (nicknamed 'Millennium man') and was found to be 6 million years old. It provides a possible link with the genus *Homo. See Ardipithecus ramidus*; *Australopithecus afarensis*; *Australopithecus africanus*; *Orrorin tugenensis*; *Paranthropus boisei*; *Paranthropus robustus.*

Australopithecus afarensis (African Eve) An early hominid fossil (*see* australopithecines) first discovered in the mid-1970s in the Hadar region, Ethiopia, by Donald JOHANSON and Maurice Taieb. They have also been found in Tanzania and Kenya and are dated between 2.9 million and 3.9 million years old. The most famous of the first fossils is the partial skeleton of 'Lucy', named for the well-known Beatles song, 'Lucy in the Sky with Diamonds'. *A. afarensis* specimens show apelike features (the small body, and the shape and size of brain), but the articulation of the pelvis shows that Lucy and her contemporaries walked upright on two legs. They also had a fully rounded dental arcade (teeth viewed from above), resembling the dental arcade of humans. They showed SEXUAL DIMOR-PHISM (males were bigger than females) and were short (only 1–1.2 m in height). The remains of animal bones and pollen associated with these fossils indicate that *A. afarensis* individuals lived in open grassland and woodland. *See also* Laetoli footprints; mitochondrial Eve; out of Africa theory.

Australopithecus africanus An AUS-TRALOPITHECINE species first discovered by Raymond DART in 1925 who found a well-preserved skull of a small child at Taung, SW of Johannesburg, in South Africa (known as the *Taung Skull* or *Taung Child*). When compared with *A. afarensis*, the teeth of *A. africanus* appear to be less primitive and the brain size/body size ratio appears to have increased. With the discovery of more fossils of this species, controversy about the lineage of *A. africanus* with other australopithecines and possible links with the *Homo* line remains. Some facial features link specimens with *Paranthropus robusta*. Comparing arm and leg lengths in *A. africanus* and *A. afarensis* indicates that *A. africanus* was more apelike. *A. africanus* lived 3–2.5 mya, compared with *A. afarensis*, fossils dated 4–2.5 mya.

Australopithecus crassidens *See Paranthropus boisei*.

autogamy 1. (*Zoology*) Reproduction in which the nucleus of an individual cell divides into two and forms two gametes, which reunite to form a zygote. It occurs in some protozoans, e.g. *Paramecium*.
2. (*Botany*) Self-fertilization in plants.

autopolyploidy A type of polyploidy involving the multiplication of chromosome sets from only one species (*see* polyploid). *Autopolyploids* may arise from the fusion of diploid gametes that have resulted from the nondisjunction of chromosomes at MEIOSIS. Alternatively, like allopolyploids, they may arise by the nondisjunction of chromatids during the mitotic division of a zygote.

Autopolyploidy was discovered by Hugo DE VRIES during his studies of the evening primrose, *Oenothera lamarckiana*, a diploid plant with 14 chromosomes. He observed a new form, *Oenothera gigas*, which has 28 chromosomes and is a TETRAPLOID. Hybrids between *O. lamarckiana* and *O. gigas* are sterile triploids (the chromosomes cannot pair up during meiosis). The tetraploid is therefore genetically different and reproductively isolated from the parent plant. *O. gigas* has evolved into a new distinct species and has adapted to living in soils that the diploid parent cannot tolerate. *Compare* allopolyploidy. *See also* adaptive radiation; speciation.

autosomes Paired somatic CHROMO-SOMES that play no primary role in sex determination. *Compare* sex chromosomes.

autotetraploid An autopolyploid that has four times the haploid number of chromosomes. *See* autopolyploidy.

autotomy Self-amputation of a damaged or trapped part of the body (e.g. tail or limb) of certain animals, such as lizards, arthropods, and worms, usually along a line of weakness. The lost part is usually regenerated (*see* regeneration).

autotrophic Describing a type of nutrition in which the principal source of carbon is inorganic (carbon dioxide or carbonate). *Photosynthesis* (photoautotrophism) uses light energy. Chemotrophism (chemoautotrophism) uses chemical energy. Autotrophic organisms are green plants and are important primary producers. Heterotrophs feed on autotrophs and are consumers. Chemotrophs include nitrifying bacteria (they obtain energy by oxidation of ammonia to nitrite or a nitrite to nitrate) and sulfur bacteria (they obtain energy by oxidation of hydrogen sulfide to sulfur). *See* photosynthesis. *Compare* heterotrophic.

Aves The class of vertebrates that contains the birds, most of whose characteristics are adaptations for *flight*. The forelimbs are modified as wings with three digits only, the third being greatly elongated. Birds have light strong hollow bones and a rigid skeleton strengthened by bone fusion. The sternum usually has a large keel for attachment of the powerful pectoral muscles, which depress the wings. Birds are homoiothermic. The short deep body is covered with feathers, which provide insulation as well as a large surface area for flight. The jaws form a horny beak and teeth are absent. They lay yolky eggs with a calcareous shell and typically have a well-developed social life, including territorial and courtship displays, nesting, parental care, and song. Many undertake long migrations. There are 28 orders, including the passerines (perching birds), which alone account for about 60% of all birds. The flightless birds (ratites) tend to be swift runners.

Birds evolved from reptiles and retain many reptilian characteristics, such as scaly legs and feet. However, in contrast to reptiles, oxygenated and deoxygenated blood are completely separated in the four-chambered heart. Two evolutionary theories exist: the *thecodont theory* proposes that birds evolved from archosaurian reptiles in the late Triassic, 200 mya; the *dinosaurian theory* proposes that birds evolved from theropod dinosaurs in the later Cretaceous, 80–110 mya – based on similarities in the structure of the pelvic girdle. The discovery of new fossils could settle the argument. Two important adaptations the ancestral reptiles must have possessed were HOMOIOTHERMY and a four-chambered heart, increasing metabolic activity for a new very active way of life. Fossil evidence shows that birds continued to have teeth in Cretaceous times, but teeth were no longer present from the Eocene onward. Well over 400 kinds of fossil birds have been found in North America: in the Cretaceous of Kansas and Montana; the Eocene of Wyoming; the Miocene of Colorado; and the Pleistocene of California and Florida.

Feathers did not arise from a single mutation but evolved through a series of intermediates between scales and feathers, which would have been useless for flight. Feathers therefore did not evolve for use in flying, but were a selective advantage because they trapped heat and then became used in flight (*see* exaptation). There are two conventional, and mutually exclusive, theories for the evolution of flight in birds. One is that flight evolved from small dinosaurs leaping into the air from the ground, and the other is that flight evolved from small dinosaurs jumping to the ground from height. However, recently the discovery of a *Microraptor* fossil throws both theories into doubt and suggests that the evolution of flight in birds may be more complex. The *Microraptor* fossil shows a small dinosaur with feathers on its arms, legs, and tail. The feathers on all four limbs are longer at the ends than near the body. The skeleton suggests *Microraptor* could have climbed up using its four limbs and glided down, but all known gliding surfaces taper away from the body, i.e. in the opposite direction to the feathers of the *Microraptor*. *See also* archosaurs; passerines; ratites.

Avicenna (98–1037) Persian physician and philosopher who wrote on a wide variety of subjects. He believed that fossils were unsuccessful attempts by a life force (which he termed *vis plastica*) to manufacture living organisms from rocks.

axolotl *See* neoteny.

Ayala, Francisco José (1934–) Spanish–American biologist who has worked extensively in the field of molecular evolution. He has also sought to measure genetic variation in natural populations, rates of evolution, and the amount of genetic change needed to produce new species. Many of his results were published in his *Molecular Evolution* (1976) and in a work he coauthored in 1977 entitled *Evolution*. Ayala has written a number of other books including *Molecular Genetics* (1984).

B

Bacillariophyta *See* diatoms.

bacillus Any rod-shaped bacterium. Bacilli may occur singly (e.g. *Pseudomonas*), in pairs, or in chains (e.g. *Lactobacillus*). Some are motile.

backbone *See* vertebral column.

background extinction *See* extinction.

Bacteria One of the three cellular kingdoms (domains) in certain classifications (ARCHAEA and EUKARYA are the other two). It was formerly named Monera or Prokaryotae. In the Five Kingdoms classification scheme, ARCHAEA and EUBACTERIA are subkingdoms of Bacteria. Lynn MARGULIS and Karlene Schwartz defended their status as subkingdoms by arguing that these two groups did not evolve by symbiosis, which sets them apart from other organisms. Bacteria are a large and diverse group of prokaryotic unicellular organisms, which, in terms of numbers and variety of habitats, include the most successful life forms. Bacterial cells are simpler than those of animals and plants. They lack well-defined membrane-bound nuclei, i.e. they are PROKARYOTES and do not contain complex organelles such as chloroplasts and mitochondria. They may divide (by binary FISSION) every 20 minutes and can thus reproduce very rapidly. They also form resistant spores.

The oldest fossils resemble bacteria, especially the present-day cyanobacteria, and are believed to be about 3.5 billion years old. It can be argued that their endurance throughout the known fossil record and their continued success could mean that when all other living organisms have perished, bacteria will persist in some form or other until the sun finally goes out.

In nature, bacteria are important in the nitrogen and carbon cycles, and some are useful to humans in various industrial processes, especially in the food industry, and in techniques of GENETIC ENGINEERING. However, there are also many harmful parasitic bacteria that cause such diseases as botulism and tetanus. *See also* Cyanobacteria; endosymbiont theory; myxobacteria; origin of life; sulfur bacteria.

bacteriophage *See* phage.

Baer, Karl Ernst von (1792–1876) German–Estonian biologist, comparative anatomist, and embryologist who is often described as 'the father of modern embryology'. In 1817 Baer became professor of zoology at Königsberg and in 1834 moved to the Academy of Sciences at St. Petersburg. It was prior to his move to St. Petersburg that Baer did most of his research, laying the foundation of comparative embryology as a separate discipline. He established that all mammals, including humans, develop from eggs. He also traced the development of the fertilized egg and the order in which the organs of the body appear and develop, showing that similar (homologous) organs arise from the same germ layers in different animals. His expounding of the 'biogenetic law' (*see* recapitulation), demonstrating the increasing similarity in the embryos of different animals as one investigates younger and younger embryos, provided Darwin with some basic arguments for his evolutionary theory. Baer was, however, opposed to the idea of a common ancestor for all animal life, although he conceded that some animals and some races of man might have had common ancestry. His great work on the mammalian egg, *De ovi mammalium et hominis genesi* (1827; On the Origin of the Mammalian and Human Ovum) was followed (1828–37) by *Über Entwickelungsgeschichte der Tiere* (On the Development of Animals), in which he surveyed all existing knowledge of vertebrate development.

balanced polymorphism *See* polymorphism.

Balanoglossus *See* Hemichordata.

Balbiani ring *See* puff.

Baldwin effect The selection of genes that strengthens the genetic basis of a particular PHENOTYPE.

Balfour, Francis Maitland (1851–1882) British zoologist. Much influenced by the work of Michael Foster, with whom he wrote *Elements of Embryology* (1883), Balfour demonstrated the evolutionary connection between vertebrates and certain invertebrates, both of which have a NOTOCHORD in their embryonic stages. Balfour proposed the term 'Chordata' for all animals possessing a notochord at some stage in their development, the Vertebrata (backboned animals) being a subphylum of the Chordata. He was also an early exponent of RECAPITULATION. Other important publications by Balfour include *On the Development of Elasmobranch Fishes* (1878) and *Comparative Embryology* (1880–81).

Banks, Sir Joseph (1743–1820) British botanist. He studied botany at Oxford, graduating in 1763, and three years later traveled abroad for the first time as naturalist on a fishery-protection vessel heading for Labrador and Newfoundland. On the voyage he collected many new species of plants and insects and, on his return, was elected a fellow of the Royal Society.

The Royal Society was organizing a voyage to the South Pacific to observe the transit of Venus across the Sun and in 1768 James Cook set sail in the *Endeavour* and Banks accompanied him. Cook landed in Australia where Banks found that most of the Australian mammals were marsupials, which are more primitive, in evolutionary terms, than the placental mammals of other continents.

After three years with the *Endeavour* Banks returned to England, with a large collection of unique specimens, to find himself famous.

Throughout his life he retained his interest in natural history. As honorary director of Kew Gardens he played a major part in establishing as many species as possible and in providing a center for advice on the practical use of plants. He also initiated a number of successful projects, including the introduction of the tea plant to India from its native China and the transport of the breadfruit from Tahiti to the West Indies.

basal body 1. (kinetosome) A barrel-shaped body found at the base of all eukaryote cilia and flagella (undulipodia) and identical in structure to the CENTRIOLE. It is essential for formation of undulipodia.
2. An assembly of thin plates found at the base of bacterial flagella.

base 1. (*Chemistry*) A compound that reacts with an acid to produce water plus a salt.
2. (*Biochemistry*) A nitrogenous molecule, either a PYRIMIDINE or a PURINE, that combines with a pentose sugar and phosphoric acid to form a nucleotide, the fundamental unit of nucleic acids. The most abundant bases are cytosine, C, thymine, T, and uracil, U, (pyrimidines) and adenine, T, and guanine G, (purines).

base pairing The linking together of the two helical strands of DNA by bonds between complementary bases, adenine pairing with thymine and guanine pairing with cytosine. The specific nature of base pairing enables accurate replication of the chromosomes and thus maintains the constant composition of the genetic material. In pairing between DNA and RNA the uracil of RNA pairs with adenine.

base ratio The ratio of adenine (A) plus

thymine (T) to guanine (G) plus cytosine (C). In DNA the amount of A is equal to the amount of T, and the amount of G equals the amount of C, but the amount of A + T does not equal the amount of C + G. The A + T : G + C ratio is constant within a species but varies between species.

Basidiomycota (basidiomycetes) A phylum of FUNGI characterized by their spore-bearing structures (basidia) borne on a fertile layer (the hymenium) on the fruiting body. The basidia produce basidiospores. Basidiomycetes may be saprophytes or parasites and include mushrooms, toadstools, puffballs, rusts, and smuts.

Bates, Henry Walter (1825–92) British naturalist and explorer. In 1844 he met Alfred WALLACE and, three years later, Wallace suggested they should travel together to the tropics to collect specimens and data that might throw light on the evolution of species.

In May 1848 they arrived at Pará, Brazil, near the mouth of the Amazon. After two years collecting together they split up, and Bates spent a further nine years in the Amazon basin. By the time he returned to England in 1859, he estimated that he had collected 14 712 species, 8000 of which were new to science.

While in the Amazon Bates had noted striking similarities between certain butterfly species – a phenomenon later to be called BATESIAN MIMICRY. He attributed this to natural selection, since palatable butterflies that closely resembled noxious species would be left alone by predators and thus tend to increase. His paper, *Contributions to an Insect Fauna of the Amazon Valley, Lepidoptera: Heliconidae* (1861) provided strong supportive evidence for the Darwin–Wallace evolutionary theory, which had been published three years earlier. Darwin persuaded Bates to write a book on his travels, *The Naturalist on the River Amazon* (1863), an objective account of the animals, humans, and natural phenomena that Bates had encountered.

Batesian mimicry *See* mimicry.

Bateson, William (1861–1926) British geneticist. Working in Cambridge, Bateson began studying variation within populations and found instances of discontinuous variation that could not be related simply to environmental conditions. He believed that this discovery was of evolutionary importance, and began a series of breeding experiments to investigate the phenomenon more fully. These prepared him to accept MENDEL's work when it was rediscovered in 1900, although other British scientists were skeptical at the time. Bateson translated Mendel's paper into English and set up a research group at Grantchester to investigate heredity in both plants and animals.

Through his study of comb shape in poultry, he was able to show that Mendelian ratios are found in animal crosses (as well as plants). He turned up various deviations from the normal dihybrid ratio (9:3:3:1), which he rightly attributed to gene interaction. He also found that certain traits are governed by two or more genes and showed that some characters are not inherited independently. This was the first hint that genes are linked on chromosomes, although Bateson never accepted T. H. Morgan's explanation of linkage or the chromosome theory of inheritance.

In 1908 he became the first professor of the subject he himself named – genetics. He was the leading proponent of Mendelian genetics in Britain and became involved in a heated controversy with supporters of biometrical genetics such as Karl PEARSON. The views of both sides were later reconciled by the work of Ronald FISHER. Bateson wrote a number of books, including the controversial *Materials for the Study of Variation* (1894) and *Mendelian Heredity – A Defence* (1902).

bats *See* Chiroptera.

bauplan *See* archetype.

bees *See* Hymenoptera.

beetles *See* Coleoptera.

behavior, animal A general term applied to any observable activity of a whole animal. Behavior includes all the processes by which an animal senses its external surroundings and the internal state of its body and responds to any changes it perceives. An animal behaves continuously in order to survive – to feed, drink, reproduce, and avoid being eaten. Some behavior is *innate* and some is learned through experience. *See also* instinct.

belemnites Extinct marine invertebrates related to squid, octopi, and chambered nautiluses, that were common along with the AMMONITES in the Jurassic and Cretaceous periods and had bullet-shaped internal chambered shells known as *guards*. Usually only the guard is found, which is in fact the back part of the shell. In *Cylindroteuthis*, for example, the hollow region in front of the guard (the *alveolus*) contains the chambered part of the shell (the *phragmocone*). *See also* Cephalopoda; nautiloids.

benefit Any change in a trait that increases FITNESS. For example, the evolution of lungs increased the ability of vertebrates to adapt to life on land. *Compare* cost.

Bennettitales (Cycadeoidales) A fossil GYMNOSPERM order (similar to the CYCADALES) that evolved in the Mesozoic, but became extinct at the end of the era. They were widespread, particularly in North America. Some had short stout trunks, others were tall and slender and both types bore tufts of long narrow leaves. The cones, formed at the ends of lateral branches (rather than on the stem tips), bear some resemblance to the angiosperm flower. They had whorls of microsporophylls resembling stamens surrounding megasporangia with ovules. However, unlike angiosperm ovules, they were not enclosed in a carpel. The microsporophylls and megasporophylls were borne on a receptacle surrounded by a series of bracts, suggesting a similarity to sepals and petals. Within the seeds was an embryo with two cotyledons and some endosperm. Examples are *Williamsonia* of the Jurassic of Yorkshire, England, and the genus *Cycadeoidia* widespread, particularly in North America. The Bennettitalean or Cycadeoidian 'flower' suggests the beginnings of the evolution of the angiosperm flower. *See* Angiospermophyta.

benthic Describing organisms that live on or in the sea bed. Benthic epifauna live upon the seafloor or upon bottom objects and benthic infauna live within the surface sediments. *Compare* pelagic.

bifurcation *See* phylogeny.

big-bang theory (superdense theory) A widely accepted theory for the formation of the Universe approximately 10×10^9 years ago. All the matter in the Universe was packed into a superdense mass followed by a cataclysmic explosion in which matter was thrown out at enormous speeds in every direction. A brief period of very rapid expansion formed a Universe of mainly hydrogen and some helium. As the Universe expanded and cooled, concentrations of gas were pulled together, by gravity, to form galaxies. Stars formed within these galaxies, synthesizing heavier elements from hydrogen and helium nuclei until they consisted mainly of iron when the larger stars exploded and created the elements heavier than iron.

bilateral symmetry The arrangement of parts in an organism in such a way that the structure can only be divided into similar halves (mirror images) along one plane. Bilateral symmetry is characteristic of most free-moving animals, where one end constantly leads during movement. However, some secondary asymmetry of internal organs has occurred in humans and other vertebrates. In plants, bilateral symmetry is seen particularly in flowers (e.g. snapdragon), the condition commonly being termed *zygomorphy*. *See also* radial symmetry.

binocular vision A type of vision in which the eyes point forward so that the image of a single object can be focused onto the fovea of both eyes at once. This allows perception of depth and distance. It is an important evolutionary adaptation, particularly for animals living in trees. Binocular vision is found in primates and other vertebrates, especially active predators, such as owls.

binomial nomenclature A system introduced by LINNAEUS, the Swedish botanist, in which each species is given two names. The first is the generic name, written with a capital letter, which designates the genus to which the species belongs. The second is the specific name, indicating the species. The generic and specific names are in Latin and are printed in italic type. For example, humans belong to the species *Homo sapiens*. *Homo* is the generic name and *sapiens* is the specific name. If an organism has already been referred to in any preceding text, it is customary to shorten the generic name to its initial capital letter followed by a full point, i.e. *Homo sapiens* can now be shortened to *H. sapiens*. The scientific name of an organism is used to enable accurate communication among scientists because an organism may have more than one common name. For example, *Bidens frondosa* has a number of common names: rayless marigold, devil's jackboot, bur marigold, etc. *See* Linnaean classification.

biochemical taxonomy The use of chemical characteristics to help classify organisms; for example, the Asteroideae and Cichorioideae, which are the two main divisions of the plant family Compositae, are separated by the presence or absence of latex. This area of taxonomy has increased in importance with the development of chromatography, electrophoresis, serology, and other analytical techniques.

biodiversity The number and variety of organisms in a given locality, community, or ecosystem. High biodiversity is typical of complex and highly productive ecosystems, such as tropical rainforests, where a small area can contain many different species of animals, plants, and other organisms. Biodiversity is often used as an indicator of the health of such ecosystems.

biogenesis The theory that living things originate only from other living things as opposed to nonliving matter. The theory became accepted as a result of the work of Redi and Pasteur, who showed that dirt, for example, does not itself produce bacteria or maggots, but that bacteria and maggots only come from spores or eggs already existing in the dirt. This theory satisfactorily explains the occurrence of existing organisms, but not the origins of the first organisms. *See* abiogenesis.

biogeography The study of the geographic distribution of species and higher taxons across the Earth. *Vicariance biogeography* shows the relationship between geographic distribution and possible geological or climatic events that cause splitting in the distribution range of a taxon (*vicariance effects*), such as CONTINENTAL DRIFT. For example, true camels live in Asia and Africa. The discovery of fossil camels in the Tertiary of North America indicates that Asia and North America were once connected and the closely related llamas of South America are the descendants of these extinct North American camels. Thus, the present-day geography of living things can be explained in part by dramatic geological events (such as continental drift) together with the fossil record. *See* biome; phytogeography; zoogeographical region.

bioherm *See* coral.

bioinformatics The use of computers to analyze biological information. Algorithms are used to compare the sequences of DNA and proteins to detect structural, functional, and evolutionary relationships between the sequences. *See* molecular phylogenetics.

biolistics *See* recombinant DNA (def. 1).

biological species concept The definition of a SPECIES as a group of organisms that can interbreed and produce viable grandchildren. This is the most widely used definition in vertebrates. *Compare* cladistic species concept; ecological species concept;

phenetic species concept; recognition species concept.

biology The study of living organisms, including their structure, function, evolution, interrelationships, behavior, and distribution.

biome A major regional terrestrial community of plants and animals with similar life forms and environmental conditions. It is the largest geographical biotic unit, and is named after the dominant type of vegetation, such as tropical rainforest, grassland, desert, tundra, etc. Biomes gradually merge into one another and are not sharply divided regions.

biometrics The quantitative study of the characteristics of living organisms.

biopoiesis The origin of organisms from replicating molecules. Biopoiesis is a cornerstone of ABIOGENESIS. Deoxyribonucleic acid (DNA) is the best example of a self-replicating molecule, and is found in the chromosomes of all higher organisms. In some bacterial viruses (bacteriophages) ribonucleic acid (RNA) is self-replicating. Various chemical and physical conditions must be met before either DNA or RNA is able to replicate.

biosphere The part of the Earth and its atmosphere that is inhabited by living organisms. The Earth's surface and the top layer of the hydrosphere (water layer) have the greatest density of living organisms. The geosphere, or nonliving world, is made up of the lithosphere (solid earth), hydrosphere, and atmosphere.

biostratigraphy The division of rocks into various zones (biostratigraphic units) based on their fossil assemblages, e.g. oolitic limestones.

biosynthesis Chemical reactions in which a living cell builds up its necessary molecules from other molecules present.

biosystematics The area of systematics in which experimental taxonomic techniques are applied to investigate the relationships between taxa (*see* taxon). Such techniques include serological methods, biochemical analysis, breeding experiments, and cytological examination, in addition to the more established procedures of comparative anatomy. Evidence from ecological studies may also be brought to bear. *See also* molecular phylogenetics.

biota The combined flora and fauna of an area.

biotype **1.** A naturally occurring group of individuals all with the same genetic composition, i.e. a clone of a pure line. *Compare* ecotype.
2. A physiological race or form within a species that is morphologically identical with it, but differs in genetic, physiological, biochemical, or pathogenic characteristics.

bipedalism Using two legs for locomotion, specifically walking upright on two hind limbs. Humans habitually walk on the hind limbs resulting in an upright posture in contrast to the anthropoid apes, which are semi-erect (*see* anthropoids). Bipedalism is advantageous to humans as it allows greater flexibility of the arms, hands, and fingers. Accompanying major changes in the skeleton (the vertebral column and pelvis) and in the muscular system have also occurred. *See also* human evolution.

bipinnaria A form of DIPLEURULA larva characteristic of starfish. It bears lobes that carry ciliated bands used for feeding and locomotion. *Compare* pluteus.

birds *See* Aves.

bisexual *See* hermaphrodite.

Biston betularia *See* industrial melanism.

bivalent A term used for any pair of homologous chromosomes when they pair up during MEIOSIS. Pairing of homologous chromosomes (SYNAPSIS) commences at one or several points on the chromosome and is clearly seen during the first division of meiosis.

bivalve mollusks   *See* Pelecypoda.

black smokers   Plumes of dark-colored dense water produced by fissures (*hydrothermal vents*) in the ocean floor consisting of metallic sulfides of copper, zinc, and lead. Volcanic eruptions on the sea floor heat the sea water and the dark sulfide minerals swirling around resemble clouds of smoke. It is believed that such vents occurred in Archean times (*see* Precambrian) and in the sulfur-rich precipitates around the vent, it is possible that primitive SULFUR BACTERIA may have evolved and may represent the most primitive life forms.

blastula   The stage in an animal embryo following cleavage. It is a hollow fluid-filled ball of cells. *See also* Hydrozoa.

blending inheritance   The historically influential but incorrect theory that organisms contain a blend of their parents' hereditary factors and pass that blend on to their offspring. It is now known that the apparent blending is the result of CO-DOMINANCE. For example, if a pure-bred *Antirrhinum* plant with a red flower is crossed with a pure-bred *Antirrhinum* plant with a white flower, the resulting F_1 generation plants have pink flowers. Both alleles for flower color are expressed equally. Selfing the pink F_1 generation results in 25% of plants with white flowers, 50% of plants with pink flowers, and 25% of plants with red flowers. *See* Mendelian inheritance.

blood vascular system   In mammals, a continuous system of vessels containing blood, which transports food materials, excretory products, hormones, respiratory gases, etc., from one part of the body to another. The blood is circulated by muscular contractions of the heart: it is first pumped to the lungs but returns to the heart to be pumped around the body.
   Certain invertebrates (mollusks and arthropods) have an open system in which blood flows in blood spaces (e.g. the *he-mocoel* of Crustacea). Vertebrates and most invertebrates have a closed system with the blood contained in blood vessels and generally circulated by muscular contractions of the vessels or a heart. In fish, the blood flows only once through the heart before circulating around the body (single circulation) but in other vertebrates blood returning to the heart is circulated to the lungs, where it is oxygenated, before being repumped around the body (double circulation).

blue-green algae   *See* Cyanobacteria.

blue-green bacteria   *See* Cyanobacteria.

B lymphocyte   *See* AIDS; immune response.

Bodo skull   *See Homo sapiens.*

body cavity   In most metazoan animals, the cavity bounded by the body wall, which contains the heart, viscera, and many other organs. The body cavity of many triploblastic animals is the coelom; the body cavity of arthropods is the *hemocoel*. *See* coelom.

bone beds   Sedimentary rocks containing a large number of fossil bones, teeth, fish scales, COPROLITES, etc. Examples include the hadrosaur (DINOSAUR) bone beds of Alaska and the bone beds of the *Rhaetic series* of the late Triassic period that contain fossil bones of the earliest mammals, e.g. *Megazostrodon*, a tiny shrewlike mammal from the Triassic Red Bed series of the Karoo, Lesotho, southern Africa.

Bone Wars   The acrimonious feud and intense rivalry that took place in the final third of the 19th century between two eminent US paleontologists – Edward Drinker COPE and Othniel Charles MARSH – and continued over several decades.
   Cope was an expert in the anatomy of lizards and snakes and as a very young man joined the Philadelphia Academy, working for Dr Joseph Leidy, and eventually becoming secretary of the Academy and also

professor of natural history at Haddonfield College. At the Academy, he worked on the fossil reptile collection, including the skeleton of *Hadrosaurus foulkii*, the first almost complete dinosaur skeleton ever to be discovered, which was found in a Cretaceous marl pit in 1858 at Haddonfield, New Jersey. In 1865, Cope discovered a second dinosaur skeleton near Haddonfield (*Dryptosaurus aquilungus*). Cope was a prolific writer and published many scientific papers throughout his life.

Marsh also had an intense interest in collecting and studying fossils and was established as the first professor of paleontology at Yale at the time he first became interested in Cope's publications. They had first met at the University of Berlin and they organized a joint expedition in 1868 when Marsh visited the New Jersey marl fields. After Marsh had returned to Yale, Cope discovered that he had secretly bribed some of the workers and managers at the marl pits to send their bones to Yale, rather than to Haddonfield. The Bone Wars had begun.

Beginning in 1870, both Marsh and Cope conducted separate expeditions to the western lands of the USA, to the site of an ancient Cretaceous seashore that had been surrounded by swamps. This extended through parts of Kansas, Nebraska, Colorado, and Wyoming. During these expeditions many wonderful fossils of all kinds were discovered and cataloged, including giant turtles and enormous pterodactyls and apatosauruses (brontosauruses).

Cope once published a paper describing an *Elasmosaurus* (a marine sauropod dinosaur), but unfortunately had placed the head on the wrong end. When Marsh discovered this, he made sure that the error was much publicized, despite Cope's attempts to withdraw the paper after discovering his mistake.

Both men used the forts belonging to the US cavalry as their bases and transported their equipment and fossils in covered wagons drawn by mules. Marsh used his political influence to acquire the protection of the US army on his expeditions and was accompanied on his first expedition in 1871 by Buffalo Bill (William F. Cody), who was a friend and also acted as a guide. He was unconcerned about the dangers posed by Native Americans, whose territories and treaties he often violated, being obsessed with his fossil finds. Marsh, however, sensibly sought the friendship of Red Cloud on his first expedition, promising to present the case for the Indian nations with the President on his return, a promise that he kept. Cody, however, had a more personal relationship with the Indians, for example, it is said that he entertained and fascinated them by taking out his false teeth.

Matters came to a head between Marsh and Cope in 1877 in Wyoming. Railroad workers had told Marsh that they had discovered large bones when excavating at Como Buffalo. In 1879, Cope turned up and accused Marsh first of trespassing and then of stealing his fossils. Marsh ordered the dinosaur pits to be dynamited rather than let Cope have them. Cope countered by directing a train containing Marsh's fossils to be delivered to Philadelphia.

Both men were wealthy, but their much publicized rivalry had resulted in Congress putting a stop to their funding and so they had to use up much of their wealth to finance their own expeditions. In spite of this, they made a massive contribution to paleontology and it is estimated that Cope discovered 56 and Marsh 86 new dinosaur species.

Bonnet, Charles

Bonnet, Charles (1720–93) Swiss naturalist who is chiefly remembered for discovering PARTHENOGENESIS (reproduction without fertilization) in the spindle-tree aphid and for the ideas on evolution that he proposed following this observation.

Bonnet believed all organisms are preformed and that the germs of every subsequent generation are contained within the female. Such thinking implied that species remain constant, leaving Bonnet to explain how species become extinct as evidenced by fossil remains. He argued that the Earth had experienced periodic catastrophes, each destroying many life forms, but the remaining species all evolved to some degree. (Bonnet was the first to use the term 'evolution' in a biological context.) Thus after the next catastrophe apes progress to men, and men become angels. The CATASTROPHISM THEORY was adopted by Georges CUVIER, and was a strong influence on geological thinking until the 1820s.

bony fishes   *See* Osteichthyes.

boot strapping   A statistical method, based on repeated random sampling, of estimating confidence in a phylogenetic tree.

Boreal period   The period from 7500–5000 BC, following the deglaciation of the last Ice Age and characterized by a warmer, improving climate. It was named Boreal for the predominantly coniferous vegetation of NW Europe where the first investigations were conducted. It was followed by the ATLANTIC PERIOD.

Boucher de Crevecoeur de Perthes, Jacques   (1788–1868) French archeologist. His hobby was investigating the fossil-rich beds of the Somme Valley near Abbeville in northern France, and in *Antiquités celtiques et antédiluviennes* (3 vols. 1847–64; Celtic Antediluvian Antiquities) he first described the existence of a prehistoric world occupied by humans. He reported finding such objects as stone axes, which he attributed to the people he called 'celtiques', and also older tools linked with the remains of extinct mammalian species. These he claimed must have belonged to 'homme antédiluvien'.

Such ideas initially received little support in France, where Georges CUVIER's views still dominated evolutionary thinking, although British scientists were more sympathetic. Later evidence that some of the finds at Abbeville were forgeries tended to discredit Boucher de Perthes' early work.

Boxgrove Man   *See Homo sapiens.*

Brachiopoda   (brachiopods)   A small phylum of marine invertebrates, the lamp shells (e.g. *Lingula*), living attached to a firm substratum in shallow waters. They are so called because they are shaped like a Roman oil lamp. Lamp shells superficially resemble bivalve mollusks in the possession of a bivalve shell, but the valves are placed dorsally and ventrally (as opposed to laterally, as in bivalves). The internal *lophophore*, a filter-feeding organ composed of ciliated tentacles, protrudes from the shell. Excretion is carried out by nephridia. The sexes are separate and there is a free-swimming larva.

The phylum was very much larger in the Paleozoic and they were one of the most common animals in the seas of that time. More than 30 000 fossil species have been identified, but by the Jurassic period only two groups were common and today only 300 species exist. The largest of all the brachiopods, *Terebratula*, became extinct at the end of the Pliocene. Individuals of the genus *Lingula* are identical to their Cambrian fossil ancestors.

brain   The most highly developed part of the nervous system, which is located at the anterior end of the body in close association with the major sense organs and is the main site of nervous control within the animal. Brain size is primarily governed by body size with intelligence a secondary factor. More intelligent animals have a larger brain size compared to their body size.

Natural selection has favored a high concentration of sense organs in the head to process the new stimuli that an organism encounters thus resulting in an enlargement of the nerve cord in this region (CEPHALIZATION). The most primitive brain probably funneled impulses from the sense organs to the nerve cords, which transmitted impulses to the appropriate motor neurons. Even in organisms such as nematodes, information began to be processed and analyzed resulting in a primitive 'brain'. This evolutionary trend has reached its highest peak yet in the vertebrates and particularly humans. The most obvious evolutionary change in the vertebrate brain is a marked increase in the size and complexity of the forebrain, particularly the cerebrum, and the decrease in size and importance of the midbrain.

In fishes and birds, the major sensory and motor centers occur in the greatly enlarged deeper regions of the cerebrum – the *corpus striatum*. This is thought to reflect the predominance of INSTINCT in bird behavior, whereas in mammals, in which learning and memory are paramount, the cerebral cortex (*neopallium*) is the dominant region of the brain.

branching evolution *See* cladogenesis.

Branchiopoda The most primitive class of the Crustacea. Most branchiopods live in fresh water (except *Artemia*, the brine shrimp), and have flat fringed appendages for filter feeding, respiration, and locomotion. The heart and nervous system resemble those of annelids. Parthenogenesis is common. The class includes *Daphnia* (water flea). Fossil branchiopods have been discovered as far back as the Cambrian period.

Branchiostoma (*Amphioxus*) A genus of small marine burrowing cephalochordates, the lancelets (*see* Cephalochordata). *Branchiostoma* has a fish-shaped body with a dorsal and caudal fin and segmentally arranged V-shaped muscle blocks (myotomes). The pharynx and pharyngeal (or gill) slits are modified for food collec-

tion as well as respiration. Excretion is by nephridia, which is unique among chordates.

breeding true Displaying the same character state in the offspring as in the parents, indicating the character is genetically determined (and therefore the parents are genetically similar).

bristle worms *See* Polychaeta.

brittle stars *See* Ophiuroidea.

broad sense heritability (*H2*) The proportion of phenotypic variation in a population due to the genetic variation between individuals. It is of limited value in estimating the response to selection and is given by: *H2 = VG / VP*. *Compare* narrow sense heritability. *See* variance.

Broken Hill 1 *See Homo sapiens*.

Brongniart, Alexandre (1770–1847) French geologist and paleontologist. His early work included his *Essai d'une classification naturelle des reptiles* (1800; Essay on the Classification of Reptiles) in which

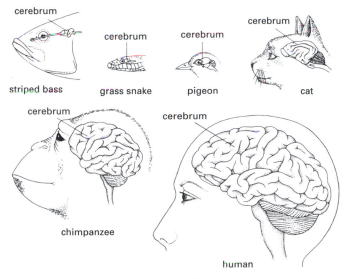

Brain

he divided the Reptilia into the Chelonia, Sauria, Ophidia, and Batrachia. In 1822 he published the first full-length account of trilobites, the important paleozoic arthropods.

His most significant research was done in collaboration with Georges Cuvier on the geology of the Paris region, published jointly by them in 1811 as *Essai sur la géographie minéralogique des environs de Paris* (Essay on the Mineralogical Geography of the Environs of Paris). In this, they were among the first to identify strata within a formation by their fossil content; earlier geologists had tended to rely on the characteristics of the rocks themselves rather than their content. Brongniart and Cuvier were also able to show a constant order of fossil sequence, mainly of mollusks, over the whole Paris region.

They also produced evidence that counted strongly against the neptunism of Abraham WERNER in their discovery of alternate strata of fresh- and sea-water mollusks. The solution to the problem of how fresh- and sea-water strata could alternate was crucial for the new science of geology and was to lead to the catastrophism of Cuvier and the evolution theory of Charles Darwin.

Brontosaurus   *See* dinosaur.

Bronze Age   *See* Neolithic.

Broom, Robert   (1866–1951) British–South African morphologist and paleontologist. Broom's major contributions have been concerned with the evolutionary origins of mammals, including humans. He excavated and studied the fossils of the Karroo beds of the Cape in South Africa, and in the 1940s discovered numbers of AUSTRALOPITHECINE skeletons in Pleistocene-age quarries at Sterkfontein in the Transvaal. These have been very important in investigations of human ancestry. Broom's account of their discovery is given in *Finding the Missing Link* (1950).

brown algae   *See* Phaeophyta.

Bryophyta   A phylum of simple, mainly terrestrial, plants commonly found in moist habitats and comprising the mosses, liverworts, and hornworts. They show a heteromorphic ALTERNATION OF GENERATIONS, the gametophyte being the dominant generation. When mature the gametophyte, especially of mosses, shows differentiation into stem and leaves but there are no roots or vascular tissues. The sporophyte, which is wholly dependent on the gametophyte, is simply a spore capsule borne on a stalk. Bryophytes lack woody tissue and are rare as fossils. The oldest have been discovered in the Carboniferous. The paucity of fossil evidence, however, does not mean that they were rare plants. *See also* Anthocerotae; Hepaticae; Musci.

Bryozoa   A phylum of mainly marine sessile invertebrates, the moss animals and sea mats, which live in colonies resembling seaweed or form an encrusting sheet on rocks and shells. The massive forms of fossil Bryozoa resemble corals and some of them were classified as corals for many years. The oval or tubular individuals live in self-secreted horny, chalky, or gelatinous protective cases, into which they retreat when disturbed. They have a coelom, a ciliated tentacular food-catching organ (*lophophore*) surrounding the mouth, and a U-shaped gut. There are two classes, often regarded as separate phyla. In the Ectoprocta, the anus lies outside the tentacles and there are no special excretory organs. The Entoprocta have the anus within the tentacles, no true coelom, and protonephridia as excretory organs.

Fossil bryozoans are found in most limestone deposits from the Ordovician to the present day. Specimens can be obtained by treating weathered limestone surfaces with a weak solution of hydrochloric acid. Specimens may also be washed out of clay deposits. Identification of most specimens is only possible by microscopic examination of thin sections. Many species had a short range in terms of geological time but a wide geographic distribution, which makes them useful in identifying the age of rocks. They are particularly important in studying the cores extracted when drilling in the quest for petroleum.

Subgroups Cryptostomata (e.g. *Archimedes*, *Polypora*) and Treptostomata (e.g. *Constellaria*) are Paleozoic fossils; Cyclostomata (e.g. *Stomatopora*, *Alveolaria*) are found from the Ordovician to the present day; subgroup Cheilostomata are post-Paleozoic (Mesozoic and Cenozoic) and include the commonest living bryozoans, e.g. *Membranipora* (Miocene to Recent) and *Lunulites* (Cretaceous to Eocene).

budding (*Phylogenetics*) Speciation forming a new side branch in a lineage and the subsequent formation of a new higher taxon by the descendants of the new species.

bugs *See* Hemiptera.

bunodont *See* molar.

Burgess shale A deposit of shale above the town of Field, just above the Burgess Pass on the slopes of Mount Wapta, in British Columbia, Canada, dating from the middle of the Cambrian period (about 550 mya) and noted for the remarkable preservation of fossils of soft-bodied marine animals. It was discovered by the US paleontologist Charles D. Walcott working in the Canadian Rockies. The fossils include not only many unique arthropods, such as the elegant spined *Marella*, but other organisms with no known relatives, either living or fossil. Such an example is the strange segmented *Opabinia*, with its prominent frontal nozzle and five eyes. Study of the Burgess fauna has led to a dramatic reassessment of life in the early Cambrian, indicating a huge diversity of marine lifeforms, both soft-bodied and hard-bodied (e.g. trilobites), and prompting speculation about why so few forms survived (10–20%) and so many others became extinct.

This evidence for a Cambrian explosion (*see* Cambrian) depicted in the Burgess shale has also been discovered in deposits in China near Chengjiang. The similarity of the fossils indicates a worldwide distribution. It is possible that the evolutionary development of segmentation of the embryos of multicellular organisms along the anterior–posterior axis triggered off differentiation of organs and appendages (*see* punctuated equilibrium). New species that were less well adapted to available niches could have been gradually selected out and become extinct. It is also possible that there may have been a catastrophic event at the end of the Cambrian, similar to the Alvarez event that occurred at the end of the Cretaceous, that resulted in a MASS EXTINCTION. *See also* Alvarez theory.

butterflies *See* Lepidoptera.

C *See* cytosine.

Caenorhabditis elegans *See* Nematoda.

Caenozoic *See* Cenozoic.

Cainozoic *See* Cenozoic.

Calamites *See* Carboniferous.

Cambrian The earliest period of the PALEOZOIC era, about 590–510 mya. It is so-named because typical rocks of this age are found in Wales (Medieval Latin: Cambria), UK. It is characterized by the appearance of marine algae, photosynthetic bacteria, such as CYANOBACTERIA, and a proliferation of marine invertebrate animal forms, including ancestors of most modern animals – the so-called *Cambrian explosion*. The climate became increasingly warm and dry with increasing levels of carbon dioxide (global warming) (*see* greenhouse effect).

The first animals with shells appeared in the Cambrian (mollusks and brachiopods) and the dominant arthropods were represented by the TRILOBITES. Many soft-bodied animals, such as annelid worms, left behind burrows, trails and tracks (*see* fossils). The shallow Cambrian seas teemed with life in contrast to the empty land, where there were no animals moving around, and with no trees or flowers, it was probably a bleak empty rocky barren place.

The extinction of 80–90% of the diverse types of marine invertebrates at the end of the Cambrian and the survival of the remainder, which were the ancestors of the majority of present-day phyla, could be due either to a period of punctuational change (*see* punctuated equilibrium) followed by gradual evolution or, alternatively, by a catastrophic event (*see* Burgess shale). The punctuational change could have resulted from major genetic alterations that might have included translocations (*see* chromosome mutations), DELETIONS, and polyploidy (*see* polyploid), which in turn affected the developmental and regulatory genes. Many authorities think that this was a period when the genetic designs of major phyla were first (accidentally) 'got right', resulting in the extinction of those forms in which the design was unsuitable for the climatic conditions that prevailed. Alternatively, it is possible that animals with other genetic designs were simply not allowed to develop as the ecological niches were all successfully filled. Since the Cambrian, only one new phylum of marine invertebrates – the Bryozoa – has evolved. *See also* geological time scale.

Cambrian explosion *See* Burgess shale; Cambrian; Paleozoic.

canalization The limitation of phenotypic variation by developmental mechanisms.

canalizing selection Selection that uses an organism's developmental mechanisms to repress deleterious phenotypic changes. It is brought about by MUTATIONS in the genes that control development.

Candolle, Augustin Pyrame de (1778–1841) Swiss botanist. In 1813 he published his *Théorie élémentaire de la botanique* (Elementary Theory of Botany), in which he introduced the term 'taxonomy' to mean classification. This work was based on the natural classificatory systems of CUVIER and Antoine Jussieu. Candolle maintained that relationships between plants could be established through similarities in the plan of symmetry of their sexual parts. He realized that the symmetry could be disguised by fusion, degeneration, or loss of sexual organs, making structures with a common ancestry appear different. Candolle thus formulated the idea of homologous parts – an important concept in the theory of evolution. Despite this, Candolle continued to believe in the immutability of species. Between 1824 and 1839 he published the first seven volumes of his huge *Prodromus Systematis Naturalis Regni Vegetabilis* (Guide to Natural Classification for the Plant Kingdom), an encyclopedia of the plant kingdom. His son, Alphonse de Candolle, saw to the publication of the remaining ten volumes after his father's death and also carried on many of his father's other schemes.

canine (eye tooth) A mammalian tooth with a single pointed crown, occuring on either side of the jaw between the INCISORS in front and the PREMOLARS behind. There is one canine on each side of each jaw, making a total of four. They are typically conical and pointed, and in carnivorous mammals, like the dog, they are long and fanglike. Canines are used for killing prey, by piercing and tearing the flesh. In rodents, such as mice and rats, they are absent. *See also* teeth.

capsid The protein coat of a VIRUS, surrounding the nucleic acid. A capsid is present only in the inert extracellular stage of the life cycle. Capsids are composed of subunits called *capsomeres*.

capsomere *See* capsid.

captorhynids *See* cotylosaurs.

carbon-14 dating *See* radioactive dating.

Carboniferous The second most recent period of the Paleozoic era, some 355–280

mya. It is characterized by the evolution on swampy land of amphibians. There were also a few primitive early reptiles, the first forms of winged insects resembling dragonflies (e.g. *Homoioptera*), primitive cockroaches, millipedes, centipedes, spiders (*see* Insecta), and giant ferns. Aquatic life included a type of king-crab (*Belinurus*), sharks, and coelacanths. The period is named for the extensive coal deposits that formed from the remains of vast forests of swamp plants. One of the commonest was *Lepidodendron* (*see* Lycopodophyta) and *Lepidocarpon*, with a reproductive structure almost approaching seed form. Giant horsetails (e.g. *Calamites*) also flourished along with the seed ferns (*see* Cycadofilicales), and the fossil order CORDAITALES (e.g. *Cordaites*), ancestral to present-day conifers and resembling the modern monkey puzzle tree. These abundant forests shed their parts, died, and fell into the swamps building up great layers of peat that were compressed and changed into bituminous coal. Subsidence caused flooding above and further sedimentation resulted in alternating seams of coal.

The Mississippian (Lower Carboniferous) is characterized by huge deposits of limestone, formed from the marine species that proliferated in the warm tropical seas. During this time, the land masses were drifting slowly toward one another and the sea levels steadily rose. The Pennsylvanian (Upper Carboniferous) is characterized on the land by swamps and evolving forests as the sea levels began to drop and fluctuate. Gradually the climate in the southern hemisphere began to cool, and the continents continued their drift toward another. *See also* geological time scale.

carcinogen Any substance that causes living tissues to become cancerous. Chemical carcinogens include many organic compounds, e.g. hydrocarbons in tobacco smoke, as well as inorganic ones, e.g. asbestos. Carcinogenic physical agents include ultraviolet light, x-rays, and radioactive materials. Some viruses are carcinogenic. Most carcinogens are mutagenic, i.e. they cause changes in the DNA; dimethylnitrosamine, for example, methylates the bases in DNA. A potential carcinogen may therefore be identified by determining whether it causes mutations, as by the Ames test, which uses bacteria.

carnassial teeth Specialized teeth found in carnivorous mammals (*see* Carnivora). They comprise the last PREMOLAR in the upper jaw, and the first MOLAR in the lower jaw, and are very large and used to cut up meat and shear it from bones. Carnassial teeth have a single line of sharp-edged points (cusps) parallel to the jaw. The smooth flat surface of the upper carnassial slides over the outer smooth surface of the lower one, like the two blades of a pair of garden shears. When carnivores eat bones or meat, they move food back in the mouth so that they can gnaw it with these teeth.

Carnivora The order that contains the flesh-eating mammals, including *Canis* (wolf, dog), *Felis* (cat), *Meles* (badger), and *Lutra* (otter). They evolved after the HERBIVORES and INSECTIVORA, became widespread in the OLIGOCENE and even more prevalent in the Miocene and Pliocene epochs. The teeth of carnivores are specialized for biting and tearing flesh. The long pointed canines are used for killing prey, two pairs of CARNASSIAL TEETH (modified cheek teeth) shear the flesh and the sharp molars and premolars crush and grind it. The claws are well developed and sometimes retractile. Carnivores are typically intelligent mammals with keen senses. Most eat flesh, but the bears are omnivorous and the panda is a herbivore.

The first 'true carnivores', the *miacids*, evolved (alongside the CREODONTS and CONDYLARTHS) from small meat-eating mammals, e.g. *Cimolester*, which had shearing teeth showing the beginnings of carnassial teeth. The two main branches that evolved from the miacids are the *vulpavines* (dog group) and the *viverravines* (cat group).

The vulpavines evolved into a number of different lineages (a few extinct ones) and include foxes, wolves, jackals, badgers, otters, raccoons, bears, and pandas. Not all of this group are carnivores, and

the *pinnipeds* (sea lions, walruses, seals) have become adapted to life in the sea.

The viverravines are all carnivores. There are four main groups: the mongooses; the hyenas; the 'tree' cats (extinct saber-tooth cats; lions, tigers, wildcats, pumas, panthers, ocelots and cheetahs); and the civets and genets.

carnivore An animal that feeds largely or exclusively on meat or other animal tissue, especially a mammal of the order CARNIVORA (e.g. dogs, cats, wolves, etc.). Carnivores generally have powerful jaws, teeth modified for tearing flesh and cracking bones, and well-developed claws. *Compare* herbivore; omnivore.

carotid arch *See* aortic arches.

carpal bone A bone in the distal region of the forelimb of TETRAPODS. In humans the carpal bones constitute the wrist (carpus).

In the typical PENTADACTYL LIMB there are 12 carpal bones, arranged in three rows. However, there are various modifications and reductions to this basic pattern; in humans there are only eight. They articulate with each other, and with the metacarpal bones distally. Three carpal bones form the wrist joint with the radius of the forearm. *Compare* tarsal bones. *See also* homologous; divergent evolution.

carpel The female reproductive organ of a flowering plant. It usually consists of an ovary, containing one or more ovules, a stalk, or style, and a terminal receptive surface, the stigma. The carpel is HOMOLOGOUS with the megasporophylls of certain pteridophytes and the ovuliferous scales of gymnosperms. It has evolved by fusion of the two edges of the megasporophyll. This development can be most clearly seen in simple carpels such as those of the Leguminosae.

cartilaginous fishes *See* Chondrichthyes.

caste One of the several specialized groups of individuals that exist in a community of social insects, especially ants, bees, wasps, or termites. They are distinguished by structural and functional differences. For example, honeybees have three castes: the queen (a fertile female) reproduces; workers (sterile females) gather food; and drones (males) mate with the queen. The caste system is an example of POLYMORPHISM in animals.

catarrhine A member of the group of *Old World Monkeys* with broad noses, from which humans evolved. *See* Primates. *Compare* platyrrhine.

catastrophism The theory, now generally thought to be false, that past geological changes have occurred as a result of a number of sudden catastrophes (*compare* uniformitarianism). A succession of catastrophes was also invoked to explain the extinction of organisms, linked to special creations to account for the appearance of new forms.

causation *See* proximate causation; ultimate causation.

Cavalli-Sforza, Luigi Luca (1922–) Italian geneticist. Cavalli-Sforza has specialized mainly in the genetics of human populations, producing with Walter Bodmer a comprehensive survey of the subject in their *Genetics, Evolution and Man* (1976). He has also done much to show how genetic data from present human racial groups could be used to reconstruct their past separations. This reconstruction, based on the analysis of 58 genes, yields a bifurcated evolutionary tree with Caucasian and African races in one branch and Orientals, Oceanians, and Amerinds in the other. The main division appeared, according to Cavalli-Sforza, some 35–40 000 years ago.

Caytoniales A Mesozoic (Jurassic) GYMNOSPERM fossil group that became extinct in the late Cretaceous (e.g. *Caytonia* and *Gristhorpia*). Members of this group had small berrylike fruits that appear to have developed from closed ovaries. They evolved at about the same time as the angiosperms, but the ovaries do not correspond to those of the latter.

cDNA *See* complementary DNA.

cecum A blind pouch at the junction of the ileum and colon. It ends in the vermiform appendix and in most mammals is very short; in HERBIVORES (e.g. the rabbit) it is large and has an important function. These animals eat only plant food consisting mainly of cellulose, which mammals are normally unable to digest. Herbivores rely on the activity of millions of symbiotic bacteria living in the cecum. These produce enzymes capable of digesting cellulose and releasing simple soluble substances that can be absorbed into the bloodstream. The cecum has no villi and its only secretion is mucus.

In insects a number of ceca are found projecting from the midgut, increasing the surface area for absorption.

cell The basic unit of structure of all living organisms, excluding viruses. Cells were discovered by Robert Hooke in 1665, but Schleiden and Schwann in 1839 were the first to put forward a clear *cell theory*, stating that all living things were cellular. There are now recognized to be three cellular kingdoms: ARCHAEA, BACTERIA, and EUKARYA. Archaea and Bacteria are prokaryotic cells and Eukarya contain eukaryotic cells. Prokaryotic cells (typical diameter 1 μm) are significantly smaller than eukaryotic cells (typical diameter 20 μm). The largest cells are egg cells (e.g. ostrich, 5 cm diameter); the smallest are mycoplasmas (about 0.1 μm diameter). All cells contain genetic material in the form of DNA, which controls the cell's activities; in eukaryotes this is enclosed in the nucleus. All contain cytoplasm, containing various organelles and are surrounded by a plasma membrane, which controls entry and exit of substances. Plant cells and most prokaryotic cells are surrounded by rigid cell walls. In MULTICELLULAR organisms cells become specialized for different functions (DIFFERENTIATION); this is called *division of labor*. Within the cell, further division of labor occurs between the organelles. *See* unicellular; eukaryote; prokaryote; endosymbiont theory.

cell cycle The ordered sequence of phases through which a cell passes leading up to and including cell division (mitosis). It is divided into four phases G_1, S, and G_2 (collectively representing interphase), and M-phase, during which mitosis takes place. Synthesis of messenger RNA, transfer RNA, and ribosomes occurs in G_1, and replication of DNA occurs during the S phase. The materials required for spindle formation are formed in G_2. The time taken to complete the cell cycle varies in different tissues. For example, epithelial cells of the intestine wall may divide every 8–10 hours.

cell division The process by which a cell divides into daughter cells. In unicellular organisms it is a method of reproduction. Multicellular organisms grow by cell division and expansion, and division may be very rapid in young tissues. Mature tissues may also divide rapidly when continuous replacement of cells is necessary, as in the epithelial layer of the intestine. In plants certain growth regulators (e.g. cytokinins) stimulate renewed cell division. *See* amitosis; meiosis; mitosis.

cell lineage The theory stating that cells arise only from pre-existing cells. The cell lineage of a structure traces the successive stages that the cells pass through from the time of their formation in the zygote to their appearance in the mature functional structure.

cell membrane *See* plasma membrane.

cell plate A structure that appears in late ANAPHASE in dividing plant cells and is involved in formation of a new plasma membrane and cell wall.

cell theory The theory that all organisms are composed of cells and cell products and that growth and development results from the division and differentiation of cells. This idea resulted from numerous investigations that started at the beginning of the 19th century and it was finally given form by Schleiden and Schwann in 1839.

cell wall A rigid wall surrounding the cells of plants, fungi, bacteria, and algae. Plant cell walls are made of cellulose fibers in a cementing matrix of other polysaccharides. Fungi differ, with their walls usually containing chitin. The walls of some algae also differ, e.g. the silica boxes enclosing diatoms. Bacterial walls are more complex, containing peptidoglycans – complex polymers of amino acids and polysaccharides. Cell walls are freely permeable to gases, water, and solutes. They have a mechanical function, allowing the cell to become turgid by osmosis, but preventing bursting. This contributes to the support of herbaceous plants. Plant cell walls can be strengthened for extra support by addition of lignin (as in xylem and sclerenchyma) or extra cellulose (as in collenchyma). Plant cell walls are an important route for movement of water and mineral salts. Other modifications include the uneven thickening of guard cells, the sieve plates in phloem, and the waterproof coverings of epidermal and cork cells.

At cell division in plants the *primary wall* is laid down on the middle lamella of the cell plate as a loose mesh of cellulose fibers. This gives an elastic structure that allows cell expansion during growth. Later the *secondary wall* grows and acquires greater rigidity and tensile strength. New cellulose fibers are laid down in layers, parallel within each layer, but orientated differently in different layers. The Golgi apparatus provides polysaccharide-filled vesicles that deposit wall material by exocytosis, guided by microtubules.

Cenozoic (Caenozoic; Cainozoic) The present geological era, beginning some 65 mya, and divided into two periods, the TERTIARY and the QUATERNARY. It is characterized by the rise of modern organisms, especially mammals and flowering plants. *See also* geological time scale.

centipedes *See* Chilopoda.

central dogma Information (in the form of precise determination of sequence) can pass from nucleic acid to nucleic acid and from nucleic acid to protein but never from protein to nucleic acid.

central nervous system (CNS) The part of the nervous system that receives sensory information from all parts of the body and, through the many interconnections that are possible, causes the appropriate messages to be sent out to muscles and other organs. In vertebrates the CNS consists of the BRAIN and spinal cord. The CNS of invertebrates consists of a connected pair of ganglia in each body segment and a pair of ventral nerve cords running the length of the body.

The development of a CNS is associated with the increasing sensory awareness and complex actions that are involved in locomotion, feeding, reproduction, etc., and the need for central integration of all sensory input and motor output. The increasing importance of the dominant head and brain is a process known as CEPHALIZATION. This compares with the simple localized integration found in the nerve net of COELENTERATES.

centriole A CELL organelle consisting of two short tubular structures orientated at right angles to each other. It lies outside the nucleus of animal and protoctist cells, but is absent in cells of most higher plants. Prior to cell division it replicates, and the sister centrioles move to opposite ends of the cell to lie within the spindle-organizing structure, the centrosome. However, the centriole is not essential for spindle formation, although an analogous structure, the basal body, is responsible for organizing the microtubules of undulipodia (cilia and flagella). Under the electron microscope, each 'barrel' of the centriole is seen to consist of a cylinder of nine triplets of microtubules surrounding two central ones.

centromere (kinomere; spindle attachment) The region of the chromosome that becomes attached to the nuclear spindle during mitosis and meiosis. Following the replication of chromosomes, resultant chromatids remain attached at the centromere. The centromere is a specific genetic locus and remains relatively uncoiled during prophase, appearing as a primary constriction. It does not stain with basic dyes.

centrosome A structure found in all eukaryotic cells, except fungi, that forms the SPINDLE during cell division. It lies close to the nucleus in nondividing cells, but at the commencement of cell division it divides, and the sister centrosomes move to opposite ends of the cell, trailing the microtubules of the spindle behind them. In animal and protoctist cells the centrosome contains two short barrel-shaped structures, the CENTRIOLE, but this is not directly involved in spindle formation. In fungi, the function of the centrosome is served instead by the spindle pole body. *See* mitosis.

cephalization The development of a head – in which sense organs, BRAIN, and feeding organs are concentrated – in animals.

The anterior end of the body is the first part to encounter new stimuli as an animal moves forward. Natural selection therefore favored this arrangement of a high concentration of sense organs in the anterior region accompanied by an increase in the number of neurones and the development of a head. The more primitive brains simply transmitted impulses from the sensory neurones to the motor neurones, but the selective advantage of processing the sensory inputs led to an increase in the number of neurons and hence to a more advanced brain. *See* central nervous system; nervous system.

Cephalochordata A marine subphylum of chordates in which the characteristics of metameric segmentation, NOTOCHORD, dorsal nerve cord, and pharyngeal (gill) slits are retained in the adult. The best-known member is BRANCHIOSTOMA (*Amphioxus*). *Compare* Urochordata.

Cephalopoda The most advanced class of mollusks, containing the cuttlefishes (e.g. *Sepia*), squids (e.g. *Loligo*), and the octopus (*Octopus*). All are marine and typically have a ring of prehensile suckered tentacles around the mouth for food capture, a well-developed nervous system, and eyes. Some can learn to distinguish various shapes.

Part of the foot is modified as a siphon through which water is forced by contraction of the muscular mantle during swimming. *Nautilus* has a large coiled shell, which acts as a buoyancy chamber, and numerous unsuckered tentacles. Squids and cuttlefishes have an internal shell and ten tentacles; in the octopus, which has only eight tentacles, the shell is absent.

Cephalopods have been prevalent in the seas and oceans since CAMBRIAN times. There are about 10 000 fossil species. NAUTILOIDS were dominant in the Paleozoic and AMMONITES in the Mesozoic. The decapods (with ten arms) have existed since the Triassic and include the now extinct BELEMNITES. The octopods (with eight arms) evolved in the Cretaceous.

ceratopsian   *See* dinosaur.

Cestoda   *See* Platyhelminthes.

Cetacea   The order that contains the only completely marine mammals – the whales, dolphins, and porpoises. They have a hairless streamlined body, no hind limbs, forelimbs modified as flippers, and a tail with horizontal flukes used for propulsion. An insulating layer of blubber beneath the skin helps to conserve heat, there are no external ears, and the respiratory outlet from the lungs is the dorsal blowhole. The toothed whales, e.g. *Delphinus* (dolphin) and *Orcinus* (killer whale), feed on fish and other animals and have many peglike teeth. The whalebone whales, e.g. *Balaenoptera musculus* (blue whale), feed on plankton filtered from the sea by baleen plates in the mouth.

The cetaceans epitomize a perfect ADAPTATION to life in the seas. Whales, for example, have evolved gradually, diverging from MESONYCHIDS before 64 mya. The oldest known fossils of *Pakicetus* (a carnivore) lived on land near shallow streams. *Ambulocetus* was discovered to have short legs, big feet, a long snout and a powerful tail. It probably swam like an otter but could still walk on land. *Rodhocetus* had legs and hips that were only just connected to the vertebral column and probably used its tail to swim. *Basilosaurus* fossils had very streamlined bodies, long snouts, and arms that had become flippers, but retained hips, hind legs, and tiny toes. It was, however, fully marine and would not have survived on land. Other fossils, including *Durodon*, show a greater resemblance to modern whales. Unlike fish, because of their early land ancestry, whales swim by undulating their tails, not moving them from side to side as do fish. *See also* missing link.

C-factor paradox   The name sometimes given to the fact that most eukaryotic cells have more DNA than they need to code for their genes. Some of this excess DNA is apparently functionless and the amount of excess varies dramatically between species. *See* selfish DNA.

chalicotheres   *See* Perissodactyla.

chalk   *See* Cretaceous; Mesozoic.

character   Any distinguishable trait, feature, or property that in any given taxon or sequence takes one of two or more different states, for example, eye color at base position 23 of a particular DNA sequence.

character displacement   The increased difference in the characters of two closely related species where they live together (SYMPATRY) compared with where they live apart (ALLOPATRY).

character state   The specific value taken by a CHARACTER in a specific taxon or sequence, for example, green eyes or guanine at position 23 of a particular DNA sequence.

Charales   *See* Chlorophyta.

chasmogamy   The production of flowers that open their petals so that cross-pollination is possible.

Chelicerata In some classifications, a phylum of arthropods (*see* Arthropoda) containing the spiders, scorpions, mites, and ticks (class ARACHNIDA); the sea spiders (class Pycnogonida); and the horseshoe crabs (king crabs) (class Merostomata). They are of ancient origin, some of their ancestors having evolved in the Cambrian. They lack antennae and are characterized by the anterior pair of clawed jointed feeding appendages (chelicerae). The head and thorax are fused to form a single unit, the cephalothorax (*prosoma*), which is distinct from the abdomen (*opisthosoma*).

Eurypterids are an extinct group of aquatic chelicerates resembling scorpions found in the Ordovician–Carboniferous. The carapace of these animals was not expanded and their abdomens consisted of 12 segments, narrowing toward the posterior and ending in a long spiky tail. *Eurypterus* grew in size to over a meter long and the fossil *Pterygotus* is the largest known arthropod, about 3 m long. They were carnivorous predators and either swam or crawled along the bottom of salty or brackish water.

The pycnogonids evolved in the Devonian (e.g. *Paleopantopus mancheri*) and certain authorities believe that they probably evolved from a land-living ancestor and returned to the water secondarily. The scorpions evolved in the Silurian and the modern genus *Limulus* has been identified since Triassic times.

Chelonia *See* Reptilia.

chemical fossils Particularly resistant organic chemicals present in geological strata that are thought to indicate the existence of life in the period when the rocks were formed. Chemical fossils (e.g. alkanes and porphyrins) are often the only evidence for life in rocks of PRECAMBRIAN age.

chemotrophic *See* heterotrophic.

chiasma (pl. chiasmata) A connection between homologous chromosomes seen during the prophase stage of MEIOSIS. Chiasmata represent a mutual exchange of material between homologous, nonsister chromatids (crossing over) and provide one mechanism by which RECOMBINATION occurs, through the splitting of linkage groups.

Chicxulub crater *See* Alvarez theory.

Chilopoda The class of arthropods that contains the centipedes (e.g. *Lithobius*), characterized by a flat body divided into numerous segments, each bearing one pair of walking legs. They are terrestrial and breathe air through tracheae. Excretion is by Malpighian tubules. Centipedes are carnivorous, with poison claws on the first body segment. They are sometimes placed with the millipedes (Diplopoda) in the group MYRIAPODA. They arose in the Carboniferous, along with millipedes, land scorpions, and spiders. Fossil chilopods have been found in the Tertiary. *Compare* Diplopoda.

chimera An individual or part of an individual in which the tissues are a mixture of two genetically different tissues. It may arise naturally due to mutation in a cell of a developing embryo, producing a line of cells with the mutant gene, and hence different characteristics compared to surrounding cells. It may also be induced experimentally. For example, two mouse embryos at the eight-cell stage from different parents can be fused and develop into a mouse of normal size. Analysis of the genotypes of the tissues and organs of such a mouse reveals that there is a random mixture of the two original genotypes.

In plants, chimeras produced from two different species are known as *graft hybrids*. For example, a bud may develop at the junction between the scion and stock with a mixture of tissues from both. Many variegated plants are examples of *periclinal chimeras*, in which a mutation has occurred in a sector of tissue derived from the tunica or corpus, resulting in subsequent chlorophyll deficiency. For example, in a white-edged form of *Pelargonium*, the outermost layer is colorless, indicating a lack of chlorophyll, and is the result of a mutation. There is no genetic mixture throughout the plant.

It is believed that the first EUKARYOTE originated from a chimera between two PROKARYOTES, a eubacterium and an archaebacterium. Possibly the prokaryote and the eukaryote live symbiotically before the resultant chimera formed. *See also* chloroplast; endosymbiont theory; mitochondrion; origin of life; symbiosis.

chimpanzee   *See* Primates.

Chiroptera   The order that contains the bats, the only flying mammals. Bats have a thin elastic hairless flight membrane (*patagium*) extending from the elongated forearm and four of the elongated fingers to the hind limbs and, usually, the tail. The first finger and the toes are smaller, free, and clawed. Bats are nocturnal. They have specialized ears and use echolocation to avoid objects and to catch food. Bats evolved very rapidly from an insectivore-like ancestor in the Paleocene. *See also* adaptation; adaptive radiation.

chlorophyll   *See* chloroplast.

Chlorophyta (green algae)   A phylum of protoctists comprising mainly freshwater algae with some marine and terrestrial forms. They contain the pigments chlorophyll *a* and *b* together with carotenes and xanthophylls. The Chlorophyta store food as starch and fat and have cell walls containing cellulose and hemicellulose. They are of interest because their pigments, metabolism, and ultrastructure resemble those of the lower plants more closely than do those of any other algal phyla. Some of the commoner orders include: Volvocales, unicellular and colonial plants, e.g. *Chlamydomonas*, *Volvox*; Chlorococcales, including unicellular and coenobic plants, e.g. *Chlorella*, *Pediastrum*; Ulotrichales, filamentous and thallose plants, e.g. *Ulothrix*, *Ulva*; Oedogoniales, e.g. the filamentous *Oedogonium*; and the Conjugales (Zygnematales), e.g. *Spirogyra*. The evolutionary changes within this group are suggested by the variety of forms that exist. For example, there is a change from unicellular forms (*Chlamydomonas*) to colonial multicellular forms as in *Gonium*, *Pando-*

rina, and *Volvox*. This is accompanied by an increase in the number of cells and increasing DIVISION OF LABOR and interdependence. In sexual reproduction, there is a change from ISOGAMY to ANISOGAMY to oogamy, which in the latter involves the retention of the female gametes on the parent plant. Fewer female gametes are produced but they store more nutrients. This is an evolutionary trend that continues in higher plants.

The less well-known class Charophyceae, especially the order *Charales* (the stoneworts), have gained much more attention in recent years as they are now known, by gene sequencing, to be very closely related to the kingdom Plantae (i.e. they are a PARAPHYLETIC group). They are a highly modified group within the Chlorophyta and are included because of their similar physiology and pigments. Unlike other green algae, cell division involves the formation of a cell plate (phragmoplast), as in plants. Sexual reproduction also resembles that of higher plants. It is oogamous and complex, the male gametes having asymmetrical flagella, not a characteristic of the other Chlorophyta except for the order Coleochaetales.

Stoneworts consist of a branched thallus with an erect stemlike structure with whorls of branches arising from nodes, resembling higher plants. They occur in shallow fresh or brackish water, especially calcium-rich water, in which they become encrusted with lime, hence their name. They are an ancient group of plants of great fossil age. Having only two genera, *Chara* and *Nitella*, which are not very varied may reflect this. Their earliest appearance (possible rhizoids and bulbils) in the RHYNIE CHERT (e.g. *Palaeonitella cranii*) is still controversial, but they are well known in the marls and limestones of the Jurassic and Cretaceous by their fossilized oogonia (*gyrogonites*). The latter are used as ZONE FOSSILS in the Purbeck limestones of southern England.

chloroplast   The organelle found in the cells of algae and higher plants where photosynthesis occurs. It is bound by a double membrane and contains photosynthetic pigments such as *chlorophyll*. Chloroplasts have their own DNA and sequence analysis of their ribosomal RNA genes show that they are closely related to CYANOBACTERIA. This supports the theory that chloroplasts are derived from symbiotic photosynthetic PROKARYOTES that colonized the cytoplasm of primitive EUKARYOTES. *See* endosymbiont theory; mitochondrion.

Choanichthyes *See* Osteichthyes.

Chondrichthyes (Elasmobranchii) The class of vertebrates that contains the cartilaginous fishes – the sharks, skates, and rays, e.g. *Scyliorhinus*, (dogfish). They are predominantly marine predators characterized by a cartilaginous skeleton, a skin covering of denticles (placoid scales) that are modified in the mouth as rows of teeth, pectoral and pelvic fins, and a heterocercal tail; lungs and a swim bladder are absent, therefore the fish sink when they stop swimming. Most have separate gill openings, not covered by an operculum, and a small spiracle. The pelvic fins in the male often bear claspers through which sperm are transmitted in internal fertilization.

The cartilaginous skeleton rarely fossilizes and the usual fossil remains are the resistant teeth, scales, and fin spines. Despite this, these fish are well represented in geological strata. Sharks first appeared in the Devonian, e.g. *Cladoselache*, discovered in the black shales of the Upper Devonian of Ohio, had no claspers and a primitive jaw suspension similar to the present-day Port Jackson shark (*Heterodontus*). *Pleurocanthus* (late Devonian to Triassic) inhabited fresh water, but most ancestral cartilaginous fish were marine. Bony fish (*see* Osteichthyes) are a more ancient group and it seems that possession of a cartilaginous skeleton is a degenerate characteristic rather than a primitive one. Chondrichthyes show a number of anatomical advances over the CYCLOSTOMATA. *See* Selachii. *See also* Placodermi.

chondrocranium The first part of the skull to form in vertebrate embryos. It consists of cartilaginous structures – plates and capsules – that protect and support the brain, olfactory organs, eyes, and the inner ear. It usually becomes ossified in adults, although it remains cartilaginous in CHONDRICHTHYES (cartilaginous fish).

Chordata A major phylum of bilaterally symmetrical metamerically segmented coelomate animals characterized by the possession at some or all stages in the life history of a dorsal supporting rod, the NOTOCHORD. The dorsal tubular nerve cord lies immediately above the notochord and a number of visceral clefts (pharyngeal (gill) slits) are present in the pharynx at some stage of the life history. The post-anal flexible tail is the main propulsive organ in aquatic chordates. The phylum includes the subphylum Craniata (Vertebrata) (*see* craniates), in which the notochord is replaced by a vertebral column (backbone).

The chordates are related to the echinoderms (*see* Echinodermata), the development of the bilaterally symmetrical larvae in echinoderms having several chordatelike features. *See also* dipleurula.

There are two other subphyla, the UROCHORDATA and CEPHALOCHORDATA (sometimes known collectively as the Acrania or Protochordata). These invertebrate chordates are marine.

chromatid One of a pair of replicated chromosomes found during the prophase and metaphase stages of mitosis and meiosis. During mitosis, sister chromatids remain joined by their centromere until anaphase. In meiosis it is not until anaphase II that the centromere divides, the chromatids being termed daughter chromosomes after separation.

chromatin The loose network of threads seen in nondividing nuclei that represents the chromosomal material, consisting of DNA and protein (mainly histone). It has a regular repeating structure with about 200 bp of DNA wrapped around the outside of a core of histone proteins to form a *nucleosome*. Nucleosomes are joined together by *linker DNA* to make a flexible chain of nucleosomes. The nucleosome chains are then coiled to form hollow fibers 30 nm in diameter, which can be further coiled into 240 nm diameter fibers. It is this that is visible as the typical looped threadlike material of the nondividing CHROMOSOME. Chromatin is classified as *euchromatin* or *heterochromatin* on the basis of its staining properties, the latter staining much more intensely with basic stains because it is more coiled and compact. Euchromatin mainly consists of the 30 nm fibers and is thought to be actively involved in transcription and therefore protein synthesis, while heterochromatin is inactive. Euchromatin stains more intensively than heterochromatin during nuclear division. *See also* chromosome.

chromomere A region of a chromosome where the chromosomal material is relatively condensed, and consequently stains darker. Clusters of chromomeres produce distinct bands, the pattern of which is characteristic for a particular chromosome and is used to distinguish the chromosomes of a particular organism.

chromosome One of a group of threadlike structures of different lengths and shapes in nuclei of eukaryotic cells. They are made of CHROMATIN and carry GENES that are linked together. Some chromosomes also have an RNA component. The name chromosome is also given to the genetic material of bacteria and viruses. During nuclear division the chromosomes are tightly coiled and are easily visible through the light microscope. After division, they uncoil and become difficult to see individually, existing as less densely packaged chromatin.

The number of chromosomes per nucleus is characteristic of the species, for example, humans have 46. Normally one set (haploid) or two sets (diploid) of chromosomes are present in the nucleus. In early prophase of MITOSIS and later prophase of MEIOSIS, the chromosomes split lengthwise into two identical CHROMATIDS held together by the CENTROMERE. In diploid cells, there is a pair of SEX CHROMOSOMES; the remainder are termed AUTOSOMES. The evolution of chromosomes is a key event because linking genes together means they can be replicated synchronously, which makes

replication easier to control. Having genes linked also makes equal segregation of genes at CELL DIVISION more likely. *See* chromomere; chromosome map.

chromosome map (genetic map) A diagram showing the order of genes along a chromosome. Such maps have traditionally been constructed from information gained by linkage studies (to give a *linkage map*) or by observations made on the polytene (giant) salivary-gland chromosomes of certain insects, e.g. *Drosophila*, to give a *cytological map*. The techniques employed differ according to the type of organism being studied. For example, many plants and animals can be crossed experimentally to study inheritance patterns of particular genes, but this is not possible in humans, where family pedigrees were, until recently, often the only available evidence. However, the advent of new molecular techniques has dramatically changed the nature of chromosome mapping in all organisms, including humans. The HUMAN GENOME PROJECT is an international project which was set up to map all the 50 000 or so genetic loci present on human chromosomes. The first draft of the map was published in 2001, covering 97% of the human genome and the project was completed in 2002.

Genetic maps of other organisms including bacteria, yeast, plants, and other animals have also been produced and the data can be used in constructing (molecular) phylogenies (*see* phylogeny). *See* DNA probe; gene library; Nematoda; restriction fragment length polymorphism; restriction map.

chromosome mutation A change in the number or arrangement of genes in a chromosome. If chromosome segments break away during nuclear division they may rejoin the chromosome the wrong way round, giving an *inversion*. Alternatively, they may rejoin a different part of the same chromosome, or another chromosome, giving a *translocation*. If the segment becomes lost, this is termed a *deficiency* or *deletion*; it is often fatal. A part of a chromosome may be duplicated and occur either twice on the same chromosome or on two different nonhomologous chromosomes: this is a *duplication*. Chromosome mutations can occur naturally but their frequency is increased by x-rays and chemical mutagens. *See also* gene mutation; mutation; genome mutation.

chronology The sequence of events in their order of occurrence over time. *See also* geological time scale.

chytrids *See* Fungi.

cichlids A group of freshwater fishes that have been intensively studied because of their enormous diversity in relatively stable environments, such as the Great Lakes of Africa. Lake Victoria, for example, dried up in the last Ice Age, but since then has filled with water to reach its present-day state. Thus the cichlids of this lake have evolved from one or two common ancestors in a very short period of geological time, with over 500 species, but no geographical barriers to isolate them. It is believed that SEXUAL SELECTION may be responsible for their diversity, as there is a great variety of color in males and also elaborate courtship rituals, i.e. there is a reproductive barrier.

With the increase in pollution, male colors are obscure in the murky waters and difficult to recognize, resulting in hybridization between different species and the formation of new species (*see* hybrid). GENE SEQUENCING may provide the answer to this fascinating collection of organisms.

Ciliata *See* Ciliophora.

Ciliophora A phylum of protoctists containing some of the best-known protozoans. All have cilia for locomotion, a contractile vacuole, and a mouth. Most have two types of nuclei, the meganucleus (macronucleus) controlling normal cell metabolism, and the smaller micronucleus controlling sexual reproduction (conjugation). Binary fission also takes place. Some (e.g. *Paramecium*) are covered with cilia. Others (e.g. *Vorticella*) have cilia only round the mouth, and in some (e.g. *Sten-*

tor) these cilia are specialized for feeding. *See* Protoctista.

cilium A whiplike extension of certain eukaryotic cells that beats rapidly, thereby causing locomotion or movement of fluid over the cell. Cilia and flagella represent the two types of eukaryotic undulipodium. Cilia are identical in structure to flagella, though shorter, typically 2–10 μm long and 0.5 μm in diameter and usually arranged in groups. Each cilium has a BASAL BODY at its base. In ciliated protoctists, sperm, and some marine larvae they allow locomotion. In multicellular animals they may function in respiration and nutrition, wafting water containing respiratory gases and food over cell surfaces, e.g. filter-feeding mollusks. In mammals the respiratory tract is lined with ciliated cells, which waft mucus, containing trapped dust, bacteria, etc., towards the throat.

Cilia and flagella have a '9 + 2' structure (the axoneme), consisting of 9 outer pairs of microtubules with 2 single central microtubules enclosed in an extension of the plasma membrane. The beat of each cilium comprises an effective downward stroke followed by a gradual straightening (limp recovery). Cilia beat in such a way that each is slightly out of phase with its neighbor (*metachronal rhythm*), thus producing a constant rather than a jerky flow of fluid. The basal bodies of cilia are connected by threadlike strands (neuronemes), which coordinate the beating of neighboring cilia. *Compare* flagellum.

circulatory system A continuous series of vessels or spaces in nearly all animals that transports materials around the body. The system is best developed in mammals. Circulatory systems developed in association with the differentiation of specific organs and tissues in multicellular animals. They enable all parts of the body to receive a constant supply of oxygen, food, etc., and to have waste products removed promptly. *See also* blood vascular system.

***cis–trans* effect** The phenomenon resulting from recombination within a gene (cistron), in which a mutation is only expressed in the phenotype if the mutant pseudoalleles are on different homologous chromosomes. *See cis–trans* test.

***cis–trans* test** A test that determines whether two mutations that have the same effect occur in the same functional gene or in different genes. The mutations may be in either the *cis* position (i.e. on the same chromosome) or the *trans* position (one on each homolog). If the mutations are in different genes then a normal phenotype results whether the mutations are in the *cis* or *trans* position, since they are masked by corresponding dominant genes on the other homolog. However, if the mutations are in the same gene then a normal phenotype will result only if the mutations are in the *cis* position. In the *trans* position the mutant phenotype is expressed, since both alleles of the locus are mutants.

cistron A segment of DNA that codes for a single polypeptide chain of a protein molecule. Its extent may be defined by the *cis-trans* test. *See* gene.

CITES (Convention on International Trade in Endangered Species of Wild Fauna and Flora) An international agreement signed in 1973 by approximately 80 nations prohibiting trade in endangered species of wild plants and animals and in any products derived from these animals. 375 species were initially covered and more have subsequently been added. 239 species could only be traded if a special permit was issued by both the exporting and importing countries. The countries (known as parties) that belong to CITES are not bound by international law, but are provided with a framework that enables them to legislate on a national level to implement the convention. In 1989 CITES imposed a total ban on the ivory trade as African elephants were being killed at an alarming rate for their tusks. Even in protected nature reserves, poachers still managed to kill these animals. The numbers of elephants in some countries (not all) began to increase again and in 1997, Botswana, Namibia, and Zimbabwe were allowed to trade in ivory once more, albeit in a very

limited way. Today, 160 countries belong to CITES and about 25 000 plant species and 5000 animal species are protected. Examples include primates, whales, orchids, corals, and cacti.

clade The branch of a phylogeny that contains all the species descended from a common ancestor. *See* monophyletic.

cladistic Describing the evolutionary pathways of taxonomic groups, particularly the relationships between organisms due to recent common ancestry. *See* cladistics.

cladistics A method of CLASSIFICATION in which the relationships between organisms are based on selected shared characteristics. These are generally assumed to have been derived from a common ancestor, in the evolutionary process of cladogenesis, although the 'transformed cladists' believe that shared characteristics alone provide a logical basis for classification without postulating evolutionary relationships. The patterns of these shared characteristics are demonstrated in a branching diagram called a *cladogram*. The branching points of the cladogram may be regarded either as an ancestral species (as in an evolutionary tree) or solely as representing shared characteristics. An *area cladogram* shows the relationships between organisms from different geographic areas.

Cladistics assumes the closeness of relationship depends on the recentness of common ancestry, indicated by the number and distribution of shared characteristics that can be traced back to a recent common ancestor. It is based on phylogenetic principles and ignores phenetic relationships. Cladistics also regards the only true natural groups (monophyletic groups) as those containing *all* the descendants of a common ancestor. *See* phylogenetic. *Compare* phenetic.

cladistic species concept The definition of a species as a group of organisms in a single lineage between two phylogenetic branch points. It defines a species throughout its existence. *See* cladistics. *Compare* biological species concept; ecological species concept; phenetic species concept; recognition species concept.

cladogenesis The branching of an evolutionary line into two or more separate lineages, i.e. evolutionary change occurring during speciation events. *Compare* anagenesis. *See* cladistics. *See also* phyletic gradualism; punctuated equilibrium.

cladogram *See* cladistics.

class A taxonomic rank that is subordinate to a phylum (or sometimes a division in plant taxonomy) and superior to an order. The Latin names of plant classes end in -ae (e.g. *Monocotyledonae*) or in -opsida (e.g. *Gnetopsida*). Classes may be divided into subclasses with Latin names ending in -idae.

classification 1. The grouping and arrangement of organisms into a hierarchical order. There are three main methods of classification: CLADISTIC, evolutionary, and PHENETIC. All three produce LINNAEAN CLASSIFICATION but are based on different evolutionary principles and can therefore result in different and conflicting classifications. Each has advantages and disadvantages and there is no universally accepted best method. Techniques in molecular biology have also proved to be useful. The nucleotide sequences of genes that encode RIBOSOMAL RNA can be compared in different organisms as they are highly conserved. New problems have arisen as a result of these techniques. *See also* systematics; taxonomy.

2. The arrangement of organisms resulting from classification procedures. An important aspect of classifications is their predictive value. For example, if a characteristic is found in one member of a group of plants, then it is also likely to be found in the other members of that group even though the characteristic in question was not used in the initial construction of the classification.

cleidoic egg (amniotic egg) An egg with

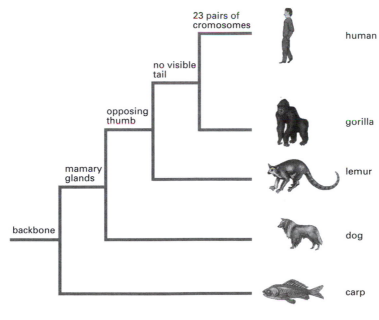

Cladistics

a tough amniotic shell, which permits gaseous exchange but restricts water loss (although it may take up water). The embryo develops in a fluid-filled cavity, in spite of being in a dry place. Characteristic of reptiles, birds, and insects, it usually has a large food store (yolk and, in birds, albumen). Its development was an important evolutionary advance for life on land.

cline A graded series of characters exhibited by a species or other related group of organisms, usually along a line of environmental or geographical transition. The populations at each end of the cline may be substantially different from each other.

clone 1. A group of genetically identical cells or organisms produced asexually from a common ancestor. In nature, clones are derived from a single parental organism or cell by ASEXUAL REPRODUCTION or PARTHENOGENESIS. Clones of sexually reproducing higher animals have been produced experimentally by new embryo-splitting techniques, and even from single adult body cells. This was first accomplished in 1997 by Ian Wilmut and his team at the Roslin Institute, Edinburgh, UK, when DNA from a sheep's udder cell was transferred to a fertilized egg from which DNA had been removed. The egg was then implanted into a ewe's womb, where it developed and a normal lamb (named Dolly) was born. Dolly died in 2003. Single mature plant cells can also be cloned when cultivated in the correct nutritive medium, a technique that is extremely important in commercial plant breeding. Cloning techniques are currently being used to attempt to 'resurrect' extinct species.
2. A homologous population of DNA molecules obtained by GENE CLONING.

cloning vector *See* gene cloning; genetic engineering; phage.

club moss *See* Lycopodophyta.

Cnidaria An ancient, large, and successful phylum of aquatic, mostly marine, invertebrates and the most primitive of the truly multicellular (metazoan) animals. Cnidarians are typically radially symmetrical and are diploblastic, the body wall having two layers separated by a layer of jelly (*mesoglea*) and enclosing the body cavity (*coelenteron*). The single opening (*mouth*) is surrounded by a circle of tentacles, which are used for food capture and defense and may bear stinging cells (*cnidoblasts*). Two structural forms occur, the sedentary polyp (e.g. the solitary *Hydra* and the sea anemones and the colonial corals) and the mobile medusa (jellyfish); either or both forms occur in the life cycle.

Fossil cnidarians have been discovered from Cambrian times onward. The most abundant fossils are the corals, because their limy or horny skeletons are well preserved in contrast to the soft-bodied delicate cnidarian forms. *See* Anthozoa; coral; coelenterate; Hydrozoa; Scyphozoa. *See also* planuloid hypothesis.

coadaptation The mutual adaptation of organisms in different species, parts of an organism, or genes at different loci in the same genome. Striking examples are the adaptations of flowering plants and their insect pollinators. Bees, which cannot see the color red, are attracted to blue or yellow flowers, or those that reflect UV light. They are also attracted to various scents, and to flowers with petals adapted as suitable platforms for landing. Bees have evolved tongues of different lengths for collecting nectar from different flower species, and have developed pollen baskets for collecting pollen.

coalescence method *See* molecular clock.

cockroach *See* Dictyoptera.

coding strand The DNA strand of a double helix that has the same sequence of bases (with T substituted for U) as the messenger RNA transcribed from that double helix. The coding strand is therefore not transcribed. *Compare* noncoding strand.

co-dominance The situation in which two different alleles are equally dominant.

If they occur together the resulting phenotype is intermediate between the two respective homozygotes. For example, if white antirrhinums (AA) are crossed with red antirrhinums (A'A') the progeny (AA') will be pink. Sometimes one allele may be slightly more dominant than the other (*partial* or *incomplete dominance*), in which case the offspring, though still intermediate, will resemble one parent more than the other.

codon A group of three NUCLEOTIDE bases (i.e. a nucleotide triplet) in a MESSENGER RNA (mRNA) molecule that codes for a specific amino acid or signals the beginning or end of the message (start and stop codons). Since four different bases are found in nucleic acids there are 64 ($4 \times 4 \times 4$) possible triplet combinations. The arrangement of codons along the mRNA molecule constitutes the GENETIC CODE. *See also* transfer RNA.

codon bias The situation in which codons for the same amino acid (*syn-*

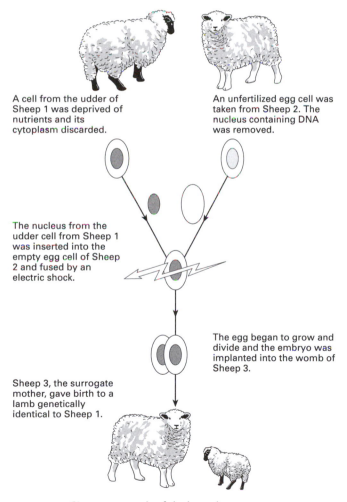

A cell from the udder of Sheep 1 was deprived of nutrients and its cytoplasm discarded.

An unfertilized egg cell was taken from Sheep 2. The nucleus containing DNA was removed.

The nucleus from the udder cell from Sheep 1 was inserted into the empty egg cell of Sheep 2 and fused by an electric shock.

The egg began to grow and divide and the embryo was implanted into the womb of Sheep 3.

Sheep 3, the surrogate mother, gave birth to a lamb genetically identical to Sheep 1.

Clone: an example of cloning a sheep

onomous codons) do not occur with the same frequency.

coelacanth A fish abundant in Devonian times and thought to have become extinct in the Cretaceous until the first live specimen of modern times was caught off East London, South Africa, in 1938. Others have since been found around islands off Madagascar and because present-day forms differ little from their ancestral fossil forms, they are often described as 'living fossils'. It belongs to an order (Coelacanthiformes) containing just a single genus, *Latimeria*. This is a large deep-sea fish with blue scales and long strong lobed fins, supported by bony skeletons, which are used to stir up the mud of the sea floor in search of prey. *Latimeria* has a SWIM BLADDER although a lung is present in fossils. There are no internal nostrils. *See also* Osteichthyes.

coelenterate Any invertebrate belonging to either of the phyla CNIDARIA (jellyfish, sea anemones, etc.) or CTENOPHORA (comb jellies), which were formerly united in the single phylum Coelenterata. Both groups possess a gastrovascular cavity (coelenteron).

coelom A fluid-filled cavity arising in the mesoderm of the more advanced animals. It functions as a *hydrostatic skeleton* in some worms (e.g. earthworm) providing an incompressible barrier for the muscles to act against. The cavity separates an internal splanchnic mesoderm from an external somatic mesoderm and is lined with the coelomic epithelium. It separates the body wall from the gut wall, allowing independent muscular movement of these structures. It allows for, and demands, greater body complexity, notably development of a blood vascular system.

In annelids, mollusks, echinoderms, and chordates it is the main body cavity, containing the viscera; in mammals it is divided into separate cavities enclosing the heart (pericardial cavity), lungs (pleural cavity), and gut (peritoneal cavity). In arthropods the coelom is reduced to cavities surrounding the gonads and excretory organs, the main body cavity being a *hemocoel*, a blood-filled cavity.

coevolution The reciprocal selective influence between two species over a prolonged period: two species evolve together and influence each other's evolution. Coevolution can be antagonistic as between parasites and hosts or predators and prey. It may also be mutualistic depending on the species and circumstances. A species usually interacts with many others so an exclusive coevolutionary relationship is hard to achieve. Natural selection continues to operate, favoring the organism that develops a selfishly beneficial characteristic. *Diffuse coevolution* describes the evolutionary interactions between a species and all its competitors and mutualists. *See* coadaptation; cospeciation; escalatory evolution; parasite. *See also* Red Queen effect.

cohesion of the genotype *See* stasis.

colchicine A drug obtained from the autumn crocus *Colchicum autumnale* that is used to prevent spindle formation in mitosis and meiosis. It has the effect of halting cell division at metaphase when the chromosomes have duplicated to give four homologs for each chromosome. If a resting nucleus forms after colchicine treatment, it is thus likely to be tetraploid.

cold-blooded *See* poikilothermy.

Coleoptera The largest order of insects (*see* Insecta) and possibly the largest order in the animal kingdom, containing the beetles and weevils. Their forewings are modified to form hard leathery *elytra*, which protect the membranous hind wings and soft abdomen when resting. The head, projected into a snout in weevils, has biting mouthparts. Beetles are found universally in a variety of terrestrial and freshwater habitats. The larvae vary between legless grubs, caterpillar-like forms, and predators. Metamorphosis is complete. Many larvae and adults are serious pests, e.g. *Anobium* larvae (woodworm), and *Elater* larvae (wire-worm). Others are beneficial, e.g. *Coccinella* (ladybird), which eats aphids. The beetles comprised only 1% of insects discovered in the Permian, but make up 40% of present-day insect species.

coliform bacteria Gram-negative rod-shaped BACTERIA able to obtain energy aerobically or by fermenting sugars to produce acid or acid and gas. Most are found in the vertebrate gut (e.g. *Escherichia coli*), but some are present in soil, water, or as plant pathogens. Many are pathogenic to humans (e.g. *Salmonella*).

colinear Describing developmental control genes whose order (along the chromosome) corresponds to the order of body parts (along the body axis) that they control. The *Hox* genes, a subset of HOMEOBOX genes, control segments along the anterio-posterior axis and are colinear.

commensalism An association between two organisms in which one, the *commensal*, benefits and the other remains unaffected either way, e.g. the saprophytic bacteria in animal guts. *Compare* mutualism; parasite; symbiosis.

common ancestor The ancestral organism from which different descendant species have evolved. The more characteristics two species have in common, the more it is likely that they have recently diverged.

common descent The theory put forward by DARWIN that all organisms on Earth had COMMON ANCESTORS and that ultimately life on Earth began with a single origin. *See* origin of life.

comparative anatomy The study of structural similarities and differences between organisms as a method of establishing evolutionary relationships.

comparative genomics *See* molecular phylogenetics.

comparative trend analysis A comparative method in which changes in two or more traits across species, or higher

groups, are compared to reveal correlated changes. These correlated changes are then examined for evidence of constraints and adaptations. *Compare* phylogenetic trait analysis.

compensation level *See* sublittoral.

compensatory hypertrophy Replacement of a lost or damaged part of an organ by an increase in size of the remainder. *Compare* regeneration.

competition The utilization of the same resources by one or more organisms of the same or of different species living together in a community, when the resources are not sufficient to fill the needs of all the organisms. The closer the requirements of two species, then the less likely it is that they can live in the same community, unless they differ in behavioral ways, such as periods of activity or feeding patterns. *See also* natural selection.

competitive exclusion principle The principle that two species cannot exist in the same area if they have identical ecological requirements.

complementary DNA (cDNA) A form of DNA synthesized by GENETIC ENGINEERING techniques from a messenger RNA (mRNA) template using a REVERSE TRANSCRIPTASE. It is used in cloning to obtain gene sequences from mRNA isolated from the tissue to be cloned. It differs from the original DNA sequence in that it lacks intron and promoter sequences. Labeled single-stranded cDNA is used as a gene probe (*see* DNA probe) to identify common gene sequences in different tissues and species and to locate specific genes within the genome. *See* gene cloning.

complementary genes Genes that can only be expressed in the presence of other genes; for example if one gene controls the formation of a pigment precursor and another gene controls the transformation of that precursor into the pigment, then both genes must be present for the color to develop in the phenotype. Such interactions between genes lead to apparent deviations from the 9:3:3:1 DIHYBRID ratio in the F_2. For example, if two complementary genes control a certain character and dominant alleles of each of the two genes must be present for the character to appear then a 9:7 ratio is seen (9:(3 + 3 + 1)). *Compare* complementation; epistasis.

complementation The production of a normal phenotype from a genotype that apparently has two mutant alleles at a given locus. It is assumed that, although the mutants have the same effect, they actually occur in different cistrons of the same gene. In a diploid cell the two different mutated regions are prevented from expression by corresponding dominant alleles on the other homologous chromosome. *Compare cis–trans effect.*

compound eye The type of eye found in crustaceans and insects. It consists of several thousands of units (*ommatidia*). The spots of light focused by these give a mosaic image, which lacks visual acuity. However, the compound eye is very efficient at detecting the slightest movement over a wide area. *See eye.*

concerted evolution The PARALLEL EVOLUTION of some of the genes in a GENE CLUSTER or GENE FAMILY, which results in different genes in the same family having the same sequence variations. The α1 and α2 globin genes in the higher primates are examples and their evolution would be almost impossible if they had evolved independently. Concerted evolution requires the same MUTATIONS to arise at different loci and these mutations to be subsequently fixed by genetic drift or selection. Unequal CROSSING OVER and GENE CONVERSION could be responsible for providing the mutational basis of concerted evolution.

condylarths An extinct order of hoofed mammals that evolved in the Paleocene. Most fossils have been found in North America, some in Europe, and a few questionable forms in Asia. The ungulates (*see* Perissodactyla; Artiodactyla) evolved from the most primitive condylarths. Like other

Paleocene mammals, they filled ecological niches vacated by the extinct dinosaurs, many becoming omnivores and herbivores. The most primitive condylarth is *Protoungatum* ('before ungulate'), contentiously of the late Cretaceous (or early Paleocene), which had teeth adapted for crushing and grinding soft vegetation, fruits, and insects. The earliest condylarths had claws and were climbers (e.g. *Chriacus*). The group diversified into squirrel-sized types (*Anischonus*), sheep-sized types (*Ectoconus*), with small hooves and teeth adapted for shredded plant material, and rat-sized forms (*Hyopsodus*). The North American genus *Mioclaemus* evolved high-crowned teeth, as did *Pleuraspidotherium* of the late Paleocene of Cernay, France, the latter having selenodont crescent-shaped ridges on their MOLAR teeth like present-day deer and camels.

The dominant (sheep-sized) condylarths of North America (e.g. *Phenacedus*) were ancestral ungulates adapted for running, and spread into Europe in the early Eocene. They had five hoofed digits, the first and fifth being reduced, similar to *Hyracotherium* (*see* horse evolution). They also had cheek teeth with cusps. A carnivorous group of condylarths, the MESONYCHIDS, were ancestral to present-day whales (*see* Cetacea). The condylarths became extinct in the Eocene, probably unable to survive competition from the evolving Perissodactyla.

congenital Present at birth. The term describes all deformities and other conditions that are present at birth, whether they are inherited or caused by environmental factors. Some congenital deformities, e.g. cleft palate and harelip, undoubtedly run in families but their occurrence is determined by environmental as well as hereditary factors.

Coniferophyta (conifers) The largest phylum of gymnosperms, comprising evergreen trees and shrubs, with many important species, e.g. *Pinus* (pine), *Picea* (spruce), *Taxus* (yew), and *Abies* (fir). They generally show a pyramidal growth form, bear simple leaves, and have the male and female reproductive structures contained in cones or strobili.

The conifers are a very ancient group of plants and evolved in the Paleozoic and were very abundant during the Mesozoic. Many forms resembling present-day conifers evolved during the Cretaceous, including the giant redwoods, firs, pines, and yew and most of the modern families and genera had evolved during the Cenozoic, along with the GNETOPHYTA. Conifers are more advanced than the CYCADOPHYTA and GINKGOPHYTA because they produce pollen grains that develop pollen tubes, thus ensuring fertilization. This is thought to be a feature that has contributed to their evolutionary success.

conodont A microscopic phosphatized toothlike structure of unknown origin, possibly a vertebrate structure, used in stratigraphic division of the Devonian and Carboniferous periods.

conservation The method of management of wild animals, plants, and other organisms to ensure their survival for future generations. Humans, unlike other species, have had a major effect on the environment as a result of their activities, often with disastrous effects on both the natural environment and on other organisms (*see* pollution). Conservationists may choose to preserve specific habitats or adopt programs to ensure the survival of individual species. There are ethical and moral reasons for conservation as well as practical ones. For example, what rights do we humans have to destroy and pollute the environment and contribute to the EXTINCTION of the organisms with whom we share our planet? It is also impractical to destroy major parts of the environment as the results will impact unfavorably on our own wellbeing; for example, destroying the tropical rainforests may be contributing to global warming (*see* greenhouse effect) and deforestation in many areas has resulted in severe soil erosion, creating dust bowls. In many countries there are national and local organizations that have been created to conserve certain areas and species, some enshrined in law, others set up on a voluntary basis. There are also international organizations dealing with environmental problems on a global level. *See* CITES; Convention on Biological Diversity.

conserved function The property shown by homologous genes from different species that code for proteins with similar functions.

conserved sequence A measure of the similarity of corresponding sequences of DNA, RNA, proteins, or other macromolecules taken from different species. Sequences showing a high degree of similarity are said to be highly conserved. *See* gene evolution; molecular phylogenetics.

continental drift The theory first proposed in 1912 by WEGENER that present-

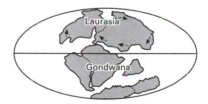

200 mya

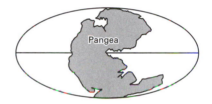

135 mya

65 mya

Continental drift

day continents have arisen by the breaking up and drifting apart of a previously existing ancient land mass (PANGEA). There is much evidence to support the theory, and it serves to explain the distribution of contemporary and fossil plants and animals. Continental drift is now believed to reflect the movement over geological time of underlying plates in the Earth's crust – the theory of PLATE TECTONICS.

A number of major events have occurred through continental drift, including: The formation of the single enormous supercontinent Pangea in the Mesozoic era, about 225 mya.
The breakup of Pangea into the northern supercontinent of LAURASIA and the southern supercontinent of GONDWANA at the beginning of the Cretaceous period, about 135 mya.
The breakup of Gondwana that began 135 mya and was completed 65 mya at the end of the Cretaceous.
After 65 mya, the continents began to take up their present positions, with Australia drifting north from Antarctica and India eventually colliding with Eurasia, about 15–20 mya in the Miocene. *See also* zoogeography.

continuous variation   *See* quantitative inheritance.

control region   *See* mitochondrion.

Convention on Biological Diversity
The world population in 1999 was estimated to be approximately six billion and is expected to rise to nine billion in the next 50 years. The demands humans make on natural resources has increased dramatically and has even eclipsed the increase in the world population. An international Convention on Biological Diversity was signed at the United Nations Rio Summit in 1992. It aims to conserve biodiversity, the sustainable use of natural resources, and the equitable sharing of the benefits arising from the exploitation of genetic resources. It covers all aspects of biodiversity, from genetic resources to ecosystems, and aims to conserve resources while promoting sustainable development and to encourage the sharing of costs and benefits between developing and developed countries. The United Nations Environment Program (UNEP) responded by commissioning the Global Biodiversity Assessment, to collect and review data, theories, and opinion relating to current issues worldwide, which provided valuable information on the rapid rate at which environmental change is taking place and natural ecosystems are being modified. The importance to human survival of implementing the aims of the convention is vital as it has been estimated that 34 000 plant species and 5200 animal species face extinction and that species have been disappearing at 50–100 times the natural rate as a result of degradation of forests, wetlands, coral reefs, mangrove swamps, and other ecosystems.

Convention on International Trade in Endangered Species of Wild Fauna and Flora   *See* CITES.

convergence   *See* convergent evolution.

convergent evolution (convergence) The development of similar structures in unrelated organisms as a result of living in similar ecological conditions. The wings of vertebrates and insects are an example of convergence, in which quite distinct groups of animals have independently adapted to life in the air. *See also* analogous; homologous. *Compare* parallel evolution.

copal   *See* amber.

Cope, Edward Drinker (1840–97) American paleontologist and comparative anatomist. Cope's early studies were mainly concerned with living fishes, reptiles, and amphibians, and in 1861 he went to Washington to study the Smithsonian Institution's herpetological collections. His interests gradually began to turn to fossils, and it was during his long association with the US Geological Survey that he made the valuable contributions to paleontological knowledge associated with his name. During explorations of western America, from Texas to Wyoming, Cope discovered many new species of extinct (Tertiary) vertebrates (fishes, reptiles, mammals, etc.). Like his rival Othniel MARSH (*see* Bone Wars), he is credited with the discovery of about 1000 species of fossils new to science. He also traced the evolutionary history of the horse and other mammals, proposed a theory for the origin and evolution of mammalian teeth (since somewhat modified), and made important contributions to knowledge of the stratigraphy of North America, indicating parallels with European strata.

Cope was a leading paleontological protagonist for the revival of Lamarck's theory of the inheritance of acquired characteristics – views that were elaborated in *The Origin of the Fittest* (1886) and *Primary Factors in Organic Evolution* (1896).

Copepoda   A large class of minute Crustacea whose members lack a carapace and compound eyes and have the first thoracic appendages modified for feeding. The remaining thoracic appendages are used for swimming. Many are important members of the PLANKTON, e.g. the marine *Celanus* and the freshwater *Cyclops*.

Cope's rule   The increase in body size of a species evolving over geological time from the lower size limit of the ancestral organisms.

coprolite   *See* fossil.

coral   A sedentary marine invertebrate belonging to the class ANTHOZOA of the phylum Cnidaria. Corals are typically colonial organisms, with the individual animals, or polyps, secreting a protective outer skeleton, which can be hard ('stony') or soft. Lime-secreting coral fossils evolved in the Ordovician, some solitary and others colonial. From Silurian times to the end of the Paleozoic, chalky limestones contained traces of corals and ancient marine coral reefs existed. There were two Paleozoic groups of corals that became extinct in the Permian. The Rugosa (rugose corals) showed bilateral symmetry, e.g. *Hexagonaria* of the Devonian and *Lithostrotion* and *Lonsdaleia* of the Carboniferous. All were colonial. The second group (the Tabulata) were colonies consisting of many tubes with horizontal cross-partitions (tabulae) evolving in the early Ordovician, e.g. *Favosites* (Silurian–Devonian) and *Halysites* (Ordovician–Silurian).

The stony corals (Precambrian–Recent) include 5000 extinct species and many species that exist today. Fossil reefs of stony corals occur in Iowa, Kansas, and Kentucky, and an enormous reef of stony coral surrounds the Michigan Basin, extending from Wisconsin to Ohio. Examples include *Acropora*, *Favia*, and *Porites*, (Miocene–Recent), *Isastrea* (Jurassic–Cretaceous), and *Thecosmilia* (Triassic–Cretaceous).

Soft corals, similar to modern forms, evolved in the Cretaceous, e.g. *Heliospora*. Ancient coral reefs (*bioherms*) are important economically as they often indicate reservoirs of petroleum in certain regions.

Cordaitales   A GYMNOSPERM fossil group that arose in the late Devonian and became extinct at the end of the Triassic. They were tall trees with large parallel-veined leaves. The leaves resembled those of cycads and their cones bore some resemblance to those of conifers. The best-known fossil (*Cordaites*), of the Upper Carboniferous, had a stem that resembled one of the present-day conifers, namely the monkey puzzle tree (*Araucaria*), but it is doubtful that the Cordaitales were the ancestors of the Coniferophyta.

corpus striatum   *See* brain.

cospeciation   The simultaneous formation of new species by hosts and parasites as a result of COEVOLUTION. It is more likely to occur if the parasite cannot move independently. Over time, cospeciation results in phylogenies that are mirror images.

cost   Any change in a trait that reduces FITNESS. *Compare* benefit.

cotylosaurs   (captorhynids; stem reptiles; root reptiles)   A group of primitive reptiles that evolved in the late Carboniferous from ancestral amphibians. They were

ANAPSIDS (*see* Reptilia) and all of the other reptile groups evolved from them. The tortoises and turtles (order Chelonia), which arose in the Triassic, are the only survivors of this ancient group. Many were displaced by the primitive mammal-like reptiles (*see* Mammalia). *Acleistorhinus*, a small lizard-like reptile from the Lower Permian is the oldest known anapsid, and the oldest turtle, *Proganochelys*, has been found in the Upper Triassic. Some of these early reptiles were either small and lizardlike or very large lumbering herbivores, most of which disappeared in the Permian extinction.

COV *See* cross-over value.

craniate (vertebrate) Any chordate animal (*see* Chordata) in which the NOTO-CHORD is replaced by a dorsal vertebral column (the backbone) and the brain is housed
in the cranium (skull). Hence craniates include the cyclostomes (Agnatha), the extinct placoderms (Placodermi), cartilaginous fishes (Chondrichthyes), bony fishes (Osteichthyes), amphibians (Amphibia), reptiles (Reptilia), birds (Aves), and mammals (Mammalia). Some authorities group all these classes together as the Craniata, which is variously given the status of subphylum or phylum. Craniates have an internal skeleton of cartilage or bone and the backbone encloses the tubular nerve cord (the spinal cord). There is a complex nervous system with a well-developed brain. The circulatory and digestive systems are located ventrally to the vertebral column. All but the most primitive vertebrates have jaws formed from the anterior pair of visceral arches.

The earliest vertebrates were the Agnatha (jawless fishes), which evolved in the Ordovician. The Placodermi, Chondrichthyes, and Osteichthyes evolved in the Paleozoic as the Agnatha declined. At the end of the Devonian, plants dominated the land and there were only a few insect and millipede groups representing land animals. A group of coelacanth (lobe-finned) fishes evolved into amphibians, which flourished during the Carboniferous. The reptiles evolved from the primitive am-phibians during the Permian and after the MASS EXTINCTION of the Permo–Triassic, the reptiles expanded and replaced the dwindling amphibians, dominating the Mesozoic era. By the early Jurassic, PTEROSAURS (flying reptiles) and birds evolved from ARCHOSAURS (*see Archaeopteryx*). Mammals evolved from the therapsid reptiles in the Triassic and the marsupials and placentals divided off very early on. The ancient placental mammals probably resembled the INSECTIVORA and mammals remained an insignificant group until the beginning of the Cenozoic (the 'Age of Mammals'), when the great diversity of forms evolved; the mammals probably being able to fill the niches left by the extinction of the dinosaurs (*see* Alvarez theory).

creationism (separate creation) The belief that species were created separately and did not change after their creation, i.e. there is no evolution. Most creationist theories stem from religious beliefs and none are accepted by evolutionary biologists in the face of overwhelming evidence for evolution.

creodonts An archaic group of meat-eating mammals that evolved in the Paleocene and competed with the evolving CARNIVORA until finally becoming extinct during the Miocene. *See also* Oligocene.

Cretaceous The most recent period of the MESOZOIC era, 145–66 mya. It is marked by continued domination of land and sea by DINOSAURS until a rapid extinction toward the end of the period. The continents continued to drift away from one another as Pangea broke up and huge limestone deposits formed in the warm humid climate. Many carnivorous dinosaurs existed in the Cretaceous including the famous *Tyrannosaurus* and *Antrodemus*, along with *Triceratops*, an enormous plant-eater with its characteristic horns, and *Iguanodon*, a bipedal herbivore. ICHTHYOSAURIA flourished in the seas. PTERODACTYLS (flying reptiles) were abundant (e.g. *Ramphorhyncus*) and Cretaceous fossils of a flightless bird

(*Hesperornis*) have also been discovered. Echinoderms flourished and sea urchin fossils were very common (e.g. *Micraster*). Arthropods were also on the increase. Primitive mammals were present, but were relatively insignificant in number, size, and variety until the Cenozoic era which followed. Birds and fishes evolved into structurally modern forms during the Cretaceous.

A group of red algae (the Corallinaceae) is found in the marine deposits of the Cretaceous, and *Lithoamnion* exists to the present day along with *Chara* (the stonewort) (*see* Chlorophyta). Ferns were also abundant with many modern characteristics, and the tree fern *Protopteris* resembles the present-day tree fern, *Dicksonia*. The flowering plants replaced the gymnosperms as the dominant terrestrial vegetation but many modern gymnosperms evolved at this time, e.g. firs, pines, yews, and giant redwoods. Butterflies and moths evolved in parallel with the evolving flowering plants (coevolution) (*see* Insecta). The Cretaceous is named for the large amounts of chalk (fossilized PLANKTON) that comprise the rocks of the period. The Alvarez event at the end of the period resulted in the extinction of the dinosaurs. The marine AMMONITES and all the aquatic reptiles also became extinct in this period. *See also* Alvarez theory; geological time scale; mass extinction.

Crinoidea   The most primitive class of the ECHINODERMATA and the only echinoderms with the mouth on the upper surface of the body. The mouth is surrounded by feathery arms bearing tube feet and ciliary grooves used in feeding. The PLUTEUS larvae (a form of dipleurula larva) are always sessile, attached to the substratum by a stalk. The deep-sea *Metacrinus* (sea lily) remains stalked as an adult but the coastal *Antedon* (feather star) is free-swimming.

Crinoids were very abundant in Paleozoic times and are found in thick limestone beds. They are important rock formers. They were mostly fixed stalked organisms (*eocrinoids*), e.g. *Macrocystella*. Fossil crinoids include *Sagenocrinites* (Silurian), *Dichocrinus* (Carboniferous), and *Mar-*

supites (Cretaceous). In the Mesozoic, crinoids were both stalked, sessile forms and also free swimming, resembling their living descendants of the present day. They are important indicator fossils in the Upper Cretaceous.

Crocodilia   *See* Reptilia.

Cro-Magnon man   A group of early representatives of the species *Homo sapiens* that lived in Europe about 40 000–13 000 years ago. They are direct ancestors of modern humans. Cro-Magnons were tall, finely built, and muscular with handsome facial features, no brow ridges on their faces, prominent noses, and a large brain. They lived alongside NEANDERTHAL MAN (whom they eventually supplanted), migrating toward the end of the last ICE AGE (wurm) in Europe, probably from northern Africa. There are likely to have been other groups that spread over other areas of the world, perhaps as far as China. They belonged to the Upper PALEOLITHIC (Stone Age) culture and were superior to the Neanderthals in their use of more specialized finely worked tools fashioned from bone and ivory as well as stone. They made parallel-sided stone blades and arrowheads. They also buried their dead with ceremony and respect. Bones of the woolly mammoth, rhinoceros, reindeer, wolf, and fox have also been found associated with Cro-Magnon settlements.

Different cultural groups have been found in different localities, for example, the *Aurignacian* culture in Spain and southern France are renowned for their exquisite cave paintings. Decorative carvings on bone and finely carved figurines have also been associated with these artistic people. *See also* human evolution; Neolithic.

crossing over   The exchange of material between homologous chromatids by the formation of chiasmata. There is normally a reciprocal exchange of material because the chromatids are aligned by sequence. If the sequences are misaligned, *unequal crossing over* occurs and the chromatids carry unequal genetic information, which can lead to gene duplication. Misalignment is more likely if there are repeated sequences along the chromatids. *See also* chiasma; gene conversion; Muller; recombination.

cross-over value (COV) The percentage of recombinations between two linked genes in the progeny of a given cross. It is a measure of the strength of linkage between two genes and can be used in the construction of linkage maps. However, if two genes are very far apart on the chromosome more than one crossover may occur between them, in which case misleading values are obtained.

Crustacea A large group of arthropods containing the mostly aquatic gill-breathing crawfish, crabs, lobsters, barnacles, water fleas, etc., and the terrestrial pill-bugs. The body is divided into a head, thorax, and abdomen. The head bears compound eyes, two pairs of antennae, and mouthparts composed of a pair of mandibles and two pairs of maxillae. The thorax is often covered with a dorsal carapace. The appendages are typically forked and specialized for different functions. The sexes are usually separate and development is indirect, via a nauplius larva. The taxon named Crustacea is variously given the rank of class, superclass, or phylum by different authorities. The BURGESS SHALE has yielded some shrimplike crustaceans along with other Middle Cambrian fauna.

Ostracods, which are bivalved crustaceans with poor segmentation, appeared in the Ordovician. They had varied forms of shell and molted many times and continue to survive to the present day. The more familiar forms of crustaceans – barnacles, crabs, and lobsters – evolved in Mesozoic seas. They are important fossil indicators used to zone the Purbeck beds of the Upper Jurassic. *See also* Arthropoda; Branchiopoda; Copepoda; Decapoda.

cryptogam In early classifications, any plant that reproduces by spores or gametes rather than by seeds. Cryptogams were thus named because early botanists considered their method of reproduction to be cryptic. They included the algae, fungi, bryophytes, and pteridophytes (ferns), the latter group often being termed vascular cryptogams. *Compare* phanerogam.

cryptophyte (geophyte) A plant in which the resting buds are below the soil surface.

Ctenophora A small ancient phylum of marine invertebrates, the sea gooseberries or comb jellies, which show similarities to the cnidarians. The transparent, often globular, saclike body bears eight rows of fused cilia (*combs* or *ctenes*) used in locomotion and the enteron forms a canal system in the body. Most have tentacles armed with adhesive cells for food capture on each side of the body. *Compare* Cnidaria. *See also* planuloid hypothesis.

Cuvier, Baron Georges (1769–1832) French anatomist and taxonomist. In 1795 he became assistant to the professor of comparative anatomy at the Museum of Natural History in Paris – then the world's largest scientific research establishment. During his lifetime he greatly enlarged the comparative anatomy section from a few hundred skeletons to 13 000 specimens. Cuvier extended Linnaeus's classification, creating another level, the phylum, into which he grouped related classes. Cuvier was also the first to classify fossils and he named the pterodactyl. His results from investigations of the Tertiary formations near Paris are published in four volumes as *Recherches sur les ossements fossiles des quadrupèdes* (1812; Researches on the Fossil Bones of Quadrupeds).

In 1799 Cuvier became professor of natural history at the Collège de France and in 1802 was also made professor at the Jardin des Plantes. In his later life he became increasingly involved in educational administration and played a large part in organizing the new Sorbonne.

Cyanobacteria A diverse phylum of bacteria containing the blue-green bacteria (formerly called blue-green algae) and the green bacteria (chloroxybacteria). They convert carbon dioxide into organic compounds using photosynthesis, generally using water as a hydrogen donor to yield oxygen, like green plants. However, under certain circumstances they use hydrogen sulfide instead of water, yielding sulfur. Cyanobacteria are an ancient group, and the oldest of their fossils (STROMATOLITES) have been dated at almost 3500 million years old and are one of the earliest known forms of cellular life. Today, most species are found in soil and freshwater. They are spherical (coccoid) or form long microscopic filaments of individual cells. Many species, e.g. *Nostoc* and *Oscillatoria*, are nitrogen fixers. They reproduce asexually by binary fission, or by releasing sporelike propagules or filament fragments. It is thought that certain ancient cyanobacteria became permanent symbionts of ancestral algae and green plants, taking up residence in their cells as photosynthetic organelles (plastids). This theory would account for the striking similarities between cyanobacteria and plastids.

Cycadofilicales

(seed ferns; Pteridospermales) Seed-bearing fossil GYMNOSPERMS that first appeared in the Devonian, flourished in the CARBONIFEROUS, but became extinct in the Cretaceous. They were originally classified as ferns (e.g. *Pecopteris*), but the discovery of seeds attached to their leaves confirms that they were indeed gymnosperms. The plant body resembled a fern and the seeds developed from megasporangia borne on the fernlike fronds. Fossil remains, especially in the coal measures (e.g. *Lyginopteris oldhamia* discovered in Oldham, England), illustrate the great diversity of this group, which is believed to be the ancestral group from which the other fossil gymnosperms and present-day gymnosperms evolved.

Cycadophyta

(cycads)   A primitive phylum of GYMNOSPERMS that grow to a height of 15 m and generally have an unbranched stem with a rosette of large pinnate leaves at the apex resembling palm trees or tree ferns. The male and female cones and micro- and megaspores are the largest of all other cone-bearing groups. Pollen dispersal is brought about by the wind or by beetles. The male sperm are also the largest known

and are motile, bearing a spiral band of flagella that enable the sperm to swim toward the megaspore to bring about fertilization. Cycads arose in the Permian and were abundant in the Mesozoic and early Cenozoic. By the beginning of the Cenozoic, several modern genera, such as *Cycas* and *Zamia*, had appeared but the most abundant gymnosperms during this period were the CONIFEROPHYTA.

Cyclostomata

The order of agnathans (*see* Agnatha) that contains the most primitive living vertebrates – the lampreys (e.g. *Petromyzon*) and the hagfish (e.g. *Myxine*). Cyclostomes are fishlike animals with no differentiated head and no scales or paired fins. Jaws are functionally replaced by a round suctorial mouth with horny teeth and a protrusible tongue. Lampreys live in the sea or rivers, attaching to fish by means of the mouth and feeding on their blood and flesh. They spawn in fresh water. Hagfishes are marine scavengers on the sea bottom.

The skeleton is secondarily cartilaginous and there is a single nasal opening and a row of spherical gill pouches. The NOTOCHORD persists throughout life. In lampreys, development is via an ammocoete larva; hagfish have no larval stage.

The *ostracoderms* were ancient jawless vertebrates that arose in the Ordovician and disappeared by the end of the Devonian. *Cephalapsis*, from the Devonian, is characterized by a massive head shield of bony scales, no paired fins, but two pectoral flaps, and ten gill openings. Cephalapsids seem to have been bottom-dwelling fish in streams and lakes. Other ostracoderms (e.g. *Birkenia*) lacked the heavy armor and were probably free swimming. Some authorities classify the cyclostomes in a separate group from the ostracoderms as modern lampreys and hagfish are so different from these Paleozoic fossils.

cynodonts

A group of extinct mammallike reptiles of the Triassic that were an intermediate stage in the evolution of modern mammals. Some cynodont fossils show a particularly interesting stage in the evolution of the mammalian jaw, having jaws articulated in both the mammalian and reptilian positions. *Cynognathus* from the Permo–Triassic Karoo Beds of South Africa had a long narrow skull with differentiated teeth (incisors, canines, and cheek teeth), a hard secondary palate, and limbs adapted for speedy locomotion as a result of mammalian-type shoulder and hip girdles. It retained a long reptilian tail. *See* Mammalia; Triassic.

Cytidine

cytidine (cytosine nucleoside)   A nucleoside formed when cytosine is linked to D-ribose via a β-glycosidic bond.

cytogenetics   The area of study that links the structure and behavior of chromosomes with inheritance.

cytokinesis   The division of the cytoplasm after nuclear division (mitosis or meiosis). In animal cells cytokinesis involves constriction of cytoplasm between daughter nuclei; in plant cells it involves formation of a new plant cell wall.

cytoplasm   The living contents of a cell, excluding the nucleus and large vacuoles, in which many metabolic activities occur. It is contained within the plasma membrane and comprises a colorless substance (*hyaloplasm*) containing organelles and various inclusions (e.g. crystals and insoluble food reserves). The cytoplasm is about 90% water. Removal of organelles and inclusions by centrifugation of cell contents leaves a soluble fraction called the *cytosol*. This is a true solution of ions (e.g. potassium, sodium, and chloride) and small molecules (e.g. sugars, amino acids, and ATP); and a colloidal solution of large molecules (e.g. proteins, lipids, and nucleic acids). It can be gel-like, usually in its outer regions, or sol-like. *See* organelle; protoplasm.

cytoplasmic inheritance   The determination of certain characters by genetic material contained in plasmids or organelles other than the nucleus, e.g. mitochondria and chloroplasts. Characters controlled by the DNA of extranuclear organelles are not inherited according to Mendelian laws and are transmitted only through the female line, since only the female gametes have an appreciable amount of cytoplasm. Cytoplasmic inheritance is known in a wide variety of animals, plants, and unicellular organisms, e.g. *Paramecium*.

Cytosine

cytosine   Symbol: C. A nitrogenous base found in DNA and RNA. Cytosine has the pyrimidine ring structure.

cytotaxonomy   The use of chromosome number, size, and shape in the classification of organisms. *See also* taxonomy.

Dart, Raymond Arthur (1893–1988) Australian anatomist. In 1924 Dart made one of the great paleontological discoveries of the century, the *Taung skull*. For this he was indebted to his student Josephine Salmons who brought him in the summer of 1924 a fossil collected from a mine at Taung, Bechuanaland. Dart named it *Australopithecus africanus*, and declared it to be intermediate between anthropoids and humans. Such a claim was far from acceptable to many scholars at the time, who claimed that the skull was that of a young anthropoid. Other and older AUSTRALOP-ITHECINE remains were later discovered by Robert BROOM in South Africa, East Africa, and Asia, making it clear that they were in fact hominid.

Darwin, Charles Robert (1809–82) British naturalist, famous as the originator of the theory of evolution by natural selection. Darwin began his university education by studying medicine at Edinburgh (1825) but, finding he had no taste for the subject, he entered Cambridge University to prepare for the Church. Here his interest in natural history was encouraged by the professor of botany, John Henslow. Their friendship led to Henslow's recommending Darwin to the admiralty for the position of naturalist on HMS *Beagle*, which was preparing to survey the coast of South America and the Pacific.

The *Beagle* sailed in 1831 and Darwin was initially occupied with the geological aspects of his work. However, his observations of animals – particularly the way in which species gradually change from region to region – led him to speculate on the development of life. He was particularly struck by the variation found in the finches of the GALÁPAGOS ISLANDS. On returning to England in 1836, Darwin first concerned himself with recording his travels in *A Naturalist's Voyage on the Beagle.* His interest in geology was reflected in *Structure and Distribution of Coral Reefs* (1842) and *Geological Observations on Volcanic Islands* (1844). These early works established his name in the scientific community and were fundamental to the development of his theories on evolution.

Darwin had realized that many questions in animal geography, comparative anatomy, and paleontology could only be answered by disregarding the theory of the

Darwin: this cartoon from the *London Sketch Book* in 1874 pictures Charles Darwin showing an ape how alike they are

immutability of the species (an idea widely held at the time) and accepting that one species came from another. The idea was not original but Darwin's contribution was to propose a means by which evolution could have occurred and to present his case clearly, backed up by a wealth of evidence. In 1838 he read Thomas MALTHUS's *An Essay on the Principle of Population* and quickly saw that Malthus's argument could be extended from humans to all other forms of life. Darwin spent over 20 years amassing evidence in support of this theory of evolution by natural selection.

The stimulus to publish came in June 1858 when Darwin received, quite unexpectedly, a communication from Alfred Russel WALLACE that was effectively a synopsis of his own ideas. The question of priority was resolved through the action of LYELL and HOOKER, who arranged for a joint paper to be read to the Linnean Society in July 1858. This consisted of Wallace's essay and a letter, dated 1857, from Darwin to the American botanist Asa Gray, outlining Darwin's theories. Darwin later prepared an 'abstract' of his work, published in November 1859 as *On the Origin of Species by Means of Natural Selection*.

The book created considerable controversy and opposition from churchmen. Darwin, a retiring man, chose not to defend his views publicly and continued quietly with his work, publishing books that extended and amplified his theories, including *The Descent of Man* (1871).

Darwin was troubled by one flaw in his theory – if inheritance were blending, i.e., if offspring received an average of the features of their parents (the then-held view of heredity), then how could the variation, so essential for natural selection to act on, come about? Fleeming Jenkin, professor of engineering at University College, London, wrote a review of the *Origin* in 1867 in which he pointed out that any individual with a useful trait mating with a normal partner, would pass on only 50% of the character to its children, 25% to its grandchildren, 12.5% to its greatgrandchildren, and so on until the useful feature disappeared. The logic of this pushed Darwin

toward Lamarckian ideas of inheritance of acquired characteristics as elaborated in his theory of pangenesis in the sixth edition of the *Origin*. The question was not resolved until the rediscovery, nearly 20 years after Darwin's death, of Gregor MENDEL's work, which demonstrated the particulate nature of inheritance, i.e., that hereditary characteristics are transmitted from parents to offspring by discrete entities, later known as genes.

Darwin, Erasmus (1731–1802) British physician. Erasmus Darwin was something of an inventor but is best remembered for his scientific writings, which often appeared in verse form. In his work *Zoonomia* (1794–96), Darwin advanced an evolutionary theory stating that changes in an organism are caused by the direct influence of the environment, a proposal similar to that put forward by Jean Baptiste LAMARCK some 15 years later. He was the grandfather, by his first wife, of Charles Robert Darwin and, by his second wife, of Francis Galton.

Darwinism DARWIN's scientific explanation of the mechanism of evolutionary change, namely, that in any varied population of organisms only the best adapted to that environment will tend to survive and reproduce. Individuals that are less well adapted will tend to perish without reproducing. Hence the unfavorable characteristics, possessed by the less well-adapted individuals, will tend to disappear from a species, and the favorable characteristics will become more common. Over time the characteristics of a species will therefore change, eventually resulting in the formation of new species (*see* natural selection).

Darwin's theory was based on painstaking and thorough study of the vast amount of evidence he had collected over many years, particularly on his voyage on HMS *Beagle*, which took him around the world enabling him to study the flora and fauna of many different countries. Although WALLACE and Darwin published a joint paper in 1858 and Wallace had come to the same conclusions as Darwin about the mechanism of evolution, Darwin had collected all his evidence and ideas together and published his seminal work in his famous book, *The Origin of Species by Means of Natural Selection* in 1859. This book has never been out of print since it was first published. The main weakness of Darwin's theory was that he could not explain how the variation, which natural selection acts upon, is generated, since at the time it was believed that the characteristics of the parents become blended in the offspring. This weakness was overcome with the discovery of MENDEL's work and its description of particulate inheritance. *See also* neo-Darwinism; pangenesis.

darwins *See* rate of evolution.

Darwin's finches The 14 species of finches, first described by Darwin, unique to the GALÁPAGOS ISLANDS of the South Pacific, but related to finches on the South American continent from which they evolved. Of particular interest is the amount of ADAPTIVE RADIATION they display, and the fact that they occupy ecological niches that, in other parts of the world, are occupied by different birds, e.g. woodpeckers.

The Galápagos finches later provided Darwin with a clear understanding of the evolutionary process. All of the finches are thought to have evolved in the Galápagos Islands except for the Cocos finch, which is restricted to Cocos Island. The finches' ancestors probably originated on the mainland and probably arrived on the islands having been blown there by very high winds. There are 25 separate islands in the group, but the smaller islands have two or more species of finch and the larger ones often ten species. Different feeding mechanisms have evolved by CHARACTER DISPLACEMENT.

There are four groups of finches:
The first comprises six species of ground finches, which belong to the genus *Geospiza*. Four of these species feed primarily on seeds of different sizes and thus a range of different finchlike beak sizes has evolved. The other two species of ground finch feed on cactus flowers, especially those of the prickly pear (*Opuntia*). They

are known as cactus finches and have evolved long straight beaks and forked tongues with which they collect nectar from the flowers.

The second group are the six species of tree finches, which belong to the genus *Camarhyncus*. Five species of tree finches feed on small insects and beetles and have beaks of similar size. Two of the insectivorous tree finches – the woodpecker finch and the mangrove finch – are rare examples of birds using tools. They use either small twigs or cactus spines to scrape or push out insects that they find in cracks and crevices in the bark of trees. The remaining tree finch is a vegetarian and feeds on fruits and buds of various plants using its curved parrotlike beak.

The third group contains a single species (*Certhidia olivacea*) and is a warbler, resembling the true warblers of the mainland.

The fourth group also consists of a single species – the isolated Cocos finch (*Pinaroloxias inornata*) that some authorities do not include with Darwin's finches. *See also* Galápagos Islands.

dating techniques Methods used in determining the age of rocks, fossils, or archeological remains. There are two main methods. *Relative dating* assesses the age of a specimen in comparison to other specimens. *Absolute dating* involves assessing the actual age of a specimen by using some reliable measure of time. *See also* dendrochronology; radioactive dating.

Dawkins, Richard (1941–) British evolutionary biologist. His book, *The Selfish Gene* (1976), was a bestseller. In 1986 Dawkins published another popular work, *The Blind Watchmaker*. The title refers to the image used by William Paley in his *Natural Theology* (1802). If anyone were to find a watch he would be able to infer from its mechanism that it had a maker; equally with nature, where the mechanisms of hand, eye, heart, and brain demand the existence of a designer just as strongly. Dawkins accepted the argument but insisted that the watchmaker was merely the operation of natural selection. In case after case he argued that the same effects could be produced by natural selection a good deal more plausibly than by a divine watchmaker.

One of the most original features of Dawkins's work was his demonstration that with few simple recursive rules, and some very simple starting points, various complex life forms or 'biomorphs' could be produced on a computer screen. The biomorphs were 'created' by the application of simple rules to a large number of apparently random initial positions.

Dawkins has continued to write on evolutionary theory, most notably in his *Climbing Mount Improbable* (1996), where he shows how such unlikely candidates as a spider's web and the vertebrate eye can have evolved under the guiding power of natural selection.

De Beer, Sir Gavin Rylands (1899–1972) British zoologist. De Beer is noted for his early publication, *Introduction to Experimental Biology* (1926), in which he disproved the germ-layer theory in embryology.

De Beer has also done work to show that adult animals retain some of the juvenile characters of their evolutionary ancestors (*pedomorphosis*), thus refuting Ernst HAECKEL's theory of RECAPITULATION. He also suggested that gaps in the evolutionary development of animals may be accounted for by the impermanence of the soft tissues of young ancestors. Studies of *Archeopteryx*, the earliest known bird, led him to propose piecemeal evolutionary changes in such animals, thus explaining the combination of reptilian and avian characters (e.g., teeth and feathers). His other books include *Embryology and Evolution of Chordate Animals* (1962, with Julian Huxley) and *The Elements of Experimental Embryology* (1962).

Decapoda The order that contains the most specialized members of CRUSTACEA. The prawns (e.g. *Palaemon*), shrimps (e.g. *Crangon*), lobsters (e.g. *Homarus*), and crawfish (e.g. *Astacus*) all have a long abdomen ending in a tail for swimming backward. The crabs (e.g. *Cancer*) have a much reduced abdomen. The head and thorax are characteristically fused and covered with a carapace. There are five pairs of walking legs, the first and second pairs often having pincers (chelae) used in feeding and defense. Crab- and lobsterlike crustaceans evolved in the Mesozoic, and in the Cenozoic crabs and lobsters resembled present-day forms.

degeneration 1. Evolution to an apparently simpler structural form. It is seen in the wings of the flightless birds (e.g. emus). Such organs are said to be vestigial. It is also common in parasites; for example, parasitic protozoa possess few organelles compared with their free-living relatives. 2. Death and deterioration of cells, nerve fibers, etc.

deletion *See* chromosome mutation; gene mutation.

deme A local population of individuals that can potentially breed with each other.

dendrochronology A method of archaeological dating by the *annual rings* of trees, used when the lifespans of living and fossil trees in an area overlap. Exact dates for sites can be calculated and the method is more accurate than RADIOACTIVE DATING techniques. Bristlecone pines, which can live for up to 5000 years, have been used in such work.

dendrogram A branched diagram used in TAXONOMY to demonstrate relationships between species, families, etc., or used to show the relationships between individuals, as in family trees. A cladogram (*see* cladistics) is a type of dendrogram.

density-dependent selection Selection that benefits different variations depending on the population density.

density-independent selection Selection that benefits the same variation at all population densities.

dentary A tooth-bearing membrane bone. In mammals, it is the lower jaw bone

Devonian

consisting of a single membrane bone on each side, fused together in front. *See* Mammalia.

deoxyribonuclease   *See* DNase.

deoxyribonucleic acid   *See* DNA.

derived homology   *See* homologous.

Dermaptera   A small order of nocturnal insects – the earwigs (e.g. *Forficula*). Earwigs have a long body covered with a hard shiny exoskeleton and are omnivorous, with biting and sucking mouthparts. The thin transparent hind-wings are folded in a complicated way and covered by the short scaly fore wings (*elytra*) when resting. The forceps-like cerci at the end of the abdomen aid in folding the wings as well as being used in attack and defense. They evolved in the Jurassic along with ants, true bugs, flies, and caddis flies. *See* Insecta.

deterministic   Describing any model in evolutionary biology in which the population is large enough to ignore random events.

Deuteromycota   (Fungi anamorphici; Fungi Imperfecti)   A phylum of so-called 'imperfect' fungi in which sexual reproduction is unknown or has been lost during evolution. Its members, for example the *Penicillium* molds, are assigned as a taxonomic convenience, rather than by any true criteria, and some authorities prefer to allocate the deuteromycotes to either the ascomycetes (the majority) or the basidiomycetes, on the basis of available evidence. Indeed, *Penicillium* is now known to have a sexual stage, formerly regarded as a quite distinct ascomycete fungus (*Talaromyces*). *See* Fungi.

deuterostomes   An evolutionary line of bilaterally symmetrical animals based on certain embryonic features. The name is derived from the Greek words: '*deuteros*' meaning 'second' or 'last' and '*stoma*' meaning 'mouth'. The blastopore becomes the anus and the mouth is formed later, hence the name, 'mouth last' or 'mouth

second'. Deuterostomes include the Echinodermata and the Chordata. *Compare* protostomes. *See also* bilateral symmetry.

developmental change   Change that occurs during the lifetime of an organism and is not considered to be evolutionary. Changes to the timing, rate, or result of development of an organism over generations are part of evolution. *See* homeotic gene.

developmental constraint   A constraint placed on the evolution of a perfectly adapted phenotype by an organism's developmental system. *See* Evo-Devo, pleiotropy. *Compare* genetic constraint; historical constraint.

developmental genetics   The study of genes that control developmental processes in organisms, i.e. regulatory genes. *See* homeobox; homeotic gene; operon.

Devonian   Named for the county of Devon in SW England, the geological period described as the 'Age of Fishes', some 405–355 mya, between the Silurian and the Carboniferous periods of the Paleozoic era. It was characterized by an enormous number and variety of fishes, most of which have become extinct without leaving any modern relatives.

There were two periods of mountain building: the Caledonian OROGENY continued from the Silurian and was followed by the Acadian orogeny, caused by the collision of what is now North America with a land mass that is now modern Scandinavia. The climate continued to warm, becoming hotter and drier.

Enormous deposits of red sediment (Old Red Sandstone) accumulated in NW Europe and North America and the fossil record reveals that the seas were abundant with fishes, including the first sharks (*see* Chondrichthyes), ostracoderms, and placoderms. The marine deposits also show that the first AMMONITES had appeared and there were abundant crinoids (*see* Crinoideae). By the end of the Devonian, however, the ostracoderms and GRAPTOLITES had become extinct and TRILOBITES were rare. During the late Devonian, prim-

65

itive amphibians were evolving from crossopterygians (lobe-finned fish) (*see* Dipnoi; Osteichthyes). Vascular land plants appeared, such as the psilophytes and pteridophytes, while terrestrial fauna included insects and spiders. The oldest fossil fern is *Iridopteris* from Devonian rocks, but the end of the period marked the rise of the tree ferns. *See also* geological time scale; mass extinction.

de Vries, Hugo (1848–1935) Dutch plant physiologist and geneticist. During the 1880s, de Vries became interested in heredity and in 1889 he published *Intracellular Pangenesis*, in which he critically reviewed previous research on inheritance and advanced the theory that elements in the nucleus, 'pangenes', determine hereditary traits. In 1892 he began a series of plant-breeding experiments and by 1896 he had obtained clear evidence for the segregation of characters in the offspring of crosses in 3:1 ratios. He delayed publishing his results, proposing to include them in a larger book, but in 1900 he came across the work of Gregor MENDEL, published 34 years earlier, and announced his own findings. This stimulated both Karl Correns and Erich von Tschermak-Seysenegg to publish their essentially similar observations.

De Vries's work on the evening primrose, *Oenothera lamarckiana*, began in 1886 when he noticed distinctly differing types within a colony of the plants. He considered these to be mutants and formulated the idea of evolution proceeding by distinct changes such as those he observed, believing also that new species could arise through a single drastic mutation. He published his observations in *The Mutation Theory* (1901–03). It was later shown that his *Oenothera* 'mutants' were in fact triploids or tetraploids (i.e., they had extra sets of chromosomes) and thus gave a misleading impression of the apparent rate and magnitude of mutations (*see* autopolyploidy). However, the theory is still important for demonstrating how variation, essential for evolution, can occur in a species.

diakinesis The last stage of prophase in the first division of MEIOSIS. Chiasmata are seen during this stage, and by the end of diakinesis the nucleoli and nuclear membrane have disappeared.

Diapsida (diapsids) *See* Reptilia.

diatomaceous earths *See* diatoms.

diatoms Unicellular algae of the phylum Bacillariophyta, found in freshwater, the sea, and soil. Much of PLANKTON is composed of diatoms and they are thus an important link in food chains. They have silica cell walls (frustules) composed of two valves ornamented with perforations, which are arranged differently in each species. The silica cell walls of dead frustules are highly resistant to decay and gradually deep sediments form on the bottoms of lakes and oceans, called *diatomaceous earths* or *kieselghur*, which consolidate to form the rock diatomite. These organisms first appeared in the Jurassic, were abundant during the Miocene, and continue to the present day. The chloroplasts contain chlorophyll *a* and *c*, carotenes, and xanthophylls.

dichopatric speciation *See* allopatric speciation.

Dicotyledonae (dicotyledons) A class of flowering plants (*see* Angiospermophyta) characterized by having two cotyledons in the seed. They include herbs, shrubs, and trees and secondary growth is normal. Examples are the buttercup and the oak. The flower parts are arranged in fours or fives, or multiples thereof, and the leaf veins are branched. The vascular bundles of the stem are arranged in a ring within a single endodermis and pericycle, giving a eustele. The dicotyledons were the first flowering plants to evolve. They first appeared in the late Jurassic and flourished in the Cretaceous. Both monocotyledons and dicotyledons evolved from the order Magnoliales. The MONOCOTYLEDONAE were also firmly established by the end of the Cretaceous period.

Dictyoptera The order of insects that contains the cockroaches (e.g. *Periplaneta*). Cockroaches are cosmopolitan nocturnal omnivorous insects; they are pests and can spread disease in dirty places. They have a flattened body enabling them to hide in crevices and the hardened fore wings protect the larger delicate hind wings. They seldom fly. The eggs are laid in capsules (*oothecae*), which may be carried about by the female. The young resemble adults but are wingless. The first fossils of winged insects are found in the Carboniferous period and include a very primitive cockroach.

dicynodonts *See* Mammalia; Triassic.

differentiation A process of change during which cells with generalized form become morphologically and functionally specialized to produce the different cell types that make up the various tissues and organs of the organism. Differentiation has been best studied in experimental organisms, such as the fruit fly *Drosophila*. Here, proteins called *morphogens*, encoded by maternal genes of follicle cells, diffuse into the developing early embryo where they lay the foundations of the general body plan. Gradients of concentration of the various morphogens cause genes in different zones of the embryo to be activated to different extents, creating a rudimentary pattern of body segments. This pattern is reinforced and refined by the embryo's own genes – the so-called *segment genes*. Within each segment the differentiation of limbs and other appendages is controlled by a class of master genes, called HOMEOTIC GENES. Mutations of these in *Drosophila* can result in, for example, legs developing on the head instead of antennae. These homeotic genes are highly conserved across a wide range of species, from plants to humans, and produce a protein that binds to DNA, acting as a switch for various other genes. *See also* conserved sequence.

diffuse coevolution *See* coevolution.

digitigrade Describing the mode of progression in some mammals in which only digits (fingers or toes) are in contact with the ground. It is seen in dogs, cats, and most fast-running animals. *Compare* plantigrade; unguligrade.

dihybrid A hybrid heterozygous at two loci and obtained by crossing homozygous parents with different alleles at two given loci: for example, Mendel's cross between yellow round (YYRR) and green wrinkled (yyrr) garden peas to give a yellow round dihybrid (YyRr). When a dihybrid is selfed a characteristic *dihybrid ratio* of 9:3:3:1 is obtained in the offspring. Nine plants (or the equivalent proportion of the offspring) exhibit both dominant characters, six plants show one dominant and one recessive character, and one plant exhibits both recessives. *Compare* monohybrid.

dimorphism *See* sexual dimorphism.

dinoflagellate A marine or freshwater protoctist of the phylum Dinoflagellata (Dinomastigota) that swims in a twirling manner by means of two undulipodia (flagella). These lie at right angles to each other in two grooves within the organism's rigid body wall (test). Many possess stinging organelles that they discharge to catch prey; and some produce potent toxins that are capable of killing fish. Roughly half of all known dinoflagellates are capable of photosynthesis. In PLANKTON, they are important as food and also for their symbiotic relationships with marine invertebrates such as corals and are known as *zooxanthellae* in some species. Nucleic acid sequencing shows that dinoflagellates are closely related to the Ciliata, but very distantly related to *Euglena* (*see* Euglenophyta), even though both have chloroplasts and flagella. *See also* endosymbiont theory.

dinosaurs The large extinct terrestrial reptiles (*see* Reptilia) that existed during the Mesozoic era. The name 'dinosaur' was coined in 1842 by the first director of the British Museum, Sir Richard Owen. There are two main orders, based on the anatomy of the pelvic girdle: the *Saurischia* (*lizard-hipped dinosaurs*) and the *Ornithischia* (*bird-hipped dinosaurs*). In the saurischians, the pubic bone of the pelvis points forward, whilst the pubic bone of ornithischians points toward the posterior, parallel with the ischium, possibly to accommodate a large gut.

The Saurischia comprised the oldest group, evolving in the early Triassic from the diapsid ARCHOSAURS (alongside the lines that evolved into the modern crocodiles, pterosaurs, and birds). The first were the *theropods*, meaning 'beast feet', which were bipedal carnivores, some of which were small delicate animals. Later forms had beaklike jaws. The most spectacular animals of this group were the giant carnivores, e.g. *Allosaurus*, which evolved in the Jurassic and was over 10 m long; and the most famous, the genus *Tyrannosaurus* from the Cretaceous, which included the largest land carnivores of all time (*see* tyrannosaurs).

The other saurischian group included the giant long-necked quadrupedal herbivores (the *sauropods*), such as *Apatosaurus* (*Brontosaurus*) and *Diplodocus*, which roamed and migrated in herds, feeding on trees and thickets. They had long balancing tails, tiny heads, and four pillarlike limbs that supported their enormous bodies, which were often almost 27 m long and weighed 50 tons. Some authorities believe that they wallowed in water because their nostrils were situated on the top of the head, as were their eyes, allowing almost complete submersion. The water supported their large bulk and also allowed them protection from such carnivores as *Allosaurus* and *Tyrannosaurus*.

The Ornithischia were more specialized than the Saurischia and evolved mainly in the Cretaceous.

The *ornithopods* included the *hadrosaurs* ('duck-billed dinosaurs'). They were bipedal herbivores with webbed feet, long tails, ducklike bills, some with about 2000 teeth for chewing. Some developed crests with long nasal passages, possibly used as 'snorkels' as they dived in the swamps (e.g. *Trachodon*). *Iguanodon*, the first dinosaur to be described, was 5 m tall and over 6 m long. Some members of this group had forelimbs that enabled them to walk on all four legs, so not all were bipedal.

Ankylosaurs were armored quadrupedal herbivores with clublike tails and squat broad tanklike bodies (e.g. *Ankylosaurus*). *Stegosaurs* evolved in the Jurassic and were armor-plated herbivorous quadrupeds, ranging from 6–10 m long, with tiny heads, high-arched backs and four spikes on the tail, e.g. *Stegosaurus*.

Ceratopsians were horned dinosaurs. They were herbivorous quadrupeds with huge bony head shields bearing horns and frills and a narrow beak. *Triceratops* was over 8 m long with a head shield of about 2 m. *Proceratops*, discovered in Mongolia, was an abundant smaller dinosaur and complete skeletons have been found in desert sandstones.

Dinosaurs were a very successful and diverse group, dominating terrestrial environments for 140 million years. Their diversity accompanied the evolution of the flowering plants. Many of them, especially the enormous herbivores, probably lived on the shores of shallow lakes and around swamps where they wallowed in the water, using it for buoyancy. There are many theories to explain the extinction of the dinosaurs at the end of the Cretaceous period, the most popular being major climatic changes induced by CONTINENTAL DRIFT or by the impact of a giant meteorite on the Earth's surface (*see* Alvarez theory).

Certain authorities have proposed a contentious theory that dinosaurs could well have been warm-blooded because some of their bones were highly vascularized, their wide variety of body coverings could possibly have been heat conserving, and the dinosaurs from which birds evolved had feathers.

dinosaurian theory   *See* Aves.

diphycercal tail   The type of tail found in lampreys, hagfish, the young stages of all fish, and the larvae of such amphibians as frogs and toads. The vertebral column extends into the tail, which has caudal fins of equal size above and below it. *Compare* heterocercal tail; homocercal tail.

diphyodont   A type of dentition (found in most mammals) in which an animal has two sets of teeth in succession. The milk (or deciduous) teeth of the young animal fall out and are replaced by the permanent teeth, which are larger and more numerous since there are molars as well as premolars. *Compare* monophyodont; polyphyodont.

dipleurula The hypothetical free-swimming larva of early echinoderms. It is believed to have been flattened and bilaterally symmetrical, with the digestive canal opening to the exterior by a mouth and anus, and the coelom opening to the dorsal surface by a narrow tube. It had large lobes on its body, fringed with bands of cilia. These were used for locomotion and for feeding. This basic form has been modified in existing echinoderms. The dipleurula larva of echinoderms is also found in hemichordates and suggests that these groups have probably evolved from a common ancestor. The fact that adult echinoderms have a radially symmetrical form suggests that the hemichordates probably have a greater similarity to the common ancestor. *Compare* trochophore. *See* bipinnaria; Echinodermata; pluteus; tornaria.

diplobiontic Describing life cycles showing a typical ALTERNATION OF GENERATIONS with haploid and diploid somatic bodies. Ferns are diplobiontic organisms. *Compare* haplobiontic.

diploblastic Describing animals in which the body wall consists of two layers, an ectoderm and an endoderm, separated by mesoglea. The CNIDARIA are diploblastic animals. *See also* planuloid hypothesis.

diploid A cell or organism containing twice the haploid number of chromosomes (i.e. 2n). In animals the diploid condition is generally found in all but the reproductive cells and the chromosomes exist as homologous pairs, which separate at MEIOSIS, one of each pair going into each gamete. In plants exhibiting an alternation of generations the sporophyte is diploid, while higher plants are normally always diploid. Exceptions are those species in which polyploidy occurs. *Compare* haploid.

diplont A diploid organism that represents the vegetative stage in life cycles in which haploidy is restricted to the gametes. *Diplontic* life cycles are found in most organisms. *See* haplobiontic. *Compare* haplont.

diplontic *See* diplont.

Diplopoda The class of arthropods that contains the millipedes (e.g. *Julus*), characterized by a cylindrical body divided into numerous segments each bearing two pairs of walking legs. Millipedes are terrestrial herbivores, breathing air through tracheae. Excretion is by Malpighian tubules. They are sometimes placed with the centipedes (Chilopoda) in the group MYRIAPODA. They appeared in the Carboniferous, along with scorpions and spiders. *Compare* Chilopoda.

diplotene In MEIOSIS, the stage in late prophase I when the pairs of chromatids begin to separate from the tetrad formed by the association of homologous chromosomes. Chiasmata can often be seen at this stage.

Dipnoi The ancient order of bony fish that contains the lungfishes. Found in fresh water in areas subject to seasonal drought, they are characterized by a functional lung and internal as well as external nostrils, allowing air-breathing at the water surface without opening the mouth. The young breathe by temporary external gills. *Neoceratodus* of Queensland rivers is the most primitive and cannot live out of water. It has paddle-shaped rayed fins, a single lung, and very large scales. *Protopterus* of the Nile and *Lepidopterus* of South America have rayless whiplike fins, paired lungs, smaller scales, and survive when rivers dry up completely by living in the mud, leaving a small opening for breathing. The heart and blood system are adapted for pulmonary respiration and resemble those of amphibians. They evolved in the Devonian period when they were very numerous (e.g. *Ceratodus*). They are often regarded as living fossils, having changed very little over millions of years. *See also* coelacanth; Osteichthyes; swim bladder.

Diptera The order of insects that contains the flies, characterized by only one pair of wings (balancing organs (*halteres*) replace the hind wings). The adults have sucking or piercing mouthparts and feed on plant juices, decaying organic matter, or blood. The legless larvae (*maggots*) feed on plants, decaying organic matter, or are carnivorous. Metamorphosis is complete and the pupa is often protected by a barrel-shaped *puparium*. Many flies are medically important as the carriers of various diseases; for example the *Anopheles* mosquito transmits malaria.

Fossil Diptera have been found in the Permian, where other groups are more abundant. They became more prevalent in the Mesozoic, and make up 27% of all insects in the Tertiary, falling to 10% of Recent fossil species.

directional selection NATURAL SELECTION that always acts in one direction, causing a consistent change in a character over time; for example, an increase in body size. *Compare* disruptive selection; stabilizing selection.

discontinuous variation *See* qualitative variation.

dispersal The movement of members of a species to new areas, altering the geographical distribution of the species. Dispersal occurs in response to the pressure of an increasing population and environmental change. Mechanisms of dispersal can be active or passive.

disruptive selection NATURAL SELECTION that favors extreme forms in a population and works to eliminate the average. *Compare* directional selection; stabilizing selection.

distance The quantitatively measured difference between the phenetic appearance of two groups of individuals, such as populations or species (*phenetic distance*),

or the difference in their gene frequencies (*genetic distance*).

divergence *See* divergent evolution.

divergent evolution (divergence) The concept that as related species evolve they become less and less similar. It can be attributed to competition, different environmental challenges, and the fact that mutations (and therefore variation) occur randomly. The ancestral stock divides into two and the new types become less and less like one another over a period of time. *See* adaptation; adaptive radiation.

diverticulum A blind tubular or saclike outgrowth from a tube or cavity. For instance, the appendix and cecum of a rabbit form a diverticulum. The primitive chordate animal, *Branchiostoma*, has such an outgrowth at the point where the esophagus meets the intestine. It projects forward beside the pharynx and may be homologous with the liver of vertebrates.

division One of the major groups into which the plant kingdom is classified: a taxonomic rank used instead of phylum in some plant and fungus classifications. Division names (and hence phylum names too) end in -*phyta* (e.g. Bryophyta, Filicinophyta). The Latin names of divisions in the fungi end in -mycota, e.g. Ascomycota. Divisions may be divided into subdivisions.

division of labor The distribution of tasks originally carried out by one unit over a number of different units. For example, all tasks in a single-celled organism are carried out by that cell, but in a multicellular organism, different tasks are carried out by different cell types. The division of labor requires functional DIFFERENTIATION, which allows an organism to carry out more tasks more effectively, but also creates scope for GENOMIC CONFLICT.

D-loop *See* mitochondrion.

DNA (deoxyribonucleic acid) A nucleic acid, mainly found in the chromosomes, that contains the hereditary information of organisms. The molecule is made up of two antiparallel helical polynucleotide chains coiled around each other to give a *double helix*. It is also known as the *Watson–Crick model* after James Watson and Francis Crick who first proposed this model in 1953. Phosphate molecules alternate with deoxyribose sugar molecules along both chains and each sugar molecule is also joined to one of four nitrogenous bases – adenine (A), guanine (G), cytosine (C), or thymine (T). The two chains are joined to each other by bonding between bases. The two purine bases (adenine and guanine) always bond with the pyrimidine bases (thymine and cytosine), and the pairing is quite specific: adenine with thymine and guanine with cytosine. The two chains are therefore complementary. The sequence of bases along the chain makes up a code – the GENETIC CODE – that determines the precise sequence of amino acids in proteins (*see* messenger RNA; protein synthesis; transcription).

DNA is the hereditary material of all organisms with the exception of RNA viruses. Together with histones (and RNA in some instances) it makes up the CHROMOSOMES of eukaryotic cells. *See* DNA repair; junk DNA; replication; selfish DNA. *See also* RNA.

DNA fingerprinting   *See* genetic fingerprinting.

DNA hybridization   *See* nucleic acid hybridization.

DNA ligase   *See* DNA repair; splicing.

DNA polymerase   *See* polymerase.

DNA probe (gene probe)   A nucleic acid consisting of a single strand of nucleotides whose base sequence is complementary to that of a particular DNA fragment being sought, for example a gene on a chromosome or a restriction fragment in a DNA digest. The probe is labeled (e.g. with a radioisotope or a fluorescent compound) so that when it binds to the target sequence, both it and the target can be identified (by autoradiography or fluorescence microscopy).

DNA repair   Any of the mechanisms by which cells mend their DNA following damage. DNA must undergo MUTATION in order to create the genetic variation on which NATURAL SELECTION acts, but it must also be maintained and replicated faithfully to prevent the build-up of deleterious mutations. Organisms could not survive the natural rate of damage to their DNA without specific enzymatic mechanisms to repair the damage. The double-stranded structure of DNA is important in DNA repair because it provides a complementary strand with the necessary information for repairs to be carried out correctly. The use of double-stranded DNA as the genetic material was an important evolutionary step that allowed for the existence of complex genomes. Spontaneous and induced DNA damage usually only affects one strand in any one place and is repaired by the excision repair system, which involves three types of enzyme: *repair nucleases*, which remove the damaged DNA; *DNA polymerases* (*see* polymerase), which fill in the gap using the complementary strand as a template; and *DNA ligase*, which seals the break. If both strands are damaged then the recombinational repair system uses a DNA segment from an identical, but separate, DNA molecule as a template. During replication, DNA polymerase proofreads the bases it adds and any incorrect nucleotides are immediately removed, by an EXONUCLEASE, and replaced. Any mistakes that are missed by proofreading are repaired by the mismatch repair system, which can also detect small additions and deletions.

DNase (deoxyribonuclease)   Any enzyme that hydrolyzes the phosphodiester bonds of DNA. DNases are classified into two groups, according to their site of action in the DNA molecule (*see* endonuclease; exonuclease).

DNA sequencing   *See* gene sequencing.

Dobzhansky, Theodosius (1900–75)

Russian–American geneticist. Dobzhansky is noted for his work on the fruit fly (*Drosophila*). He was able to show that the genetic variability within populations was greater than had been thought. The high frequency of potentially deleterious genes had previously been overlooked because their effects are masked by corresponding dominant genes. Dobzhansky showed that such debilitating genes actually conferred an advantage to the organism when present with the normal type of gene, and therefore they tended to be maintained at a high level in the population. Populations with a high GENETIC LOAD – i.e., many concealed lethal genes – proved to be more versatile in changing environments. This work profoundly influenced the theories on the mathematics of evolution and natural selection with regard to Mendelism. Dobzhansky wrote a number of influential books, including *Genetics and the Origin of Species* (1937).

dodo   A large extinct flightless bird (*Raphus cucullatus*) that inhabited the island of Mauritius off the coast of East Africa and became extinct when the last one was killed in 1681. It was discovered in 1598 and lived in the dense forest feeding on fallen nuts and laying its eggs in nests in the ground. The dodo and other bird species flourished with few predators as no mammals lived on the island.

Mauritius was first discovered by the Portuguese in 1505 and soon became an important stopping-off place for ships involved in the spice trade. The sailors killed large numbers of dodos for meat. Worse, when the Dutch established a penal colony on the island, rats escaped from the convict ships and together with cats, pigs, and macaque monkeys, fed on the eggs of the dodo. It took less than 100 years for the dodo to become extinct.

Certain authorities believe that the Mauritian 'calvaria' tree is also a victim of the extinction of the dodo. Many trees in the rainforests of Mauritius, like the calvaria tree, are long-lived (300 years old). Many of these trees are now dying out. It is thought that the nuts of the calvaria tree could only germinate if they passed through the gut of a dodo first, i.e. this is how the dormancy was broken. Creative experiments feeding these nuts to turkeys have resulted in the egested nuts germinating into seedlings, possibly saving this species from extinction. This tree is now known as the dodo tree.

domain   1. A taxonomic grouping of organisms that ranks higher than kingdom. there are generally considered to be three domains: ARCHAEA, BACTERIA, and EUKARYA. The FIVE KINGDOMS CLASSIFICATION recognizes only two 'superkingdoms': Prokarya (which includes the single kingdom Bacteria, comprising both archaea and the bacteria) and Eukarya.
2. A discrete part of the tertiary structure of a PROTEIN that has a particular function, e.g. as the binding site for the substrate of an enzyme.

dominant   An ALLELE that, in a heterozygote, prevents the expression of another (recessive) allele at the same locus. Organisms with one dominant and one recessive allele thus appear identical to those with two dominant alleles, the difference in their genotypes only becoming apparent on examination of their progenies. The dominant allele usually controls the normal form of the gene, while mutations are generally recessive. *Compare* recessive.

double helix   *See* DNA.

double recessive   An organism containing both RECESSIVE alleles of a particular gene and thus expressing the recessive form of the gene in its phenotype. Double recessives, being of known genotype, are often used in *test crosses* to establish whether the organism to which it is crossed is heterozygous or homozygous for the same gene.

Down's syndrome   *See* nondisjunction.

dragonflies   *See* Odonata.

drift   *See* genetic drift.

Drosophila melanogaster   The banana fruit fly (insect order Diptera), which has been used for decades in experimental genetics and later in developmental biology. It is suited for this purpose because it displays phenotypic variants of numerous characters, which can be used as markers in breeding experiments (red eyes and white eyes, long wings and vestigial wings, for example). The discovery of giant chromosomes (*polytene chromosomes*) in its salivary glands was instrumental in the first attempts at chromosome mapping. It has a short life cycle that takes two weeks to complete and is easy to keep in large numbers. *Drosophila* cells have four pairs of chromosomes, a pair of SEX CHROMOSOMES and three pairs of AUTOSOMES. The

entire genome has now been sequenced, consisting of about 165 million bases and about 14 000 genes. *See* chromosome map; homeotic gene; puff.

Dryopithecus *See* human evolution; primates; Pilbeam; *Ramapithecus*.

duplex Double, or having two distinct parts. The term is particularly used to describe the double helix of the Watson–Crick DNA model.

duplication The occurrence of extra genes or segments of a chromosome in the genome. *See* chromosome mutation.

E *See* environmental effect.

ear ossicles In mammals, three small bones in the middle ear – the malleus, incus, and stapes. They form a series of levers whereby vibrations induced by sound waves falling on the eardrum (tympanum) are transmitted to the oval window (fenestra ovalis) and so to the inner ear. They are HOMOLOGOUS with certain jaw bones of lower vertebrates. *See* Meckel's cartilage. *See also* Weberian ossicles.

Earth, age of By comparing the amounts of uranium and lead isotopes in rocks from the Earth and meteorites, the latest estimate of the age of the Earth is 4500 million years. *See* Acasta rocks; origin of life.

earthworms *See* Lumbricus.

earwigs *See* Dermaptera.

East African Rift Valley A rift valley formed in East Africa as a result of the collision of tectonic plates. Many of the HOMINID fossils (*Homo* species and AUSTRALOPITHECINES) have been found in this valley. The large number of inland lakes and rivers have provided lush vegetation and resources for many populations of animals and eventually humans. During the PLIOCENE and PLEISTOCENE, the mountain range that formed as a result of the collision sank downward and formed the rift valley. Hot boiling springs are indicators of continuing volcanic activity in this area. Abundant jungle vegetation remained on the western side of the rift, but on the eastern side, grassland and savannah developed. Major paleoanthropological sites in this area include: the Olduvai Gorge, Laetoli, Lake Turkana, Koobi Fora, Hadar, Omo, and Aramis. *See also* plate tectonics.

Echinodermata A phylum of marine invertebrates containing the starfishes, sea urchins, feather stars, sea cucumbers, and brittle stars. Most echinoderms exhibit radial symmetry, with typically five rays extending from a central disk. All have calcareous skeletal plates and most have spines. Part of the coelom is modified as the water vascular system, which extends into hydraulic *tube feet*, used typically in locomotion. The water vascular system has an external opening, the *madreporite*. The nervous system is simple and there are no excretory organs. The development of the bilaterally symmetrical larvae (*see* dipleurula) shows affinities to the Chordata.

The Echinodermata are an ancient group, fossil remains of starfishes, sea cucumbers, and the crinoids (*see* Crinoidea) having been found in Cambrian rocks. Sea urchin fossils have been found in the Ordovician and echinoderms are represented up to the present day. Echinoderms flourished during the Mesozoic when many of the modern forms began to appear. There are a number of extinct groups of echinoderms that had their heyday in the Paleozoic, for example: the edrioasteroids (Cambrian–Carboniferous, e.g. *Stromatocystites*); the eocrinoids (Cambrian–Ordovician, e.g. *Macrocystella*); the Cystoidea (Ordovician–Devonian, e.g. *Echinosphaerites*); and the Blastoidea (Ordovician– Permian, e.g. *Pentremites*).

The echinoderms were once joined with the COELENTERATES as a group known as the *Radiata*, because of their radial symmetry. However, they are now linked with the HEMICHORDATA and CHORDATA. Their ancient origin is reflected in their calcareous endoskeleton, their water vascular system, and their *pedicellareae* (with tiny 'jaws' that keep the body surface free of debris). Chordatelike features include: a mesodermal endoskeleton (not external or ectodermal in origin like other invertebrates); the embryonic blastopore becomes the adult anus (not the mouth as in annelids and mollusks); the mouth is formed from an ectodermal invagination that connects with the endodermal esophagus; the mesoderm forms from pouches of the primitive gut (not from mesoblast cells as in annelids and mollusks); and radial and indeterminate cleavage. These features as well as the similarity of echinoderm larvae to hemichordate larvae provide strong evidence that chordates and echinoderms are relatives. The two groups probably diverged from a common ancestor in the remote past. The phylum is divided into five classes. *See* Asteroidea; Crinoidea; Echinoidea; Holothuroidea; Ophiuroidea.

Echinoidea The class of the Echinodermata that contains the sea urchins (e.g. *Echinus*), found on the sea bed or buried in sand. The spherical, heart-shaped, or flattened body lacks arms and is covered by a rigid shell (*test*) bearing movable spines used in locomotion and defense. The mouth, with a complicated jaw apparatus (*Aristotle's lantern*), is on the ventral surface. The larva is a form of DIPLEURULA larva (*see* pluteus).

Echinoids made their first appearance in the Ordovician and some fossils have been found in the early Carboniferous. Sea urchin fossils are very common in Cretaceous rocks and many are used as fossil indicators (*zonal indices*). The genus *Micraster*, the burrowing heart urchin, has a continuous record in the chalk deposits of the Cretaceous. Heart urchins were also abundant in the Oligocene.

ecological niche (niche) The functional role of an organism in a community. If two species occupy the same niche then competition occurs until one has replaced the other. A similar niche may be occupied by different species in different areas, for example the fallow deer of Africa occupies the same niche as the red deer of Eurasia. Conversely one type of organism may evolve by ADAPTIVE RADIATION to fill several different niches, such as the finches of the Galápagos Islands.

ecological role The contribution of a character to the survival of an organism.

ecological species concept The definition of a SPECIES as a group of organisms adapted to a particular niche. *Compare* biological species concept; cladistic species concept; phenetic species concept; recognition species concept.

ecological system *See* ecosystem.

ecosystem (ecological system) A unit made up of all the living and nonliving components of a particular area that interact and exchange materials with each other. The concept of the ecosystem differs from that of the community in that more emphasis is placed on abiotic factors. Various studies have been made to attempt to itemize the energy flow of an entire ecosystem, taking into account factors such as incoming radiation, photosynthetic efficiency, etc.

ecotype A group of organisms within a species adapted genetically to the combination of environmental factors in their habitat, but able to reproduce with other ecotypes belonging to the same species. Differences between ecotypes may be physiological or morphological. *Compare* biotype. *See also* adaptive radiation; speciation.

ectoderm The germ layer of metazoans (including vertebrates) that remains on the outside of the embryo and develops into the epidermis and its derivatives (e.g. hairs, glands, feathers, enamel) and the lining of the mouth and cloaca. *See* germ layers.

Ediacaran fauna The oldest known group of multicellular animal fossils found in PHOSPHORITES in Australia, Canada, and

China. They date back to approximately 570 million years ago (PRECAMBRIAN) and comprise a wide variety of soft-bodied aquatic animals, including ancestors of sponges, jellyfish, and worms, most of which became extinct before the Cambrian. Fossil Ediacaran embryos have also been found. They show individual cells and are almost identical to the embryos of modern-day insects and worms.

egg cell   *See* ovum.

elasmobranch   *See* Chondrichthyes.

electrophoresis   A method of distinguishing and identifying molecules, such as proteins and nucleic acids, according to their motility in an electric field. The motility of a molecule is influenced by its size, shape, and electric charge.

embryo   1. (*Zoology*) The organism formed after cleavage of the fertilized ovum and before hatching or birth. In mammals the embryo in its later well-differentiated stages is called a fetus.
2. (*Botany*) The organism that develops from the zygote of bryophytes, pteridophytes, and seed plants before germination.

embryology   The study of the structure and development of embryos of living organisms. In certain organisms, the study of developmental stages of an embryo may suggest what the ancestors of these organisms may have been like. *See* Haeckel; ontogeny; recapitulation.

endangered species   A species that is likely to become extinct as a result of human activities that have caused disastrous effects on parts of the environment and the organisms that live there (*see* pollution). The numbers of these species are so depleted, that the likelihood of increasing these populations is unlikely unless steps are taken to protect them (*see* conservation). In 1973 in the US, the government

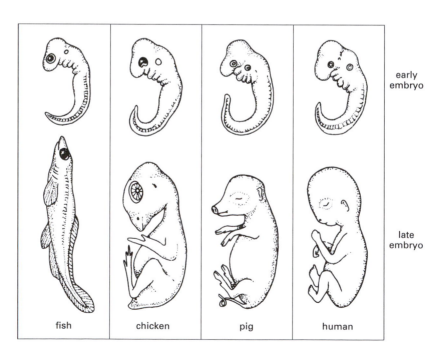

early embryo

late embryo

fish   chicken   pig   human

Embryo: in the early stages the different species have similar embryos

took steps to help to conserve these species by passing the Endangered Species Act. The animals and plants considered to be in danger must first be entered on the Federal list of endangered and threatened wildlife and plants before a program of action is devised. *Threatened species* (which are threatened with extinction in the forseeable future) can also be listed. If there is a successful outcome, the species can be delisted. Examples of endangered species in the US are the Florida panther, the grizzly bear, the autumn buttercup, and Smith's blue butterfly.

endoderm (entoderm) The innermost germ layer of most metazoans (including vertebrates) that develops into the gut lining and its derivatives (e.g. liver, pancreas). It also forms the yolk sac and allantois in birds and mammals. *See* germ layers.

endomitosis The duplication of chromosomes without division of the nucleus. Endomitosis may take two forms: the chromatids may separate causing endopolyploidy, e.g. in the macronucleus of ciliates such as *Paramecium*, or the chromatids may remain joined leading to multistranded chromosomes or *polyteny*, e.g. during larval development of dipteran flies. Both processes lead to an increase in nuclear and cytoplasmic volume. *Compare* amitosis; mitosis.

endonuclease An enzyme that catalyzes the hydrolysis of internal bonds of polynucleotides, such as DNA and RNA, producing short segments of linked nucleotides (oligonucleotides). *See also* DNase; restriction endonuclease.

endoplasmic reticulum (ER) A system of membranes forming tubular channels and flattened sacs (cisternae), running through the cytoplasm of all eukaryotic cells and continuous with the nuclear membrane. Rough ER is covered with RIBOSOMES and contains sites of protein synthesis. Smooth ER lacks ribosomes and is involved with lipid synthesis. *See also* endosymbiont theory.

endoskeleton A skeleton that occurs inside the animal body, such as the bony or cartilaginous skeleton of vertebrates (*see* craniate). It is comprised of a skull, vertebral column, pectoral and pelvic girdles, ribs, and limb or fin elements. It gives shape and support to the body, protects vital organs, and provides a system of rigid levers to which muscles can attach and produce movement. An endoskeleton also allows the steady growth in size of the animal. An endoskeleton is also present in echinoderms and certain other invertebrates. *Compare* exoskeleton.

endosperm The nutritive tissue that surrounds the embryo in angiosperms. In nonendospermic seeds most of the endosperm is absorbed by the developing embryo and the food stored in the cotyledons. In endospermic seeds the endosperm replaces the nucellus and is often a rich source of growth-regulating substances. Many endospermic seeds (e.g. cereals and oil seeds) are cultivated for their food reserves. The endosperm develops from the primary endosperm nucleus and is therefore TRIPLOID.

In the gymnosperms the female prothallial tissue is sometimes termed the endosperm. However, this tissue develops before fertilization and in fact is the haploid female GAMETOPHYTE. It is therefore not homologous with the angiosperm endosperm although it does have a nutritive function.

endosymbiont theory (endosymbiotic theory) The theory (advocated by Lynn Margulis), that eukaryotic organisms evolved from symbiotic associations between bacteria. It proposes that integration of photosynthetic bacteria, for example purple bacteria and cyanobacteria, into primitive eukaryotic cells led to their permanent incorporation as forerunners of the mitochondria (*see* mitochondrion) and plastids (e.g. CHLOROPLASTS) seen in modern EUKARYOTES. There is compelling supporting evidence for the theory, particularly from studies of mitochondrial and plastid inner membranes, DNA, and ribosomes, which demonstrate remarkable similarities with those of bacteria. Such organelles also divide by binary fission. Other structures such as the nuclear membrane and endoplasmic reticulum may also have formed by infolding of the plasma membrane and eventual isolation.

endothermy *See* homoiothermy.

entoderm *See* endoderm.

environment The complete range of external conditions under which an organism lives, including physical, chemical, and biological factors, such as temperature, light, and the availability of food and water.

environmental effect (E) A quantitative measure of the effects of the environment on phenotypic variation. *See* quantitative genetics; variance. *Compare* genotypic effect.

enzyme A protein that acts as a very efficient catalyst for biochemical reactions. An enzyme is unchanged in a reaction, its presence allowing the reaction to take place. Enzymes are very sensitive to their environment, for example, to changes in temperature, pH, and the presence of other substances. The region of an enzyme molecule that combines with or acts on a substrate is the *active site* in which amino acids are arranged so that they are specific to a particular substrate or type of substrate. *See also* functional constraint.

Eoanthropus dawsoni *See* Piltdown man.

Eocene The second oldest epoch of the TERTIARY period, 55–38 mya. This long epoch is characterized by a warm tropical to subtropical climate. The Alpine OROGENY began and toward the end of the Eocene and Australia split off from Antarctica. There was intense volcanic activity around the Pacific Ocean, termed the Pacific 'Ring of Fire'. The tropical climate gave rise to rainforests consisting of cycads, lianas, etc. as exemplified in the Eocene of both North America and the

London Basin in England. Early hoofed mammals, the ungulates (mainly perissodactyls, some artiodactyls), were dominant feeders on this vegetation, including *Eohippus*, the 'dawn horse' (now known as *Hyracotherium*). The largest mammal was *Uintotherium*, which was rhinolike and had an assemblage of horns on its skull and very large canine tusks. The first grasses had appeared by the end of the Eocene, providing a greater range of food for the herbivorous mammals. CREODONTS were the dominant carnivores and the first whales evolved from the MESONYCHIDS. Bats and birds were also present. *See also* geological time scale.

Eohippus *See* horse evolution.

eon *See* geological time scale.

epigenesis The process by which a developing organism increases in complexity, which is brought about by interaction between parts of the nuclear genetic program, the organized cytoplasm of the developing egg, and the egg's environment. *Compare* PREFORMATION.

epigenetic Describing any process that modifies gene expression without changing the DNA sequence, particularly during development; for example, inherited patterns of DNA methylation.

episome A genetic element that exists inside a cell, especially a bacterium, and can replicate either as part of the host cell's chromosome or independently. Homology with the bacterial chromosome is required for integration, therefore a plasmid may behave as an episome in one cell but not in another. Examples of episomes are temperate phages. *See* plasmid.

epistasis The action of one gene (the *epistatic gene*) affecting the expression of another, nonallelic, gene (the *hypostatic gene*). Epistatic and hypostatic genes are analogous to dominant and recessive alleles. In *epistatic fitness interaction* the fitness of a genotype varies depending on the genotypes of the loci with which it interacts. Epistasis requires heterozygosity at more than one locus. *Compare* complementary genes.

epistatic fitness interaction   *See* epistasis.

epoch   *See* geological time scale.

Equus   *See* horse evolution.

ER   *See* endoplasmic reticulum.

era   *See* geological time scale.

escalatory evolution   The theory that improvements in predatory adaptations are matched by improvements in prey defenses and vice versa in a so-called evolutionary 'arms race' caused by antagonistic COEVOLUTION.

Escherichia coli   A purple bacterium widely used in genetic research, occurring naturally in the intestinal tract of animals and in soil and water. It is Gram-negative and the cells are typically straight round-ended rods, usually occurring singly or in pairs. Some strains are pathogenic, causing diarrhea or more serious gastrointestinal infections. *See* genetic engineering.

essentialism (typology)   The belief that variation in the natural world can be sorted into a limited number of basic classes, representing constant, sharply delineated types. It was founded by the ancient Greeks and became a doctrine adopted by most philosophers and Christians up until Darwin's time. Any variation within the basic classes was believed to be accidental and largely ignored. Just before the publication of Darwin's theory, a less strict form of essentialism had begun to be adopted that allowed for gradual changes over time, known as transformations. *See also* creationism.

Ethiopian   One of the six zoogeographical regions of the Earth. It encompasses Africa south of the Sahara Desert, the southern half of Arabia, and (according to certain authorities) Madagascar. The animals characteristic of this region are the gorilla, chimpanzee, African elephant, rhinoceros, lion, hippopotamus, giraffe, certain antelopes, ostrich, guinea fowl, secretary bird, and, in Madagascar, the lemur. The main species barrier to this region is the Sahara Desert. *See* continental drift; Palearctic; zoogeographical region.

Eubacteria   A major subkingdom of the BACTERIA in the FIVE KINGDOMS CLASSIFICATION, containing a large and diverse group of bacteria, principally distinguishable from the other major subkingdom, the ARCHAEA, by differences in the base sequences of RNA subunits of the ribosomes, which are thought to reflect the very early evolutionary divergence between the two groups. Most are unicells that divide by binary fission. The cells can be spherical, rod-shaped, or helical, and some form assemblages of cells, such as branching filaments. Most are immotile, but some possess flagella. They are a ubiquitous group, some being found in extreme environmental conditions (*see* black smoker). Cell-wall structure, morphology, and metabolic features are used to distinguish the different phyla. The Eubacteria contains both Gram-positive and Gram-negative bacteria, and bacteria with no cell walls at all.

eucaryote   *See* eukaryote.

euchromatin   *See* chromatin.

eugenics   The theory that the human race could (or should) be improved by controlled selective breeding between individuals with 'desirable' characteristics – health, physique, intelligence, etc. It is a controversial subject, partly because of difficulties in judging the relative importance of genetic and environmental factors. More fundamentally, it is thought by many to be a moral issue involving the freedom of the individual and the danger of its use for sinister political ends.

Euglenophyta   A phylum of aquatic single-celled protoctists that swim using one or more flagella (undulipodia). It contains both photosynthesizing and nonphotosynthesizing members. For example, members of the genus *Euglena* possess a flexible pellicle surrounding the cell, and a single undulipodium. Many species contain chloroplasts, with pigments similar to those found in plants, although these organisms may also consume dissolved or particulate food from their surroundings. Reproduction is asexual, by binary fission. *E. gracilis* is a popular laboratory organism, in which the chloroplasts regress and are effectively turned off in sustained darkness, a process reversed when light is reintroduced. Some individuals may lose their chloroplasts permanently. Although in their possession of flagella and chloroplasts, they are similar to dinoflagellates, nucleic acid sequencing shows that they are in fact more distantly related than once supposed.

Eukarya One of the three cellular kingdoms (domains) in certain classifications (ARCHAEA and BACTERIA are the other two). It is a subkingdom of the Bacteria in the FIVE KINGDOMS CLASSIFICATION scheme. Eukaryotic cells are distinguished by the presence of a membrane-bound nucleus that contains chromosomes. *See* eukaryote.

eukaryote An organism whose cells have their genetic material packaged in chromosomes within a membrane-bound nucleus. Eukaryotic cells possess mitochondria and (in plants and other photosynthetic eukaryotes) chloroplasts in the cell cytoplasm. The oldest known eukaryotic cells in the fossil record are 1800 million years old. The oldest known prokaryote cells are 3500 million years old and the length of time between the two suggests the evolution of eukaryotic cells was difficult and probably occurred in stages. According to the theory of three cellular kingdoms, the eukaryotic cell did not evolve directly from prokaryotes, but from an ancient ancestor that could possibly be more than 3500 million years old. *Compare* prokaryote. *See also* endosymbiont theory; Eukarya; photosynthesis.

Eumetazoa *See* Metazoa.

Euryapsida (eurapsids; Parapsida; parapsids) *See* Reptilia.

eusociality An advanced social system, seen in some HAPLO-DIPLOID SPECIES (e.g. Hymenoptera) in which sterile workers assist the reproduction of the queen. *See also* division of labor.

eusporangiate Describing the condition, found in certain club mosses, in which the sporangia develop from a group of initial cells. *Compare* leptosporangiate.

Eutheria The infraclass that contains the placental mammals – the most advanced and the majority of living mammals, including humans. Placental mammals have a complex and well-developed brain. Their young are born at a comparatively advanced stage of development after a long gestation period in the maternal uterus (womb), where they are nourished by the placenta. The group shows great adaptive radiation, being found in terrestrial, aquatic, and aerial habitats. *See* Artiodactyla; Carnivora; Cetacea; Chiroptera; Insectivora; Lagomorpha; Perissodactyla; Primates; Proboscidea; Rodentia. *See also* Mammalia.

Evo-Devo The study of the evolution of developmental mechanisms by comparing gene sequences. Sequence analysis has revealed that the genes that regulate development are highly conserved from invertebrates to vertebrates, showing that a basic developmental regulatory system evolved in a common ancestor more than 600 mya. *See* conserved sequence; differentiation; homeobox; homeotic gene; sequence alignment.

evolution The gradual process of change that occurs in populations of organisms over a long period of time. It manifests itself as new characteristics in a species, and the formation of new species. Evolution predicts that all life shares a single origin. The idea of evolution is almost universally accepted in the face of overwhelming evidence. There are three lines of evidence for evolution: 1) Nonfunctional similarities between species, from the molecular level, e.g. the universal genetic code, to the morphological, e.g. the pentadactyl limb. 2) Direct observation of change on a small scale, e.g. the change in color of the peppered moth (*see* industrial melanism). 3) The fossil records. Evolution also explains ADAPTATION. The areas of biology usually studied that reveal evolutionary relationships or evidence include geographical distribution of organisms; comparative anatomy; embryology; paleontology; taxonomy; and molecular biology. Recent research in the latter has supported and confirmed many of the existing ideas revealed by the study of the other older disciplines. *See* Darwinism; Lamarckism; natural selection. *Compare* adaptive evolution; creationism.

evolutionary biology The study and interpretation of all kinds of biological diversity. The development of MOLECULAR BIOLOGY has solved many problems, but many questions remain unanswered.

evolutionary causation *See* proximate causation; ultimate causation.

evolutionary classification A method of classification that incorporates PHENETIC and PHYLOGENETIC principles. It allows MONOPHYLETIC groups (as does CLADISTICS) and PARAPHYLETIC groups (as does phenetic classification). *See also* polyphyletic.

evolutionary computing Computer programs that have been devised to create artificial living organisms that imitate the process of evolution by natural selection. The organisms in some research programs are allowed to reproduce, mutate, and even eat and are subjected to various environmental changes, including being subjected to harmful bugs. This technology is beginning to show how natural selection can even create new types of technology, such as new designs for machines, robots, and even computer software.

evolutionary conflict The situation that arises when two interacting genes have different evolutionary interests.

evolution of dominance Selection acting to make favorable alleles dominant and unfavorable alleles recessive. If a recessive gene becomes advantageous then selection acts at other loci to make the gene advantageous in heterozygotes and therefore makes it dominant. *See* epistasis.

exaptation (preadaptation) The use of an existing structure to perform a new function. It is a common feature in evolution in which a new structure evolves because it confers a selective advantage by performing a function but later becomes able to perform a different function, which confers a different selective advantage. An example is the evolution of feathers in birds. *See* Aves.

exon A segment of DNA that is both transcribed and translated and hence carries part of the code for the GENE PRODUCT. Most eukaryotic genes consist of exons interrupted by noncoding sequences – INTRONS. Both exons and introns are transcribed to HETEROGENEOUS NUCLEAR RNA (hnRNA), an intermediary form of messenger RNA (mRNA); the introns are then removed leaving mRNA, which has only the essential sequences and is translated into the protein. Recombination can create novel combinations of exons – a process known as *exon shuffling*. *See* splicing.

exon shuffling *See* intron.

exonuclease An enzyme that catalyzes the hydrolysis of the terminal linkages of polynucleotides, such as DNA and RNA, thereby removing terminal nucleotides. *See also* DNase.

exoskeleton The hard outer covering of the body of certain animals, such as the thick cuticle of arthropods (e.g. insects and crustaceans). It forms a rigid skeleton, which protects and supports the body and its internal organs and provides attachment for muscles. Growth of the body may only occur in stages, by a series of molts (ecdyses) of the cuticle. The term is also applied to other hard external protective structures, including a mollusk shell and the shell of a tortoise.

exothermy *See* poikilothermy.

expression system *See* gene cloning.

expression vector *See* gene cloning.

extinction The dying out of a lineage that leaves no descendants behind. It is a natural process and throughout the history of life on earth, millions of new species have evolved and millions have disappeared. Extinction may occur if a rival species is more successful in a particular environment or through other factors such as disease, fluctuations in the environment, CHARACTER DISPLACEMENT, and predation. Environmental changes impose pressures on species to adapt. Inability to adapt results in mortality and extinction. Human activities have also caused species to become extinct as a result of POLLUTION and the destruction of many habitats. This has led to scientists and governments across the world to try to protect ENDANGERED SPECIES and also to attempt to strike a balance between obtaining resources that humans need with the needs of animal and plant species to survive (CONSERVATION). *See* mass extinction. *Compare* pseudoextinction.

extrachromosomal DNA In eukaryotes, DNA found outside the nucleus of the cell and replicating independently of the chromosomal DNA. It is contained within self-perpetuating organelles in the cytoplasm, particularly mitochondria and plastids (e.g. chloroplasts), and is responsible for cytoplasmic inheritance.

extrapolative theory of macromutation *See* macroevolution.

eye An organ of sight, or light perception. Invertebrates usually have eyes that are simple photoreceptors (ocelli), sensitive to the direction and intensity of light. The higher mollusks and arthropods have COMPOUND EYES that form images. The vertebrate eye is a complicated spherical structure, connected to the brain by the optic nerve. It has an outer white sclerotic coat with a transparent front called the cornea. This is lined by the vascular pigmented choroid, continuous with the iris in front. In the center of the iris is the pupil, through which light enters, to be focused by the lens onto the retina. This is the innermost layer and contains light-sensitive cells (rods and cones).

The complex structure of eyes, especially the vertebrate eye, has often been used by anti-Darwinists to cast doubt on the process of natural selection, but it is known that eyes have evolved at least 40 times in many diverse species. Researchers discovered that the regulator gene – *Pax6* – is present in all animals with eyes and concluded that all eyes developed from an ancestral form with this gene. Subsequent research revealed that organisms without eyes also contained *Pax6* – the same structure was found in bacteria – suggesting a very ancient origin. The conformation of this gene had been conserved for billions of years. It is now known that in many organisms with eyes, *Pax6* activates the program that leads to the development of eyes. Its original function is unknown.

Research on *Drosophila* (the fruit fly) had revealed the existence of a *Pax6* gene *Ey* (eyeless), but recently a second *Pax6* gene has been discovered named *Toy* (twin of eyeless). Therefore, at some stage in the evolution of flies, there must have been duplication of the *Pax6* gene. *Toy* has subsequently been found to be more closely related to vertebrate *Pax6*, which means that *Toy* is the ancestral form and mutated to produce *Ey*. Each gene regulates two different events in eye development in *Drosophila*.

Recently, computer modeling has been used to find out how much time it would take complex structures, such as the vertebrate eye, to evolve by directional selection from a patch of photosensitive tissue. 'Descendants' were only allowed to survive if there was an improvement in structure before proceeding to the next stage. Very tiny morphological changes were allowed at each stage. It was found that eyes could evolve very quickly indeed, in fewer than

2000 generations, which is equivalent to 2000–20 000 years, representing a miniscule amount of time in evolutionary terms. *See also* evolutionary computing; homeobox; *hox* genes.

eyespot (stigma)   A light-sensitive structure of certain protoctists and invertebrate animals. The eyespot of unicellular and colonial algae and their gametes and zoospores contains globules of orange or red carotenoid pigments. It controls locomotion, ensuring optimum light conditions for photosynthesis. Its location varies. In *Chlamydomonas* it is just inside the chloroplast; in *Euglena* it is near the base of the flagellum. A light-sensitive pigmented spot is also found in the cells of some jellyfish and flatworms, e.g. the miracidium larva of liver fluke.

F

F_1 The first filial generation; i.e. the first generation that results from a particular cross.

F_2 The second filial generation, obtained by crossing within the F_1 generation. It is in the F_2 that the characteristic MONOHYBRID and DIHYBRID ratios become apparent.

family A collection of similar genera (*see* genus). Families may be subdivided into subfamilies, tribes, and subtribes. Plant family names generally end in -aceae, whereas animal family names usually end in -idae. Similar families are grouped into orders. *See also* tribe.

fauna All the animal life characteristic of a given place or time.

feathers *See* Aves.

female choice *See* sexual selection.

ferns *See* Filicinophyta.

fertilization (syngamy) The fusion of a male gamete with a female gamete to form a zygote; the essential process of sexual reproduction. In animals, a fertilization membrane forms around the egg after the penetration of the sperm, preventing the entry of additional sperm. *External fertilization* occurs when gametes are expelled from the parental bodies before fusion; it is typical of aquatic animals and lower plants. *Internal fertilization* takes place within the body of the female and complex mechanisms exist to place the male gametes into position. Internal fertilization is usually an adaptation to life in a terrestrial environment, although it is retained in secondarily aquatic organisms, such as pondweeds or sea turtles.

Internal fertilization is necessary for terrestrial animals because the male gametes are typically very small and require external water for swimming toward the female gametes. In addition, the propagules produced on land require waterproof integuments, which would be impenetrable to male gametes, so they must be fertilized before being discharged from the female's body. Internal fertilization also allows a considerable degree of nutrition and protection of the early embryo, which is seen in both mammals and seed plants. As plants are relatively immotile, they are dependent on other agents, such as wind or insects, to carry the male gamete to the female plant.

Filicinophyta (ferns) A phylum of seedless vascular plants comprising the ferns. It is divided into the orders Ophioglossales, Marattiales, Filicales (e.g. *Dryopteris*), Marsileales, and Salviniales, the latter two orders sometimes being included in the Filicales. There are also a number of fossil genera. Ferns have large spirally arranged leaflike fronds (megaphylls) bearing sporangia on their margins or undersurfaces. The sporangia develop from one cell (leptosporangiate) or a number of cells (eusporangiate) and develop into thin- or thick-walled sporangia respectively.

The Filicinophyta probably evolved from the PSILOPHYTA and have a rich fossil record beginning in the Devonian and increasing in importance in the CARBONIFEROUS. The oldest known fossil is *Iridopteris* from the Devonian. Important Carboniferous fossils include tree ferns (*Megaphyton*) similar to present-day Dicksonia. Petrified remains of important fossil genera such as *Etapteris* display great details of their anatomical structure. At the end of the Paleozoic, ferns were more successful than the declining psilophytes, LYCOPODOPHYTA, and SPHENOPHYTA, although some orders became extinct (Cladoxylales and Coenopteridales, which seem to have been homosporous). Ferns continued to be dominant in the Jurassic and Cretaceous. At this time, the fossil genera closely resemble modern ferns, for example, *Osmunda* (the royal fern) closely resembles the fossil *Osmundites*. As some of the PTERIDOPHYTES declined, the seed-bearing plants began to be dominant. In the Cenozoic many modern genera had evolved (e.g. *Dryopteris* and *Marattia*) and by the Quaternary, modern vegetation had been well established. The Ice Ages probably caused certain ferns to go extinct and forced others into warmer areas.

finalism Belief in a built-in trend in nature toward a preordained final goal, such as the attainment of perfection. It had existed since Aristotle and along with ESSENTIALISM continued to flourish in Darwin's time and beyond. Both ideologies prevented immediate acceptance of Darwin's theory, although Darwin himself rejected them.

Fisher, Sir Ronald Aylmer (1890–1962) British statistician and geneticist. Fisher made a number of important contributions to statistics theory. His major researches in genetics were brought together in *The Genetical Theory of Natural Selection* (1930), in which he argued that Mendelism, far from contradicting Darwinism as some people believed, actually provides the missing link in the theory of evolution by natural selection by showing that inheritance is by means of particulate entities (genes) rather than by physical blending of parental characteristics. (In 1936 Fisher published a paper arguing that probabilistically Mendel's famous results were "too good to be true.") The book also summarizes Fisher's views on eugenics and on genes controlling dominant characteristics. He believed that dominance develops

gradually by selection, showing selection rather than mutation to be the driving force in evolution.

Fisher's theory A theory of female choice in which a male character that is harmful or disadvantageous in the present was previously advantageous to survival and was a preferential choice for some females when deciding on a mate. Offspring will possess the maternal genes for preference and the paternal genes for the character. Thus the two reinforce each other and the character becomes a mating advantage as well as a survival advantage. Over time, therefore, a majority of females will prefer the character and it will be maintained by female choice even after it has become a disadvantage. *Compare* handicap theory. *See* parasitic theory of sexual selection; sexual characters; sexual selection.

fishes *See* Chondrichthyes; Osteichthyes.

fission A type of asexual reproduction in which a parent cell divides into two (binary fission) or more (multiple fission) similar daughter cells. Binary fission occurs in many unicellular organisms (protoctists, bacteria); multiple fission occurs in apicomplexans (sporozoans), such as the malaria parasite (Plasmodium).

fitness In an evolutionary context, the ability of an organism to produce a large number of offspring that survive to a reproductive age. 'Fit' in this sense has nothing to do with being healthy although healthy animals and plants are more likely to leave more offspring than weak individuals. In human populations fitness is affected more by social conditions and traditions than by health and indeed large families are more often found in the poorer developing countries in which people are generally less healthy. The phrase 'survival of the fittest' summarizes the principles of the theory of NATURAL SELECTION.

fitness surface *See* adaptive topography.

Five Kingdoms classification A classification system proposed by the US biologist Robert H. Whittaker in 1959 that recognizes at least 96 phyla in five kingdoms. It was based on nutrition methods and levels of organization. There are two superkingdoms, the Prokarya (PROKARYOTES) and Eukarya (EUKARYOTES). The Prokarya consists of a single kingdom, the BACTERIA (formerly Prokaryotae; equivalent to the former kingdom Monera, divided into two subkingdoms, the ARCHAEA and EUBACTERIA), which fed by various methods. The Eukarya consists of four kingdoms: Animalia (multicellular organisms feeding heterotrophically by ingestion); Plantae (multicellular organisms that feed by photosynthesis); Fungi (multicellular organisms feeding heterotrophically by absorption); and PROTISTA (unicellular organisms with different feeding methods).

The Protista proved problematical because it contained unicellular organisms formerly classified as plants or animals, plus organisms such as *Euglena*, that could be placed in both kingdoms. Two US biologists, Lynn MARGULIS and Karlene Schwartz, suggested a modification of Whittaker's scheme in which the multicellular green algae are removed from the Plantae and placed with all the unicellular organisms in the Protista into a new kingdom, the PROTOCTISTA. The system is successful up to a point, but the Protoctista remains an odd mixture of groups that cannot be fitted in elsewhere.

fixation probability The probability that a mutation will become FIXED.

fixation time The time taken for a new mutation to become FIXED, measured in generations.

fixed Describing a gene or mutation that is present in 100% of the population.

flagellum A whiplike extension of prokaryote cells with a basal body at its base, whose beat causes locomotion of the cell. Strictly the term is now reserved for the bacterial flagellum. The flagella and cilia of eukaryote cells have a quite different structure and are called *undulipodia*.

Bacterial flagella are much simpler than undulipodia, being hollow cylinders about 15 nm in diameter, consisting of subunits of a protein (flagellin) arranged in helical spirals. Unlike eukaryote flagella they are not membrane-bounded, are rigid, and function by a complex rotation of their bases.

flat-faced Kenya man *See* australopithecines.

flatworms *See* Platyhelminthes.

fleas *See* Siphonaptera.

flies *See* Diptera.

flight *See* Aves.

flora All the plant life characteristic of a given place or time.

flowering plants *See* Angiospermophyta.

Foraminifera An order of the phylum RHIZOPODA that consists mainly of marine species. They are single-celled organisms with outer shells known as *tests* through which long pseudopodia (*reticulopodia*) stream in and out. Some are fixed to seaweeds, hydroids, or the ocean bottom to catch food, others creep using their pseudopodia, while yet others are PELAGIC. They range in size from 0.1 to 100 mm in diameter. They feed on a variety of organisms, such as bacteria, diatoms, and other phytoplankton. The shape of the tests varies considerably (e.g. spherical, spiral, tubular). They are usually divided into chambers, which are added to as they grow. The shells are made of gelatinous, limy, or chitinous material or of sand grains, sponge spicules, or other debris cemented together.

Foraminifera have inhabited the seas since Cambrian times. Their tests accumulate on the sea bottom and the deposits become compressed to form rock strata. The chalk of the Upper Cretaceous of SE England contain foraminiferans. The great pyramids of Giza in Egypt were carved from limestone that contained *Nummulites*, a foraminiferan from the early Tertiary. Many species are important ZONE FOSSILS in the Carboniferous and older strata. Foraminiferans are also important zone fossils in oil-bearing strata.

form 1. (*Botany*) The lowest taxonomic group, ranking below the variety level. Subforms may also be recognized.
2. (*Zoology*) A vague term used when the appropriate taxonomic rank is not clear. It may also be applied to seasonal variants and the different forms found in polymorphic series.

fossil The remains of, or impressions left in rocks by, long dead animals and plants. Of the countless millions of organisms that ever existed on Earth, only comparatively few are represented in the *fossil record*. Nevertheless, paleontologists have been able to chart the pattern of life from earliest times and detailed studies of fossils and the rocks in which they are found have provided crucial evidence for evolution and information about the climatic conditions in which they lived.

Most fossils consist of hard skeletal material because soft tissues and organs rot away very quickly. Mineral salts from surrounding rocks gradually replace the hard organic material, to give a cast in a process termed *petrification* (permineralization), e.g. the petrified forests and the ancient PSILOPHYTA of the Rhynie Chert, many fossil shells, and the fossilized giant horsetails (e.g. *Calamites*) of the Carboniferous. Alternatively, the organic material dissolves away leaving an impression, cast, or mold in the surrounding rocks. Generally, the best fossils formed in this way are found in fine-grained sediments.

Trace fossils provide indirect evidence of prehistoric life forms, e.g. dinosaur footprints, casts of worm and mollusk burrows, and trails left by creeping animals. *Coprolites* are fossilized fecal pellets and serve as indicators of feeding habits of animals, especially when they contain undigested scales or teeth.

Preservation of organisms in an almost perfect state sometimes occurs, but only when there is no microbial decomposition and in conditions in which no organic matter can be dissolved away, e.g. woolly mammoths and rhinoceroses preserved in ice. Also there are insects preserved in resin (*see* amber), skeletons of saber-toothed tigers preserved in oily or tarry substances as in the 'asphalt lakes' of California, and skeletons and plants in peaty areas formed from acid bogs. *See also* Burgess shale; chemical fossils; Remanié fossil; taphonomy; zone fossil.

fossil record See fossil.

founder effect A type of GENETIC DRIFT caused by the loss of genetic variation when a new population is formed by only a small number of individuals from a larger parental population. As a result, the members of the new population will carry in their genotypes a relatively small fraction of the genetic variability that is available in the large population resulting in a different genetic potential. *See also* allopatric speciation; Galápagos Islands. *See* gene mutation.

frameshift mutation *See* gene mutation.

frequency-dependent selection A type of selection in which the FITNESS of the genotype or phenotype depends on its frequency. There are two main types of frequency-dependent selection. *Positive frequency-dependent selection* favors common genotypes and *negative frequency-dependent selection* favors rare genotypes. *See* polymorphism.

frogs *See* Amphibia; Jurassic.

functional constraint The constraint placed on the rate of molecular evolution by the function of a molecule or part of molecule. Functionally more important parts of molecules, such as the active site of an ENZYME, are consistently found to evolve more slowly than functionally less important parts. Molecules with specialized and localized functions tend to evolve more rapidly than molecules with general

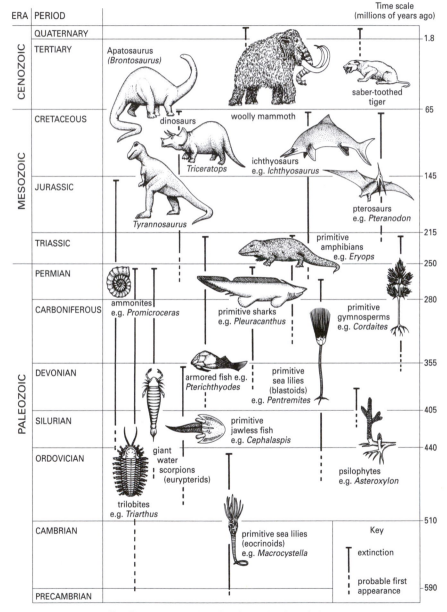

ERA	PERIOD		Time scale (millions of years ago)

QUATERNARY

CENOZOIC

TERTIARY — Apatosaurus (*Brontosaurus*), woolly mammoth, saber-toothed tiger

1.8

CRETACEOUS — dinosaurs, *Triceratops*, ichthyosaurs e.g. *Ichthyosaurus*

65

MESOZOIC

JURASSIC — *Tyrannosaurus*, pterosaurs e.g. *Pteranodon*

145

TRIASSIC — primitive amphibians e.g. *Eryops*

215

PERMIAN — ammonites e.g. *Promicroceras*

250

CARBONIFEROUS — primitive sharks e.g. *Pleuracanthus*, primitive gymnosperms e.g. *Cordaites*

280

DEVONIAN — armored fish e.g. *Pterichthyodes*, primitive sea lilies (blastoids) e.g. *Pentremites*

355

SILURIAN — primitive jawless fish e.g. *Cephalaspis*

405

PALEOZOIC

ORDOVICIAN — giant water scorpions (eurypterids), psilophytes e.g. *Asteroxylon*

440

trilobites e.g. *Triarthus*

CAMBRIAN — primitive sea lilies (eocrinoids) e.g. *Macrocystella*

510

Key
| extinction
¦ probable first appearance

PRECAMBRIAN

590

Fossil: some examples of extinct animals and plants

and widespread functions. PSEUDOGENES evolve more rapidly than genes. *See* molecular clock; neutral theory.

Fungi A kingdom of nonphotosynthetic mainly terrestrial organisms that are now regarded as quite distinct from plants or other living kingdoms. As fungi are heterotrophic, they are more like animals than plants. Comparisons of nucleotide sequences in RNA and DNA indicate that they have a separate evolutionary development from plants. They are characterized by having cell walls made chiefly of chitin, not the cellulose of plant cell walls, and they all develop directly from spores without an embryo stage. Moreover, cilia or flagella (undulipodia) are never found in any stage of their life cycles. Fungi are generally saprophytic or parasitic, and may be unicellular or composed of filaments (termed hyphae) that together comprise the fungal body or mycelium. Hyphae may grow loosely or form a compacted mass of pseudoparenchyma giving well-defined structures, as in toadstools.

Fossil fungi are usually microscopic and very few fungal bodies, such as mushrooms, have been found.

In the Proterozoic, certain authorities maintain that animals and fungi diverged from a more recent common ancestor than plants. In the Ediacara of Australia, fossil lichens have been found and ribosomal DNA sequencing indicates that an ASCOMYCOTA–BASIDIOMYCOTA lineage evolved followed by the Glomales (ZYGOMYCOTA). In the Cambrian, it is believed that terrestrial fungi evolved from the *chytrids* (parasitic protoctists of eukaryotic and blue-green algae). Early terrestrial plants were established in the Ordovician and some plant fossils contain symbiotic MYCORRHIZAE. By the Devonian, mycorrhizal associations were firmly established, based on studies of fossils of the Rhynie Chert in Aberdeenshire, Scotland (e.g. *Paleomyces* within the silicified stems of *Agalophyton*). During this period, the Basidiomycota and Ascomycota separated, and by the Carboniferous period the fungi had become a more diverse kingdom based on evidence provided by fossil spores and fruiting bodies. Gilled mushrooms and rust fungi appeared in the Cretaceous. Throughout the Cenozoic, fossil fungi began to resemble present-day species, mushrooms and puffballs having been established.

Fungi anamorphici *See* Deuteromycota.

Fungi Imperfecti *See* Deuteromycota.

G

G *See* genotypic effect; guanine.

Gaia hypothesis The hypothesis first put forward by James Lovelock in 1972 that the interactions between organisms and the world they inhabit are regulated by a control program, called Gaia (*Gaia* is the Greek word meaning 'Mother Earth'). It is not an opposing theory to natural selection, which also embraces the interdependence of living organisms and the environment, but it takes interdependence to an even greater degree. For example, the balanced relationship between organisms and the environment is so close that it has had a profound influence on the way life has evolved on Earth. According to advocates of Gaia, if certain human activities persist in harming the environment (e.g. by continued pollution), then humans as a species, will eventually die out.

Galápagos Islands A group of over 25 separate volcanic islands on the equator in the South Pacific approximately 950 km to the west of Ecuador and formed about 7 million years ago. They were visited by DARWIN on his voyage aboard HMS *Beagle*. After their formation, these uninhabited islands were colonized by a few species that arrived by chance and natural means from the mainland of South and Central America. These ancestral organisms (founder species) reached all the islands and founded new colonies, all of which were able to exploit different ecological niches (*see* founder effect). The location of the islands also meant that they were geographically isolated. The colonies on different islands eventually diverged, having been subjected to different SELECTION PRESSURES, MUTATIONS, and GENETIC DRIFT. In addition, the founder species were immediately different as they carried only a small percentage of the genetic variability available to the larger mainland population.

The most famous example of the effects of geographical isolation on the evolution of species is the existence on these islands of DARWIN'S FINCHES. Other famous inhabitants of the Galápagos Islands encountered by Darwin on his voyage were the giant land tortoises, after which the islands were named: *galápagos* is the Spanish word for tortoise. Other reptiles included the well-known IGUANA LIZARDS (one marine and one terrestrial species), five other lizard species, and one or two snakes. Mammals that he encountered included two species of bat and five rat species. In addition to the finches, he noted other birds: two owl species, a warbler, a martin, two species of flycatcher, four species of mocking bird, and a cuckoo.

There are 560 plant species. They include cotton, pepper, guava, passion flower, and tomato. The native species *Scalesia*, the daisy tree, has evolved into many different species paralleling Darwin's finches. Unique cacti include the lava cactus and the candelabra cactus. The original pioneer species were hardy plants equipped to survive the harsh volcanic conditions. The native species are threatened by introduced species, especially the quinine tree, guava plants, and the thorny shrub lantana. The native vegetation is also threatened by the activities of feral goats.

The government of Ecuador has legislated to protect these unique islands since 1934 and the establishment of the Darwin Research Station on Santa Cruz has subjected them to intensive scientific study.

Restricted tourism is used to educate visitors about CONSERVATION.

gamete   A cell capable of fusing with another cell to produce a zygote, from which a new individual organism can develop. Gametes may have similar structure and behavior (*isogametes*), as in many simple organisms, but are usually dissimilar in appearance and behavior (*anisogametes*). The typical male gamete is small, motile, and produced in large numbers. The typical female gamete is large because of the food reserves it contains, immotile, and is produced in small numbers. Fusion of gametes results in the nucleus of the zygote having exactly twice the number of chromosomes present in the nucleus of each gamete. *See also* ovum; spermatozoon.

gametogenesis   The formation of sex cells or gametes, i.e. ova or spermatozoa. *See also* oogenesis; spermatogenesis.

gametophyte   The generation of a plant life cycle that is HAPLOID and produces sex organs. It is the main generation in the life cycle of bryophytes, in which the sporophyte is completely or partially dependent upon it. The prothallus of pteridophytes is the gametophyte. *Compare* sporophyte. *See also* alternation of generations; diploid.

Gastropoda   A large class of mollusks comprising the terrestrial slugs (e.g. *Limax*) and snails (e.g. *Helix*), which lack gills and have an air-breathing lung, as well as many marine and freshwater members, e.g. *Patella* (limpet) and *Limnaea* (pond snail).

Gastropods are characterized by a well-developed head with tentacles and eyes, a single shell, and a large flat foot. They always undergo torsion during their development, i.e. the visceral hump twists through 180° so that the mantle cavity, gills, and anus are anterior and the other organs are asymmetrically arranged. The shell and visceral hump are often spirally coiled.

Gastropods are the oldest group of mollusks and range from the Cambrian to Recent. The more primitive gastropods were marine, possessing one or two gills, some migrating to fresh waters and others invading the land and developing gills. These are members of the order Pulmonata. Some of the latter returned to fresh-water habitats and because they evolved lungs, must rise to the surface to breathe. Early gastropods were usually small and conical (e.g. *Helcionella*). A large swimming snail (*Bellephoron*) evolved in the Carboniferous, but disappeared at the end of the Paleozoic. The oldest land snails have been found in the Upper Carboniferous of Nova Scotia, discovered in the fossilized stumps of trees. In the Jurassic, fresh-water snails were very common. The remains of one species (*Viviparus*) resulted in the formation of the rock known as Purbeck Marble, used to decorate churches. In the Cenozoic marine gastropods evolved that resembled cowries, and land snails and fresh-water snails continued to flourish. Gastropods have been used as ZONE FOSSILS in the Tertiary.

gastrula   *See* gastrulation; Hydrozoa.

gastrulation   The stage of animal embryonic development at which the gut cavity and germ layers first appear. In most animals gastrulation follows cleavage and precedes neurulation (development of the nervous system); the embryo at this stage is called a *gastrula*. In most animals gastrulation is the stage when the embryo's main features are established or determined by interaction of the primary organizer with other tissues of the embryo. In some animals (e.g. nematodes), however, there are no such interactions, and gastrulation is simply a mechanical folding in of gut and the other internal structures. *See* organizer.

Gegenbaur, Karl   (1826–1903) German comparative anatomist. Gegenbaur's work was important in emphasizing the importance of COMPARATIVE ANATOMY to the concept of evolution. One of the leading champions of Darwinism in Europe, he may be said to have laid the foundations of modern comparative anatomy with his embryological investigations, which led to his demonstration (1861) that all vertebrate eggs and sperm are unicellular, thus developing an earlier supposition of Theo-dor Schwann. In his standard textbook on evolutionary morphology, *Grundriss der vergleichenden Anatomie* (1859; Elements of Comparative Anatomy), Gegenbaur expounded his view that the most reliable clues to animal evolutionary relationships lay in homology; e.g., the arm of a man as compared to the foreleg of a horse or the wing of a bird. *See* homologous.

gene In classical genetics, a unit of hereditary material located on a chromosome that, by itself or with other genes, determines a phenotypic characteristic in an organism. It corresponds to a segment of the genetic material, usually DNA (although the genes of some viruses consist of RNA). Genes may exist in a number of forms, termed ALLELES. For example, a gene controlling the characteristic 'height' in peas may have two alleles, one for 'tall' and another for 'short'. In a normal diploid cell only two alleles can be present together, one on each of a pair of homologous chromosomes: the alleles may both be of the same type, or they may be different. The segregation of alleles at meiosis and their dominance relationships are responsible for the particulate nature of inheritance. However, many phenotypic characteristics are now known to be caused by multiple genes and also environmental factors.

Although the DNA molecules of the chromosomes account for the great majority of genes, genes are also found as PLASMAGENES in certain DNA-containing cytoplasmic bodies (e.g. mitochondria, plastids).

A gene has also been defined as the smallest hereditary unit capable of recombination, or of mutation, or of controlling a specific function. These three definitions do not necessarily describe the same thing and a unit of function, a CISTRON, may be much larger than a unit of recombination or mutation. Research with bacteria has shown that the smallest unit of recombination or mutation is one base pair.

Molecular genetics now defines three types of gene:

1. *structural genes*, which code for polypeptides of enzymes and other proteins
2. *RNA genes*, which code for ribosomal RNA and transfer RNA molecules used in polypeptide assembly
3. *regulator genes*, which regulate the expression of the other two types.

Many genes of higher eukaryotes e.g. mammals, have a mosaic structure composed of coding regions (EXONS) and noncoding regions (INTRONS). *See also cis–trans* test; genome mutation; operon; splicing.

gene cloning (DNA cloning; molecular cloning) A technique of genetic engineering whereby a gene sequence is replicated, giving many identical copies. The gene sequence is isolated by using RESTRICTION ENDONUCLEASES or by making a COMPLEMENTARY DNA. It is then inserted into the circular chromosome of a *cloning vector* – a plasmid or a bacteriophage. The hybrid is used to infect a bacterium, usually *Escherichia coli*, and is replicated within the bacterial cell. A culture of such cells produces many copies of the gene, which can subsequently be isolated and purified.

Genes can also be cloned into so-called *expression vectors*, which allow expression of that gene in a different cellular system (known as an *expression system*) from which it originated. Bacterial cells cannot always express eukaryotic proteins and eukaryotic cells, e.g. yeast, are required.

Entire genomes can be cloned at one go using *shotgun cloning*. The DNA is randomly broken into fragments, which are then cloned into vectors. This technique was used in sequencing the human genome. *See also* genetic engineering.

gene cluster A group of functionally related genes with highly conserved sequences that are closely linked on a single chromosome. Gene clusters are common in mammals and are thought to have arisen by repeated duplications of a common ancestral gene. Individual genes in a cluster often show CONCERTED EVOLUTION. *See* chromosome mutation; crossing over; gene family. *See also* repeated gene.

genecology The study of POPULATION GENETICS in relation to the environment.

gene conversion The conversion of one allele at a locus to the other as a result of mismatch repair of a HETERODUPLEX after CROSSING OVER. The sequence of one of the DNA strands is altered so it is complementary to its partner, which converts one allele into the other. If genes in a cluster or family with similar sequences come into physical contact, the sequences can align to form a heteroduplex. The more similar the sequences, the more likely is heteroduplex formation. Alteration of one of the sequences will either cause a mutation to disappear or to appear in two genes at different loci simultaneously. *See* concerted evolution; DNA repair.

gene duplication Duplication of a chromosomal DNA sequence that corresponds to a gene. Gene duplication occurs in higher organisms and is probably the result of unequal CROSSING OVER at recombination. Repeated duplications are responsible for the formation of GENE CLUSTERS. Gene duplication is thought to have played an important role in the evolution of higher organisms because duplicated genes can acquire mutations independently and acquire new functions. The importance of gene duplication in evolution is also seen in the high number of gene clusters in mammalian genomes. *See also* chromosome mutation.

gene evolution All of the processes by which the number of genes and gene functions possessed by living organisms have increased and diversified over evolutionary time. Increase in gene number arises by GENE DUPLICATION. Errors in RECOMBINATION are responsible for duplication of single genes, leading to the formation of GENE CLUSTERS and GENE FAMILIES, which are common in higher eukaryotes. Selection pressure on a duplicated gene is relieved because one version can mutate and acquire a different function without depriving the organism of the protein. This produces so-called sister, or PARALOGOUS genes, that is, structurally related genes

that fulfill quite different functions in the same species. Additional DNA also arises by multiplication of chromosomes, leading to POLYPLOIDY. The chromosomes can be derived from one species (autopolyploidy) or from two or more species (allopolyploidy). Both autopolyploidy and allopolyploidy have played significant roles in the evolution of certain plant species, for example, bread wheat. Polyploidy also occurs in animals, including fishes, reptiles, amphibians, flatworms, and leeches. Existing arrangements of genes can also be altered by transposable elements (*see* transposon), segments of DNA that move about within the genome. Usually disruption of a gene by such an element is harmful to the organism, but occasionally gene function might be modified in a way that introduces a new function.

At the dawn of evolutionary history, the earliest genes were probably made of RNA rather than DNA. It is postulated that individual RNA molecules either encoded a protein or a functional RNA (a primitive tRNA or rRNA) and therefore acted as 'RNA genes', with each one being translated and replicated separately and independently. As proteins took over from RNA as enzymes and became bigger (*see* protein evolution), the genetic code needed to be more stable and it is thought that RNA genes became double stranded. Evidence for this is provided by modern RNA viruses, which are regarded as fossils of the RNA world. All double-stranded RNA virus genomes are segmented, that is, they consist of several RNA molecules, each coding for a single polypeptide. As the enzymes increased in size further, DNA took over as the genomic material, leaving RNA involved with protein synthesis. As cells evolved and became more complicated, they came to have more genes. It would have been a selective advantage to be able to replicate genes synchronously, so genes became linked together forming chromosomes. Another advantage of having genes linked together is that equal segregation of genes at cell division is more likely because there are less individual parts to segregate. The appearance of chromosomes required the evolution of codons to start and stop

TRANSCRIPTION in order that genes could be transcribed individually. With expansion of the genome, it became an advantage to be able to express genes selectively, leading to the evolution of negative and positive control systems.

Bacterial genomes consist of a single circular chromosome. Eukaryotes are more complex than prokaryotes and have more genes, which are distributed over several chromosomes. Eukaryotic genes consist of INTRONS and EXONS, and it is thought that this interrupted structure of eukaryotic genes is a remnant of the ancient mechanism of constructing novel proteins by combining smaller polypeptide modules. The gene that encoded these modules became the exons of larger genes, and their duplication and rearrangement played an important role in evolution. As eukaryotes became multicellular, they evolved advanced systems to regulate gene expression both temporally and spatially.

gene expression The exhibition of genetic information in the phenotype. For example, every cell in the body of multicellular organisms receives the same genetic information from the parent organisms – the entire evolutionary inheritance from their ancestors. But many cells look and behave differently from one another. This is because only a small fraction of the total DNA in a cell is active at any one time. The degree of gene expression is tightly controlled, which is essential to the functioning of living organisms. For genes that encode proteins, it involves TRANSCRIPTION and TRANSLATION.

gene family (multigene family) A group of functionally related genes with highly conserved sequences that are spread throughout the genome. A gene family can be made of several clusters on different chromosomes. Gene families are thought to have arisen by chromosome duplication, translocation (*see* chromosome mutation), or the incorrect separation of chromosomes during cell division. Individual genes in a family often show CONCERTED EVOLUTION. An example is the globin gene family. *See* chromosome mutation; conserved sequence; crossing over; nondisjunction; repeated gene.

gene flow The movement of alleles between populations through interbreeding.

gene frequency The proportion of an allele in a population in relation to other alleles of the same gene.

gene library A collection of cloned DNA fragments derived from the entire genome of an organism. The genetic material of the organism is first broken up randomly into fragments using restriction enzymes, for example. Then each fragment is cloned using a vector (e.g. plasmid or bacteriophage) inside a suitable host, such as the bacterium *E. coli*. Particular genes or DNA sequences are identified by a suitable DNA probe.

gene mutation A change in one or more of the bases in DNA, which can result in the formation of an abnormal protein. There are three types of gene mutation: *deletions*, in which a base or a number of bases are lost; *additions*, in which a base or number of bases are gained; and *substitutions*, in which a base or number of bases are replaced by or converted into different bases. Substitutions are divided into *transitions* (the replacement of a purine by the other purine or a pyrimidine by the other pyrimidine) and *transversions* (the replacement of a purine by a pyrimidine or vice versa). A mutation to a single base is called a *point mutation*. If an addition or deletion mutation causes an alteration in the READING FRAME, it is known as a *frameshift mutation* and usually leads to a drastically altered gene product. The genetic code is read in continuous triplets so any addition or deletion that is not a multiple of three will result in a frameshift. The addition or deletion of a single base can therefore have a dramatic effect.

A mutation that does not produce an altered amino acid in the protein is called a *silent mutation*. Mutations can be spontaneous, caused by the action of a MUTAGEN, or result from errors in DNA replication and are inherited only if they occur in the cells that give rise to the gametes. Somatic mutations may give rise to CHIMAERAS and CANCERS. Mutations result in new allelic forms of a gene and hence new variations upon which natural selection can act. Most mutations are harmful but are often retained in the population because they also tend to be recessive and can thus be carried in the genotype without affecting the viability of the organism. Selection acts to remove deleterious mutations so genetic variation is a balance between the two but further factors may also be involved as the natural mutation rate does not appear to be high enough to maintain observed levels of genetic variation. Although the natural rate of mutation is low, organisms could not survive without specific enzymes to repair damaged DNA. *See also* chromosome mutation; DNA repair; genome mutation; mutational load.

gene pool   The total number and variety of genes existing within a breeding population or species at a given point in time.

gene probe   *See* DNA probe.

gene product   Any RNA (TRANSCRIPTION product) or protein (TRANSLATION product) synthesized from genetic information.

generation time   The average time between the cell division of parent and daughter cells within a population of cells.

gene sequencing (DNA sequencing)   Determination of the order of bases of a DNA molecule making up a gene. Sequencing requires multiple cloned copies of the gene; long DNA sequences are cut into more manageable lengths using restriction enzymes (*see* restriction endonuclease). Since these cleave DNA at specific points, it is possible to reconstitute the overall sequence once the constituent fragments have been analyzed individually by the methods outlined below.

There are two methods of sequencing DNA. One is the *chemical cleavage method*, or *Maxam–Gilbert method*. This involves firstly labeling one end of the DNA of the gene or DNA segment with radioactive ^{32}P. The segment is then subjected to a chemical reaction that cleaves the sequence at positions occupied by one of the four bases, say, adenine. Starting with numerous cloned DNA segments, the result is a set of radioactive fragments extending from the ^{32}P label to each successive position of adenine in the segment. This process is repeated for the other three bases, and the four sets of fragments are then separated according to the number of nucleotides they contain by gel electrophoresis, in adjacent lanes on the gel. The sequence can then be deduced directly from the autoradiograph of the gel. This method is used for sequences of more than 150 nucleotides.

The second method is the *chain-termination* or *dideoxy method* (also called the *Sanger method*). A single-stranded segment of DNA taken from the gene is used as a template to replicate a new DNA strand using the enzyme DNA polymerase. The enzyme is provided with the four normal nucleoside triphosphates (ATP, GTP, CTP, TTP), plus the dideoxy (dd) derivative of one of them, say ddATP. Incorporation of the dideoxy derivative causes replication of the new strand to cease at that point. The result is a set of new strands of varying length, terminating at all the different positions where adenine, say, normally occurs in the sequence. The process is repeated in turn for each of the three remaining bases, and the set of fragments from each incubation are separated according to size by gel electrophoresis. The sequence of bases in the newly synthesized strand can be deduced directly from the gel. This method is used for sequences of less than 200 nucleotides.

Automation of both procedures, for example by using laser scanning of fluorescent dye markers instead of autoradiography, has greatly increased the speed with which DNA can be sequenced, and made possible the sequencing of entire genomes, including the human genome (*see* Human Genome Project.

gene splicing   *See* splicing.

genetically modified organisms (GMOs) *See* genetic engineering.

genetic assimilation The (hypothetical) process by which an acquired character that appears in response to an environmental stimulus during development eventually appears in the population without the stimulus. The effect has been shown in experiments with fruit flies (*Drosophila*). *See* Waddington.

genetic bottleneck The change in genetic composition of a population caused by a reduction in population size over a prolonged period. Some alleles are lost while others increase in frequency.

genetic code The sequence of bases in either DNA or MESSENGER RNA that conveys genetic instructions to the cell. The basic unit of the code consists of a group of three consecutive bases, the base triplet or CODON, which specifies instructions for a particular amino acid in a polypeptide, or acts as a start or stop signal for translation of the message into polypeptide assembly. The genetic code is almost universal with the only differences being found in some mitochondrial DNA. There are 64 different triplet combinations but only 20 amino acids; thus many amino acids can be coded for by two or more triplets. The code is therefore said to be *degenerate*, and it appears that only the first two bases, and in certain cases only one base, are necessary to insure the coding of a specific amino acid. Three triplets (UAA, UAG, and UGA), termed 'nonsense triplets', do not code for any amino acid and mark the end of a polypeptide chain. AUG (or sometimes GUG) is the signal to start TRANSLATION. *See also* wobble hypothesis.

genetic constraint A constraint placed on the evolution of a perfectly adapted population by the mechanisms of inheritance. *See* heterozygous advantage. *Compare* developmental constraint; historical constraint.

genetic distance *See* distance.

genetic diversity (h) A quantitative measure of the amount of genetic VARIATION in a population defined as the probability that two alleles chosen at random from all the alleles at that locus are different. It has now been superseded by molecular methods of measuring genetic variation such as restriction mapping and DNA sequencing. *See* gene sequencing; nucleotide diversity; restriction map.

genetic drift (neutral drift; Sewall Wright effect) The fluctuation of allele frequencies in a population due entirely to chance. It can randomly produce evolutionary change. If the number of matings is small then the actual numbers of different types of pairing may depart significantly from the number expected on a purely random basis. Genetic drift has a larger effect on smaller populations and is one of the factors that can disturb the HARDY–WEINBERG EQUILIBRIUM. Certain authorities believe that the color variation of male CICHLID fishes may be the result of genetic drift in the absence of selective forces in the stable environments they inhabit. *See* neutral theory; Wright.

genetic effect *See* genotypic effect.

genetic engineering (recombinant DNA technology) The direct introduction of foreign genes into an organism's genetic material by micromanipulation at the cell level. Genetic engineering techniques bypass crossbreeding barriers between species to enable gene transfer between widely differing organisms. Gene transfer can be achieved by various methods, many of which employ a replicating infective agent, such as a virus or plasmid, as a vector (*see* gene cloning). Other methods include microinjection of DNA into cell nuclei and direct uptake of DNA through the cell membrane. Recognizing whether or not transfer has occurred may be difficult unless the new gene confers an obvious visual or physiological characteristic. Consequently the desirable gene may be linked to a marker gene, e.g. a gene conferring resistance to an antibiotic in the growth medium. The transferred gene must also be

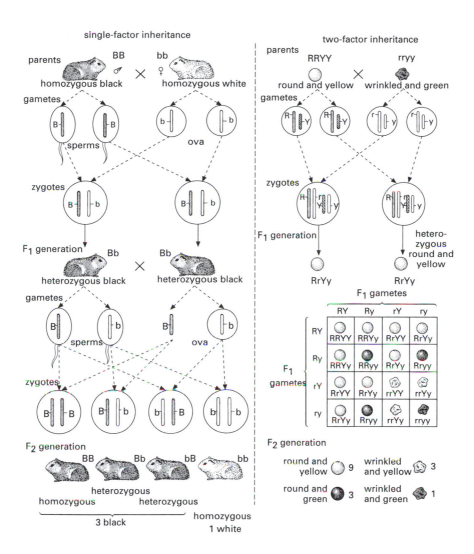

single-factor inheritance

parents **BB** ✕ **bb** ♀
homozygous black   homozygous white ♀

gametes

sperms   ova

zygotes

F₁ generation **Bb** ✕ **Bb**
heterozygous black   heterozygous black

gametes

sperms   ova

zygotes

F₂ generation
BB   **Bb**   **bB**   **bb**

homozygous   heterozygous   heterozygous   homozygous

3 black ⎫⎭   1 white

two-factor inheritance

parents **RRYY** ✕ **rryy**
round and yellow   wrinkled and green

gametes

zygotes

F₁ generation   hetero-zygous round and yellow

RrYy   **RrYy**

F₁ gametes

	RY	Ry	rY	ry
RY	RRYY	RRYy	RrYY	RrYy
Ry	RRYy	RRyy	RrYy	Rryy
rY	RrYY	RrYy	rrYY	rrYy
ry	RrYy	Rryy	rrYy	rryy

F₁ gametes (row label, left side)

F₂ generation

round and yellow 9   wrinkled and yellow 3

round and green 3   wrinkled and green 1

Genetics: Single-factor inheritance: when a purebred (homozygous) black guinea pig (BB) mates with a purebred white one (bb) all the offspring (F₁ generation) will be black (Bb) since the gene for black is dominant. Mating of this heterozygous F₁ generation will produce both black and white guinea pigs (F₂ generation) in the ratio 3:1, since each of the parents carries a white recessive gene.

Two-factor inheritance: seed color and texture – in pea plants. When a plant with round yellow seeds (RRYY – dominant) is crossed with one producing wrinkled green seeds (rryy – recessive) the offspring will all have round yellow seeds (RrYy – heterozygous). Crossing of this generation results in the segregation and reassortment of the genes so that their offspring will show all four possibilities of seed color and texture in the proportions 9:3:3:1. These examples of inheritance obey Mendel's laws.

linked to appropriate regulatory DNA sequences to insure that it works in its new environment and is regulated correctly and predictably.

Initial successes in DNA transfer were achieved with bacteria and yeast. Genetic manipulation of higher animals and plants has been achieved more recently. Transgenic mammals, including mice, sheep, and pigs, have been produced by microinjection of genes into the early embryo, and it is also now possible to clone certain mammals from adult body cells. Such technology may have considerable impact on livestock production, e.g. by injection of growth hormone genes. Dicotyledonous plants, including tobacco and potato, have been transfected using the natural plasmid vector of the soil bacterium *Agrobacterium tumefaciens* (*see Agrobacterium*). Genes have been introduced into a number of organisms (genetically modified organisms (GMOs)) for various reasons, for instance to reduce damage to crops during harvest or to make them resistant to the herbicides used in controlling weeds. Genetically modified tomatoes and soya beans are now widely available. It is also hoped that in future many genetic diseases will be treatable by manipulating the faulty genes responsible. However, genetic engineering raises many legal and ethical issues, and the introduction of genetically modified organisms into the environment requires strict controls and monitoring. *See also* recombinant DNA.

genetic fingerprinting (DNA fingerprinting; genetic profiling)   A technique for identifying individuals by means of their DNA. The DNA being tested is extracted from cells (from blood, semen, tissue fragments, etc.) and broken into fragments of 600–700 bases each, using restriction enzymes. The human genome contains many loci (known as MINISATELLITES) where short base sequences are repeated in tandem, with great variation between individuals in the number of such repeats. These so-called *variable number tandem repeats* (*VNTR*) can be identified using special DNA probes, thus providing a virtually unique set of markers for any given individual. This technique is used in veterinary and human medicine to establish the parentage of individuals, and in forensic science to identify individuals from traces of body tissue or fluids. Even minute amounts of DNA can now be amplified, using the POLYMERASE CHAIN REACTION, to provide sufficient material for genetic fingerprinting.

genetic imprinting   The phenomenon in which the expression of genes is determined by their maternal or paternal origin. Only a few genes are imprinted and many that are, are involved in controlling growth. One theory for the evolution of genetic imprinting is GENOMIC CONFLICT between maternal and paternal genes resulting from the different interests of the father and mother.

genetic load   The reduction in mean FITNESS of a population caused by harmful or disadvantageous genetic variations. *See* mutational load.

genetic map   *See* chromosome map.

genetic polymorphism   *See* polymorphism.

genetic profiling   *See* genetic fingerprinting.

genetics   The term coined by BATESON to describe the study of inheritance and variation and the factors controlling them. Today the subject has three main subdivisions – Mendelian genetics, population genetics, and molecular or biochemical genetics.

genetic separation   A characteristic of speciation where one gene pool is split into separate gene pools between which there is no exchange of genetic information. It can be caused by geographical isolation as in ALLOPATRIC SPECIATION or by REPRODUCTIVE ISOLATION.

genetic variation   *See* variation.

genome   The complete genetic information of an organism. The genome is not simply a series of discrete genes joined together on chromosomes. There are groups of related genes, GENE FAMILIES, clustered together on one or more chromosomes and there is also a large amount of NONCODING DNA, much of which consists of repeated sequences. The genomes of several organisms, including humans, have been completely sequenced and the data can be used to look at evolutionary relationships between diverse organisms. *See also* concerted evolution; gene cluster; gene conversion; selfish DNA.

genome mutation An alteration in the number of chromosomes. *See* nondisjunction.

genomic conflict A possible result of MULTILEVEL EVOLUTION in which different genes, or alleles, affecting the same character experience conflicting selection pressures. It may also occur when a variation is advantageous at one biological level but disadvantageous at another. Different biological levels are created when units capable of independent replication join together to form a larger whole; for example, genes on a chromosome, mitochondria in eukaryotic cells, individual cells in a multicellular organism. *See also* division of labor.

genomics The branch of molecular genetics concerned with the study of genomes. It has emerged since the 1980s as one of the fastest-growing fields in all biology, following the development of automated techniques for nucleic acid and protein sequencing, and computerized systems for handling and analyzing the resultant data. It can be divided into three main areas. *Structural genomics* deals with determining the DNA sequence of all the genetic material of a particular organism. Such a definitive physical map of the genome is the ultimate objective of all genome projects. *Functional genomics* focuses on characterizing all the messenger RNAs produced by transcription of an organism's genome, and the polypeptides that they encode. Complementary DNAs can be constructed from such transcripts, and com-

pared with the genome sequence data to identify corresponding coding regions. *Comparative genomics* is concerned with comparing the genomic sequences of different species, to see how genomes change in the course of evolution, and which parts remain unchanged. The presence of such highly conserved sequences sheds light on their functional significance, and helps in making predictions about similar sequences in other organisms.

genotype The genetic make-up of an organism. The actual appearance of an individual (the phenotype) depends on the dominance relationships between alleles in the genotype and the interaction between genotype and environment.

genotypic effect (genetic effect; G) A quantitative measure of the effect of the genotype on phenotypic variation. It is divided into the part that is inherited, the *additive genetic effect* (A), and the part that is not. Noninheritable effects include allele dominance and epistatic interactions. The additive effect can be estimated by breeding experiments and is the key to understanding the evolution of quantitative characters. *See* quantitative genetics; variance. *Compare* environmental effect.

genotypic redundancy Different genotypes specifying the same phenotype and having the same FITNESS. The genetic variation between these phenotypes is therefore selectively neutral. *See* neutral evolution.

genus (*pl.* genera) A taxonomic unit comprising a collection of similar species. Genera may be subdivided into subgenera, and also, especially in plant taxonomy, into sections, subsections, series, and subseries. Similar genera are grouped into families. *See also* binomial nomenclature.

Geoffroy Saint-Hilaire, Etienne (1772–1844) French biologist. In 1798 Geoffroy accompanied Napoleon on his conquest of Egypt, where he examined a number of mummified cats taken from ancient tombs. They were, he noted, identical to the animals of his day. Did this mean that species were fixed? If they were fixed why were there so many similarities between different forms? Why, for example, despite differences in external form, do the skeletons of bats, whales, and dogs resemble each other so closely?

Geoffroy derived his answer from German *Naturphilosophie* (nature philosophy), which claimed to see beneath an apparent diversity of form mere variations on a single plan. There was a vertebrate type which could be identified in all vertebrates. Thus he demonstrated in 1807 that pectoral fins in fish and the bones of the front limbs of other vertebrates were morphologically and functionally similar. By 1830 Geoffroy had begun to argue that there was a universal 'unity of composition', quoting in evidence work claiming to have detected a unity in crustacea, fish, and mollusks. Such views brought a savage onslaught from CUVIER who insisted that there were distinct forms in nature, and that parts were formed to meet functional needs.

But, once having accepted a unity of composition, it becomes possible to see how one species can be transformed into another. If birds and reptiles are built to the same plan, then "an accident that befell one of the reptiles ... could develop in every part of the body the conditions of the ornithological type." Geoffroy was thus moving late in his career to some form of evolutionary theory. A stroke in 1840 which left him blind and paralyzed brought such work to an end.

geographic distribution   The areas in which a particular taxonomic group lives. It is influenced by ecology, dispersal, climate, continental drift, and speciation. *See* biogeography.

geographic isolation   *See* allopatric speciation. *See also* genetic separation; reproductive isolation.

geographic speciation   *See* allopatric speciation.

geological time scale   A history of the Earth in the form of a table that shows the sequence of geological time units, the length of time that each period probably occupied, and sometimes, showing the main groups of animals and plants that existed in those times. It is constructed by studying rocks that have been exposed by various means, for example, where rivers have deeply cut into (eroded) the Earth's crust, where the sea has eroded the land exposing cliffs, or where excavations of the land have taken place in mines, etc.

Most fossils occur in SEDIMENTARY ROCKS. These are formed from deposits of sand, silt, clay, or calcium carbonate, which harden and are compressed when other layers of sediment are deposited on top. Gradually, layers or *strata* are formed, containing fossil animals and plants that lived at that time. Unless there are major earth movements (e.g. folding of the rocks and other distortions), generally speaking, the lower the rock layer, the older it is, and the more ancient are the fossils it contains. By measuring the rate of erosion and deposition of known particles, the intervals of time occupied by different periods can be roughly estimated.

More accurate dating can now be provided by various methods. *Absolute geological time* (expressed in years) is established by RADIOACTIVE DATING, i.e. by measuring the rates of decay of radioactive material in the rocks. *Relative geological time* is measured by comparing fossil contents. There is no complete agreement on the terminology used but the geological time scale is divided into: *eons* (e.g. ARCHEAN), subdivided into *eras* (e.g. Mesozoic), subdivided into *periods* (e.g. Carboniferous), subdivided into *epochs* (e.g. Oligocene), subdivided into *ages* (e.g. Puercan age of the Paleocene epoch). A period may also be termed a *system*; an epoch may also be termed a *series*; an age may also be termed a *stage*. The different time units are recognized on the basis of changes in the types of fossils and the occurrence of major geological events, e.g. periods of mountain building, and changes in sea level and climate. *See also* Lyell.

germ cell   Any of the cells in animals that give rise to the gametes.

ERAS	Periods	Years x 10^6	Angiosperms	Gymnosperms	Pteridophytes	Bryophytes	Bacteria, Algae, Fungi	Protoctists, Poriferans, Simple Metazoa	Myriapods	Insects, Mollusks	Echinoderms	Fish	Amphibians	Reptiles	Birds	Mammals
CENOZOIC	Tertiary	65														
MESOZOIC	Cretaceous	145						Ammonites								
MESOZOIC	Jurassic	215														
MESOZOIC	Triassic	250														
PALEOZOIC	Permian	280						Trilobites								
PALEOZOIC	Carboniferous	355														
PALEOZOIC	Devonian	405														
PALEOZOIC	Silurian	440														
PALEOZOIC	Ordovician	510														
PALEOZOIC	Cambrian	590														

Geological time scale

germ layers The three major body layers – ECTODERM, MESODERM, and ENDODERM – that develop in the embryos of most animals during gastrulation. These layers do not include special cells or groups of cells that may be migratory (e.g. neural crest cells of vertebrates) or perform special functions (e.g. germ cells).

germ line The lineage of cells from which gametes arise, continuous through generations.

germ plasm 1. The part of an organism that, according to WEISSMANN at the beginning of the 20th century, passed its characters on to the next generation. It is now known that most of this information is carried by DNA in the chromosomes.
2. The special cytoplasm of the eggs of most animals that becomes the germ cells when provided with nuclei. It lies at one end of the eggs of insects, under the gray crescent of amphibian eggs, and in the endodermal area of amniotes.

gill 1. (*Zoology*) An organ in aquatic animals that effects the exchange of respiratory gases between the blood or body fluids of the animal and the water in which it lives. External gills (e.g. in amphibian larvae) trail in the water so that the water around them is renewed as the animal swims along. Most groups have evolved a means of mechanically renewing the water supply; for example by respiratory movements of appendages in crustaceans and aquatic insect larvae. The internal gills of fish are situated in gill slits. They are ventilated by forcing water from the pharynx past the gills and out through the gill slits.
2. (*Botany*) (lamella) One of many thin platelike spore-producing structures radiating outwards from the stalk on the undersurface of the cap of agaric fungi, such as mushrooms and toadstools. The spores (basidiospores) are produced on the outer layer (hymenium). Not every gill extends to the edge of the cap.

gill slits Openings in the pharyngeal (throat) region of the alimentary canal of aquatic vertebrates, leading to the gills. In cartilaginous fish the first gill slit is modified as the spiracle. Traces of gill slits appear in the embryos of all vertebrates but persist only as the Eustachian tube in adult terrestrial vertebrates.

Ginkgo *See* Ginkgophyta.

Ginkgophyta The genus comprising only one species, *Ginkgo biloba* (the maidenhair tree), which is the sole living representative of the GYMNOSPERM phylum, the Ginkgophyta. It is a deciduous dioecious tree with fan-shaped leaves and motile male sperms, native to the Far East. The phylum evolved in the Paleozoic, and was abundant in the Upper Triassic (e.g. *Baiera* and *Ginkoites*). The genus *Ginkgo* first appeared in the Jurassic and has survived to the present day. It occurs rarely in the western forests of China, but has been cultivated as a sacred tree and is commonly planted in cities because of its robustness. *G. biloba* is considered to be a living fossil, remaining unchanged over many millions of years.

Glires A name (superorder) used to group rabbits, hares, pikas, RODENTIA, and extinct ancestral groups (mimotonids and anagalids).

global warming *See* greenhouse effect.

Glossopteris *See* Permian.

GMOs *See* genetic engineering.

Gnathostomata A superclass used in some classifications and containing all the vertebrates that possess jaws, i.e. the Chondrichthyes and Osteichthyes (sometimes grouped as the Pisces), the Amphibia, Reptilia, Aves, and Mammalia. Members typically have paired olfactory organs and nostrils and paired limbs, although these are secondarily lost in some groups. The NOTOCHORD is not retained throughout life.

Gnetophyta A highly specialized GYMNOSPERM phylum of cone-bearing desert plants that evolved during the Cenozoic era. The fossil history is sparsely represented mainly by pollen grains and twigs. The phylum includes large-leafed trees, shrubs, and vines and is represented by three genera: *Ephedra* (a shrub of arid regions), *Gnetum* (a tropical vine), and *Welwitschia* (a desert plant from Southern Africa). They are thought to be closely linked to the ANGIOSPERMOPHYTA.

Golgi apparatus (Golgi body; Golgi complex) An organelle of eukaryotic cells discovered by Camillo Golgi in 1898. It is associated with ENDOPLASMIC RETICULUM but lacks RIBOSOMES. It consists of stacks of flattened membrane-bounded sacs (cisternae) associated with vesicles. In the cisternae, materials such as enzymes and polysaccharides are processed and leave the apparatus inside vesicles for transport, often to the PLASMA MEMBRANE for secretion. *See also* lysosome.

Gondwana (Gondwanaland) One of the two enormous land masses that formed from PANGEA during the Mesozoic consisting of South America, Africa, Madagascar, India, Antarctica, and Australia. During the mid-Jurassic India separated and by the end of the late Cretaceous, South America had separated from Africa and Australia was separating from Antarctica. *See* continental drift; Laurasia.

Gould, Stephen Jay (1941–2002) American biologist. He is widely known for the volumes of essays on natural history that he began publishing in 1978, usually about some aspect of evolution.

Gould also published a number of influential monographs. In *Ontogeny and Phylogeny* (1977) he examined the notion of RECAPITULATION. *The Mismeasure of Man* (1984) sought to demonstrate that attempts to measure human intelligence were often designed to serve political rather than scientific ends. In a further monograph, *Wonderful Life* (1990), Gould surveyed the fossils of the BURGESS SHALE to illustrate a familiar theme of his work that evolution is not "a ladder of predictable progress," it is rather "a copiously branching bush, continually pruned by the grim reaper of extinction."

In the fields of paleontology and ecology Gould worked for many years on the West Indian land snail, *Cerion*. As an evolutionary theorist he is best known for proposing in 1972, along with Nils Eldredge, the PUNCTUATED EQUILIBRIUM hypothesis.

Shortly before his death Gould published a large book, *The Structure of Evolutionary Theory*, which summarized his life's work on this topic.

gracile australopithecines *See* australopithecines.

gradualism (gradual evolution) *See* phyletic gradualism.

graptolites Often included in the phylum HEMICHORDATA, extinct colonial marine organisms characteristic of dark shales that appear in the Upper Cambrian and become extinct in the Carboniferous. They were originally classified as coelenterates. They consisted of one or more branches (stipes), the individuals of the colony housed in chitinous cup-shaped tests (thecae). The dendroid graptolites (Upper Cambrian–Lower Carboniferous) are the most primitive, the earliest consisting of 64 branches, the more advanced forms having 16 stipes. The *graptoloids* (Lower Ordovician–Lower Devonian) have eight stipes in more primitive forms ranging to a single stipe in more advanced forms. They are used as ZONE FOSSILS in the Ordovician and Silurian because they evolved quickly and were very widespread. Examples are: *Nemagraptus gracilis* (Ordovician), *Didymograptus* (Ordovician), and *Monograptus* (Silurian). The name means 'writing on rock' derived from their appearance on black shiny rock.

Great American Interchange *See* Pliocene.

Great Chain of Being (scala naturae) An 18th-century theory to describe the natural world. It was a response to certain scientific discoveries (e.g. the vast age of the

Earth and extinct animal fossils) that appeared to contradict prevailing religious beliefs in the Creation. A linear ladderlike arrangement of living and nonliving entities was envisaged, beginning with rocks and minerals at the base, then rising through lower to higher plants, lower to higher animals, finally culminating in humans. It was believed that God had planned this sequence and it would eventually lead to perfection.

Great Ordovician radiation *See* Ordovician; Paleozoic.

green algae *See* Chlorophyta.

greenhouse effect The rise in temperature of the atmosphere, analogous to that in a greenhouse. Solar (short-wave) radiation passes easily through the atmosphere (or glass in a greenhouse) and is absorbed by the Earth's surface. It is re-emitted in the form of infrared (long-wave) radiation, which is absorbed by water vapor and carbon dioxide in the atmosphere with a consequent increase in the atmospheric temperature. Many scientists believe that increasing atmospheric pollution by carbon dioxide is leading to a rise in global temperatures (*global warming*), which will eventually affect other aspects of climate and have profoundly damaging effects on natural ecosystems. There is a growing consensus of opinion that the MASS EXTINCTION at the end of the PERMIAN was caused by a vast increase in atmospheric carbon dioxide levels. *See also* snowball Earth.

group adaptation An adaptation produced by GROUP SELECTION that is advantageous to the entire group, rather than the individual. Like group selection, group adaptations are controversial.

group selection Selection operating between groups that favors characters beneficial to a population as a whole in competition with other populations, rather than characters beneficial to an individual. *See also* kin selection; species selection.

guanine Symbol: G. A nitrogenous base found in DNA and RNA. Guanine has a purine ring structure.

Guanine

gymnosperm Any vascular plant bearing naked seeds. Gymnosperms include the cycads (phylum CYCADOPHYTA), *Ginkgo* (phylum GINKGOPHYTA), conifers and yews (phylum CONIFEROPHYTA), and phylum GNETOPHYTA (e.g. *Gnetum* and *Welwitschia*). In older classifications, the Gymnospermae constituted a class, but the term gymnosperm is a more general term that includes these four phyla in certain modern classifications. These groups of gymnosperms show considerable diversity. For example, cycads and ginkgo have motile sperm, unlike gnetophytes and conifers. Most gymnosperms retain archegonia (*see* archegonium) except for the most advanced genera, *Gnetum* and *Welwitschia*. These genera and another gnetophyte *Ephedra* also have advanced TRACHEIDS with a structure reminiscent of angiosperm VESSELS, whereas in other gymnosperms the xylem is composed solely of more primitive tracheids.

The first gymnosperms appeared in the late Devonian and were especially abundant in the Carboniferous. They dominated the Jurassic and early Cretaceous, but by the late Cretaceous, the angiosperms became the dominant vegetation (*see* Angiospermophyta).

There are several extinct orders of gymnosperms: CAYTONIALES (early Mesozoic to late Cretaceous); CORDAITALES (late Devonian to Triassic); CYCADOFILICALES (Devonian to Triassic), also known as the pteridosperms or seed ferns and believed to be the ancestral stock of all the other gymnosperm groups; and BENNETTITALES (Mesozoic).

gyrogonites *See* Chlorophyta.

H

h   *See* genetic diversity.

h2   *See* narrow sense heritability.

H2   *See* broad sense heritability.

habitat   The place where a particular organism lives, described in terms of its climatic, vegetative, topographic, and other relevant factors. Habitats vary both in space and time. For example, in a forest the conditions at ground level are very different from those in the leaf canopy. Conditions also vary between seasons. However the conditions found in a specific habitat at a given time are unique to that habitat even though they may resemble conditions found in other similar habitats. The term *microhabitat* describes a small area, perhaps only a few square millimeters or centimeters in size, e.g. the undersurface of a stone.

habitat isolation   *See* prezygotic isolation.

Hadean   *See* Precambrian.

hadrosaur   *See* dinosaur.

Haeckel, Ernst Heinrich   (1834–1919) German biologist. Haeckel argued that the embryological stages of an animal were a RECAPITULATION of its evolutionary history, and indeed that there had once been complete animals resembling the embryonic stages of higher animal forms living today. He formulated a scheme of evolution for the whole animal kingdom, from inorganic matter upward. His studies of marine life, particularly the radiolarians, encouraged him to compare the symmetry of crystals with the simplest animals, and led him to postulate an inanimate origin for animal life. In 1866 Haeckel anticipated later proof of the fact that the key to inheritance factors lies in the cell nucleus, outlining this theme in his *Die Perigenesis der Plastidule* (1876; The Generation of Waves in the Small Vital Particles).

Haeckel also proposed the idea that all multicellular animals derived from a hypothetical two-layered (ectoderm and endoderm) animal, the *Gastraea* – a theory that provoked much discussion. He was also the first to divide the animal kingdom into unicellular (protozoan) and multicellular (metazoan) animals. An ardent Darwinist, Haeckel made several zoological expeditions and founded the Phyletic Museum at Jena and the Ernst Haeckel Haus, which contains his books, archives, and other effects.

In 1906 the Monist League was formed at Jena with Haeckel as its president. The League held a strong commitment to social Darwinism.

Haldane, John Burdon Sanderson   (1892–1964) British geneticist. His early research was on respiration, investigating how the levels of carbon dioxide in the blood affect the muscles regulating breathing. He subsequently did some important work on enzymes. In 1933 Haldane became professor of genetics at University College, London, a position he exchanged in 1937 for the chair of biometry. While at London he prepared a provisional map of the X sex chromosome and showed the genetic linkage between hemophilia and color blindness (*see* sex linkage). He also produced the first estimate of mutation rates in humans from studies of the pedigrees of hemophiliacs, and described the effect of recurring deleterious mutations on a population. Haldane's books include *Enzymes* (1930), *The Causes of Evolution* (1932), and *The Biochemistry of Genetics* (1954); he also wrote a number of books popularizing science.

Haldane's rule   A form of incomplete POSTZYGOTIC ISOLATION in which, if only one sex of the offspring of mating between closely related species is inviable or infertile, then it will be the HETEROGAMETIC SEX, that is, the sex with unlike chromosomes, X and Y. In most animals, the male is the heterogametic sex, and male F_1 hybrids are often either inviable or infertile, unlike their fertile female siblings. In birds, butterflies, and moths, the females are the heterogametic sex and in hybrids, the females are often sterile and there may be a large number of males. The genetic mechanism is not known but is thought to be an important process in SPECIATION.

hallux   The first digit of the hindfoot of tetrapods; it forms the big toe in humans. In the typical PENTADACTYL LIMB it contains two phalanges, however there are reductions and modifications to this general plan and in some mammals, e.g. the rabbit, it is absent. It is directed backwards in most birds as an adaptation to perching. *Compare* pollex.

Hamilton, William Donald   (1936–2000) British theoretical biologist. In the *Origin of Species* (1859) Darwin raised a "special difficulty," which he at first considered unsurmountable. How could natural selection ever lead to the evolution of neuter or sterile insects? Darwin's answer was that selection may be applied to the family, as well as the individual. In a series of papers, beginning in 1964 with *The Genetical Theory of Social Behaviour*, Hamilton pursued these implications and opened the way for the emergence of sociobiology. The key concept deployed by Hamilton was that of inclusive fitness, which covers not only an individual's fitness to survive but also the effects of its behavior on the fitness of its kin.

Hamilton's rule   *See* kin selection.

handicap theory   A theory of female choice in which only males with genes that confer high FITNESS can survive with characters that reduce survival (a handicap), e.g. secondary sexual characters, so a female will preferentially mate with a handicapped male. *Compare* Fisher's theory; parasitic theory of sexual selection. *See* sexual selection.

Handy man   *See Homo habilis.*

haplobiontic   Describing life cycles in which only one type of somatic body is formed, which may be either haploid or diploid. Haplobiontic is thus a collective term for *haplontic* and *diplontic*. The life cycle lacks a sporophyte or gametophyte generation, i.e. there is no ALTERNATION OF GENERATIONS. *Compare* diplobiontic.

haplo-diploid species   A species in which males develop from unfertilized eggs and are haploid, but females develop from fertilized eggs and are diploid. A female therefore has three-quarters of her genes in common with her sisters, but only half with her daughters. In normal diploid species a female has half her genes in common with both. Haploid-diploid species occur in the HYMENOPTERA, where sterile females spend their lives looking after their sisters. *See* inclusive fitness.

haploid   (monoploid)   A cell or organism containing only one representative from each of the pairs of homologous chromosomes found in the normal diploid cell. Haploid chromosomes are thus unpaired and the haploid chromosome number (n) is half the diploid number ($2n$). Meiosis, which usually precedes gamete formation, halves the chromosome number to produce haploid gametes. The diploid condition is restored when the nuclei of two gametes fuse to give the zygote. In humans there are 46 chromosomes in 23 pairs and thus the haploid egg and sperm each contain 23 chromosomes. Gametes may develop without fertilization, or meiosis may substantially precede gamete formation. This is especially true in plants, and leads to the formation of haploid organisms, or haploid phases in the life cycles of organisms.

Various multiples of the haploid number, e.g. the tetraploid ($4n$), hexaploid ($6n$), and octaploid ($8n$) conditions, are common in some plant groups, especially in certain cultivated plants.

haplont A haploid organism that represents the vegetative stage in life cycles in which diploidy is restricted to the zygote. *Haplontic* life cycles are typical of the filamentous green algae. *Compare* diplont.

haplontic *See* haplobiontic; haplont.

haplotype 1. A set of genes located on a single chromosome inherited from a parent. An organism produced by outbreeding will have two haplotypes because the maternal and paternal chromosomes are different.
2. In population genetics, a combination of ALLELES at more than one locus.

Hardy–Weinberg equation If a pair of ALLELES, A and a, have the frequencies p and q in a population, and p + q = 1, then random crossing among individuals in the population will give genotypes AA, Aa, and aa in the frequencies p^2, pq, q^2 respectively. The Hardy–Weinberg equation $p^2 + 2pq + q^2 = 1$ is obtained from the expansion of $(p+q)^2$, the total of the frequencies making up the GENE POOL being unity. *See* Hardy–Weinberg equilibrium.

Hardy–Weinberg equilibrium The situation in a large randomly mating population in which the proportion of DOMINANT to RECESSIVE genes remains constant from one generation to the next. It is described by the equation $p^2 + 2pq + q^2 = 1$, where p^2 and q^2 are the frequencies of the double dominant and double recessive respectively, and 2pq is the frequency of the heterozygote. The law was formulated in 1908 and disproved the then current theory that dominant genes always tend to increase in a population at the expense of their equivalent recessive alleles. The equilibrium only holds providing that the population is sufficiently large to avoid chance fluctuations of allele frequencies in the gene pool (GENETIC DRIFT) and providing there is no mutation, selection, or migration. The fact that allele frequencies may be seen to change fairly rapidly in large populations that show minimal mutation and migration, emphasizes the important role NATURAL SELECTION must play. Until the Hardy–Weinberg law was formulated, the extent of natural selection was not fully appreciated.

heart A muscular organ – essentially a specialized region of a blood vessel – that pumps blood around the body. In mammals and birds, it consists of four chambers (two upper atria and two lower ventricles) with the right and left sides totally separate.

The form of the heart varies greatly throughout the animal kingdom (reaching its greatest complexity in birds and mammals). Mammals and birds are warm-blooded (HOMOIOTHERMIC) and maintain both a high body temperature and metabolic rate. The separate systemic and pulmonary circulations have evolved to maximize the oxygen level in blood entering the systemic circulation that supplies all the cells of the body.

In annelids there are a number of lateral contractile vessels known as hearts. Crustaceans have a single heart with openings (ostia) possessing valves. In insects the heart is a long dorsal tube divided into 13 chambers, also with ostia. Molluscs and fish have two-chambered hearts. The single circulation means that the blood leaving the respiratory organs, such as gills, is under a lower pressure, but this is compensated for by the efficiency of respiratory organs at picking up oxygen from water.

Amphibians have two atria and one ventricle. In reptiles there is one ventricle, with a septum that completely separates the ventricle into two in crocodiles. The air-breathing amphibians and reptiles have evolved a second pump to increase efficiency. Amphibians, however spend much of their time in water and the mixing of oxygenated and deoxygenated blood reduces available oxygen, which is compensated for by blood capillaries in the skin performing a surface gas exchange independently of the lungs.

Heidelberg man *See Homo sapiens.*

helper T lymphocyte *See* AIDS.

Hemichordata A small but evolutionary important phylum of marine invertebrates. Hemichordates have an unsegmented body divided into three regions, the proboscis, collar, and trunk, each containing part of the coelom. The collar bears pharyngeal (gill) slits. Development is via a TORNARIA larva similar to that of the ECHINODERMATA. The relationship between these two groups is confirmed by DNA sequencing. The phylum includes the free-living wormlike Enteropneusta (acorn worms), e.g. *Balanoglossus*, which live in sand and mud, and the often colonial Pterobranchia, e.g. *Cephalodiscus*, which live in transparent tubes and have only one pair of gill slits and tentacles for feeding. The pharyngeal slits and a dorsal nerve cord (sometimes hollow) are important chordate characteristics. The extinct GRAPTO-LITES are often included in this phylum.

Hemiptera A very large order of insects, the true bugs, characterized by piercing and sucking mouthparts modified into a beak (*rostrum*). The plant bugs (e.g. *Aphis*) feed on plant sap and are serious pests, both damaging plants and carrying disease. They have uniform fore wings and membranous transparent hind wings, which are folded over the back when resting. Wingless parthenogenetic generations are common. Insects evolved in the Mesozoic and fossil bugs have been found in the Upper Pensylvanian, the Triassic, Cretaceous, and the Baltic amber of the Oligocene. *See* Insecta.

hemizygous Describing genetic material that has no homologous counterpart and is thus unpaired in the diploid state. Both single genes and chromosome segments may be hemizygous; for example, the X chromosome in the heterogametic sex, and whole chromosomes in aneuploids.

hemocoel *See* blood vascular system.

Hepaticae (liverworts) A class of BRYOPHYTA, in some classifications placed in a separate phylum, Hepatophyta, containing prostrate thallose dichotomously branching plants bearing unicellular rhizoids. They are simpler than the mosses with leafy axes only developing in more advanced species. There are seven orders of liverworts, including the Metzgeriales, e.g. *Pellia*, and the Marchantiales, e.g. *Marchantia*. The hornworts (*Anthoceros*) are sometimes included in the Hepaticae, but differ in having a photosynthetic, and thus partially independent, sporophyte. Spore formation is also different in *Anthoceros* and they are thus usually placed in a separate class, the Anthocerotae, or in a separate phylum, Anthocerophyta. Liverworts are nonwoody and thus are poorly represented in the fossil record. They were found in the Carboniferous but the oldest fossil is believed to be *Pellavicinites devonicus* from the Devonian. *Marchantites*, a Jurassic-fossil, consists of a flat forked thallus with a midrib, closely resembling present-day *Marchantia*. Liverworts preserved in Dominican and Baltic AMBER from the Tertiary are representatives of present-day genera.

herbivore A plant-eating animal, especially one of the herbivorous mammals, such as cows, rabbits, etc. Herbivores show various adaptations associated with this diet including to the teeth and digestive system. *Compare* carnivore; omnivore.

heredity The process by which characteristics are passed from one generation to the next.

heritability Symbol: h^2 The proportion of phenotypic variation due to additive genetic factors. It can be estimated from measurements of individuals from different generations, and is used in animal and plant breeding to predict how successful genetic selection will be in improving a particular trait. The heritability of a character determines its evolutionary response to selection.

heritable Capable of being passed from an individual to its offspring. A heritable character is therefore partly or wholly determined by genes.

hermaphrodite (bisexual) **1.** An animal possessing both male and female reproductive organs. The earthworm is a common example.
2. A plant bearing stamens and carpels in the same flower.

Herto man *See Homo sapiens.*

heterocercal tail The type of tail found in the cartilaginous fish, in which the vertebral column extends into the tail, bending upwards as it does so. The caudal fin below the vertebral column is much larger than that above; when the fish is swimming the lower caudal fin contributes lift, preventing the fish from sinking (which it does immediately it stops swimming). *Compare* homocercal tail; diphycercal tail.

heterochromatin *See* chromatin.

heterochronic mutation *See* heterochrony.

heterochrony A change in the rate or timing of the development of some types of cell relative to other types. A mutation that causes such a change is called a *heterochronic mutation*. The most important evolutionary heterochronic change is a change in the timing of reproduction. *See* paedomorphosis.

heterodont A type of dentition found in mammals in which there are four different types of TEETH, adapted for different functions.

heteroduplex A double-stranded DNA molecule in which the two strands do not have completely complementary sequences.

heterogametic sex The sex with dissimilar SEX CHROMOSOMES, one (in mammals the Y chromosome) being shorter than the other (the X chromosome). *See* sex determination.

heterogeneous nuclear RNA (hnRNA) *See* exon; messenger RNA; transcription.

heterokaryon A cell (common in fungi) with two genetically different haploid nuclei formed by the fusion of two individual haploid cells. It is probable that the fusion of gametes seen during sexual reproduction evolved from the formation of heterokarya.

heteromorphism The existence of more than one form, used especially with reference to life cycles in which the alternating generations are markedly different morphologically, as in ferns (*see* Filicinophyta) and jellyfish (*see* Cnidaria). *Compare* isomorphism.

heterosis (hybrid vigor) The condition in which the expression of a characteristic is greater in the heterozygous offspring than in either of the homozygous parents. The effect arises from an accumulation of dominant genes in the F_1. Thus, if height is controlled by two genes, A and B, and tall and short forms are determined by dominant and recessive alleles respectively, then the cross AAbb × aaBB would give an F_1 AaBb, containing both dominant genes for tallness. Usually the more unlike the parents are the more hybrid vigor is released, but the effect diminishes in subsequent generations as more recessive homozygotes reappear. *See also* heterozygous advantage.

heterospory The production of two different sizes of spore: microspores and megaspores. Heterospory is found in *Selaginella* species and shows this genus to be more advanced than the *Lycopodium* species (*see* Lycopodophyta) and most of the ferns. The microspores develop into male gametophytes whereas the megaspores produce female gametophytes. Moreover, gametophyte development is completed inside the spore and the gametophytes of both sexes are totally dependent nutritionally on the sporophyte. The evolution of heterospory is seen as a significant stage in the development of the seed habit.

heterotrophic Describing a type of nutrition in which the principal source of carbon is organic, i.e. the organism cannot make all of its own organic requirements from inorganic requirements from inorganic starting materials. Most heterotrophic organisms are *chemotrophic* and include animals, fungi, and most bacteria. *Compare* autotrophic.

heterozygous Having two different alleles at a given locus. Usually only one of these, the dominant allele, is expressed in the phenotype. Mating between heterozygotes inevitably produces viable homozygotes and reduces the heterozygosity of the population. Heterozygosity is maintained by outbreeding and results in a more adaptable population. *See also* heterozygous advantage; genetic constraint. *Compare* homozygous.

heterozygous advantage The situation in which the heterozygote is fitter than either of the homozygotes (*see* heterosis). A POLYMORPHISM that confers a heterozygous advantage will therefore be retained by natural selection even if it appears to be a disadvantage, for example, the SICKLE-CELL ANEMIA allele in malarial areas. If there is a heterozygous advantage in a sexually reproducing population there will always be homozygotes because of the GENETIC CONSTRAINT of independent assortment.

Hirudinea The class of the ANNELIDA that contains the leeches, mostly terrestrial or fresh-water carnivorous or bloodsucking invertebrates (e.g. *Hirudo medicinalis*, the European medicinal leech). Leeches have a flat body, each segment being subdivided externally into narrow rings (*annuli*), and anterior and posterior suckers for attachment to a host. Leeches can swim strongly. They are hermaphrodite, the eggs developing in cocoons produced by the clitellum. Fossil annelids are soft-bodied and not well represented in fossil fauna.

historical constraint A past evolutionary event that prevents an organism from adapting in the present. *Compare* developmental constraint; genetic constraint.

hitchhiking The effect of selection at one locus influencing gene frequencies at linked loci.

hnRNA (heterogeneous nuclear RNA) *See* exon; messenger RNA; transcription.

Holarctic *See* Nearctic; Palearctic.

holistic *See* reductionism.

Holocene (Recent) The present epoch in the geological time scale, being the second epoch of the QUATERNARY period, dating from the end of the last glaciation, about 10 000 years ago, to the present day.

It is an interglacial period, another ice age predicted to occur in 5000–10 000 years' time, unless human activities upset the natural equilibrium (e.g. as a result of global warming or deforestation). At the beginning of the period, the Arctic polar ice sheets melted and sea levels rose. The impact of human activities (which makes this epoch unique) began about 8000 years ago when settled farming began: land was cleared for growing crops and for grazing domesticated livestock, and huge tracts of forests were cut down for fuel and timber. This led to increased human populations that migrated and colonized new areas. Large-scale industrialization has led to the POLLUTION of entire ecosystems. Human action has been responsible for most modern extinctions of plants and animals, and many species are at risk. *See* Ice Age. *See also* endangered species; greenhouse effect; extinction.

Holothuroidea The class of the ECHINODERMATA that contains the sea cucumbers (e.g. *Cucumaria*), which have a long cylindrical body showing secondary bilateral symmetry and covered with tough leathery skin in which the skeletal plates are reduced to spicules. There are no arms, but tube feet modified as food-catching tentacles surround the mouth. Other tube feet are suckered for locomotion or pointed for burrowing. Many holothurians extrude eggs and sperm into the sea, and the resulting larva is known as an *auricularia*, a type of DIPLEURULA larva.

Holothurians first appeared in the Ordovician and more modern forms appeared in the Mesozoic. Their soft bodies mean that they are not common as fossils, but in the middle Paleozoic, they have left behind abundant tiny spicules.

homeobox　A segment of DNA found in many so-called HOMEOTIC GENES concerned with controlling the development of organisms. It consists of 180 base pairs, and the sequence of bases is remarkably similar across a wide range of species, from yeasts to humans. This suggests that it arose early in evolutionary time and has been little changed since. The sequence encodes the amino acids of a peptide sequence that enables the parent protein to bind to DNA. This is consistent with the suggested role of homeotic proteins as genetic switches, binding to genes to control their expression. The *Hox* genes are a subset of homeobox genes (*see* colinear). *See also* differentiation.

homeostasis　The maintenance of a constant internal environment by an organism. It enables cells to function more efficiently. Any deviation from this balance results in reflex activity of the nervous and hormone systems, which tend to negate the effect. The degree to which homeostasis is achieved by a particular group, independent of the environment, is a measure of evolutionary advancement.

homeotic gene　Any of a class of genes that are crucial in determining the DIFFERENTIATION of tissues in different parts of the body during development. They encode proteins that regulate the expression of other genes by binding to DNA. This binding capability can be pinpointed to a characteristic base sequence known as a HOMEOBOX. Homeotic genes have been intensively studied in the fruit fly, DROSOPHILA MELANOGASTER. They come into play when the basic pattern of body seg-ments has been established in the fly embryo, and direct the development of particular groups of cells in each segment. In *Drosophila* there are two major clusters of homeotic genes: the *antennapedia* complex controls development of the head and front thoracic segments, while the *bithorax* complex governs the fate of cells in more posterior segments. The physical order of the genes in these complexes corresponds to the order in which they are expressed from anterior to posterior in the developing embryo. This, together with studies of homeotic mutants, has prompted the theory that differentiation in each segment requires expression of the homeotic gene regulating that particular segment in combination with the gene for the preceding segment. A similar ordered arrangement of homeotic genes is seen in other species, including humans.

homeotic mutation　A mutation (to any of the HOMEOTIC GENES) that results in one body part growing in the place of another. Homeotic mutations are developmental macromutations and are nearly always lethal. They produce large phenotypic variations, but not adaptations and have a small role in evolution.

hominid　A member of the primate family Hominidae, which includes modern humans (*Homo sapiens*) as well as extinct forms found in great number and variety as fossils (AUSTRALOPITHECINES and HOMO SPECIES). Diagnostic features of fossil hominids include smaller canines, hyperbolic tooth rows, and smaller lower jaws than in fossil apes. The presence of stone tools associated with a fossil can also help in identification.

hominoid　A term loosely used to group the apes with humans and their ancestors.

Homo　A genus of the family Hominidae of which modern humans, *Homo sapiens*, is the only surviving species. The species of the *Homo* line had a larger cranial capacity than their AUSTRALOPITHECINE ancestors. They had greater manual dexterity, not only in using stones and tools, but also in shaping them for different purposes. Later species had a more erect gait. Gradually humans began to use fire, and speech areas developed in the brain of later types. *See* Cro-Magnon man; *Homo erectus*; *Homo ergaster*; *Homo habilis*; *Homo rudolfensis*; *Homo sapiens*; human evolution.

Homo antecessor *See Homo sapiens.*

homocercal tail The type of tail found in adult bony fish, in which the vertebral column does not extend to the end of the tail and the caudal fin has two lobes of equal size. *Compare* diphycercal tail; heterocercal tail.

homodont A type of dentition in which the teeth are all alike. This is found in such animals as frogs, in which all the teeth are similar small conical structures, cemented to the maxillae, premaxillae, and vomers of the upper jaw.

Homo erectus (Upright man) An extinct early human species and the first early human fossil remains to be discovered on an expedition led by Eugene Dubois in 1890–94 in Java and Indonesia. It was named *Pithecanthropus erectus* (nicknamed *Java man*) and later identified as *Homo erectus* when it was associated with fossils excavated in China at Zhoukoudian, near Beijing (Peking) by Gunnar Anderson between 1927 and 1937. The bones of 40 individuals – men, women, and children were found, together with animal bones, some of which were burned, suggesting cooking. At first this species was named *Sinanthropus pekinensis* (Peking man). Unfortunately, most of these fossils were destroyed in World War II when the Japanese invaded China and only two teeth remain. Other *H. erectus* material has been excavated in China, in Lantian County, Shensi Province, that are even older than the Zhoukoudian fossils.

In 1960, Louis and Mary LEAKEY first discovered part of the cranium of a specimen at Olduvai Gorge in Tanzania. More fossils were discovered there and also eventually at other sites in South, East, and Northwest Africa. In 1984, Richard Leakey's team discovered the 'Turkana Boy' at Nariokotome, Lake Turkana dated 1.6 mya. These later remains, together with discoveries in the 1990s in Eastern Europe at Dmanisi in Georgia, have been placed in a separate species *(see Homo ergaster)*. *H. erectus* had a robust but human skeleton, a flat thick skull with large eye sockets and brow ridges, largish jaws in larger individuals, and smaller teeth than HOMO HABILIS. The pelvis and leg bones resembled those of modern humans, implying that they could walk and run on two legs. Unlike humans, their foreheads were shallow and sloped back from the brow ridges and the skull was elongated from front to back. *See also* human evolution.

Homo ergaster An extinct early human species. Many researchers believe that later fossils found in 1984 (e.g. Turkana Boy) and discoveries made in the 1990s in Eastern Europe of HOMO ERECTUS should be placed in a separate species, *Homo ergaster*. There is much controversy, certain authorities grouping all early African material as *H. ergaster*. *H. ergaster* and *H. erectus* are very similar, but *H. ergaster* specimens have a higher cranial vault, increased body size, and a larger brain, although the latter characteristics probably indicate that the relative brain size/body size has increased little. The most famous fossil is Turkana Boy, which most researchers believe to be *H. erectus*. Dated at 1.6 million years, the skeleton was almost complete, except for the hands and feet. He was tall and thin with long arms and legs, typical of humans living in an open tropical environment. He was over 5 ft tall when he died at the age of about 11 or 12, but if he had lived longer, he would probably have reached a height of over 6 ft.

homogametic sex The sex with homologous SEX CHROMOSOMES, in mammals, designated XX. *See* sex determination.

Homo habilis (Handy man) An extinct early human species, the first fossils of which were discovered by Louis LEAKEY at Olduvai Gorge in Tanzania, East Africa, together with stone tools. They were thought to be older than *Paranthropus boisei* (also discovered at that site), dated 2.0–1.6 mya and overlapped with the robust AUSTRALOPITHECINES. The fossil remains showed unique *Homo* characteristics, such as an increase in the size and thickness of the cranium, reduced jaw size, reduction in size of molars and premolars, and most important, an increase in brain size. *Homo habilis* individuals had small faces and a nose had developed. The skeleton was significantly human, but also quite robust. It is unclear whether this species evolved into later *Homo* species. *See also* Oldowan industrial complex.

Homo heidelbergensis *See Homo sapiens.*

homoiothermy (endothermy) The maintenance of the body temperature at a constant level, irrespective of environmental conditions. Birds and mammals are homoiothermic ('warm-blooded'). *Compare* poikilothermy.

homologous Describing structures that, though in different species, are believed to have the same origin in a common ancestor. Thus the forelimbs and hindlimbs of all land vertebrates are said to be homologous, being constructed on the same five-digit (pentadactyl) pattern. *See illustration overleaf.* An *ancestral homology* is a character that developed before the common ancestor of a set of species and so is present in other, more distantly related species. A *derived homology* is a character that developed in the common ancestor of a set of species and is therefore unique to those species. Whether a homology is ancestral or derived can depend on the species being compared.

The phrase 'homologous sequence' is often used in molecular biology to refer to similar sequences of nucleotides (in genes) or amino acids (in proteins), but it should only be used for sequences that have derived from a common ancestor. *See also* conserved sequence. *Compare* orthologous; paralagous. *See also* analogous.

homologous chromosomes Chromosomes that pair at meiosis. Each carries the same genes as the other member of the pair but not necessarily the same alleles for a given gene. During the formation of the germ cells only one member of each pair of homologs is passed on to the gametes. At fertilization each parent contributes one homolog of each pair, thus restoring the diploid chromosome number in the zygote. The members of each homologous pair are similar to one another in size and shape. The exceptions are the sex chromosomes, for example in mammals the Y chromosome is much smaller than the X chromosome.

homoplastic Describing similarity due to convergent or parallel evolution. *Compare* patristic.

homoplasy Shared characters for reasons other than inheritance from a common ancestor. The most common cause of morphological homoplasy is CONVERGENT EVOLUTION. Mutation is the most likely cause of homoplasy in nucleic acid sequences because they consist of only four different bases and there is therefore a 25% chance that two bases are the same due to mutation. *See* analogous; homologous; plesiomorphy; sequence alignment.

Homo rudolfensis An extinct early human species first discovered in 1993 near Lake Malawi in East Africa (dated 2.4–1.6 mya). *Homo rudolfensis* resembles HOMO HABILIS and exists alongside fossils of the latter also found at Lake Turkana as well as at the Olduvai Gorge. It had a larger cranium, larger molars and premolars with more complex roots and crown, and a larger flatter face. It is doubtful whether this species gave rise to later *Homo* species, even though the brain and skull were larger than that of *H. habilis*. *See also* Oldowan industrial complex.

Homo sapiens (humans) The species that includes archaic and modern humans. The earliest and regarded as the type specimen was a mandible found in 1907 at Mauer, near Heidelberg in Germany that

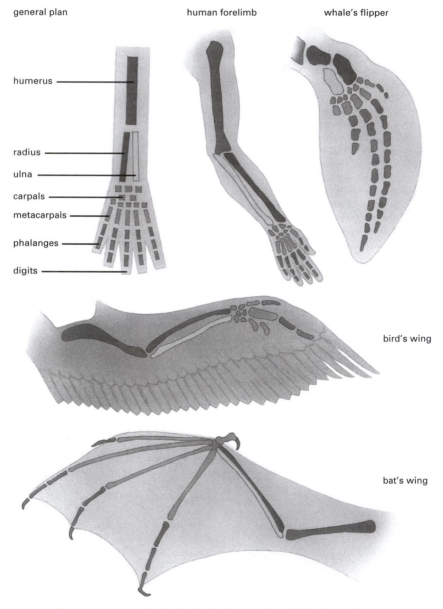

general plan

human forelimb

whale's flipper

humerus

radius

ulna

carpals

metacarpals

phalanges

digits

bird's wing

bat's wing

Homologous: showing similarities in the pentadactyl limb of vertebrates

combined some modern features (size of molar teeth) with the primitive robustness of the jaw. It was named *Homo heidelbergensis* (nickname: Heidelberg man) and later assigned to the subspecies *Homo sapiens heidelbergensis*. Excellent specimens of this archaic *Homo sapiens* were found in 1997 at Atapuerca in NE Spain, dated at 780 000 years old. However, the discoverers of the Atapuerca specimens have decided to rename these fossils *Homo antecessor*, believing that they are transitional between earlier *Homo* species and modern *H. sapiens*. The specimens have a more prominent nose and face, and there may be changes at the base of the cranium that could be associated with the development of the voice box. Certain authorities believe that *H. antecessor* gave rise to two lines: *H. heidelbergensis*, which evolved into *H. neanderthalis* and *Homo sapiens* (*see* out of Africa theory).

Other specimens also assigned to *H. heidelbergensis* include the *Kabwe skull* (*Broken Hill 1, Rhodesian man*) discovered in 1921 at Kabwe, Zambia. Also, a tibia from Boxgrove, Sussex, England in 1994, 524 000–478 000 years old, was named *Boxgrove man*. The latter was associated with ACHEULIAN TOOLS, and is roughly contemporaneous with the *Mauer mandible*. The *Bodo skull* from Ethiopia is dated at 600 000 years old and the *Qatzeh skull* from Israel is dated as 100 000 years old. The discovery in 1997 (published in 2003) of three well-preserved skulls by Professor Tim White at Herto, in the Middle Awash, Ethiopia, are the most significant finds yet. They are 160 000 years old, resemble the younger Qatzeh skull (although the back of the skull resembles the Kabwe skull), but match the exact age that *Homo sapiens* is said to have diverged from its ancestral line based on DNA analysis in the out of Africa theory. It is named for the village of Herto (nickname: Herto man), and is placed in the subspecies: *Homo sapiens idaltu* ('idaltu' means 'elderly' in the Afar language).

When the archaic *H. sapiens* spread worldwide, they migrated across the Bering land bridge into North America 40 000 years ago, and reached Australia

about 33 000 years ago. The more modern humans (often assigned to the subspecies *Homo sapiens sapiens*) were able to survive the last Ice Age because they were able to develop specialized tools, weapons, hunting techniques, and other intelligent strategies. *See also* multiregional theory.

homospory The production of only one kind of a sexual spore, which then develops into a hermaphrodite gametophyte. In the vascular plants the condition is seen in the ferns and *Lycopodium* species. *Compare* heterospory.

homozygous Having identical alleles for any specified gene or genes. A homozygote breeds true for the character in question if it is selfed or crossed with a similar homozygote. An organism homozygous at every locus produces offspring identical to itself on selfing or when crossed with a genetically identical organism. Homozygosity is obtained by inbreeding, and homozygous populations may be well adapted to certain environments, but slow to adapt to changing environments. *Compare* heterozygous. *See* pure line.

Hooker, Sir Joseph Dalton (1817–1911) British plant taxonomist and explorer. Hooker studied medicine at Glasgow University, where his father William Hooker was professor of botany. After graduating in 1839, he joined the Antarctic expedition on HMS *Erebus* (1839–43), nominally as assistant surgeon but primarily as naturalist. Between 1844 and 1860, using collections made on the expedition, Hooker produced a six-volume flora of the Antarctic Islands, New Zealand, and Tasmania.

When he returned from the Antarctic expedition Hooker was congratulated on his work by Charles DARWIN, who had been following his progress, and in 1844 Darwin confided to Hooker his theory of evolution by natural selection. This communication later proved important in establishing Darwin's precedence when his theory – together with Alfred Russel WALLACE's essentially identical conclusions – was presented by Hooker and George Lyell at the famous Linnaean Society meeting of July 1858.

In 1855 Hooker was appointed assistant director at Kew Gardens and in 1865 succeeded his father as director. With George Bentham he produced a world flora, *Genera Plantarum* (1862–83; Genera of Plants) – a major work describing 7569 genera and 97 000 species.

hornworts   *See* Anthocerotae.

horse evolution   One of the most complete evolutionary sequences from the fossil record, beginning with the genus *Hyracotherium* (formerly called *Eohippus*) and ending with the modern horse, genus *Equus*. The main stages (omitting evolutionary sidelines) are as follows, based on major changes in the teeth and limbs:
Hyracotherium fossils of the Eocene of North America show that these horses were 0.4 m tall, had low-crowned nonserrated teeth, and walked on four digits on the forefoot and three on the hind foot. They browsed on the fruit and soft vegetation of the woodlands and marshes. They were small fleet-footed horses.
Mesohippus from the Oligocene was 0.6 m tall and also browsed on vegetation. These horses had low-crowned molar teeth, but the amount of cement had increased. They were three-toed and the third digit had become slightly larger. The fifth digit was now much smaller.
Merychippus from the Miocene was 1 m tall. The molar teeth had developed higher crowns (*hypsodont*) completely covered with cement, which as they wore down left serrated edges caused by the exposed harder enamel appearing as ridges (*lophodont* teeth). These horses had now become grazing animals, indicating a change in the vegetation to grasses with a high silica content, which eroded the teeth. *Merychippus* walked on one long stout toe (the third digit), the others not reaching the ground, the fifth having disappeared. The third metacarpals and metatarsals had also increased in length. The second and fourth metacarpals and metatarsals had disappeared.

Pliohippus from the Pliocene was also 1 m high. These horses were also grazers, the teeth similar to those of *Merychippus*. The third digit was even larger, as were the third metacarpals and metatarsals. The other metatarsals and metacarpals had disappeared.
Equus, modern horses from the Pleistocene to the present day, had teeth with even higher crowns and ridges, adapted to continuous grazing. The third metacarpals and metatarsals had become even longer and stouter and the last phalange of the third digit (really the nail) had evolved into a hoof.

The ancestral horses had evolved in response to a changing environment, particularly in the Miocene where the vegetation had changed from woodland to open savanna with the evolution of grasses. Browsing habits changed to grazing habits, with corresponding changes in the teeth. The limbs increased in length and proportion to support the increasing bulk of the animal, and also probably to enable the animals to increase their speed to escape from predators in the open grasslands. The increased elevation of the head, together with the position of the eyes positioned farther back on the skull (an advantage to animals cropping grass), enabled horses to spot their predators more easily. The hooves were a better adaptation for speed on the harder ground, the splayed-out digits now unnecessary for support on such terrain. These adaptations were also accompanied by an increase in both the complexity and size of the brain. The changes were probably sporadic and irregular (*see* punctuated equilibrium) as evidenced by the intermediate forms and evolutionary sidelines in the history of this animal.

horsetails   *See* Sphenophyta.

***hox* genes**   *See* colinear; homeobox.

human evolution   The earliest humans (hominids) evolved from an ancestral ape 12 mya, which also produced the orang-utan, gorillas, and chimpanzees. Recent DNA sequencing and analysis of amino acid sequences of proteins have shown that humans and chimpanzees share 99% of their genes. These two groups diverged 5–8 mya.

There are many characteristics that make modern human beings unique and remarkable in the animal kingdom and we differ from our ape ancestors as the result of many anatomical changes: walking on two legs with an upright posture (*see* bipedalism); opposable thumbs (shared by chimpanzees) that possibly made it easier for carrying and manipulating tools, and later, many other skills, as a result of an upright posture; the point of attachment of the skull moved from the back of the cranium to its base thus allowing the skull to balance on top of an erect vertebral column; the brain and cranium became larger; the jaw became shorter, the teeth smaller, and the forehead more prominent and vertical; the eyebrow ridges reduced and the nose became more prominent; the arms became shorter; the feet flattened and an arch developed; the big toe ceased being opposable and moved in line with the foot; the

gestation period is long (40 weeks) and there is no estrous cycle so breeding can occur at will; and body hair is much reduced.

In addition, speech has developed, humans often live in large societies, live for a long time, inhabit most of the world, and can exercise control over the environment and also over other animals. Humans are a dominant species, speech and communication playing an important part in evolution accompanied by an increase in brain size and neural coordination and the mental ability to think and to predict and solve problems. Learning from parents over a long period of time has also contributed to human success. The reasons for the evolution of bipedalism continues to be controversial, but this characteristic has enabled human hands to perform many intricate and also creative activities.

The fossil record shows that the ancestral ape was probably similar to *Proconsul* from the early MIOCENE of Africa, Asia, and Europe. It first appeared about 23 mya.

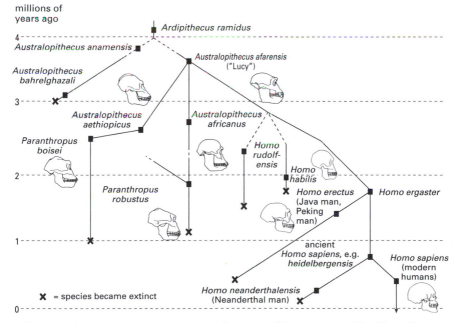

Human evolution: this chart shows some of the more well-known relationships. Those that are less certain are indicated by the broken lines.

(*Proconsul* is often now assigned to the genus *Dryopithecus*.) The discovery of a very ancient fossil from China (*Eosimias sinensis*) is the most ancient anthropoid ever found and is from the middle Eocene, dated about 40 mya, indicating that PROSIMIANS and anthropoids probably diverged even earlier than once thought (*see* anthropoids).

The earliest hominids were the AUSTRALOPITHECINES. One of the most famous species (AUSTRALOPITHECUS AFARENSIS, exemplified by 'Lucy') is believed to be the ancestor of the HOMO genus. A number of species evolved in the *Homo* genus, including *Homo habilis* and later *Homo erectus*. Both species used tools and *H. erectus* individuals had discovered fire and lived in caves (Java man and Peking man). Two theories exist for the origin of *Homo sapiens*. The MULTIREGIONAL THEORY envisages *H. erectus* spreading out from Africa and evolving into *H. sapiens* as a result of adaptations and GENETIC DRIFT. The OUT OF AFRICA THEORY based on studies of African mitochondrial and nuclear DNA indicates that a speciation event may have taken place in African *H. erectus* individuals, which evolved into *H. sapiens* (modern

man). Modern humans then migrated out of Africa and gradually replaced existing *H. erectus* species in other parts of the world (*see* mitochondrial Eve). The discovery of Herto man (*see Homo sapiens*) is the best evidence yet for the out of Africa theory because it matches the exact age at which *H. sapiens* has been calculated (by DNA analysis) to have diverged from its ancestral line. *See Homo erectus*; *Homo ergaster*; *Homo habilis*; *Homo rudolfensis*; *Homo sapiens*.

Human Genome Project An international project launched in 1989 with the aim of mapping and sequencing the entire human genome. The results will help in the diagnosis and possibly the treatment of a wide range of diseases. These include not only hereditary disorders, such as Huntington's disease, but also many common ailments with a genetic component, such as heart disease and breast cancer. Sequencing the genes responsible for the development of these diseases enables the design of DNA PROBES that will identify susceptible individuals, so allowing preventive measures or routine check-ups. However, such knowledge has profound ethical and com-

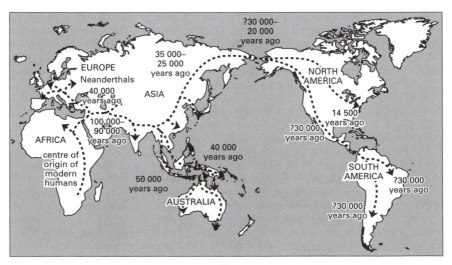

Human evolution: modern humans (*Homo sapiens*) probably evolved in Africa 150 000–100 000 years ago and subsequently spread from there to other parts of the world. The map shows possible routes of dispersal of these early humans.

mercial implications. For example, insurance companies may insist on a full genome check before agreeing terms for life insurance, even in healthy applicants. The project was completed in 2002. *See* chromosome map.

humerus The long bone of the upper forelimb in tetrapods; the upper arm bone in humans, extending from the shoulder to the elbow. Its rounded upper head articulates with the glenoid cavity of the scapula in a ball-and-socket joint. The lower end is modified to form an articular surface (condyle) for the radius and ulna, which produces the hinge joint of the elbow. *See illustration at* pentadactyl limb.

Hutchinson, John (1884–1972) British botanist. Hutchinson's most significant work was his *Families of Flowering Plants* (2 vols. 1926–34; 2nd edition 1959), which contains details of 342 dicotyledon and 168 monocotyledon families. Hutchinson drew most of the illustrations for this work himself. In it he concentrated on the different plant families that various workers had considered the most primitive. He concluded that bisexual flowers with free petals, sepals, etc., as seen in the magnolia and buttercup families, are more ancient than the generally unisexual catkinlike flowers found in the nettle and beech families, which lack these parts. Furthermore Hutchinson stated that families with apparently more simple flowers are in fact more advanced, and have evolved by reduction from more complex structures; that is, the families show retrograde evolution (*see* Angiospermophyta; Dicotyledonae; Monocotyledonae).

Hutchinson also published, with John Dalziel, the standard work, *Flora of West Tropical Africa* (1927–36) and at the time of his death was engaged in a revision of the *Genera Plantarum* (Genera of Plants) of Bentham and Hooker.

Hutton, James (1726–97) British geologist. Hutton's uniformitarian theories were first published as a paper in 1788 and later extended into a two-volume work, *Theory of the Earth* (1795). This work reached a wide audience only when his friend John Playfair edited and summarized it as *Illustrations of the Huttonian Theory* (1802). It marked a turning point in geology. The prevailing theory of the day, the neptunism of Abraham Werner, was that rocks had been laid down as mineral deposits in the oceans. However, Hutton maintained that water could not be the only answer because it was mainly erosive. The water could not account for the nonconformities caused by the foldings and intrusions characteristic of the Earth's strata. Hutton showed that the geological processes that had formed the Earth's features could be observed continuing at the present day. The heat of the Earth was the productive power, according to Hutton, that caused sedimentary rocks to fuse into the granites and flints, which could be produced in no other way. It could also produce the upheaval of strata, their folding and twisting, and the creation of mountains.

In the 19th century Charles LYELL expanded the theories of uniformitarianism and these were to influence Charles DARWIN in his theory of evolution.

Huxley, Thomas Henry (1825–95) British biologist. Huxley is best remembered as the main advocate of Charles DARWIN's theory of evolution, and in 1860 – the year following the publication of *The Origin of Species* – he took part in a famous debate with the bishop of Oxford, Samuel Wilberforce, at the Oxford meeting of the British Association for the Advancement of Science. During the discussion Wilberforce asked whether Huxley traced his ancestry to the apes on his mother's or father's side of the family. Huxley answered witheringly that given the choice of a miserable ape and a man who could make such a remark at a serious scientific gathering, he would select the ape.

hybrid An organism derived from crossing genetically dissimilar parents. Thus most individuals in an outbreeding population could be called hybrids, but the term is usually reserved for the product of a cross between individuals that are markedly different. If two different species are crossed the offspring are often sterile; for example, the mule, which results from a cross between a horse and a donkey. The sterility results from the nonpairing of the chromosomes necessary for gamete formation. In plants this is sometimes overcome by the doubling of the chromosome number, giving an allopolyploid.

hybrid belt   *See* parapatric speciation.

hybrid breakdown   Offspring produced by viable, fertile hybrids are either inviable or have drastically reduced viability and do not reproduce. *See* postzygotic isolation.

hybrid inviability   *See* postzygotic isolation.

hybridization analysis   *See* nucleic acid hybridization.

hybrid speciation   *See* sympatric speciation.

hybrid sterility   *See* postzygotic isolation.

hybrid swarm   A very variable series of organisms resulting from the continual crossing, recrossing, and backcrossing of the hybrid generations of two species.

hybrid vigor   *See* heterosis.

hybrid zone   *See* parapatric speciation.

Hydra   *See* Hydrozoa.

hydrostatic skeleton   *See* coelom.

hydrothermal vent   *See* black smokers.

Hydrozoa   A class of the Cnidaria in which alternation of generations of polyps and medusae typically occurs in the life cycle. Fossil relics have been found from Cambrian times onward. Most are marine, with colonial sedentary polyps (e.g. *Obelia*). The polyps reproduce asexually, forming either new polyps or free-swim-

ming sexually-reproducing medusae. The best-known exception, the freshwater *Hydra*, exists as a solitary polyp with no medusa phase. It reproduces both sexually and also asexually (by budding). After fertilization in sexual reproduction the zygote gives rise to a hollow ball of cells (a blastula). The ectodermal cells give rise to endodermal cells that fill up the cavity (the *blastocoel*). The solid embryo is then described as a *gastrula*, which develops into an elongated ciliated free-swimming larva called a *planula*. The larva eventually becomes fixed at one end and develops a mouth and tentacles at the other, forming a new organism. *See* planuloid hypothesis. *See also* Burgess shale; Edicara fauna.

Hymenoptera   A large order of insects containing the bees (e.g. *Apis*), wasps (e.g. *Vespula*), and ants (e.g. *Formica*). They evolved in the CENOZOIC, in parallel with the evolution of flowering plants (*see* Angiospermophyta). Most are carnivorous, with biting mouthparts, although some (e.g. bees) have additional sucking mouthparts. The hind wings are coupled to the larger fore wings by small hooks for a more stable flight, and the thorax is usually joined to the abdomen by a narrow waist. The female's ovipositor may be modified as a saw, drill, or sting. The larvae are either caterpillar-like, feeding on plants, or legless and helpless, being cared for by the adults. Metamorphosis is complete. Although some hymenoperans are solitary, the order also includes social insects, such as honeybees and ants, living in highly organized colonies.

A colony of honey bees, for example, consists of thousands of workers (sterile females), a few hundred drones (fertile males), and a single queen (fertile female). The queen lays eggs, the drones fertilize queens, and the workers build the hive, rear the young, forage for food (collecting nectar and pollen from flowering plants), and guard the hive. The workers and the queen are DIPLOID, but the males are produced from unfertilized eggs and are HAPLOID.

The idea of KIN SELECTION can be applied to honey bees and other social insects, e.g. ants and also termites, which belong to the insect order Isoptera. W. D. HAMILTON considered that the altruistic behavior (*see* altruism) of social insects can only evolve if the alleles that code for this behavior are found in even more individuals in the next generation. The altruistic behavior that results in an individual not reproducing and passing its own alleles on must result in the recipients of this behavior being able to do so (i.e. it increases their FITNESS to carry the alleles). Male hymenopterans develop from unfertilized eggs and have only ½ of the chromosomes, all of which they pass on to their daughters. Thus all the daughters have exactly the same set of paternal alleles. The female is diploid and so there is a 50% chance of any allele going to an offspring, i.e. ½. Multiply ½ of these shared genes by ½ of the total genome and the result is ¼ of the offspring's alleles being identical through the mother. Ant or bee daughters are therefore ¾ genetically identical to their sisters, so alleles for altruism could increase in frequency and are di-rected toward siblings (in this case, the workers).

hyoid arch The second visceral arch, lying between the jaws and spiracle. In tetrapods, its ventral elements form the *hyoid apparatus*, which supports the tongue. In fish, its dorsal element is modified to form the hyomandibular.

hyomandibular One of a pair of cartilages or bones in fish that attaches the ends of the upper and lower jaws to the rest of the skull. In tetrapods, with the changes in jaw articulation, the hyomandibular is modified to form an ear ossicle.

hypostasis The situation in which the expression of one gene (the *hypostatic gene*), is prevented in the presence of another, nonallelic, gene (the *epistatic gene*). See epistasis.

hypsodont *See* molar; horse evolution.

Hyracotherium *See* horse evolution.

Ice Age A period in the latter part of the PLEISTOCENE characterized by successive coolings and warmings of the earth. In at least four major glaciations (cold periods), ice caps spread south from the Arctic and north from the Antarctic. Large areas of Europe and North America were covered by ice from the North. The cause of the Ice Ages is not known, but it is assumed that others will occur in the future. The rapid reversal between glacial and *interglacial* conditions resulted in many repeated extinctions of plants and animals on the land and in the oceans and also caused their major redistribution. In North America, the ice ages are named: Nebraskan, Kansan, Illinoian, and Wisconsinian. In Europe, they are named: Donau, Günz, Mindel, Riss, and Würm.

Ichthyosauria The only order of the extinct subclass of marine euryapsid reptiles, the Ichthyopterygia, which lived from the Triassic to the Cretaceous and are known as the fish-lizards. *Ichthyosaurus*, common in the Jurassic, was a large predaceous marine reptile with a long snout, numerous teeth, a streamlined sharklike body, four paddle-shaped limbs, and dorsal and caudal fins. Ichthyosaurs were probably ovoviviparous and never left the water. *See also* plesiosaurs; pliosaurs; placodonts; Reptilia.

idiogram *See* karyogram.

iguana lizards Giant plant-eating lizards encountered by Darwin on the GALÁPAGOS ISLANDS. One species is terrestrial, the other marine. The latter is the only known aquatic lizard, adapted to life in water by possessing webbed feet and a flattened tail.

Certain authorities believe that the marine species evolved as a result of competition for vegetation and overcrowding on the land. The marine species feeds on seaweed; the land species feed on especially the prickly pear (*Opuntia*).

immune response A response by living organisms to withstand invasion by harmful disease-causing organisms such as bacteria, fungi, viruses, and other pathogens, and resulting in *immunity*. In animals, the response is carried out by the *immune system*. There are two main types of immunity. The first is *natural immunity*, which is inherited and nonspecific. For example, in humans, white cells (*leukocyctes*) in blood, lymph, and certain other tissues engulf, ingest, and destroy any foreign material that has entered the body, a process known as *phagocytosis*. The second type of immunity is *adaptive immunity*, which is acquired during the lifetime of an individual, either as the result of specific responses by certain specialized proteins (*antibodies*) or by immune cells (lymphocytes), both of which recognize and combine with foreign substances, e.g. the surface molecules of the invading organisms or the toxins produced by the invaders. The foreign substances are known as *antigens*. Antibodies are *immunoglobulins* (of which there are five types), and it has been discovered that they have evolved from ancient proteins that have been present in animals for hundreds of millions of years.

All the cells involved in the immune system are derived from *stem cells* in the bone marrow. Stem cells produce two types of lymphocyte: *B lymphocytes* (*B cells*) and *T lymphocytes* (*T cells*). B lymphocytes are produced by the stem cells during embryonic development and in a newborn child millions of B lymphocytes exist. This is because the stem cells divide by mitosis extremely rapidly to form clones, all having the potential to recognize most types of antigen that could ever exist. The genes responsible for the antibody sites on the surface of the B lymphocytes can mutate very rapidly at random producing this enormous variety and so the recognition mechanism to counteract antigens is ready and waiting. Many mutations will be unsuccessful and the cells will die, but successful B lymphocytes will rapidly proliferate. After an attack, B lymphocytes can also produce so-called *memory cells*, which can remain in the body for months or years to counteract further infection.

In addition, there are three types of T lymphocytes: *killer T cells*, which are phagocytes and destroy infected cells and invading pathogens; *helper T cells*, which are needed to stimulate the B lymphocytes (otherwise they cannot function); *suppressor T cells*, which stop the B lymphocytes and all the other phagocytic cells from working unnecessarily – otherwise the immune system could overreact. Thus the immune system of higher vertebrates has evolved by selection into a self-regulating system, but random mutation of the genes within the developing B lymphocytes provides variation, which is the basis of the evolutionary process. *See also* AIDS; Sarich.

inbreeding   Breeding between closely related individuals. The most extreme form of inbreeding is self-fertilization, which occurs in some plants. In animals mating between siblings or between parents and offspring is generally the closest form of inbreeding. Inbreeding increases homozygosity so that deleterious recessive genes are expressed more often in the phenotype, and decreases heterozygosity and hence the potential genetic variability of the population. There is also a general lowering of vigor in inbred stock (*inbreeding depression*), which is especially pronounced amongst normally outbreeding populations. In human societies there are usually cultural restraints on marriage between close relatives. *Compare* outbreeding.

inbreeding depression   *See* inbreeding.

incisor   A tooth in the very front of the jaw of a mammal. It has a single crown and root and is usually chisel-shaped with a sharp cutting edge. Most mammals have four incisors on the upper jaw and four on the lower jaw.

inclusive fitness   An indirect benefit of ALTRUISM in which the altruistic behavior of an individual does not benefit the individual itself but it does increase the frequency of some of the individual's genes in the population. It is seen in HAPLO-DIPLOID SPECIES (e.g. in the HYMENOPTERA) where the ratio of females to males is 3 to 1 and females take more care of female larvae than male larvae.

incompatibility   **1.** The rejection of grafts, transfusions, or transplants between animals or plants of different genetic composition.
2. A mechanism in flowering plants that prevents fertilization and development of an embryo following pollination by the same or a genetically identical individual. It is due to interaction between genes in the pollen grain and those in the stigma, in such a way that the pollen is either unable to grow or grows more slowly on the stigma. It results in self-sterility, thus preventing inbreeding.
3. A genetically determined mechanism in some fungi that prevents sexual fusion between individuals of the same race or strain.

incomplete dominance   *See* co-dominance.

incus (anvil)   The anvil-like bone forming the middle ear ossicle in mammals. It is homologous with the QUADRATE bone of other vertebrates.

independent assortment   The law, formulated by MENDEL, that genes segregate independently at meiosis so that any one combination of alleles is as likely to appear in the offspring as any other combination. The work of T. H. MORGAN later showed that genes are linked together on chromosomes and so tend to be inherited in groups. The law of independent assortment therefore only applies to genes on different chromosomes as it is the maternal and paternal chromosomes that are randomly sorted into gametes at meiosis. *See* linkage; Mendel's laws.

index fossil   *See* zone fossil.

indicator fossil   *See* zone fossil.

indigenous   Describing an organism that is native to an area, rather than introduced.

individual selection   Selection operating on individuals that favors characters beneficial to the reproductive success of an individual, regardless of the effect on the group or species. Individual selection produces adaptations and occurs over a generational time scale. *Compare* species selection. *See also* kin selection; group selection.

induced response   A change in the phenotype, resulting in an improvement in growth, reproduction, or survival, in response to a specific environmental signal.

industrial melanism   An increase in dark forms, for example in the peppered moth (*Biston betularia*), in industrial soot-polluted environments. Natural selection against normal pale forms by predators results in dark offspring being at a selective advantage in such environments. This results in an increase in the numbers of the better camouflaged dark forms.

It is one of the most widely studied examples of cryptic coloration in animals and an excellent example of transient POLYMORPHISM. The first black (melanic) forms were noticed in Manchester, England in 1848 and by the late 1890s, 98% of the moths in these populations were black. The resting black forms in the day were protected from predators (mainly birds) by the soot-blackened trees and rocks. In con-

trast, before industrialization had blackened the environment, the pale forms of the moth had been protected from predators by the presence of light-colored lichens. The pale forms were soon killed off by the pollution.

In the mid-1950s, Bernard KETTLEWELL carried out investigations in Dorset, England in a particular rural area where the tree trunks were light colored and encrusted with pale lichens and the moth population was pale-colored. He released equal numbers of pale and black forms. Of a total of 190 moths captured by birds, 164 were black forms and 26 were pale moths. In a different experiment in which hundreds of marked moths were used of each type, twice as many pale moths as melanic moths were captured, showing that the black moths were more easily seen by predators. The experiments were reversed in a polluted wood near Birmingham, England, where the dark moth prevailed and the results were the reverse of the experiments carried out in Dorset. In industrial areas that have been cleaned up and pollution controls imposed, the population has shifted back to the pale morph.

infinite allele model   (unique mutation model)   The assumption that every new mutation is unique and does not already exist in the population.

initiation factors   *See* translation.

innate behavior   *See* instinct.

innominate artery   An artery in mammals and some birds that arises from the arch of the aorta and divides to form the right carotid and right subclavian arteries. In fish, the innominate arteries arising from the ventral aorta divide into the first and second pairs of afferent branchial arteries. *See* aortic arches.

Insecta   The largest class of arthropods and the largest in the animal kingdom. Most insects can fly. The body is characteristically divided into a head, thorax, and abdomen. The head bears a pair of antennae, compound eyes, and simple eyes (ocelli). The MOUTHPARTS are modified in different way according to the diet. The thorax bears three pairs of five-jointed legs and, typically, two pairs of wings. The abdomen is usually limbless. Most insects are terrestrial and respiration is carried out by tracheae with segmentally arranged spiracles. Excretion is by Malpighian tubules. Usually the life history includes METAMORPHOSIS but in some metamorphosis is incomplete – the larvae (nymphs) resemble the adult and there is no pupal stage. Many insects are beneficial, being pollinators of flowers and predators of pests; others are harmful, being pests of crops, disease carriers, and destroyers of clothes, furniture, and buildings.

The most primitive insects were wingless and evolved in the early and middle Devonian, for example, *Rhyniella praecursor* discovered in the Rhynie Chert of Scotland. They represent the order Collembola (springtails) that probably scavenged in the organic detritus. Some may have been herbivores. The first dramatic adaptive radiation of winged insects took place in the CARBONIFEROUS and by its end, a number of familiar groups were established. The earliest included primitive cockroaches (order Orthoptera) and dragonflies (e.g. *Homoioptera*) (*see* Odonata). By the end of the Permian period, most of the modern forms had begun to appear and dominated the air. They included lacewings, beetles, stoneflies, mayflies, cicadas, and thrips. About ten insect orders that evolved in that period became extinct during geological events at the end of the Permian.

In the Mesozoic, true bugs, flies, caddis flies, ants, and earwigs evolved in the next large adaptive radiation in the CRETACEOUS and in the CENOZOIC, butterflies, moths, and bees evolved. The insects were rapidly evolving in parallel with the evolution of flowering plants (*see* Angiospermophyta; Hymenoptera). The fossil remains include wings, and also pupal cases, larval chambers, and borings in fossil wood. Many have been found preserved in Baltic AMBER of the Oligocene.

The oldest fossils of primitive dragonflies are over 300 million years old and have wings that are almost identical to present-day dragonflies. DNA sequence analysis shows that shrimp genes (*see* Crustacea) expressed in specialized limbs used as gills and fruitfly genes expressed in wing development are highly conserved, indicating that insect wings developed from specialized limbs used to help primitive invertebrates obtain oxygen. *See also* Coleoptera; Dermaptera; Dictyoptera; Diptera; Hemiptera; Hymenoptera; Lepidoptera; Siphonaptera.

Insectivora An order of small primitive insectivorous or omnivorous and generally nocturnal mammals, e.g. *Sorex* (shrew), *Erinaceus* (hedgehog), and *Talpa* (mole). Insectivora have a long tapering snout with sensitive vibrissae and numerous small teeth with pointed cusps for crushing insects. Most have five-clawed digits and locomotion is plantigrade.

The oldest fossil mammals have been found in the Jurassic and Triassic. They resembled the present-day Insectivora, feeding probably on insects, many of them being shrewlike, for example, *Eozostrodon* and *Megazostrodon*. The Insectivora are the ancestral group from which all the main groups of mammals evolved in the Cenozoic, 'The Age of Mammals'. The fossil *Deltatheridium* resembles a present-day opossum and may have been a possible ancestor of the kangaroo. The heterodont dentition of mammals had already evolved. *See* Eutheria; Mammalia.

instinct A response to an external stimulus that an animal is born with and performs involuntarily, i.e. *innate behavior*. Instinct provides an animal with adaptive responses that have evolved over a long time and appear the very first time the stimulus is perceived. Usually instinctive responses are fixed stereotyped movements that are the same in all individuals of the species every time they are performed. Instinctive responses are most important in animals with short lifespans and little or no parental care and which have little opportunity to modify their behavior as a result of experience. Also, when it is essential for immediate action to be taken in response to a particular stimulus, it is an advantage for these actions to be instinctive. For example, the alarm calls of birds given when a predator approaches are performed instinctively whereas the courtship song is learnt by listening to other birds.

intensity of selection A measure of how many individuals in a population die because they are not as well adapted as the fittest members in the population.

interglacial *See* Ice Age.

internal environment The medium surrounding the body cells of multicellular animals, i.e. the intercellular fluid. In vertebrates its composition is kept relatively constant by the mechanisms of HOMEOSTASIS.

interphase The stage in the CELL CYCLE when the nucleus is not in a state of division. Interphase is divisible into various stages each characterized by a differing physiological activity.

introgression *See* introgressive hybridization.

introgressive hybridization (introgression) The introduction of genetic material from one gene pool to another by hybridization and subsequent backcrossing to one or other of the parents. It is thought that *hybrid speciation* involves a number of generations of introgression. It forms the basis of most livestock- and crop-breeding programs.

intron A noncoding DNA sequence that occurs between coding sequences (exons) in many eukaryote genes. Mature RNA does not contain introns, these being removed during the transcription process by SPLICING. Some introns are spliced by an autocatalytic process in which the RNA acts as its own enzyme (*see* ribozyme). However, in the case of mRNA in the nucleus the process is regulated by a complex of proteins called a *spliceosome*. Different mRNAs can be produced from a DNA transcript by the splicing together of different exons – a process known as *alternative splicing*.

The function and evolution of introns is a highly contentious subject. One view is that by acting as 'spacers' for exons in mRNA they enable *exon shuffling* – recombination or rearrangement of exons – and hence the rapid evolution of proteins with different combinations of functional groups. Another view is that they represent SELFISH DNA, which confers no advantage on the host. It is now known that introns also occur in some bacteria, particularly Cyanobacteria, in ARCHAEA and even in certain viruses. *Compare* exon.

inversion *See* chromosome mutation.

invertebrate Any animal that does not possess a vertebral column. Invertebrates (the term is a general one, not used in zoological classification) include such widely differing animals as cnidarians, mollusks, worms, and arthropods (including insects).

Iron Age *See* Neolithic.

island continents *See* zoogeographical region.

isogamy The sexual fusion of gametes of similar size and form. It occurs in fungi and some protoctists.

isolating mechanism Structural, physiological, behavioral, genetic, geographical, or other factors that restrict the interbreeding of one population with another and cause REPRODUCTIVE ISOLATION. The development of isolating mechanisms promotes the formation of new varieties and species. *See* prezygotic isolation; postzygotic isolation.

isomorphism A condition seen in certain algae (e.g. *Ulva*, the sea lettuce) in which the alternating generations of the life cycle are morphologically identical. *Compare* heteromorphism.

iteroparous Having several discrete reproductive structures in a lifetime.

J

Java man   *See* Homo erectus.

jawless fishes   *See* Agnatha.

jellyfish   *See* Scyphozoa.

Johanson, Donald Carl (1943–)
American paleoanthropologist. In 1973 Johanson led his first expedition to Hadar about 100 miles northeast of Addis Ababa, Ethiopia. There he found a hominid knee joint. The following year he discovered further remains of a new species of fossil primate that challenged the existing theories of the evolution of modern man (*Homo sapiens*) and other hominids. The remains were reconstructed to form, remarkably, a complete skeleton, revealing a female hominid about three and a half feet tall with a bipedal stance and a relatively small brain. The fossil proved to be some 3 million years old, making it the oldest known fossil member of the human tribe. Johanson named it *Australopithecus afarensis*, after the Afar triangle of northeast Ethiopia where the find was made. The skeleton is popularly called 'Lucy', prompted by the Beatles' song 'Lucy in the Sky with Diamonds', which was playing in the camp site of Johanson's team on the evening following their discovery.

During the 1975 season Johanson's team made another dramatic find. Scattered in a single hillside were more than 350 fossil pieces from a group of thirteen men, women, and children, all dating from the same time as Lucy. The 'first family', as it was later called, was Johanson's last major find at Hadar. Following the 1976 expedition a series of military coups, civil wars, and famines closed Ethiopia to scientific expeditions.

The findings of Johanson's team were published in 1979. Johanson's account of the discovery of Lucy was published as *Lucy: The Beginnings of Humankind* (with Maitland A. Edey; 1981). Johanson and Edey have also written *Blueprints: Solving the Mystery of Evolution* (1989).

jumping gene   *See* transposon.

junk DNA   Repetitive noncoding DNA that apparently has no useful function. *See* selfish DNA.

Jurassic   Named for the Jura Mountains of Switzerland, the middle period of the MESOZOIC era, 215–145 mya. In Britain, the Jurassic rocks were originally called 'lias', meaning 'layers' and 'oolite'. *Oolites* were so named because they contain spherical rock particles that have grown concentrically around a nucleus (a sand grain or piece of shell, for example). The *Lias* consisted of alternate beds of clay and limestone, above which were thick layers of oolitic limestone. These beds spread from the northeast of England to southern England. In Europe the Lower, Middle, and Upper Jurassic are divided into three distinct parts: the Lias, the Dogger (oolitic limestone), and the Malm (oolitic limestone).

The climate in the Jurassic period was warm and humid, and there was a widespread expansion of forests, which produced thick deposits of coal. The Jurassic has been described by botanists as the 'Age of Cycads' (*see* Cycadophyta). The seed ferns declined and the cycads and conifers increased in number and diversified. However, the Jurassic is best known as the 'Age of the Dinosaurs', which are the most familiar and spectacular fossils. The DI-NOSAURS were becoming large and abundant. Fossils of ARCHAEOPTERYX (part bird, part dinosaur), the first frog, and the first mammals have been discovered in Jurassic rocks. In the seas, new types of phytoplankton evolved and extensive tropical reefs developed from new coral species. AMMONITES and BELEMNITES flourished: the ammonites in particular have been used as ZONE FOSSILS, because they evolved very rapidly and became very widespread. The BRACHIOPODA still flour-ished but there were only two groups: the rhynconellids and the terebratlids. Echinoderms, lamellibranchs (*see* Pelecypoda), and gastropods were also abundant. Bony fishes (teleosts) were also evolving rapidly (*see* Osteichthyes).

In the Jurassic period, the ancient supercontinent of PANGEA was beginning to break up and new seas and oceans started to form between what would become present-day Africa, North America, and South America. *See* geological time scale. *See also* Morrison formation; Bone Wars.

Kabwe skull *See Homo sapiens.*

karyogram (idiogram) The formalized layout of the KARYOTYPE of a species, often with the chromosomes arranged in a certain numerical sequence.

karyokinesis *See* mitosis.

karyotype The physical appearance of the chromosome complement of a given species. A species can be characterized by its karyotype since the number, size, and shape of chromosomes vary greatly between species but are fairly constant within species.

Kettlewell, Henry Bernard Davis (1907–79) British geneticist and lepidopterist. Kettlewell is best known for his work on the occurrence of melanism – black pigmentation in the epidermis of animals. In 1953 he set out to explain why, in the mid-19th century, certain moth species had a light coloration, which camouflaged them on such backgrounds as light tree trunks where they sat motionless during the day. However, by the 1950s, of 760 species of larger moths in Britain 70 had changed their light color and markings for dark or even totally black coloration. Kettlewell suspected that the success of the melanic form was linked with the industrial revolution and the consequent darkening of the trees by the vast amounts of smoke produced by the 19th-century factories. To test his hypothesis he released large numbers of the dark and light forms of the peppered moth (*Biston betularia*) in the polluted woods around Birmingham and in a distant unpolluted forest. As many of the released moths as possible were recaptured

and when the results were analyzed it was found that the light form had a clear advantage over the dark in the unpolluted forest but in the polluted Birmingham woods the result was just the opposite. From this Kettlewell concluded that if the environment of a moth changes so that it is conspicuous by day, then the species is ruthlessly hunted by predators until it mutates to a form better suited to its new environment. His work was seen as a convincing and dramatic confirmation of the Darwinian hypothesis of natural selection.

kidney One of a pair of major excretory organs of vertebrates, which may also function in osmoregulation (controlling the amount of water in the body cells). They are made up of nephrons (excretory units), which are responsible for the filtration and selective reabsorption of materials (water, mineral salts, glucose, etc.) and the production of (especially nitrogenous) waste. *See* mesonephros; metanephros; pronephros.

Kimura, Motoo (1924–94) Japanese population geneticist. From 1968 Kimura developed a cogent alternative to the neo-Darwinian synthesis as it emerged in the 1930s in the works of such scholars as J. B. S. Haldane. He gathered evidence to show that certain mutations can increase in a population without necessarily having any selective advantage. Kimura examined a number of mutant genes whose effects were not apparent in the phenotype and could be detected only by advanced chemical techniques. He found that adaptively they were neither better nor worse than the genes they replaced, concluding that, at the molecular level, most evolutionary changes are the result of 'random drift' of selectively equivalent mutant genes.

Kimura allowed that at the level of the phenotype evolution is basically Darwinian but insisted that the laws governing molecular evolution are clearly different. Such views have met with much opposition from Darwinians. They have argued that many of the apparently neutral mutations are, on closer examination, found to be selective; also many cases, such as human hemoglobin, do not seem to show the variants expected from Kimura's theory.

Kimura's formula   A formula for the amount of genetic variation that should be seen if it is solely a balance between MUTATION and STABILIZING SELECTION.

kinetochore   *See* centromere.

kinetosome   *See* basal body.

kingdom   Formerly, the highest ranking category in most classification systems. Most taxonomists today recognize the rank of DOMAIN as being higher than that of kingdom. *See* Five Kingdoms classification.

kin selection   Natural selection operating on a close genetic relative that can explain ALTRUISM. It occurs in groups of close genetic relatives where the BENEFIT to the relatives is greater than the COST to the individual (*Hamilton's rule*). *See also* group selection; species selection.

Kovalevski, Aleksandr Onufrievich (1840–1901) Russian zoologist and embryologist. One of Kovalevski's most notable contributions to zoological science and the fuller understanding of evolution lay in his demonstration that all multicellular animals display a common pattern of physiological development. His research into the embryology of primitive chordates, such as *Amphioxus* (the lancelet), *Balanoglossus* (the acorn worm), and the sea squirts, particularly his demonstration of the links between them and the craniates, provided the basis for later studies of the evolutionary history of the vertebrates and led to HAECKEL's theory that all multicellular animals are derived from a hypothetical ancestor with two cell layers.

K–T event   The period at the end of the CRETACEOUS marked by a MASS EXTINCTION, including the extinction of the dinosaurs. 'K' is the initial letter of 'Kreide', the German word for Cretaceous and 'T' is the initial letter for the Tertiary. It marked the end of the MESOZOIC. A number of theories exist to explain this mystery. One is the Alvarez event, which suggests that the Earth was hit by a meteorite, causing worldwide catastrophic effects (*see* Alvarez theory). Another is that there was volcanic activity on a massive scale. A third possibility is that the meteoric impact of the Yucatán Peninsula in Mexico triggered off the volcanic activity that also occurred at this time in India – the Deccan Traps (near the Seychelles) formed at the end of the Cretaceous consists of lava 1 km thick. Or it is possible that two meteorites struck the Earth in both of these areas at about the same time.

The gradualist theories of the K–T event envisage a sudden drop in sea level causing the climate to become cooler and drier making conditions very difficult for very large animals to thrive. Land bridges reappearing might have enabled more migrations of plants and animals, possibly bringing in diseases to new areas. Dinosaurs were already disappearing from Europe and the ammonites, for example, had already become extinct. The reason for this mass extinction may yet be found to embrace both gradualist and catastrophic theories.

Lacerta (lizard)   *See* SQUAMATA.

Laetoli footprints   A discovery by Mary LEAKEY in 1974 of footprints of two (or possibly three) individuals of *Australopithecus afarensis*. They were discovered at Laetoli in N Tanzania and dated about 3.6 mya. Their importance is a demonstration of evidence that early humans walked on two legs (*see* bipedalism). The big toes hardly diverged from the foot, in contrast to chimpanzees, that have very divergent big toes. The footprints were preserved as a result of being made in wet volcanic ash following a volcanic eruption. The ash dried rather like cement, so preserving the footprints.

lagging strand   *See* replication.

Lagomorpha   An order of herbivorous mammals that evolved in the EOCENE and includes the pikas (conies) (e.g. *Ochotona*), hares (e.g. *Lepus*) and rabbits (e.g. *Oryctolagus*). Lagomorphs resemble rodents, differing principally in the possession of two pairs of incisor teeth in the upper jaw, a small pair of peglike teeth lying behind the larger pair of chisel-like teeth.

They are believed to have evolved from an ancient group, the *mimotonids*, in Asia and North America (e.g. *Mimotona*). Rabbits and hares diversified in the Oligocene and early Miocene in North America. The first pikas appeared in Asia in the middle Oligocene and spread to North America and Europe in the Pliocene. *Compare* Rodentia. *See* Mammalia.

Lamarck, Jean Baptiste, Chevalier de (1744–1829) French biologist. Lamarck was originally employed as botanist at the Jardin du Roi until the institute was reorganized during the French Revolution. In the newly named Muséum National d'Histoire Naturelle he was placed in charge of animals without backbones – a group he later named 'invertebrates'. Lamarck wrote a seven-volume *Natural History of Invertebrates* (1815– 22). He was also interested in meteorology, geology, chemistry, and paleontology and his observations in these fields probably contributed to the formulation of his evolutionary theory, which he first put forward in *Zoological Philosophy* (1809). Until the late 1790s, he had believed that species remained unchanged, but fossil evidence, and his nonbelief in extinction, combined to change his mind. He saw evolution as a natural tendency to greater complexity and put forward four laws to explain how such complexity is brought about. The second law states that "the production of a new organ in an animal body results from a new need that continues to make itself felt," and the fourth law, for which he is best remembered, states that such acquired characteristics are inherited. A much-quoted example of this view is the neck of the giraffe, which, through stretching for the uppermost leaves, becomes gradually elongated, and this adaptation is passed on to its offspring. Today Lamarckism has largely been rejected in favor of DARWIN's theory of evolution by natural selection, especially in the light of knowledge gained about genetic mutation as a source of the variation on which Darwin's theory is based.

Lamarckism (transformism)   Lamarck's theory of evolution (1809) postulating that acquired characteristics can be inherited, so resulting in permanent changes in populations.

The classic example is the evolution of the long neck of the giraffe. Lamarck believed that giraffes with short necks stretched them to reach leaves higher up on the trees and so their offspring had slightly longer necks. He believed this was repeated in successive generations.

This theory, which was widely accepted during the 19th century, fell from favor with the rediscovery in 1900 of MENDEL's work on inheritance. This and subsequent genetic discoveries showed that characteristics are inherited at fertilization, and that inheritance is thus unaffected by the life of the organism. *Compare* natural selection.

lamellibranchs Bivalved molluscs, formerly in some classifications placed in class Lamellibranchiata and now grouped into class PELECYPODA, also known as Bivalvia.

lampbrush chromosome An extended chromosome structure found in the oocytes of certain animals, notably amphibians, during the prophase of MEIOSIS. In those species that show a great increase in nuclear and cytoplasmic volume during prophase, the lampbrush chromosomes may measure up to 1 mm in length and 0.02 mm in width. Such chromosomes consist of two central strands along which fine loops extend laterally. The loops are associated with an RNA matrix and are sites of active TRANSCRIPTION.

lamp shells *See* Brachiopoda.

land bridge A connection between two land masses, especially continents, that allows migration of plants and animals from one land mass to the other; for example, the Bering land bridge linking Alaska and Siberia across the Bering Strait. Before the widespread acceptance of CONTINENTAL DRIFT, the existence of former land bridges was often invoked to explain faunal and floral similarities between continents that are now widely separated. On a smaller scale, the term may be applied to land connections that have now been removed by recent tectonics or sea-level changes, for

example, between northern France and southeastern England.

Lankester, Sir Edwin Ray (1847–1929) British zoologist. Lankester was an ardent Darwinist, and his work on invertebrate morphology and embryology (e.g., of the mollusks) did much to strengthen arguments in favor of evolution. He believed that an inherited ability to learn played an important part in the evolution of humans, and he expounded this controversial idea in *The Significance of the Increased Size of the Cerebrum in Recent as Compared with Extinct Animals* (1899). Lankester was also one of the first to describe the protozoan parasites in the blood of vertebrate animals, a crucial step in the diagnosis and treatment of diseases such as malaria. His publications include both purely scientific works such as *Comparative Longevity in Man and the Lower Animals* (1870) and popular works such as *Science from an Easy Chair* (1910–12).

latent virus (provirus) A virus that can remain inactive in its host cell for a considerable period after initial infection. The viral nucleic acid becomes integrated in the host chromosome and multiplies with it. Eventual replication inside the host cell may be triggered by such factors as radiation and chemicals. An example of a latent virus is *Herpes simplex*, which causes cold sores. *See also* provirus.

Laurasia One of the two major blocks of land formed when PANGEA split at the end of the Permian, consisting of North America, Europe, and most of Asia except for India, i.e. north of the Himalayas. *See* Gondwana; continental drift.

Law of Constant Extinction *See* Red Queen effect.

Law of Independent Assortment *See* Mendel's laws.

Law of Segregation *See* Mendel's laws.

leading strand *See* replication.

Leakey, Louis Seymour Bazett (1903–72) British anthropologist and archeologist. Leakey was born at Kabete in Kenya. Apart from anthropological studies, notably of the Kikuyu people, he is best known for his excavations of fossils of early humans, notably in Tanzania's Olduvai Gorge. Here, in 1959, the jaw, skull, and huge teeth fragments of a species that Leakey called *Zinjanthropus* (*Australopithecus*) were uncovered by his wife Mary. The following year his son Jonathan discovered remains of the larger-brained *Homo habilis*. Both have been estimated at between 1 750 000 and 2 000 000 years old, but Leakey considered that only *H. habilis* was the true ancestor of modern humans, *Zinjanthropus* having died out, a view not shared by other researchers. Leakey also found, in western Kenya, remains of the earliest known hominid *Proconsul africanus*. Leakey's work not only provided evidence for the greater age of man but suggested that Africa, and not, as was previously thought, Asia, may have been the original center of human evolution.

Leakey, Richard Erskine (1944–) Kenyan anthropologist. Richard Leakey was born at Nairobi in Kenya, the son of the famous scholars Louis and Mary Leakey. His parents had spent much of their lives exploring the Rift Valley and working at Olduvai in Northern Tanzania. In contrast Leakey undertook his first field trip to the Omo valley in Ethiopia. In 1965 he shifted his interest to Lake Turkana in northern Kenya, concentrating his work in the Koobi Fora area. At the same time he was appointed to the directorship of the Kenya National Museum, Nairobi. In 1972 he made his first major find at Koobi Fora. This was a skull with a brain capacity of about 800 cm^3, given the number 1470. Leakey identified 1470 as *Homo* rather than an australopithecine precursor, and took it to be *Homo habilis*. The age of the skull, however, was in dispute, varying from 1.8 to 2.4 million years; the former age was eventually accepted. In 1975 a second skull was found, this time *Homo erectus*, a more advanced form than 1470. Leakey subsequently became interested in

conservation and, later, became active in Kenyan politics.

leeches *See* Hirudinea.

lek A territory that is defended by a male for displaying courtship behavior in the breeding season. This form of mating behaviour (*lekking*) occurs in bird species and some mammals. *See* sexual selection.

lemur *See* Primates; prosimians.

Lepidocarpus *See* Carboniferous.

Lepidodendron *See* Carboniferous.

Lepidoptera A large order of insects that evolved in the Jurassic, containing the butterflies and moths, characterized by a covering of scales, often brightly colored, over their wings and bodies. Mandibles are usually absent and the maxillae form a tube (proboscis) for sucking nectar or fruit juices. The wings are coupled together in flight. The larvae (caterpillars) are mostly herbivores; some are serious plant pests. Metamorphosis is complete, with a pupal stage (the chrysalis). Butterflies are diurnal, have slim bodies and clubbed antennae, and rest with the wings folded over the back. Moths are mostly nocturnal, never have clubbed antennae, and rest with the wings in various positions. In the Cretaceous, these pollinating insects evolved in parallel with the evolution of flowering plants.

Lepidosauria *See* Reptilia; Squamata.

leptosporangiate Describing the condition found in certain ferns in which the sporangium develops from a single initial cell. *See* Filicinophyta.

leptotene In MEIOSIS, the stage in early prophase I when the chromosomes, already replicated, start to condense and appear as fine threads, although sister chromatids are not yet distinct. The spindle starts to form around the intact nucleus.

Lias *See* Jurassic.

lichens Symbiotic associations between an alga or cyanobacterium (the *photobiont*) and a fungus (the *mycobiont*). They are slow-growing but can colonize areas too inhospitable for other plants. Usually the fungus is an ascomycete but occasionally it is a basidiomycete. Reproduction in lichens may be asexual by soredia (algal cells enclosed by fungal hyphae) or by sexual fungal spores, which can only survive if some algal cells are also present. Examples include *Peltigesa* and *Xanthoria*.

Lichens probably evolved in the Silurian, when the first colonization of the barren landscape by land plants began to take place. Their tolerance of cold conditions also enabled them to survive during glacial periods and they probably provided much-needed food (along with mosses) for reindeer, elk, oxon, and small herbivores of the PLEISTOCENE epoch.

life cycle The sequence of changes making up the span of an organism's life from the fertilization of gametes to the same stage in the subsequent generation. The cycle may involve only one form of the organism, as in higher animals and plants. In lower plants, and some animals, two or more different generations exist and there is an alternation of generations, usually between haploid and diploid forms. Various terms exist to describe the different types of life cycle and take into account which generation is dominant and whether the generations differ morphologically. *See also* polymorphism; diplobiontic; diplont; haplobiontic; haplont.

lineage An ancestor–descendant sequence of populations, cells, or genes.

linkage The occurrence of genes together on the same chromosome so that they tend to be inherited together and not independently. Groups of linked genes are termed *linkage groups* and the number of linkage groups of a particular organism is equal to its haploid chromosome number. Linkage groups can be broken up by crossing over at meiosis to give new combinations of genes. Two genes close together on a chromosome are more strongly linked, i.e. there is less chance of a cross over between them, than two genes further apart on the chromosome. Linked genes are symbolized Ab...Y/aB...y, indicating that Ab...Y are on one homolog while aB...y are on the other homolog. *See* cross-over value.

linkage disequilibrium A common term for the deviation in HAPLOTYPE frequency in a population from the value it would have if all loci were combined at random. If there is no deviation, the population is said to be in *linkage equilibrium*. Linkage disequilibrium can exist because equilibrium has not yet been reached, or can be due to nonrandom mating, GENETIC DRIFT, or epistatic fitness interactions operating in natural selection. It can be advantageous or disadvantageous. *See* epistasis; recombination.

linkage equilibrium *See* linkage disequilibrium.

linkage map *See* chromosome map.

Linnaean classification A hierarchical system of classification invented by LINNAEUS in the 18th century in which individuals are assigned to a species, genus, family, order, class, phylum, and kingdom. *See* binomial nomenclature.

Linnaeus, Carolus (1707–78) Swedish botanist. Linnaeus began studying medicine at the University of Lund in 1727, transferring to Uppsala University the following year. While at college he investigated the newly proposed theory that plants exhibit sexuality and, by 1730, had begun formulating a taxonomic system based on stamens and pistils. He extended his knowledge of plants on travels through Lapland in 1732, and around Europe from 1733 to 1735.

In 1735 he settled in Holland and published his first major work, *Systema Naturae* (The System of Nature), in which he systematically arranged the animal, plant, and mineral kingdoms. In it, he classified whales and similar creatures as mammals and recognized man's affinity to the apes to the extent of naming the orang-utan *Homo troglodytes*. The flowering plants were divided into classes, depending on the number and arrangement of their stamens, and subdivived into orders, according to the number of their pistils. Linnaeus's lasting contribution to TAXONOMY was his introduction, in 1749, of BINOMIAL NOMENCLATURE, which he applied in *Species Plantarum* (1753; Species of Plants) by giving each plant a generic and a specific name.

littoral 1. The zone of the seashore (the beach) between the high and low tide mark. The littoral deposits consist of sand and/or pebbles, sometimes boulders, rarely mud. The term is also applied to organisms living in this zone. *Compare* benthic; sublittoral.
2. The zone between the water's edge and a depth of about six meters in a pond or lake. Rooted hydrophytes, both emergent and submergent, are found in this zone. *Compare* profundal; sublittoral.

liverworts   *See* Hepaticae.

living fossil   Modern organisms with anatomical or physiological features that are normally characteristic of extinct ancestral species. They are often associated with highly restricted, remote, and almost unchanging environments, and so evolve very slowly. Examples are the deep-sea fish, the coelacanth, and the *Ginkgo* tree.

lizards   *See* Squamata.

local mate competition   *See* sex ratio.

locus   (*pl.* loci) The position of a particular gene, or one of its alleles, on all homologous chromosomes.

lophodont   *See* horse evolution; molar.

lophophore   *See* Brachiopoda; Bryozoa.

Lubbock, John, 1st Baron Avebury (1834–1913) British biologist, politician, and banker. Lubbock benefited greatly from his contact with DARWIN from an early age. He left school at 14 to enter his father's banking business and his knowledge of natural history was almost entirely self-taught. His first published papers were on specimens collected by Darwin during his voyage on HMS *Beagle* and he also provided illustrations for Darwin's work.

A convinced evolutionist, Lubbock became interested in primitive humans and the origin of civilization. He introduced the terms 'Paleolithic' and 'Neolithic' for the Old and New Stone Ages respectively, and also found the first fossil remains of the musk ox in Britain, providing evidence for the existence of an ice age. However, Lubbock's best-remembered biological researches are those on insect behavior. He set up an artificial ants' nest bounded by two panes of glass, which enabled him to study the ants without undue disturbance. In this way he was the first to witness the 'farming' of aphids by ants. He also studied insect vision and the detection of color by bees, and he tested insect intelligence by setting up obstacle courses and mazes. His observations are collected in *Ants, Bees and Wasps* (1882).

Lucretius   (*c.* 95 BC–*c.* 55 BC) Roman philosopher. Little is known of the life of Lucretius, who was born in Rome, apart from his materialistic (Epicurean) philosophy as set forth in his *De rerum natura* (On the Nature of Things), published in 56 BC. One of his main aims was to demonstrate the natural origin of the universe and its physical, biological, and social development, in which he may be said to have anticipated modern evolutionists. Dismissing ideas of the immortality of man, he denounced beliefs in divine guidance as the one great source of human misery and evil.

Lucretius also believed in the atomic structure of all living things, although he also extended this to include the mind, wind, etc. He recognized the virtual indestructibility of matter, had a notion of gravity and of the nature and speed of light, and demonstrated that the Earth is but one of many worlds in a boundless Universe. Lucretius also recognized the incessant struggle for existence in the natural world, and in this again anticipated Darwin and other evolutionists.

Lucy *See Australopithecus afarensis*; human evolution; Johanson.

Lumbricus A genus of earthworms that burrow in soil and whose only appendages are a few chaetae. The burrow walls are stiffened with mucus secreted from the skin and the worms feed by swallowing soil and digesting the organic matter in it. These activities are important in soil aeration and drainage. *See also* OLIGOCHAETA.

lung The respiratory organ of air-breathing vertebrates, including aquatic forms (such as turtles and whales). A pair of lungs is situated in the thorax. Air enters and leaves each lung through a bronchus. The lung contains a thin moist membrane of large surface area, folded so that it occupies relatively little volume. Gases can diffuse readily through this membrane, between the air on one side and the blood in the capillaries that are on the other side. In amphibians and reptiles the lung is a simple elastic sac with folds on its inner walls (deeper in reptiles) to increase the surface area. In birds and mammals the lung has a spongy texture. In mammals the bronchus branches repeatedly into bronchioles, which end in clusters of alveoli, where the main exchange of gases occurs. Lungs contain no muscular tissue. They are inflated either by air being pumped from the mouth cavity (amphibians), by the action of intercostal muscles (reptiles, birds, and mammals), or by the action of the diaphragm (mammals). Lungs are deflated by their own elasticity.

In lungfish the lung is an outgrowth from the pharynx, thought to be homologous with the SWIM BLADDER of teleosts. In birds, tubes from the bronchi lead to air sacs between the organs of the body and in the larger bones. This provides highly efficient ventilation of the lungs during flight. The mantle and mantle cavity of terrestrial gastropods (*see* Gastropoda) is also termed a lung and has the same function. *See* respiration.

lungfish *See* Dipnoi.

Lycopodium (club moss) A genus of lycopods (*see* LYCOPODOPHYTA). Species of *Lycopodium* are generally found in moist habitats, and have both creeping and erect stems. Numerous small leaves (microphylls) are borne spirally and the fertile leaves (sporophylls) are borne in strobili.

Lycopodophyta (Lycophyta; Lycopsida) A phylum of spore-bearing vascular plants containing about 1000 living species, most of which constitute two genera: *Lycopodium* and *Selaginella*. There are five orders, three of which – the Lycopodiales, Selaginellales, and Isoetales – contain both living and fossil representatives. The remaining orders – Lepidodendrales and Pleuromeiales – are represented only by fossils. The Pleuromeiales were known in the Triassic and are intermediate between the Lepidodendrales and Isoetales. The extinct trees of the genus *Lepidodendron* were once distributed widely and contributed largely to the coal seams of the CARBONIFEROUS. Living club mosses are typically small plants that favor damp habitats; some are epiphytes. They have shoots bearing microsporophylls and may be either homosporous or heterosporous. They differ from the whisk ferns (*see* Psilophyta) in having roots, and differ from other vascular plants in having a dichotomous rather than monopodial branching system.

Lyell, Sir Charles (1797–1875) British geologist. He originally studied law and was called to the bar in 1825, but because of poor eyesight he turned increasingly to geological investigation. During the following years Lyell traveled extensively in Europe, his studies culminating in the publication of his three-volume masterpiece *The Principles of Geology* (1830– 33). This was to be published in 11 editions in his lifetime and established him as a leading authority. Lyell established the doctrine of UNIFORMITARIANISM already stated by James Hutton and John Playfair, and the first volume, published in 1830, was subtitled 'Being an Attempt to Explain the

Former Changes of the Earth's Surface by Reference to Causes Now in Operation.' Lyell explicitly rejected the work of Abraham Werner, in which some unique deluge is the chief agent producing the Earth's topography. Uniformitarianism also involved the rejection of the catastrophism theory followed by zoologists such as CUVIER to explain dramatic changes in the flora and fauna of the Earth. Instead Lyell saw the crust of the Earth as being shaped by forces operating over unlimited time. Lyell contributed considerable knowledge and analysis to geology. In 1833 he introduced the structure of the Tertiary in which it spread from the Cretaceous to the emergence of humans and was subdivided on the basis of the ratio of living to extinct species – Eocene, Miocene, Pliocene, and Pleistocene. His other works included *Elements of Geology* (1838) describing European rocks and fossils from the most recent to the oldest then known. Charles DARWIN, in his work *Origin of Species* (1859), drew heavily on Lyell's *Principles*. Lyell did not at first share Darwin's views and it was not until the tenth edition of the *Principles* (1867–68) that he expressed any support for evolutionary theory. Even then in his *The Antiquity of Man* (1863), which was published in four editions before 1873, Lyell denied that the theory could be applied to humans.

Lysenko, Trofim Denisovich (1898– 1976) Ukrainian agriculturalist. Lysenko began work at the Kirovabad Experimental Station in 1925, after completing his studies at the Kiev Agricultural Institute. In 1929 he became a senior specialist in the physiology department at the Institute of Selection and Genetics in Odessa and in the same year he first claimed success using vernalized grain on his father's farm. *Vernalization* is the cold treatment of soaked grains and it promotes flowering in springsown plants that might otherwise take two years to flower. Lysenko claimed that the effects of vernalization could be inherited and so the treatment need not be repeated each year. This reversion to a belief in the inheritance of acquired characteristics was the hallmark of his career, and he is remembered for his single-minded application of this belief to Soviet biology. The validity of the chromosome theory of inheritance had been generally accepted in the West, especially since the publication of T. H. MORGAN's results. Naturally, many Soviet scientists also followed the MENDEL–Morgan theory of heredity, notably Nikolai Vavilov, who was president of the Lenin All-Union Academy of Agricultural Sciences and head of the Institute of Plant Protection. Vavilov was publicly discredited by Lysenko and in 1940 exiled to Siberia, Lysenko taking over his scientific posts. Other dissenting scientists were brought into line at the genetics debate held at the Lenin All-Union Academy of Agricultural Sciences in 1948. At this meeting Lysenko announced that he had the backing of the central committee of the communist party, and a motion was passed directing all textbooks and courses to be changed in accordance with his views. This state of affairs continued until 1964, and Lysenko was finally ousted from his powerful position in 1965.

lysosome An ORGANELLE of plant and animal cells that contains a range of digestive enzymes whose destructive potential necessitates their separation from the rest of the cytoplasm. They have many important functions in different organisms; they may contribute to food vacuoles, for example, in *Ameba*. They are also involved in destruction of other organelles within the cytoplasm, or even entire cells when they are old or damaged, or they are involved in development, for example, the loss of tadpole tails during metamorphosis.

M

macroevolution An imprecise term sometimes used to refer to evolution over long periods of time or of large groups of taxa above the species level. An example is the adaptive radiation of vertebrates. There is some question as to whether macroevolution is microevolution happening over a long time scale (the *extrapolative theory of macromutation*) or whether it requires large-scale mechanisms such as macromutation or paedomorphosis. The fossil record for the evolution of mammals from reptiles shows gradual adaptational changes consistent with natural selection and there is also fossil evidence for the gradual evolution of birds from reptiles. However, other macroevolutionary changes could have been brought about by sudden nonadaptive events. *See also* Aves; Mammalia; punctuated equilibrium; phyletic gradualism. *Compare* microevolution.

macromutation A mutation that produces a large effect, resulting in a phenotype that differs widely from the usual variations within a population.

magma Molten rock in the Earth's crust. It also has solid and gaseous components. When magma moves toward the crust, the increased pressure increases the gaseous component, often resulting in a volcanic eruption.

male competition *See* sexual selection.

Malthus, Thomas Robert (1766–1834) English economist. Malthus grew up at a time when many people believed that humans were progressing toward an ideal society. His father was a keen follower of the philosophy of the French philosopher Jean-Jacques Rousseau. Malthus suggested that any technological advances would always be accompanied by increases in the human population, and, moreover, that while the means of subsistence would tend to increase arithmetically, population growth would be geometric. Thus, overall the human condition would remain unimproved and numbers would still be controlled by famine, disease, and war. Others had already proposed similar ideas, but Malthus presented his case so well in *An Essay on the Principle of Population* (1798) that much controversy was aroused. Many people were later to use his arguments as an excuse for neglecting social reform and to justify laissez-faire. The population essay later helped Alfred WALLACE and Charles DARWIN reach the theory of evolution by natural selection.

Mammalia The class of vertebrates that contains the most successful tetrapods. The mammals are homoiothermic, with an insulating body covering of hair and usually with sweat and sebaceous glands in the skin. The socketed teeth are differentiated into incisors, canines, and grinding premolars and molars. Mammals have relatively large brains and external ears (pinnae), and three auditory ossicles in the middle ear. Oxygenated and deoxygenated blood are separated in the four-chambered heart and a diaphragm assists in respiratory movements. Typically, the young are born alive and are suckled on milk secreted by mammary glands. A bony secondary palate allows the retention of food in the mouth while breathing. There are two subclasses: *Prototheria*, which comprises a single order (MONOTREMATA) containing all the egg-laying mammals; and *Theria*, which contains all the mammals that bear live young. The subclass Theria is divided into two infraclasses: METATHERIA, which comprises the marsupials (pouched mammals); and EUTHERIA, which contains the placental mammals.

The mammals evolved from the mammal-like reptiles of the Permian. The COTYLOSAURS (stem reptiles) evolved into distinctive groups: the diapsids were the ARCHOSAURS (or 'Ruling Reptiles') and the synapsids (*see* Reptilia), which evolved into the order PELYCOSAURIA (carnivores with powerful teeth) by the end of the Carboniferous. The name 'Pelycosauria' means 'basin reptile', referring to the basin-shaped pelvis of these animals. They were mainly carnivores. Some retained a lizardlike appearance but others were characterized by the development of tall spines protruding from their backbones enclosed in highly vascularized skin forming a 'sail', e.g. *Dimetrodon*. The sail may have been used for signaling purposes. However, certain authorities believe that it functioned as a temperature-regulation device. The sail absorbed heat when the Sun rose in the morning, enabling hunting activities to begin. It was used as a fan to cool the animal when the desert heat was at its maximum. Pelycosaurs died out before the end of the Permian, but some had already evolved into the order *Therapsida*, which were mammal-like reptiles. The therapsids flourished in the Permian. There were lizardlike forms, but an ADAPTIVE RADIATION occurred throughout the world to produce burrowing forms, enormous rhinoceros-like forms, and carnivorous wolflike animals. As with most other animal and plant groups at the end of the Permian, most of them became extinct.

The two suborders of the Therapsida that survived were the *dicynodonts* and the CYNODONTS. They flourished in the Triassic and gradually became more mammal-like, developing specialized heterodont teeth, hairy coats, and suckling their young. The dicynodonts were mainly herbivores, ranging in size from rabbitlike animals to enormous animals as big as hippopotamuses. The cynodonts were mainly wolflike carnivores, and this group evolved more effective methods of chewing and gave rise to the true mammals.

By the end of the Triassic, the true mammals had a single lower jawbone (the DENTARY) as well as other typical mammalian features, including two OCCIPITAL CONDYLES instead of one (in Reptilia) and articulation of the dentary directly with the skull instead of through the QUADRATE. Early mammals resembled shrews (e.g. *Megazostrodon* of the Triassic) or opossums, and persisted through the Mesozoic, albeit as an insignificant group, until they became the dominant animals throughout the Cenozoic Era – the 'Age of Mammals'.

The mass extinction at the end of the Cretaceous wiped out all the larger land animals – the dinosaurs, flying reptiles, marine reptiles, and many other groups, including AMMONITES and BELEMNITES and many orders of fish. The environment drastically changed: oceans cooled and tropical forests were replaced by open grasslands. Mammals evolved to occupy all the niches vacated by the Mesozoic animals. Their homoiothermy enabled them to survive colder conditions and to develop efficient methods of locomotion. In the late Jurassic, the MONOTREMATA evolved. Insectivores and marsupials (*see* Metatheria) evolved in the Cretaceous (the marsupial–placental split). From the beginning of the Cenozoic, many new orders of mammals emerged, including whales, bats, horses, dogs, cows, elephants, etc. By the EOCENE, there were almost 100 families. Some groups were very unusual by today's standards, e.g. the now extinct titanotheres (*see* Perissodactyla), MULTITUBERCULATES, CONDYLARTHS, AMBLYPODS, TILLODONTS, and TAENIODONTS.

Eventually, all the now-familiar groups of mammals became established and diversified leading to the present-day mammals, culminating with the evolution of humans, who, as a result of their activities, may have a more profound effect on the Earth than the changing climates of the past had on their own evolution. *See also* macroevolution.

Mandibulata In some classifications, a

phylum of arthropods containing the insects, centipedes, and millipedes. Members of the Mandibulata are characterized by having mouthparts (mandibles) adapted for crushing and grinding food, a feature they share with crustaceans. Unlike crustaceans, they possess one rather than two pairs of antennae. See Arthropoda.

Manicouagan event   See Triassic.

Margulis, Lynn   (1938–) American biologist. With the success of modern biochemistry, genetics, and cytology it became apparent that there was a fundamental division in nature between cells with nuclei (EUKARYOTES) and those without (PROKARYOTES). In terms of metabolism, chemistry, genetics, and structure, higher organisms differ radically from bacteria and cyanobacteria, the prokaryotes. Margulis studied the question of how eukaryotes evolve and her answer, in terms of hereditary endosymbiosis, was fully formulated in her *Origin of Eukaryotic Cells* (1970). She argued that eukaryotes are basically colonies of prokaryotes and that such features of cells as mitochondria were once free-living bacteria but have, 'over a long period of time, established a hereditary symbiosis with ancestral hosts that ultimately evolved into animal cells." Similarly she proposes that chloroplasts and flagella evolved in the same way.

The actual evolutionary sequence proposed begins with a 'fermenting bacterium' entering into a symbiotic relationship with some oxygen-using bacteria, the first mitochondria. Such a complex might join with 'a second group of symbionts, flagellum-like bacteria comparable to modern spirochaetes,' which, attached to the host's surface, would greatly increase its motility. See endosymbiont theory.

As Margulis points out, the proof for such an imaginative model requires that the cell organelles are separated, cultured independently, and then brought back into symbiotic association again. So far no one has managed to grow an organelle outside the cell. In 1982 Margulis published (with Karlene Schwartz) *Five Kingdoms*, "a cat-alog of the world's living diversity." See Five Kingdoms classification.

marker gene   A gene of known location and function, which can therefore be used to establish the relative positions and functions of other genes. During gene transfer, a marker gene may be linked to the transferred gene to determine whether or not the transfer has been successful. See chromosome map; genetic engineering.

Marsh, Othniel Charles   (1831–99) American paleontologist. Marsh worked at Yale, from 1866 until his death, as professor of vertebrate paleontology, the first to hold such a post in America. From 1870 onward Marsh organized and led a number of paleontological expeditions to parts of North America, during which were unearthed a large number of fossils of considerable importance in enlarging the knowledge of extinct North American vertebrates. In 1871 Marsh discovered the first American pterodactyl, as well as remains of Cretaceous toothed birds and ancestors of the horse. These finds were described in a number of monographs, published by the U.S. Government. Marsh's other publications include *Fossil Horses of America* (1874) and *The Dinosaurs of North America* (1896). Marsh's appointment as head of the U.S. Geological Survey's vertebrate paleontology section in 1882 contributed toward bitter rivalry with his fellow paleontologist Edward COPE. See Bone Wars.

marsupials   See Metatheria.

mass extinction   Massive and rapid extinction that kills many species simultaneously and leads to a dramatic change in flora and fauna. There are thought to have been about 20 mass extinctions in the history of the earth and five clear mass extinctions have been identified: End Ordovician (about 440 mya) in which 60% of marine invertebrate genera disappeared; Late Devonian (about 370 mya); End Permian (about 280 mya) was the largest in which 80% of marine invertebrate genera disappeared; End Triassic (about 200 mya); End Cretaceous (about 65 mya) in which 50% of marine invertebrate genera and the dinosaurs disappeared. There are various theories for possible causes of mass extinctions. The End Permian may have been caused by increased atmospheric carbon dioxide levels and the End Cretaceous may have been caused by an asteroid collision. *See* Alvarez theory; K–T event. *See* extinction.

Mauer mandible   *See Homo sapiens.*

maximum likelihood method   A method for estimating the phylogenetic tree that is the most likely to have occurred, given the observed data and the assumed model of evolution. *See* phylogeny.

maximum parsimony   *See* parsimony; phylogeny.

Maynard Smith, John (1920–   ) British biologist. Maynard Smith, known to a wide public for his lucid *Theory of Evolution* (1958), emerged as one of the leading theorists of evolution in the postwar years. Using concepts taken from the theory of games formulated by the US mathematician John von Neumann in the 1940s, he introduced in the 1970s the idea of an evolutionary stable strategy (ESS). Assuming that two animals are in conflict, then an ESS is one that, if adopted by the majority of the population, prevents the invasion of a mutant strategy. Stable strategies by definition thus tend to be mixed strategies. Much of Maynard Smith's work on ESS was published in his *Mathematical Ideas in Biology* (1968). He also discussed why sexual modes of reproduction predominate over other means in *The Evolution of Sex* (1978). Maynard Smith has continued to write on evolutionary theory in such works as *Evolutionary Genetics* (1989) and *The Major Transitions of Evolution* (1995).

Mayr, Ernst Walter (1904–   ) German–American zoologist. As a field zoologist Mayr worked extensively on the birds of the Pacific. Beginning with his *New Guinea Birds* (1941), he published a number of surveys and monographs on the ornithology of the area. He is, however, better known for such works as *Systematics and the Origin of Species* (1942), *Animal Species and Evolution* (1963), and *The Growth of Biological Thought* (1982) in which he attempted to establish a neo-Darwinian synthesis.

mechanical causation   *See* proximate causation.

Meckel's cartilage   A paired cartilage forming the lower jaw in cartilaginous fish, such as sharks, skates, and dogfish. In bony fish (Osteichthyes), reptiles, and birds it is ossified to form the articular bone. In mammals it persists as an ear ossicle, the malleus.

median eye   An eye in the middle of the head, found in some crustaceans, such as the microscopic pond animal *Cyclops*. It is a simple light receptor (ocellus). Some insects, such as the locust, have a median ocellus as well as a pair of compound eyes. The New Zealand lizardlike reptile, *Sphenodon* (*see* Reptilia), has a median third eye that is functional. *See also* pineal eye.

Megazostrodon   *See* Insectivora; Mammalia.

meiosis   The process of cell division leading to the production of daughter nuclei with half the genetic complement of the parent cell. Cells formed by meiosis give rise to gametes and fertilization restores the correct chromosome complement.

Meiosis consists of two divisions during which the chromosomes replicate only once. Like MITOSIS the stages prophase, metaphase, and anaphase can be recognized. However, during prophase homologous chromosomes attract each other and become paired forming bivalents. At the end of prophase genetic material may be exchanged between the chromatids of homologous chromosomes. Meiosis also differs from mitosis in that after anaphase, instead of nuclear membranes forming, there is a second division, which may be divided into metaphase II and anaphase II.

The second division ends with the formation of four haploid nuclei, which develop into gametes.

The origin of meiosis is unknown and remains one of the largest unsolved problems of evolutionary biology. *See also* sexual reproduction.

meiotic drive (segregation distortion) The tendency of the ALLELES of some nuclear genes to distort segregation at MEIOSIS to increase their representation in gametes. It results in a violation of Mendel's Laws and generates GENOMIC CONFLICT.

membrane A structure consisting mainly of lipid combined with protein (lipoprotein) surrounding all living cells as the *plasma membrane*, or PLASMALEMMA, and also found surrounding organelles within cells. Membranes function as selectively permeable barriers, controlling the passage of substances between the cell and its organelles, and the environment, either actively or passively. They are typically 7.5–10 nm in thickness with two regular layers of lipid molecules (a *bilayer*) containing various types of protein molecules. Short chains of sugars may be associated with the proteins or lipids forming glycoproteins or glycolipids.

The particular types of carbohydrates, lipids, and proteins determine the characteristics of the membrane, affecting, for example, cell–cell recognition (as in embryonic development and immune mechanisms), permeability, and hormone recognition. Membranes may also contain efficient arrangements of molecules involved in certain metabolic processes, e.g. electron transport and ATP production in mitochondria and chloroplasts.

Mendel, Gregor Johann (1822–84) Austrian plant geneticist. Mendel studied at Olmütz University before entering the Augustinian monastery at Brünn (now Brno in the Czech Republic) in 1843. His childhood experience of horticultural work as the son of a peasant farmer had given him an interest in the role of hybrids in evolution, and in 1856 he began plant-breeding experiments. He studied seven characters in pea plants and obtained important results after much laborious recording of character ratios in the progeny of crosses. From his experiments Mendel concluded that each of the characters he studied was determined by two factors of inheritance (one from each parent) and that each gamete (egg or sperm cell) of the organism contained only one factor of each pair. Furthermore he deduced that assortment into gametes of the factors for one character occurred independently of that for the factors of any other pair. Mendel's results are summarized today in his law of segregation and law of independent assortment (MENDEL'S LAWS).

Mendel's work is now recognized as providing the first mathematical basis to genetics but in its day it stimulated little interest. He read a brief account of his research to the Brünn Natural History Society in 1865 and asked members to extend his methods to other species, but none did. In 1866 he published his work in the society's *Verhandlungen* (Proceedings), a journal distributed to 134 scientific institutions, and sent reprints of the paper to hybridization 'experts' of the time. Karl NAEGELI, the Swiss botanist, was skeptical of his results and suggested that he continue work on the hawkweeds (*Hieracium*), a genus now known to show reproductive irregularities and with which Mendel was bound to fail.

Mendel's work with peas, and later with *Matthiola*, *Zea*, and *Mirabilis*, had shown that characters do not blend on crossing but retain their identity, thus providing an answer to the weakness in Charles Darwin's theory of natural selection. Mendel read a copy of Darwin's *Origin of Species*, but unfortunately, Darwin never heard of Mendel's work.

Mendel became abbot of the monastery in 1868 and thereafter found less time to devote to his research. It was not until 1900, when Hugo de Vries, Karl Correns, and Erich von Tschermak came across his work, that its true value was realized.

Mendelian inheritance The method of inheritance of all diploid species. Characteristics are determined by GENES, which are passed on to the next generation in the same form as they were inherited from the previous generation. An individual has two genes at each LOCUS, one inherited from each parent. Genes are transmitted to the next generation via the gametes, which have equal proportions of maternal and paternal genes. *See* Mendelism; Mendel's laws.

Mendelism The theory of inheritance according to which characteristics are determined by particulate 'factors', or genes, that are transmitted by the germ cells. It is the basis of classical genetics and is founded on the work of MENDEL in the 1860s. *See* Mendelian inheritance; Mendel's laws.

Mendel's laws Two laws formulated by Mendel to explain the pattern of inheritance he observed in plant crosses. The first law, the *Law of Segregation*, states that any character exists as two factors, both of which are found in the somatic cells but only one of which is passed on to any one gamete. The second law, the *Law of Independent Assortment*, states that the distribution of such factors to the gametes is random; if a number of pairs of factors is considered each pair segregates independently.

Today Mendel's 'characters' are termed genes and their different forms (factors) are called alleles. It is known that a diploid cell contains two alleles of a given gene, each of which is located on one of a pair of homologous chromosomes. Only one homolog of each pair is passed on to a gamete. Thus the Law of Segregation still holds true. Mendel envisaged his factors as discrete particles but it is now known that they are grouped together on chromosomes. The Law of Independent Assortment therefore only applies to pairs of alleles found on different chromosomes.

Merychippus *See* horse evolution.

mesoderm The germ layer from which muscles, connective tissues, and the blood system usually develop. At gastrulation the mesoderm comes to lie between ectoderm on the outside and endoderm lining the gut. In most animals the COELOM divides the mesoderm into an outer *somatopleure* under the skin and an inner splanchnopleure around the gut; other regions include the SOMITES. *See* germ layers.

Mesohippus *See* horse evolution.

mesonephros The second type of vertebrate kidney: it develops after the pronephros, to which it is posterior, forming the functional kidney of adult fish and amphibians. It is formed of segmentally arranged ducts that end in cup-shaped Bowman's capsules. Sometimes the ducts have open-ended side branches. They are drained by the mesonephric or Wolffian duct, which replaces the pronephric duct. In reptiles, birds, and mammals it is functionally replaced by the metanephric kidney, forming instead the epididymis of the male testis. *See also* KIDNEY.

mesonychid A primitive mammal of the PALEOCENE. The mesonychids resembled ungulates with their hoofed five-toed feet, but had large specialized teeth for ripping flesh. An example is *Mesonyx*, which was wolflike. They were a group of carnivorous CONDYLARTHS. The last-known is *Andrewsarchus*, with an enormous skull, over twice the size of a modern bear. They had become extinct by the late Eocene. *See* Cetacea; missing link.

Mesozoic Meaning 'middle life', the middle era in the most recent (Phanerozoic) eon of the geological time scale, dating from about 230–66 mya. It is also known as the 'Age of Reptiles' and is divided into three main periods: the TRIASSIC, JURASSIC, and CRETACEOUS.

The PALEOZOIC ended with the PERMIAN mass extinctions and in the Mesozoic, the surviving plants and animals transformed dramatically. The land had formed into one vast supercontinent, PANGEA, and this enormous land mass caused temperatures to rise, especially in the central regions. Animal and plant life was only possible along the margins of Pangea, which was surrounded by shallow seas. The unification of the land mass, however, enabled species to migrate and colonize new areas. Seed ferns were the dominant species in the early Triassic, but as the climate warmed, cycads became dominant and botanists often refer to the Mesozoic as the 'Age of Cycads'. In the seas, modern reef-building corals, bivalves, and ammonites evolved and enormous marine reptiles swam in the waters. On land, the reptiles came into their own, epitomized by the dinosaurs, small carnivores and large long-necked herbivores. Mammal-like reptiles evolved and spread, and then declined.

In the Jurassic period, Pangea began to break up. Large rift valleys formed across the supercontinent. New oceans formed between the new separating continents. The more comfortable tropical and temperate climates supported forests of palm-like cycads, conifers, and ginkgoes. The dinosaurs flourished, pterodactyls dominated the air and the first birdlike reptile *Archaeopteryx* appeared. In the seas, phytoplankton, corals, sea lilies, ammonites, belemnites, and fish abounded.

In the Cretaceous, the continents continued to drift apart and became separate land masses. South America became an island, but North America was still attached to Asia. The enormous ocean *Panthalassa* on the other side of the world to the continents began to develop into the Pacific Ocean. Sea levels rose, flooding the land, resulting in the largest limestone deposits of all time, including the *chalk*. In the warm climates, the first angiosperms (flowering plants) appeared, diversified very quickly, and by the end of the Mesozoic became the dominant vegetation as the climate became cooler and drier. The dinosaurs and other reptiles continued to dominate, but mammals had now evolved, although they remained an insignificant group.

The mass extinction that occurred at the end of the Mesozoic, although not the largest, is the most famous, as it heralded the end of the dinosaurs (*see* K–T event). The flying and swimming reptiles, the ammonites, and the belemnites also became extinct and many other groups were affected to a greater (birds and marsupials) or lesser extent (placental mammals, fish, lizards, snakes, turtles, and crocodiles). Amphibians were unaffected. *See also* geological time scale.

messenger RNA (mRNA)   The form of RNA that transfers the information necessary for protein synthesis from the DNA in the nucleus to the ribosomes in the cytoplasm. One strand of the double helix of DNA acts as a template along which complementary RNA nucleotides become aligned. These form a polynucleotide identical to the other DNA strand, except that the thymine bases are replaced by uracil. This polynucleotide is called *heterogeneous nuclear RNA* (hnRNA) and it contains both coding and noncoding sequences (*see* exon; intron); the introns are then removed to produce mRNA. The whole process is termed TRANSCRIPTION. The new mRNA molecule thus has a copy of the genetic code, which directs the formation of proteins in the ribosomes.

metacarpal bone   A rod-shaped bone in the lower forelimb or forefoot of tetrapods. The metacarpal bones form the palm of the hand in humans. They articulate with the carpal bones proximally and phalanges distally. In the typical PENTADACTYL LIMB there are five, although there are modifications to this basic plan: in fast-running mammals (e.g. the horse) they are greatly elongated and raised off the ground. *Compare* metatarsal bone.

metacarpus   The collection of metacarpal bones forming part of the forefoot or lower forelimb in tetrapods; the palm of the hand in humans.

metamere   *See* metameric segmentation.

metameric segmentation (metamerism; segmentation)   The repetition of body parts of an animal along the longitudinal axis of the body to produce a series of similar units (called *segments* or *metameres*). Metameric segmentation is most clearly seen (externally and internally) in annelids; for example, in the earthworm, in which most segments contain blood vessels, ganglia, nephridia, and muscle blocks. It is also seen in arthropods, but has been obscured by CEPHALIZATION at the anterior end. In chordates, external segmentation is lost and internal segmentation is best seen in the embryo, although it is confined mainly to the muscular, skeletal, and nervous systems.

metamerism *See* metameric segmentation.

metamorphosis A phase in the life history of many animals during which there is a rapid transformation from the larval to the adult form. Metamorphosis is widespread among invertebrates, especially marine organisms and arthropods, and is typical of amphibians. It is normally under hormone control and usually involves widespread lysosome-mediated destruction of larval tissues.

metanephros The third type of vertebrate kidney. It develops from the mesonephros, to which it is posterior, forming the functional kidney of reptiles, birds, and mammals. The metanephros consists of a concentrated group of ducts drained by a different duct, the ureter, which leads to the cloaca or bladder. *Compare* pronephros; mesonephros.

metaphase The stage in MITOSIS and MEIOSIS when the chromosomes become aligned along the equator of the nuclear spindle.

metatarsal bone A rod-shaped bone in the lower hindlimb or hindfoot of tetrapods. The metatarsal bones form the arch of the foot in humans. They articulate with the tarsal bones proximally and phalanges distally. In the typical PENTADACTYL LIMB there are five, although there are modifications to this basic plan; in fast-running mammals (e.g. the horse) they are greatly elongated and raised off the ground. *Compare* metacarpal bone.

metatarsus The collection of metatarsal bones forming part of the hindfoot or lower hindlimb in tetrapods; the arch of the foot in humans.

Metatheria (marsupials) The mammalian infraclass that contains the marsupials (pouched mammals). Marsupials are more primitive than the placental mammals. The brain is relatively small and there are often more than three incisor teeth on each side of the jaw. The young, born after a brief gestation period and in a very immature state, typically continue to develop in a pouch (*marsupium*) on the abdomen of the mother, where they are suckled. Epipubic bones in the pelvis assist in supporting the pouch. Marsupials (e.g. kangaroos, koala bears) are confined to Australasia, where they fill the niches occupied elsewhere by the placental mammals, and to North and South America (e.g. opossums). The Australasian marsupials exhibit syndactyly, i.e. the second and third toes of the hind foot are encased in a sheath of skin at their base, forming a comb for grooming.

The marsupials split off from the placental mammals in the early Cretaceous (e.g. *Alphadon*) in North America and spread southward across the world to all the continents. In the early Paleogene, the continents were connected by means of island chains between North America and South America, North America and Europe, and South America and Antarctica. Marsupial fossils have been found in many places, including Eocene deposits in Antarctica. Today's dispersal of marsupials is the result of migrations across land bridges or island chains, the destruction and re-emergence of the latter, and continental drift. For example, after the breakup of Pangea, North and South America separated, but then gradually rejoined about 3 million years ago when Panama joined Nicaragua to North America. The South American marsupials had evolved and diversified like the Australian marsupials, but when the land bridge was re-established, the marsupials from South America could move north and North American fauna could move south.

Australia broke away from Antarctica in the Eocene and so the marsupials evolved in isolation, occupying ecological niches usually taken by placental mammals. The marsupials included carnivores (Tasmanian devil), burrowing insectivores (marsupial mole, bandicoot, wombat), arboreal animals (flying phalanger, tree kangaroo), and herbivores (koalas, wallabies, kangaroos). There are no very large marsupials equivalent to elephants. *Compare* Eutheria; Monotremata.

Metazoa (Eumetazoa) In some older classifications, a subkingdom of multicellular animals whose bodies are composed of specialized cells grouped together to form tissues and that possess a coordinating nervous system. This subkingdom included all animals except the PROTOZOA and PARAZOA (sponges). In more recent classifications the term Eumetazoa embraces all members of the kingdom Animalia except the Parazoa. *See also* planuloid hypothesis.

miacids *See* Carnivora; Oligocene.

Micraster *See* Echinoidea.

microbiology The study of microscopic organisms (e.g. bacteria and viruses), including their interactions with other organisms and with the environment. Microbial biochemistry and genetics are important branches, due to the increasing use of microorganisms in biotechnology and genetic engineering.

microevolution Evolution on the small scale – below the species level, such as changes in gene frequency within a population and NATURAL SELECTION acting on variations within a population to produce adaptations. *Compare* macroevolution.

microhabitat *See* habitat.

Microrapter *See* Aves.

microsatellite A NONCODING DNA sequence of very short (2–5 base pairs) TANDEM REPEATS. The number of repeats varies between individuals and between homologous chromosomes. Microsatellites evolve very rapidly and are used in molecular phy-

logenetics. *See* junk DNA; repetitive DNA; selfish DNA. *Compare* minisatellite; satellite DNA.

migration 1. An instinctive regular two-way movement of part or all of an animal population to and from a given area, usually along well-defined routes. It is closely linked to the cycle of the seasons and is triggered off by seasonal factors such as increasing and decreasing daylengths in spring and autumn. Many birds, hoofed mammals, bats, whales, fish, and insects migrate, often covering immense distances. For example, the Arctic tern breeds on the northernmost coasts of Eurasia and North America and winters around the Antarctic pack-ice 11 000 miles to the south. Migratory mammals such as the wildebeest live in habitats with fluctuating climatic conditions and migrate in order to find an adequate food supply.
2. Any movement of an animal population, not necessarily a regular two-way movement. Such migrations may occur in response to environmental changes.

Millennium man *See* australopithecines; *Orrorin tugenensis*.

Miller, Stanley Lloyd (1930–) American chemist. Stanley Miller is famous for an experiment, the results of which he published in 1953, concerning the possible ORIGIN OF LIFE. Miller, who was then a graduate student of Harold Urey, mixed water vapour, ammonia, methane, and hydrogen in a flask so as to simulate the early atmosphere of the Earth, and then put a powerful electric discharge through it to simulate lightning. He discovered that after a short time organic molecules of biological interest, including some simple amino acids, were formed. Because amino acids are the 'building blocks' for proteins it has been suggested that this experiment may give a clue as to the origin of life on Earth.

mimicry The resemblance of one animal or plant to another (or to an inanimate object) by which the mimic gains advantage from its resemblance to the model. For example, in *Batesian mimicry* certain edible insects mimic the warning coloration of noxious insects and so are avoided by their predators. Natural selection produces more accurate mimicry as only those individuals closely resembling the model will be mistaken for it and tend to be left alone. In *Müllerian mimicry* a group of poisonous animals resemble each other, for example, bees, wasps, and hornets, increasing the likelihood that potential predators will learn to avoid them.

minisatellite A NONCODING DNA sequence made up of short (about 15 base pairs) TANDEM REPEATS. Minisatellites have a high mutation rate and the number of repeats varies considerably between individuals, making them useful in GENETIC FINGERPRINTING. *See* junk DNA; repetitive DNA; selfish DNA. *Compare* microsatellite; satellite DNA.

Miocene An epoch of the TERTIARY and the first part of the Neogene, 25–7 mya. The climate became drier and the grasses evolved and spread rapidly, perhaps caus-

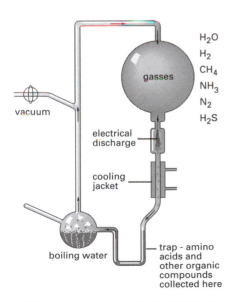

Miller: the apparatus used in his experiment on the origin of life

ing the replacement of early mammals by more modern forms. About half to three-quarters of existing mammalian families are represented in rocks of the Miocene. The Alpine orogeny continued and as India collided with Eurasia, the Himalayas began to form. The Australian plate moved northward (*see* Wallace's line). The ice sheets spread in Antarctica and later in the Arctic. The climate also became considerably cooler. Forests declined and were replaced by open woodlands, grasslands, and deserts. DIATOMS were also widespread in the seas and oceans, their siliceous remains contributing to the formation of diatomaceous earths (kieselguhr). The mammals evolved as a response to these changing conditions. Herbivores (e.g. horses, cattle, antelopes) developed teeth with higher crowns to withstand the effects of chewing grasses, which have a high silica content. Their limbs evolved to enable them to run fast in the open grasslands and to escape from carnivores (e.g. saber-toothed cats), which also diversified as the numbers of their herbivore prey increased. Smaller animals also diversified very widely (rats, mice, birds), possibly as a response to the availability of vast numbers of seeds and pollinating insects were available (butterflies, bees, ants, dragonflies, craneflies).

In the seas, whales and dolphins began to evolve. Whales included toothed whales and baleen whales (e.g. *Pelocetus*), feeding on the plankton and withstanding the cold by their homoiothermic method of regulating body heat.

The primitive monkeylike ape *Proconsul* evolved in the Miocene. Australian marsupials, having been cut off from Antarctica in the Eocene, continued to diversify (*see* Metatheria).

missing link A fossil that bridges a large gap between ancestral and derived higher groups. An example is *Archaeopteryx*, which is a primitive fossil bird that retains characteristics of its reptilian ancestors. The discovery of complete fossil lineages is very rare. One example comprises a group of fossils that are transitions between present-day whales and their UNGULATE ancestors the *mesonychids*. The descendants of this ancestral group gradually became adapted to life in water beginning about 40 million years ago. Their limbs and tails gradually became modified into fins and their body shape became more streamlined. DNA sequencing has shown that the genes of whales are most closely related to those of the hippopotamus (*see also* Cetacea).

Another example involves the wormlike animals belonging to the present-day ONY-CHOPHORA (velvet worms). For example *Peripatus* suggest a link between the annelids and the arthropods. Annelid features include simple eyes, short unjointed legs, a simple gut, and ciliated reproductive ducts. Arthropod features include jaws derived from appendages, a body cavity that is a hemocoel, a dorsal heart, a coelom reduced to cavities in the reproductive tract, and tracheae for respiration resembling those of insects. Many of the soft-bodied fossils of the early CAMBRIAN are onychophorans and some authorities believe that the arthropods evolved very early on from ancestors that resembled annelids.

Mississippian The US name for the Lower Carboniferous period.

mitochondrial DNA *See* mitochondrion.

mitochondrial Eve The name given to the common molecular ancestor of human mitochondrial DNA (mtDNA), which sequencing studies indicated existed 200 000 years ago. The research was carried out by Allan Wilson and colleagues at the University of California, Berkeley and the results published in 1987. A journalist described the putative founder individual as 'African Eve'. Because mtDNA is inherited from the mother and unlike nuclear DNA is not subjected to recombinations, etc. involved in meiosis, it is an ideal molecule (a MOLECU-LAR CLOCK) to use to reconstruct a phylogenetic tree. Samples of mtDNA were taken from different races of modern humans and the results showed two branches: one containing the modern populations of Africa, and the other containing the different races worldwide. The common ances-

tor of both branches implies that modern humans first lived in Africa 200 000 years ago. The dating method is based on several assumptions and should be viewed with caution. That there was a single molecular ancestor for human mtDNA does not necessarily mean that all humans share a single ancestor because that conclusion can only be made by studying nuclear DNA. *See also* mitochondrion; out of Africa theory.

mitochondrion A self-replicating organelle present in the cytoplasm of virtually all eukaryotic cells (*see* eukaryote). It is the site of RESPIRATION and is therefore responsible for generating energy. Mitochondria are transmitted solely through the female line and have their own DNA (mtDNA). Mitochondrial DNA is easy to extract from cells and evolves more rapidly than nuclear DNA and thus is useful in molecular phylogenetics.

In mtDNA analysis of ancient bones (e.g. those of NEANDERTHAL MAN), a part of the molecule known as the *control region* is usually used for sequencing. It is also known as the *D-loop* (displacement loop) from its shape. Unlike the rest of the molecule, this region does not code for proteins.

Analysis of mitochondrial ribosomal RNA (rRNA) genes indicates mitochondria are closely related to the purple bacteria and supports the theory that mitochondria are derived from symbiosis between purple BACTERIA and primitive EU-KARYOTES. Mitochondrial rRNA genes also suggest that plant cells acquired mitochondria after other eukaryotes. *Compare* chloroplast. *See also* endosymbiont theory.

mitosis (karyokinesis) The ordered process by which the cell nucleus divides in two during the division of body (i.e. nongermline) cells. The chromosomes replicate prior to mitosis and are then separated during mitosis in such a way that each daughter cell inherits a genetic complement identical to that of the parent cell. Although mitosis is a continuous process it is divided into four phases; prophase, metaphase, anaphase, and telophase. *Compare* meiosis; amitosis; endomitosis.

modern synthesis   *See* neoDarwinism.

molar   A large cheek tooth, two or more of which are found at the back of the jaws of a mammal. The crown has several pointed cusps or, in herbivorous animals, ridges. These teeth are used for crushing, chewing, or grinding the food. They are not present in the milk teeth, and in humans, the third molar on each side of the upper jaws do not appear until later in life (wisdom teeth).

In HERBIVORES the molars are high-crowned (*hypsodont*) teeth. In the ARTIO-DACTYLA (deer, cattle, and camels), the hypsodont teeth have moon-shaped cusps and are described as *selenodont*. In the PERISSODACTYLA, a second kind of hypsodont molar tooth has elongated cusps that form narrow ridges for grinding grasses with a high silica content and are described as *lophodont*.

OMNIVORES, e.g. pigs, bears, and primates including humans, have lower-crowned molar teeth with rounded cusps for crushing fruits, vegetables, grains, and meat. They are described as *bunodont*. *See also* teeth.

molecular biology   The study of the structure and properties of the molecules within the cells of living organisms.

molecular clock   (coalescence method) The constant rate of molecular evolution over geological time. Every molecule (or part of molecule, if different parts of the same molecule have different rates of evolution), has its own molecular clock so molecular differences can be used to infer phylogenetic relationships. *See* functional constraint; mitochondrial Eve; neutral theory.

molecular evolution   Evolution at the molecular level observable as changes in molecular sequence such as the base sequence of DNA or the amino acid sequence of a protein. Molecular evolution is rapid but constant and is driven by GENETIC DRIFT and NATURAL SELECTION though the relative importance of the two is a matter of controversy. *See* functional constraint; molecular clock; neutral theory.

molecular fossils   *See* virus.

molecular phylogenetics   (comparative genomics; phylogenomics; molecular systematics)   The reconstruction of phylogenies based on alignments of homologous sequences of DNA, RNA, or proteins. Sequences are analyzed and mutation patterns inferred by complex computer algorithms and theoretical models (*alignments*) of evolutionary relationships produced. It is not always possible to unambiguously identify the best model. Molecular and classical phylogenetics should be used together to reconstruct phylogenies. *See* phylogenetic. *See also* molecular clock.

Mollusca   A phylum of bilaterally symmetrical unsegmented invertebrates, including the aquatic bivalves, mussels, octopuses, squids, etc., and the terrestrial slugs and snails. The body is divided into a head, a ventral muscular locomotory organ (foot), and a dorsal visceral hump that houses most of the body organs and is covered by a tissue layer (*mantle*), which typically secretes a calcareous shell into which the head and foot can retract. The mantle extends into folds forming a cavity containing the gills (ctenidia). The rasping radula is used for feeding. The coelom is restricted. Development in marine species usually occurs via a TROCHOPHORE larva. Land snails and slugs lay eggs that hatch into miniature versions of the adult.

Members of the class Monoplacophora have been well-known as fossils and were believed to have become extinct in the Carboniferous. The discovery of living members (*Neopilina*) in the Pacific Ocean in 1952 enabled their close examination. Unlike other mollusks, they have a type of internal segmentation and the cleavage pattern of their larvae resembles the pattern of development in phylum ANNELIDA (segmented worms). It is thus possible that the ancestors of mollusks may have evolved from primitive annelids. Mollusks are well represented in the fossil record (*see* Cephalopoda; Gastropoda; Pelecypoda; ammonite; belemnites). The two classes, Amphineura (chitons) and Scaphopoda (tusk shells) are rarely found as fossils.

Monera An alternative name for the kingdom Prokaryotae. It was originally used by the German biologist Ernst HAECKEL to refer to BACTERIA and blue-green algae (now called cyanobacteria) as a group within the kingdom Protista, in his three-kingdom classification scheme. These prokaryotic organisms were later transferred to their own kingdom, in recognition of the fundamental differences between prokaryotes and all other organisms. *See also* eukaryote; prokaryote.

Monocotyledonae (monocotyledons) A class of the flowering plants (*see* Angiospermophyta) characterized by having a single cotyledon in the seed. They are usually herbaceous plants and do not show secondary growth. Examples of monocotyledons are the grasses and lilies. Generally the flower parts are borne in threes or multiples thereof and the leaf veins are parallel. The vascular tissue occurs as scattered bundles in the stem giving an atactostele. Monocotyledons are thought to have evolved from the ancestors of the order Magnoliales (magnolias, tulip tree), a primitive order of the Dicotyledonae, and believed to be the basal group of the families of the dicotyledons also. Grasses evolved in the MIOCENE and this had a significant effect on the evolution of mammalian herbivores and other animals of that epoch. *Compare* Dicotyledoneae.

monogamous species A species in which one male and one female mate and reproduce exclusively with each other. *Compare* polyandrous species; polygynous species.

monohybrid A hybrid heterozygous at one locus and obtained from crossing parents that are homozygous for different alleles at a given locus; for example, Mendel's cross between tall (TT) and dwarf (tt) gar-

den peas to give a tall monohybrid (Tt). When a monohybrid is selfed, dominant and recessive phenotypes appear in the offspring in the ratio of 3:1 (the *monohybrid ratio*). *Compare* DIHYBRID.

monophyletic Describing a group of species that includes an ancestor and all of its descendants. Monophyletic groups are the only groups allowed in cladistic classification. *Compare* paraphyletic; polyphyletic.

monophyodont Describing a type of dentition in which an animal has only one set of teeth during its lifetime, which are not replaced if they fall out. *Compare* diphyodont; polyphyodont.

monoploid *See* haploid.

monosomy *See* aneuploidy; nondisjunction.

Monotremata (monotremes; Prototheria) The order that contains the most primitive mammals – the only mammals that lay eggs. After hatching the young are transferred to a pouch on the abdomen and are nourished by milk secreted by primitive mammary glands whose ducts do not form nipples. Other primitive features include poor temperature control, and possession of a cloaca and a primitive pectoral girdle, but the brain, hair, heart, and diaphragm are typically mammalian. Monotremes include *Ornithorhynchus* (duck-billed platypus), only found in Australia. It is aquatic, with webbed feet and a bill for crushing invertebrates. *Tachyglossus* and *Zaglossus* (spiny anteaters) are terrestrial insectivores. They are also found in New Guinea. Most authorities believe that the monotremes were not direct ancestors of the marsupial and placental animals, and that they evolved from an even more primitive reptilelike mammal (*see* Mammalia). *Compare* Eutheria; Metatheria.

Morgan, Thomas Hunt (1866–1945) American geneticist. Morgan carried out his most important work between 1904 and 1928, while professor of experimental zoology at Columbia University. Here he became involved in the controversy that followed the rediscovery, in 1900, of Gregor MENDEL's laws of inheritance. In 1908 Morgan began breeding experiments with the fruit fly DROSOPHILA MELANOGASTER, which has four pairs of chromosomes. Morgan's early results with mutant types substantiated Mendel's law of segregation, but he soon found evidence of LINKAGE through his discovery that mutant white-eyed flies are also always male. He thus formulated the only necessary amendment to MENDEL'S LAWS – that the law of independent assortment only applies to genes located on different chromosomes.

Morgan found that linkages could be broken when homologous chromosomes paired at meiosis and exchanged material in a process known as 'crossing over'. Gene linkages are less likely to be broken when the genes are close together on the chromosome, and therefore by recording the frequency of broken linkages, the positions of genes along the chromosome can be mapped. Morgan and his colleagues produced the first CHROMOSOME MAPS in 1911. For his contributions to genetics, Morgan received the Nobel Prize for physiology or medicine in 1933.

morphogen *See* differentiation.

morphogenesis The development of form and structure.

morphological species concept (typological species concept) Pre-neoDarwinian definition of a species in which the members of a species are defined by their similarity to the standard bodyform for that species. The PHENETIC SPECIES CONCEPT is a modern version of the morphological species concept.

morphology The study of the form of organisms. The term may be used synonymously with 'anatomy' although generally the study of external form is termed 'morphology' while the study of internal structures is termed 'anatomy'. The morphology of organisms is used to infer phylogenetic relationships. The first step

is to distinguish homologies (reliable evidence) from analogies (unreliable evidence). Homologies have the same fundamental structure, have the same relationships to surrounding characters, and have the same embryonic development. Homologies are then divided into ancestral and derived (more reliable). Derived homologies can be distinguished by comparison with closely related species (*outgroup comparison*), embryology, and the fossil record. *See* homologous; phylogenetic.

Morrison formation A vast late JURASSIC deposit in the USA stretching from Montana in the north to New Mexico in the south and from Nebraska in the east to Idaho in the west, named for the town of Morrison, Colorado. It was formed from flat areas of lowland swamps, lakes, and a network of rivers. Although the climate was semi-arid, seasonal rains running off from the emerging Rocky Mountains in the west caused the rivers to flood the area and deposit silt and mud, burying animals and plants in these sediments. The formation consists of conglomerate, mudstones, sandstones, shales, and siltstones ranging in depth from 30 m to 275 m. It is one of the largest fossil beds in the world and is famous for its spectacular dinosaur fossils (at least 70 species), including *Allosaurus*, *Brachiosaurus*, *Stegosaurus*, and *Diplodocus*. Herds of apatosaurs (brontosaurs) have famously left their tracks in the mud of this formation. This formation is also noted for the so-called BONE WARS between two rival paleontologists.

mosaic evolution Evolutionary change in a taxon that occurs at different rates for different phenotypic characters.

mosquitoes *See* Diptera.

mosses *See* Musci.

moths *See* Lepidoptera.

Mousterian tools Stone tools (200 000–40 000 years ago) found at sites in Africa, Europe, and the Near East, most closely associated with NEANDERTHAL MAN but sometimes also associated with early *Homo sapiens*. The tools were more refined than ACHEULIAN TOOLS and included cutters and scrapers involving shaped blades, and spears with handles. *See also* Oldowan industrial complex; Upper Paleolithic tools.

mouthparts Jointed appendages on the heads of arthropods, modified in various ways for dealing with food. They consist of the *labrum* (upper lip), which is a single plate; a pair of *mandibles* (upper jaws), which have serrated edges; and a pair of *maxillae* (lower jaws), which also have serrated regions. In insects the second pair of maxillae is specialized to form the *labium* (lower lip), which is a single plate. The labium and maxillae have sensory feelers (*palps*) concerned with the tasting of food, and in crustaceans the second maxillae may also be used for producing respiratory water currents. The basic system of mouthparts found in the more primitive groups (e.g. cockroaches and locusts) is highly modified in other groups to suit the mouthparts for one particular kind of food. For example, the tubular mouthparts of butterflies and moths are adapted for sucking nectar; the piercing and sucking mouthparts of mosquitoes are adapted to feed on blood or plant juices. In many insects, the evolution of mouthparts corresponds closely with the evolutionary adaptations of specific floral parts, an example of CO-EVOLUTION.

mRNA *See* messenger RNA.

mtDNA *See* mitochondrion; mitochondrial Eve.

Muller, Hermann Joseph (1890–1967) American geneticist. Muller received his PhD in 1916 for his now classic studies on the crossing over of chromosomes. He was also a coauthor of *The Mechanism of Mendelian Heredity* (1915), a fundamental contribution to classical genetics.

In 1915 he began studying mutation. By 1918 he had found evidence that raising the temperature increases MUTATION RATE. In 1926 he found that x-rays induce muta-

tions, a discovery for which he eventually received the 1946 Nobel Prize for physiology or medicine.

Muller also made important theoretical contributions to genetics. He visualized the gene as the origin of life, because only genes can replicate themselves, and he believed all selection and therefore evolution acted at the level of the gene. He was also concerned about the increasing number of mutations accumulating in human populations.

Muller is seen by many as the most influential geneticist of the 20th century, mainly through his appreciation of genetic mutation as fundamental to future genetic research. He published over 350 works, the most important paper being *Artificial Transmutation of the Gene* (1927).

Müllerian duct The oviduct of female jawed vertebrates. It develops in both sexes from embryonic mesoderm, in association with the Wolffian duct, but becomes vestigial in the male. In most vertebrates it is paired (single in birds) and extends from a ciliated funnel, which opens into the coelom near the ovary, to the cloaca (when present). In mammals it is usually differentiated into Fallopian tube, uterus, and vagina. Ova entering the funnel are conveyed along the duct towards the exterior by muscular and ciliary movements. If spermatozoa are present at this time, fertilization may occur.

Müllerian mimicry *See* mimicry.

multicellular Consisting of many cells. The oldest fossils of multicellular organisms are about 550 million years old (the start of the Cambrian). Large more complex multicellular organisms with specialized cell types require mechanisms to transport substances between cells, mechanisms of gene regulation, and an epigenetic system of cellular memory. *See* unicellular.

multifactorial inheritance *See* quantitative inheritance.

multigene family *See* gene family.

multilevel evolution Simultaneous evolution at more than one level of a hierarchy of replicating units, for example, nuclear and mitochondrial genes and individual cells within a multicellular organism.

multilocus model A complex model in POPULATION GENETICS in which natural selection acts simultaneously on several loci. It is applied to systems in LINKAGE DISEQUILIBRIUM and is also concerned with recombination and multiple-peaked fitness surfaces. The equations of a multilocus model measure changes in HAPLOTYPE frequencies. *See also* one-locus model. *Compare* quantitative genetics.

multiple allelism The existence of a series of alleles (three or more) for one gene. In humans, for example, there are three alleles (A, B, and O) governing blood type. Only two alleles of the series can be present in a diploid cell. Dominance relationships within an allelic series are often complicated.

multiregional theory (of evolution) A theory to explain the origin of *Homo sapiens* (modern humans). It is based on the discovery of HOMO ERECTUS fossils in a number of separate geographical regions throughout the world. The theory proposes that *H. erectus* first spread from Africa at least a million years ago, and evolved into *H. sapiens*. Different traits developed through GENETIC DRIFT and ADAPTATION in separate geographical locations. It contrasts with the single-origin hypothesis embodied in the OUT OF AFRICA THEORY. *See also* mitochondrial Eve; Mungo man; Nanjing man.

multituberculates (multis) A major order of rodentlike mammals that spread throughout the world. Multituberculates first appeared late in the Jurassic and became extinct in the early Oligocene 100 million years later. They are not related to any of the groups of living mammals and it is believed that they evolved from primitive mammals even earlier than the monotremes. Their narrow pelvises suggest that they gave birth to tiny pups, rather like marsupials. They are named for their tooth structure, because their molars have many cusps or tubercles. They ranged in size from tiny mouselike forms to those the size of beavers. Some lived in burrows (*Lambdopsalis* from China) and were adapted for digging; others (*Ptilodus* from North America) climbed trees like squirrels.

Their incisors were enlarged. They lacked canines, and there was a gap (a diastema) between the incisors and molars. The molars with their small cusps were adapted for grinding. The last lower premolars form large serrated blades (the plagiaulacoid teeth) named for the multituberculate *Plagiaulax*. The largest, the beaverlike *Taeniolabis* (early Paleocene), had a massive skull, gnawing teeth and complex molars, indicating a herbivorous diet. However, certain authorities suggest that some multituberculates may have been insectivorous.

A very odd group of fossil multituberculates discovered in the Upper Cretaceous deposits of Madagascar, India, and South America (e.g. *Gondwanatherium*) have high-crowned molars, like grass-eating herbivores, but as grasses did not evolve until the Miocene, this remains an enigma. *See also* Mammalia.

Mungo man A skeleton discovered at Lake Mungo in New South Wales, Australia, in 1974. DNA analysis has shown that these bones are older than the 100 000–200 000-year-old *Homo sapiens* population that is believed to have emerged from Africa to replace the then existing *Homo erectus* populations all over the world (*see* out of Africa theory). The Australian researchers believe that these findings support the MULTIREGIONAL THEORY of evolution, in which it is believed that modern humans evolved from *H. erectus* ancestors in separate populations in different parts of the world. Opponents of this theory argue that DNA analysis of such old bones could well be unreliable.

murids *See* Rodentia.

Musci (mosses) A class of BRYOPHYTA, in

some classifications elevated to the status of a phylum (Bryophyta), containing erect leafy plants with multicellular rhizoids. Mosses are far more widely distributed than liverworts. They differ in that they have greater differentiation of the gametophyte and also complex mechanisms of capsule dehiscence, with no formation of elaters in the capsule. Orders include the Bryales (e.g. *Funaria, Polytrichum, Mnium*) and the Sphagnales (e.g. *Sphagnum*).

Mosses, like other bryophytes, are poorly represented in the fossil record because of their delicate structure. The oldest fossil is *Muscites plumatus* from the Carboniferous. Mesozoic fossils include representatives from most present-day orders and fossils from the Baltic, Dominican, and Mexican AMBER from the Tertiary contain present-day genera.

Mosses are believed to have evolved from the CHLOROPHYTA (green algae) because they have protonemata (juvenile filaments that develop from spores) resembling algal filaments and, like the Chlorophyta, they contain chlorophylls *a* and *b*, store carbohydrates in the form of starch, have similar cell wall constituents, and their antherozoids have two forwardly directed flagella.

mutagen Any physical or chemical agent that induces mutation or increases the rate of spontaneous mutation. Chemical mutagens include ethyl methanesulfonate, which causes changes in the base pairs of DNA molecules, and acridines, which cause base pair deletions or additions. Physical mutagens include ultraviolet light, x-rays, and gamma rays.

mutation A detectable change in the genetic material. There are three types: CHROMOSOME MUTATION, GENE MUTATION, and GENOME MUTATION.

mutational load A form of GENETIC LOAD caused by disadvantageous mutations.

mutation rate The frequency at which mutations occur in a population. In general, the rate is very low – possibly between 1 and 30 for every million gametes. However, genes at different loci have different mutation rates and so averages are difficult to calculate.

mutation–selection balance *See* variation.

mutualism A close relationship between two or more species in which all benefit from the association. There are two types of mutualism: *obligatory mutualism*, in which one cannot survive without the other, for example, the algal/fungal partnership found in lichens; and *facultative* or *nonobligatory mutualism*, in which both species can survive independently, for example marine crabs and their associated invertebrate fauna of sponges, cnidarians, etc., that attach to the crab shell and act as camouflage. Facultative mutualism is sometimes termed *protocooperation*. *Compare* symbiosis.

mya An abbreviation for *million years ago*.

mycetozoa A taxon name used for SLIME MOLDS in certain classifications.

mycorrhiza The beneficial association between the hyphae of a fungus and the roots of a higher plant. Two main types of mycorrhiza exist: ectotrophic, in which the fungus forms a mantle around the smaller roots, as in trees; and endotrophic, in which the fungus grows around within the cortex of the roots, as in orchids and heathers.

Myriapoda A group of terrestrial arthropods containing the classes CHILOPODA (centipedes) and DIPLOPODA (millipedes), characterized by a distinct head, bearing antennae, mandibles, and maxillae, and numerous body segments bearing walking legs. They evolved in the Devonian but were not widespread until the Carboniferous period. Some authorities place the centipedes, millipedes, and insects into a subphylum known as the *Uniramia*, or into a phylum, Mandibulata. It has been shown that although centipedes and millipedes show a superficial resemblance, they are not closely related.

myxobacteria (slime bacteria) A group of bacteria in which individual cells are typically rod-shaped and covered in slime, but which may congregate to form gliding swarms or various upright reproductive structures under certain conditions. For example, the reproductive body of *Stigmatella aurantiaca* consists of a stalk bearing several cysts. These open when wetted to release masses of individual gliding bacteria that move together over the substrate as discrete colonies. In some species the reproductive structures are brightly colored and just visible to the naked eye. Myxobacteria are common in soil, animal dung, and decaying plant matter.

Myxomycetes *See* slime molds.

Myxomycota *See* slime molds.

Naegeli, Karl Wilhelm von (1817–91) Swiss botanist. In 1842 Naegeli published an essay on pollen formation in which he accurately described CELL DIVISION, realizing that the wall formed between two daughter cells is not the cause but the result of cell division. He noted the division of the nucleus and recorded the chromosomes as 'transitory cytoblasts'.

In 1845 he began investigating apical growth, which led to his distinguishing between formative (meristematic) and structural tissues in plants. Naegeli's micellar theory, formulated from studies on starch grains, gave information on cell ultrastructure.

In the taxonomic field, Naegeli made a thorough study of the genus *Hieracium* (hawkweeds), investigating crosses in the group. He had strong views on evolution and inheritance, which led him to reject Mendel's important work on heredity and hybrid ratios.

Nanjing man An example of HOMO ERECTUS evidenced by two skulls (male and female) discovered in Tangshan Cave near Shanghai, China, in 1993. They were estimated to be between 580 000 and 620 000 years old based on uranium dating of the rocks above and below the fossils using a thermal ionization mass spectrometer. It has been claimed that the male skull shows evidence of a transition between *Homo erectus* and *Homo sapiens*, thereby supporting the MULTIREGIONAL THEORY. This view is controversial.

nanoplankton *See* plankton.

narrow sense heritability (*h2*) The proportion of total phenotypic variation V_P in a character due to the additive genetic variance (effect), V_A. It is a useful measure of the potential response to selection and is given by: $h2 = V_A/V_P$. Narrow sense heritability can also be estimated from the values of the SELECTION DIFFERENTIAL, S, and the SELECTION RESPONSE, R, resulting from TRUNCATION SELECTION experiments: $h2 = R/S$. *Compare* broad sense heritability. *See* genotypic effect; variance.

natural selection The process, which Darwin called the 'struggle for survival', by which organisms less adapted to their environment tend to perish, and better-adapted organisms tend to survive and enjoy greater reproductive success. Natural selection is not a random process and over time it generates adaptations and is the only process that can explain why organisms show adaptations to their environment. It can produce evolutionary change (but is not the only process that can do so) when there is environmental change or when a new fitter form emerges. But if neither happens then natural selection acts to keep a population the same. For natural selection to operate, there must be reproduction and inheritance, but the most important condition is variation, both in characters and fitness. *See* adaptive evolution; Darwinism; directional selection; disruptive selection; evolution; fitness; genetic drift; mutation; neoDarwinism; stabilizing selection. *See also* molecular evolution; neutral theory. *Compare* Lamarckism.

nature and nurture The interaction between inherited and environmental factors (*nature* and *nurture* respectively) in determining the observed characteristics of an organism. It is often applied in a discussion of behavioral characteristics, such as intelligence, in which the relative importance of inherited and environmental factors, including such factors as social background, is a matter of great controversy. The term *heritability* is sometimes used as an alternative, meaning the proportion of the total variation caused by genetic influences alone.

Naudin, Charles (1815–99) French experimental botanist and horticulturist. Naudin's most significant work began in 1854 with experiments in plant hybridization, from which he found that first-generation HYBRIDS display relative uniformity while second-generation hybrids obtained by crossing within the first generation show great diversity of characters. He recognized, in his theory of disjunction, that inheritance is particulate and not blending. However, unlike his contemporary Gregor Mendel, he failed to recognize the statistical regularity with which different characters appear.

Naudin proposed hybridization to be the prime agent of evolutionary change and not natural selection or environmental action. He held that the present diversity of species is the product of a smaller number of basic forms and might or might not exhibit permanence.

nautiloids Cephalopod mollusks (*see* Mollusca) with about 2500 fossil representatives and only one living genus, the pearly nautilus (*Nautilus pompilius*) found in depths of almost 700 m in the Indian and Pacific Oceans. Nautiloids were dominant in the Paleozoic. Like the AMMONITES they had external limy chambered shells, the animal probably living in the outer chamber. Early fossils had conical shells varying from a few centimeters to a few meters. The largest invertebrate with a shell is *Endoceras*, an Ordovician fossil that can measure up to 5m long. *See* Cephalopoda.

Neanderthal man A species of early humans, *Homo neanderthalensis*, that lived in Europe from about 150 000 years ago in the Pleistocene and was replaced by modern humans, *Homo sapiens*, about 30 000 years ago. Neanderthals were dominant in western Europe during the first stages of the last glaciation, and were cave-dwelling, and made regular use of fire and tools.

They had large long faces, probably to accommodate their large canine and incisor teeth (their smaller molar and premolar teeth resembled those of modern humans). They also retained the brow ridges and short chins of their ancestors. The details of their hand bones and their powerful arms suggest that they were adapted largely for powerful movements rather than for the precision movements of modern humans. Neanderthals were named for the Neander Valley in Germany where their remains were first discovered.

In recent years, their bones have been subjected to DNA analysis. Thus far, only mitochondrial DNA (mtDNA) has been analyzed (*see* mitochondrion); nuclear DNA sequence analysis has not proved possible for such ancient material. As each cell contains many mitochondria, many copies of mtDNA exist, in contrast to nuclear DNA, where there is only one copy per cell. Also, mtDNA is inherited only through the female line (*see* mitochondrial Eve), which could be problematical in comparing populations with, for example, different marriage customs. The mtDNA of the PALEOLITHIC humans who lived after the Neanderthals has been compared with that of living humans. They have been shown to be similar, but that of the Neanderthals has proved to be quite different from either type. This shows that the mtDNA lineage of Neanderthals branched off before the common ancestor of modern humans. The first bone used in mtDNA sequencing was the upper arm bone from a Neanderthal in the Feldhofer Cave in the Neander Valley. Other samples have come from Neanderthals at the Vindija Cave in Croatia, and from an infant found in the Mezmaiskaya Cave in the northern Caucasus, Russia. The first two show 35 differences from present-day human sequences, the Russian sample, less so (22 differences). *See also* Mungo man; *Homo*; human evolution; Out of Africa theory; multiregional theory.

Nearctic Literally 'new northern', one of the six zoogeographical regions of the Earth, including North America from the Central Mexican Plateau in the south to the Aleutian Islands and Greenland in the north. The fauna include mountain goat, prong-horn antelope, caribou, and muskrat. North America and Eurasia remained connected throughout much of geological time because when the northern Atlantic Ocean formed, a land-bridge between Siberia and Alaska remained until comparatively recently. Humans migrated across the bridge about 50 000 years ago. Some authorities group the Nearctic and PALE-ARCTIC together as the *Holarctic* as they are biologically very similar. *See* zoogeography; continental drift.

Nebraska man *See* Piltdown man.

negative frequency-dependent selection *See* frequency-dependent selection.

neighbor joining An important method of constructing ADDITIVE TREES that can deal with different rates of evolution in different branches of a tree.

nekton Animals of the pelagic zone of a sea or lake that are free-swimming and independent of tides, currents, and waves, such as fish, whales, squid, crabs, and shrimps. Nekton are limited in distribution by temperature and nutrient supply, and decrease with increasing depth. *See also* benthic; plankton.

Nematoda A large phylum of marine, freshwater, and terrestrial invertebrates, the roundworms. They are very small, often microscopic, occurring in their millions in soil and water. Most are free-living, e.g. *Anguillula* (vinegar eel), but many are parasites, e.g. *Heterodera* (eelworm of potatoes) and *Ascaris* (found in pigs' and human intestines). Some cause serious diseases in humans, e.g. *Wuchereria* (causing elephantiasis). Nematodes are bilaterally symmetrical with an unsegmented smooth cylindrical body pointed at both ends and covered with a tough cuticle. The body cavity is not a true coelom and is a remnant of the embryonic blastocoel. There are no blood or respiratory systems. The muscular and excretory systems and embryonic development are unusual.

Nematodes are not closely related to any other phylum. Their soft bodies mean that fossil remains are difficult to discover. However, fossil nematodes have been found in Carboniferous rocks and have also been preserved in Cenozoic amber (Dominican, Mexican, and Baltic amber). As some related groups date from the Cambrian, it is possible that nematodes may have evolved at that time.

In 1998, the sequencing of the entire genome (97 million base pairs) of the soil-dwelling free-living nematode *Caenorhabditis elegans* was announced by a team headed by John Sulston and Bob Waterston on December 11. This nematode thus became the first animal to have its entire genetic blueprint unraveled.

neoDarwinism (modern synthesis; synthetic theory of evolution) Darwin's theory of evolution through NATURAL SELECTION, modified and expanded by modern genetic studies arising from the work of MENDEL and his successors. Such studies have answered many questions that Darwin's theory raised, but could not adequately explain because of lack of knowledge at the time it was formulated. Notably, modern genetics has revealed the source of variation on which natural selection operates, namely mutations of genes and chromosomes, and has provided mathematical models of how alleles fluctuate in natural populations, thereby quantifying the process of evolution.

Neogene *See* Tertiary.

Neolithic The recent Stone Age, dating from about 10 000 years ago at the end of the Pleistocene until the beginning of the Bronze Age. It is characterized by Neolithic humans who were able to make more advanced and often polished stone tools and also by the development of agriculture. The stone tools were gradually supplanted by bronze (Bronze Age) and later by iron (Iron Age). *See also* Paleolithic.

neopallium *See* brain.

neoteny The retention of larval or other juvenile features beyond the normal stage in the development of an animal. It may be either temporary, because of climatic or other factors, or permanent, in which case the animal breeds in the larval stage (*see* paedogenesis). Neoteny is thought to be important in the evolution of some groups, including humans, who have certain resemblances to young stages of apes. It also occurs in plants; for example, it is believed that herbaceous plants may have evolved from trees by neoteny.

Neotropical Literally meaning 'new tropics', one of the six main zoogeographical regions of the Earth. It includes South and Central America, the West Indies, and the Mexican lowlands. The characteristic fauna includes sloths, armadillos, anteaters, cavies, vampire bats, llama, alpaca, peccary, rhea, toucan, curassows, and certain hummingbirds. South America, like Australia, was isolated throughout much of geological history, and similarly there was a prevalence of marsupial fauna, probably from the time when Australia, South America, and Antarctica were joined and experienced a much warmer climate. North America and South America were joined by a land bridge about 60 million years ago, allowing placental mammals into South America. These two types of mammals evolved in isolation when the land bridge disappeared. The Panamanian land bridge was then established, allowing further migrations. *See* Pliocene; zoogeography; continental drift.

neritic The marine environment from low water level to a depth of about 200 m, a zone that in many areas corresponds to the extent of the continental shelf. It makes up less than 1% of the marine environment. Nutrients are relatively abundant in this zone and it is penetrated by sunlight. *Compare* oceanic.

nervous system A ramifying system of cells, found in all animals except sponges, that forms a communication system between receptors and effectors and allows varying degrees of coordination of information from different receptors and stored memory, producing integrated responses to stimuli.

At its simplest, as found in the Cnidaria, the nervous system is merely a diffuse net with little concentration of function, but higher animals, which have bilateral symmetry, possess groups of neurones (ganglia) within which integration can take place. The major ganglion develops in the head, as the brain, and becomes increasingly important as a control center in more advanced types. The brain communicates with the body through the spinal cord, which is composed mostly of long axons transmitting impulses to and from the brain but also contains the circuits for body reflexes, and the peripheral nervous system, which contains sensory or motor neurones running from receptors or to effectors. *See also* central nervous system; cephalization.

neutral drift *See* genetic drift.

neutral evolution Random evolutionary change driven by GENETIC DRIFT. It shows little or no correlation between heritable variation and reproductive success. *Compare* adaptive evolution.

neutral mutation A MUTATION that does not cause a change in FITNESS. It has no positive nor disadvantageous effects.

neutral theory The theory that MOLECULAR EVOLUTION is driven mainly by GENETIC DRIFT, making it random and nonadaptive. The opposing theory is that NATURAL SELECTION is largely responsible for molecular evolution. Both genetic drift and natural selection can in principle explain molecular evolution. The neutral theory was proposed in 1968 with evidence from the MOLECULAR CLOCK, the rapid rate of molecular evolution, the functional constraint of molecular evolution, and the high degree of natural variability in proteins to support it. It is now considered unlikely that genetic drift is the main driving force as recent evidence from sequence analysis indicates that the relative importance of genetic drift and natural selection in molecular evolution depends on the type of molecule and the region of molecule involved. *See* protein evolution.

New Red Sandstone *See* Permian; Triassic.

New World monkeys *See* platyrrhine; Primates.

niche *See* ecological niche.

noncoding DNA A DNA sequence that does not code for RNA and is not transcribed. *See* junk DNA.

noncoding strand The DNA strand of a double helix that is the template for TRANSCRIPTION and synthesis of RNA. Its sequence is therefore complementary to the RNA sequence (with T substituted for U). *Compare* coding strand.

nondisjunction The failure of homologous chromosomes to move to separate poles during anaphase I of MEIOSIS, both homologs going to a single pole. This results in two of the four gametes formed at telophase missing a chromosome (i.e. being $n - 1$). If these fuse with normal haploid (n) gametes then the resulting zygote is *monosomic* (i.e. $2n - 1$). The other two gametes formed at telophase have an extra chromosome (i.e. are $n + 1$) and give a *trisomic* zygote (i.e. $2n + 1$) on fusion with a normal gamete. If two gametes deficient for the same chromosome fuse then *nullisomy* ($2n - 2$) will result, which is almost always lethal, and if two gametes with the same extra chromosomes fuse, *tetrasomy* ($2n + 2$) results. All these abnormal chromosome conditions are collectively referred to as ANEUPLOIDY. In humans the condition of Down's syndrome is due to trisomy of chromosome 21.

nonMendelian processes Processes in which DNA sequences are copied laterally through the genome of one individual rather than vertically from parent to off-spring. *See* crossing over; gene conversion; transposon.

nonrandom elimination Elimination of less fit individuals by NATURAL SELECTION.

normalizing selection *See* stabilizing selection.

nothosaurs A group of extinct fish-eating marine reptiles that evolved in the Triassic, became extinct in the late Triassic, and may have evolved into the PLESIOSAURS. Nothosaurs had long thin heads with sharp teeth, long thin necks, and four paddlelike limbs. They breathed air, but spent time in the water, e.g. *Nothosaurus* (from Europe and North America), which was about 3 m long. *See also* Icthyosauria; placodonts; plesiosaurs; pliosaurs; Reptilia.

notochord The flexible dorsal supporting rod characteristic of the CHORDATA. The notochord is equivalent to the vertebral column in vertebrates.

nuclear envelope *See* nucleus.

nuclear membrane *See* nucleus.

nuclear pore *See* nucleus.

nuclease *See* endonuclease; exonuclease.

nucleic acid hybridization The pairing of a single-stranded DNA or RNA molecule with another such strand, forming a DNA–DNA or RNA–DNA hybrid. In order to achieve hybridization the base sequences of the strands must be complementary. This phenomenon is exploited in many techniques, notably in gene probes (*see* DNA probe), which are designed to bind to particular complementary base sequences among a mass of DNA fragments. Hybridization can also be used in comparative biology to assess the degree of similarity of base sequences between, say, corresponding genes from different organisms.

nucleic acids Organic acids whose molecules consist of NUCLEOTIDES – chains of alternating sugar and phosphate units, with nitrogenous bases attached to the sugar units. They occur in the cells of all organisms. In DNA the sugar is deoxyribose; in RNA it is ribose. *See* DNA; RNA.

nucleolar organizer *See* nucleolus.

nucleolus (*pl.* nucleoli) A more or less spherical structure found in nuclei of eukaryote cells, and easily visible with a light microscope. One to several per nucleus may occur. It is the site of ribosome manufacture and is thus most conspicuous in cells making large quantities of protein. Nucleoli disappear during cell division. The nucleolus synthesizes ribosomal RNA (rRNA) and is made of RNA (about 10%) and protein. It forms around particular loci of one or more chromosomes called *nucleolar organizers*. These loci contain numerous tandem repeats of the genes coding for ribosomal RNA.

nucleoprotein A compound consisting of a protein associated with a nucleic acid.

nucleoside A molecule consisting of a purine or pyrimidine base linked to a sugar, either ribose or deoxyribose. Adenosine, cytidine, guanosine, thymidine, and uridine are common nucleosides.

nucleosome *See* chromatin.

nucleotide The compound formed by condensation of a nitrogenous base (a purine, pyrimidine, or pyridine) with a sugar (ribose or deoxyribose) and phosphoric acid. The coenzymes NAD and FAD are *dinucleotides* (consisting of two linked nucleotides) while the nucleic acids (DNA and RNA) are *polynucleotides* (consisting of chains of many linked nucleotides).

nucleotide diversity (p) A quantitative measure of the variability of DNA sequences defined as the average number of nucleotide differences per site between randomly chosen pairs of sequences. It can be measured using restriction analysis and DNA sequencing. *See* gene sequencing; restriction endonuclease.

nucleus (*pl.* nuclei) An ORGANELLE containing the genetic information (*see* DNA) that is found in virtually all eukaryotic living cells (exceptions include mature sieve tube elements of the phloem of angiosperms and mature mammalian red blood cells). DNA replication and transcription occur exclusively in the nucleus. It is the largest organelle, typically spherical and bounded by a double membrane, the *nuclear envelope* or *nuclear membrane*, which is perforated by many pores (*nuclear pores*) that allow exchange of materials with the cytoplasm. The outer nuclear membrane is an extension of the ENDOPLASMIC RETICULUM. In the nondividing (interphase) nucleus the genetic material is irregularly dispersed as CHROMATIN; during nuclear division (MITOSIS or MEIOSIS) this condenses into densely staining CHROMOSOMES, and the nuclear envelope disappears as do the nucleoli (*see* nucleolus) that are normally present.

nullisomy *See* aneuploidy; nondisjunction.

numerical taxonomy (taxometrics) The assessment of similarities between organisms by mathematical procedures, often involving the use of computers. It involves statistical analysis of some measurable characteristic and uses phenetic rather than phyletic evidence. *See also* evolutionary computing.

O

Obelia *See* Hydrozoa.

occipital condyle A rounded prominence on the posterior portion of the tetrapod skull. There are two in mammals; they
articulate with the first (atlas) vertebra to
allow nodding of the head. There are also
two in amphibians, but only one in reptiles
and birds.

oceanic The marine environment beyond the continental shelf, which is usually
deeper than 200 m. It makes up about 99%
of the total marine environment. *Compare*
neritic.

ocellus A simple eye of some invertebrates (e.g. arthropods). It consists of a
group of light-sensitive cells (photoreceptors). Ocelli are concerned with perceiving
the direction and intensity of light and do
not form an image.

Odonata The order of insects (*see* Insecta) that contains the dragonflies,
brightly colored carnivorous insects with a
long thin abdomen and two pairs of equal-
sized elongated wings. The head bears
large compound eyes, reduced antennae,
and biting mouthparts and the legs are set
well forward for catching the smaller insects that they prey on. The aquatic
nymphs are also carnivorous, with an enlarged labrum (the *mask*) for catching
prey. Dragonflies have been known from
Late Carboniferous times. Some fossil
members had a wingspan of 70 cm (e.g.
Meganeura).

Oenothera lamarckiana *See* autopolyploidy; de Vries.

Okazaki fragments *See* replication.

Oldowan industrial complex The
oldest stone tool assemblage in the Lower
PALEOLITHIC period at *Olduvai Gorge* in
Tanzania, E. Africa (dated 1.5–2 mya).
They include choppers, scrapers, and flake
tools. They have also been found at the
Gona and Oma Basins in Ethiopia. Basalt,
quartz, and chert were used to make the
tools. Bones were also used as diggers, indicated by scratch marks. These tools are
associated with *Homo habilis* and *Homo
rudolfensis*, but robust AUSTRALOPITHE-
CINES overlapped with these species, and so
some uncertainty remains. *See also* Acheulian tools; Mousterian tools; Upper Paleolithic tools.

Old Red Sandstone *See* Devonian.

Olduvai Gorge *See* Oldowan industrial
complex.

Old World monkeys *See* catarrhine;
Primates.

olfactory organ The organ involved in
the detection of smells, which consists of a
group of sensory receptors that respond to
air- or water-borne chemicals. Vertebrates
possess a pair of olfactory organs in the
mucous membrane lining the upper part of
the nose, which opens to the exterior via
the external nares (nostrils). Chemicals
from the environment are dissolved in the
mucus secreted by the nasal epithelium and
information is transmitted to the brain by
the receptors via the olfactory nerve. Ancestral vertebrate brains were probably
only a pair of small swellings concerned
with the sense of smell, which became and

remains important in the environment of higher vertebrates.

Olfactory organs are found on the antennae in insects and in various positions in other invertebrates.

Oligocene The epoch of the Tertiary period 38–25 mya. It is characterized by the gradual disappearance of earlier mammal groups, including primitive insectivores and primates, and their replacement by more modern forms. A major cooling down of the Earth began as the ice around Antarctica increased. The Alpine orogeny continued from the Eocene into this epoch. In the seas, modern CORALS (stony corals) evolved, along with the baleen whales. On land, grasses began to flourish and continued into the MIOCENE. The first monkeys evolved and the 'true' carnivores became the top predators. There were marsupial carnivores in South America and the CREODONTS (archaic carnivores) competed with the emerging 'true' carnivores, characterized by their large carnassial teeth and canines. The first carnivores (*miacids*) split into two groups: doglike (*vulpavines*) and catlike (*viverravines*), which then evolved into modern forms. True rodents also appeared, with grinding molars and chisel-shaped incisors with self-sharpening edges. *See* Carnivora. *See also* geological time scale.

Oligochaeta A class of annelid worms containing the terrestrial earthworms (e.g. LUMBRICUS) and many freshwater species. Earthworms are adapted for burrowing and have no parapodia or head appendages and only a few chaetae. They are hermaphrodite but cross-fertilization is usual. The eggs develop in cocoons and development is direct, with no larva. *See* Annelida.

ommatidium (*pl.* ommatidia) *See* compound eye.

omnivore An animal that eats both animal and plant material, e.g. humans. *Compare* carnivore; herbivore.

omomyids *See* Primates; prosimians.

one-locus model A simple deterministic model in POPULATION GENETICS in which NATURAL SELECTION acts on a single locus with two alleles, one dominant and one recessive. Equations derived from this model can be used to calculate changes in gene frequency at a given fitness and changes in fitness at a given change in frequency. It shows that natural selection can produce evolutionary change rapidly (on a geological timescale). Although it is a simplified model it can be used in real cases; for example, INDUSTRIAL MELANISM in the peppered moth. The one-locus model can also be used for a multi-locus system in linkage equilibrium but cannot be used if there is LINKAGE DISEQUILIBRIUM. *See also* multi-locus model. *Compare* quantitative genetics.

ontogeny The course of development of an organism from fertilized egg to adult. Occasionally ontogeny is used to describe the development of an individual structure. *See also* Haeckel; recapitulation.

Onychophora A small invertebrate phylum comprising the velvet worms. They have some annelid and some arthropod features and are often referred to as a MISSING LINK between the two groups. Onychophorans (e.g. *Peripatus*) live mainly in tropical forests and have an elongated body covered with a soft cuticle and bearing short unjointed segmentally arranged clawed legs. Cilia, which are absent in arthropods, are present in the reproductive system and the excretory organs are segmentally arranged ciliated coelomoducts. However, in common with arthropods, the body cavity is a hemocoel and respiration is carried out by tracheae. *See also* missing link.

oocyte A reproductive cell in the ovary of an animal that gives rise to an ovum. The primary oocyte develops from an oogonium, which has undergone a period of multiplication and growth. It divides by MEIOSIS and the first meiotic (or reduction) division produces a secondary oocyte, containing half the number of chromosomes, and a small polar body. The secondary oocyte undergoes the second meiotic division to form an ovum and a second polar body. In many species the second meiotic division is not completed until after fertilization. *See also* oogenesis.

oogamy *See* anisogamy.

oogenesis The formation of ova within the ovary of female animals. Precursor cells in the germinal epithelium multiply by MITOSIS to form oogonia, even before the animal is born. After the onset of sexual maturity, ova are produced from oogonia at regular intervals.

The oogonium grows in size and becomes a primary oocyte, which then undergoes MEIOSIS. The first meiotic division or reduction division results in the formation of a secondary oocyte and a small polar body. The second meiotic division of the secondary oocyte produces an ovum and a second polar body. However, the female gamete may be released at the secondary oocyte stage and the second meiotic division may not be completed until after fertilization.

oogonium 1. A cell in the ovary of an animal that undergoes a period of multiplication and growth to give rise to an oocyte. *See* oogenesis.
2. The female reproductive organ of certain protoctists and fungi, often distinctly different in shape and size from the male reproductive organ (the antheridium). This unicellular gametangium contains one or more large nonmotile haploid eggs called oospheres. These may be liberated prior to fertilization, e.g. *Fucus*, or remain within the oogonium, e.g. *Pythium*.

oolite *See* Jurassic.

oomycete Any member of a phylum (Oomycota) of funguslike protoctists (pseudofungi) that includes the water molds, downy mildews, and white rusts. They are mainly parasites or saprophytes, and feed by extending hyphae into the tissues of their host, releasing digestive enzymes and absorbing nutrients through the hyphal walls. The oomycetes were for-

merly classified as fungi, but are now grouped with the PROTOCTISTA because they possess flagella.

operator *See* operon.

operon A genetic unit found in prokaryotes and comprising a group of closely linked genes acting together and coding for the various enzymes of a particular biochemical pathway. At one end is an *operator*, which may under certain conditions be repressed by another gene outside the operon, the *regulator gene*. The regulator gene produces a substance that binds with the operator, renders it inoperative, and so prevents enzyme production. The presence of a suitable substrate prevents this binding, and so enzyme production can commence. Another site in the operon, the PROMOTER, initiates the formation of the messenger RNA that carries the code for the synthesis of the enzymes determined by all the *structural genes* of the operon.

Ophiuroidea The largest class of the Echinodermata, containing the brittle stars (e.g. *Ophiothrix*). The body is covered by articulating skeletal plates and consists of a small central disk with long fragile arms, which are used in locomotion. Feeding is effected by tube feet, which convey food to the ventral mouth. The larva is a form of DIPLEURULA larva (*see* pluteus).

Brittle stars made their appearance in the Ordovician, but have little importance as fossil indicators, although when they are discovered, they are usually found in abundance.

opposable thumb *See* pollex.

order A taxonomic unit comprising a collection of similar families. Plant orders generally end in -ales (e.g. Liliales) but animal orders do not have any particular ending. Orders may be divided into suborders. Similar orders constitute a class.

Ordovician The second oldest period of the Paleozoic era, some 510–440 million years ago. It is characterized by an abundance of marine invertebrates but an almost total absence of vertebrates apart from some jawless fish. Many of the invertebrates were primitive forms of life that have no living representatives. The sea levels of the Ordovician were usually high, and by the middle of this period, very little land was exposed. In the first half of the period, the climate became warmer with an increase in carbon dioxide levels, but it then began to cool down, ending in a period of glaciation and a mass extinction. The Cambrian fauna declined and were replaced by a much more diverse fauna that dominated the seas for the next 250 million years (the *Great Ordovician radiation*). Articulate brachiopods, with a hinged calcareous shell, echinoderms, foraminiferans, and bivalve mollusks (pelecypods) flourished. The first corals (both tabulate and rugose forms), bryozoans, stomatoporoid sponges, ostracods, and jawless fishes appeared. Graptolites (e.g. *Didymograptus*), trilobites (e.g. *Triarthus*), and cephalopods abounded and individuals became larger in size. Nautiloids (e.g. *Heracloceras*) developed a number of differently designed shells, often reaching lengths of 6 m. They were adapted to a wide variety of niches in the seas and on the continental shelves. Reef-building became more complex. When the climate cooled, the more specialized organisms died out. The Caledonian OROGENY began in the Ordovician and continued into the Silurian. The name comes from an ancient Celtic tribe from North Wales, Great Britain, known as the Ordovices. *See also* geological time scale; mass extinction.

organ A part of an organism that is made up of a number of different tissues specialized to carry out a particular function. Examples include the lung, stomach, wing, and leaf.

organelle A discrete subcellular structure with a particular function. The largest organelle is the nucleus; other examples are chloroplasts, mitochondria, Golgi apparatus, vacuoles, and ribosomes. Organelles allow division of labor within the CELL. Prokaryotic cells have very few organelles compared with eukaryotic cells.

organizer A part of an embryo whose presence causes neighboring tissue to develop in a particular way. The term *primary organizer* is restricted to the first or most important initiator at gastrulation; for example, the dorsal lip of the amphibian blastopore or Hensen's node in mammals and birds. Determinants of major systems (e.g. notochord) are called *secondary organizers*; local centers of developmental activity (e.g. dermal papillae) are *tertiary organizers*.

Oriental One of the six zoogeographical regions of the Earth. It includes the southern Asian countries of India, Southeast Asia, and the western Malay archipelago. The characteristic fauna include the Indian elephant, rhinoceros, macaque, gibbon, orang-utan, jungle fowl, and peacock. The boundary between this region and the Australasian region has been the subject of contention in the past. The Oriental is separated from the Palearctic by mountain ranges going from east to west including the Himalayas, which separated warm-adapted species in the south from cold-adapted species in the North. The Himalayas were formed when India collided with southern Asia in the MIOCENE. *See* zoogeography; continental drift; Wallace's line.

origin of life The process by which living cells evolved from nonliving precursors. Geological evidence strongly suggests that life originated on earth at least 4000 mya with the oldest known fossils being approximately 3500 million years old. The basic components of organic matter – water, methane, ammonia, and related compounds – were abundant in the atmosphere. Energy from the sun (cosmic rays) and lightning storms caused these to recombine into increasingly complex organic molecules, e.g. amino acids, nucleotides, and sugars, which formed a prebiotic chemical soup (*primordial soup*). Particular combinations of these molecules formed a replicating molecule, now thought to be RNA. The next step was probably the enclosure of the replicating molecule inside a membrane, creating a primitive cell. Once enclosed, metabolic and replicating enzymes evolved, giving a simple prokaryotic cell. Within 500 million years cells were also capable of photosynthesis.

Silica-rich rocks (cherts) in South Africa and Western Australia (dated 3500 mya) have been found to have contained microfossils similar to present-day CYANOBACTERIA, which can photosynthesize (see photosynthesis), and in Greenland organic compounds have been found dated 3800 mya, indicating an even earlier origin. The oldest bacteria (see Archaea) cannot survive if oxygen is present, and forms such as these possibly preceded the photosynthesizing organisms. However, the bacteria continued to exist even when the oxygen levels increased by photosynthesis, by inhabiting mud and ocean bottoms, where there is no oxygen.

Certain authorities ascribe to the theory that life did not originate on Earth, but started elsewhere in the solar system and was brought to Earth when asteroids containing primitive prokaryotes crashed into Earth. See also black smokers; Miller.

Ornithischia   See dinosaur.

ornithopods   See dinosaur.

orogeny   A period of mountain building in geological time leading to the formation of mountain ranges, often lasting for tens of millions of years. Examples are the Laramide orogeny, which began in the Cretaceous and gave rise to the Rocky Mountains, and the Alpine orogeny of the Tertiary, which happened when Europe collided with Africa and led to the formation of the Alps.

Orrorin tugenensis   An extinct AUSTRALOPITHECINE comprised of 12 fossil fragments found in the Tugen Hills of Kenya, dated about 6 mya. Their discovery in the year 2000 by Birgett Senut and Martin Pickford on the Kenya Paleontology Expedition led to the nickname *Millennium man*. *Orrorin* means 'original man' in the Tugen language and the species is named after the Tugen Hills. Characteris-

tics of the femurs of *O. tugenensis* suggest bipedalism, and the teeth with small molars and thick dentine are more like those of the genus *Homo* than the Australopithecines. However, the link between this species and *Homo sapiens* is tenuous and continues to be very controversial.

orthogenesis   An early theory of evolution in which evolutionary change was envisaged as occurring in a definite direction and along a predetermined route, irrespective of natural selection. Orthogenesis therefore conflicts with conventional evolutionary theory such as NEODARWINISM.

orthologous   Describing genes of similar sequence, or function, from different species. *See* conserved sequence; homologous. *Compare* analogous; paralagous.

osmoregulation   The process by which animals regulate their internal osmotic pressure by controlling the amount of water and the concentration of salts in their bodies, thus counteracting the tendency of water to pass in or out by osmosis. In freshwater animals, water tends to enter the body and various methods have evolved to remove the excess, such as the contractile vacuole of protoctists, nephridia and Malpighian tubules in invertebrates, and kidneys with well-developed glomeruli in freshwater fish. Marine vertebrates prevent excess water loss and excrete excess salts by having kidneys with few glomeruli and short tubules. Terrestrial vertebrates avoid desiccation by having kidneys with long convoluted tubules, which increase the reabsorption of water and salts.

Osteichthyes   The class of vertebrates that contains the bony fishes, characterized by a skeleton of bone and only one external gill opening, which is covered by an operculum. The spiracle is greatly reduced or absent and the body is covered by overlapping scales. Bony fishes are first found as fossils in the Devonian, often described as the 'Age of Fishes', and today are the dominant fishes, invading all types of waters. Primitive forms possessed functional lungs and these are still present in members of the order DIPNOI (lungfish). The order TELEOSTEI contains most of the modern bony fishes, in which the lung has become modified to form the swim bladder.

Most of the earliest fossil representatives of the Middle Devonian lived in fresh water. There were two main groups: the ray-finned fishes (*actinopterygians*) and the air-breathing fishes (*Choanichthyes*). The actinopterygians were rather insignificant in the Paleozoic, but in the Mesozoic expanded very rapidly and diversified enormously to occupy the seas and inland waters; they include the Teleostei. The main trends in their evolution were the development of thinner, more rounded scales, a homocercal tail, complete ossification of the skeleton, and changes associated with the jaws.

The Choanichthyes can be divided into the lungfish (Dipnoi) and the lobe-finned fishes (coelacanths), the latter thought to have been extinct until living representatives were found near Madagascar in 1939. The large fleshy bases of the lobe-fins enabled them to pull themselves out of the water on to the land, sparsely inhabited by animals and thus with a host of different habitats to exploit. The Devonian fossil *Eusthenopteron* had many amphibian features similar to those of *Ichthyostega*, the oldest fossil amphibian, and it is likely that a group of these ancient lobe-finned fishes evolved into the first land-living vertebrates. *Compare* Chondrichthyes. *See also* Amphibia; coelacanth; Placodermi.

ostracoderms *See* Cyclostomata.

ostracods *See* Crustacea.

outbreeding Breeding between individuals that are not closely related. In plants the term is often used to mean cross-fertilization, and various methods (e.g. stamens maturing before pistils) exist to promote it. In animals behavioral mechanisms often promote outbreeding. The most extreme form – crossing between species – usually results in sterile offspring and there are various mechanisms to discourage it. Outbreeding increases heterozygosity, giving more adaptable and more vigorous populations. *Compare* inbreeding.

outgroup comparison *See* morphology.

out of Africa theory (African Eve theory) The theory that modern humans (*Homo sapiens*) originated in Africa and migrated to Asia and Europe, in so doing causing other human species, e.g. *H. erectus* and *H. neanderthalis*, to go extinct. This theory was partly derived from the discovery of MITOCHONDRIAL EVE, a supposed ancestor of all modern humans who existed in Africa. There is more variation in African mitochondrial and nuclear DNA than in Asian, American, and European DNA, which could indicate that African DNA is older, but it is not the only explanation. The best support for the out of Africa theory comes from fossil evidence. This is especially so with the discovery of the Herto skull (*see Homo sapiens*) discovered in 1997 in Ethiopia, and dated at 150 000 years old, the exact match calculated from the genetic analysis of DNA. *Compare* multiregional theory. *See also* Mungo man; Nanjing man.

oviparity The production of undeveloped eggs, which are laid or spawned by the female. Fertilization may occur before their release, as in birds and some reptiles, or after, as in most invertebrates, fish, and amphibians. Large numbers of eggs are usually produced because of their poor chances of survival, due to lack of maternal protection. Each egg contains a large yolk store to nourish the developing embryo. *Compare* ovoviviparity; viviparity.

ovoviviparity The condition in invertebrates, fish, and reptiles in which eggs are produced and retained within the body of the female during embryonic development. The embryo derives nourishment from the yolk store and so only depends on the mother for physical protection. Ovoviviparity is presumed to be an evolutionary stage leading to viviparity. *Compare* oviparity; viviparity.

ovulation The release of an egg (ovum) from a Graafian follicle at the surface of a vertebrate ovary. Ovulation actually occurs before the ovum is fully mature; i.e. at the oocyte stage. The process is stimulated by luteinizing hormone (LH) produced by the pituitary gland in the presence of estrogen.

ovum (egg cell) The immotile female reproductive cell (gamete) produced in the ovary of an animal. It consists of a central haploid nucleus surrounded by cytoplasm, containing a variable amount of yolk and a vitelline membrane. Size varies between species; in humans, it is about 0.15 mm in diameter. In chickens it is about 30 mm in diameter and further enlarged by a layer of albumen, more membranes, and a shell to become a true egg. A single ovum is released from the ovary at regular intervals; in humans, about once every 28 days. If fertilized by a spermatozoon it develops into a new individual of the same species. Sometimes fertilization occurs before the ovum is fully developed, i.e. at the oocyte stage. *See also* ovulation.

ozone layer *See* pollution.

P

p   *See* nucleotide diversity.

pachytene   In MEIOSIS, the stage in mid-prophase I that is characterized by the contraction of paired homologous chromosomes. At this point each chromosome consists of a pair of chromatids and the two associated chromosomes are termed a tetrad.

paedomorphosis   A form of HETE-ROCHRONY in which an organism repro-duces in what was a juvenile form in an ancestor. It can be brought about by *prog-enesis*, speeding up the development of germ cells, or NEOTENY, slowing down the development of somatic cells. The Mexican axolotl is a classic example of neoteny. There is a theory that many higher taxa have evolved by paedomorphosis from the larval stage of ancestors because larval stages are more flexible, but there is no real evidence for this. *See* macroevolution; ter-minal addition; von Baer's law.

pairing   *See* synapsis.

palate   The roof of the mouth; a parti-tion that separates the nasal passage from the buccal cavity in mammals. The anterior portion is supported by bone and is called the *hard palate*. Behind this is the *soft palate* ending in the uvula. The bones forming the hard palate are projections from the premaxillae and maxillae, and posteriorly, the palatines complete the shelf.

In Amphibia, the skin covering the palate is adapted as a respiratory surface.

Palearctic   Literally 'old northern', one of the six zoogeographical regions of the Earth, including Europe, the former USSR, northern Arabia, and the Mediterranean coastal strip of Africa. The fauna include the hedgehog, wild boar, and fallow and roe deer. This region has remained part of the original supercontinent of PANGEA, and later, of LAURASIA. The Palearctic had al-ways been connected with the NEARCTIC because even after the northern part of the Atlantic Ocean had separated these land masses, they were still connected by the land bridge across the Bering Straits in the east, which existed on and off from about 75 000 to 11 000 years ago. Certain au-thorities link the Nearctic and Palearctic into the *Holarctic* region. *See* zoogeogra-phy; continental drift.

paleoanthropology   The use of fossil evidence to study early human ancestors.

paleobiology   The biological study of fossils.

paleobotany   *See* paleontology.

Paleocene   The oldest epoch of the Ter-tiary, 65–55 mya. There was an initial pe-riod of cooling, followed by gradual warming to a tropical or subtropical cli-mate at the end of the epoch. The Laramide OROGENY of the Cretaceous continued the formation of the Rocky Mountains and Greenland split off from America and Eurasia. There was an ADAPTIVE RADIATION of the mammals, filling the niches that had been occupied by the extinct dinosaurs. Many of these strange primitive mammals became extinct, e.g. the hoofed carnivo-rous MESONYCHIDS that were the ancestors of the whales. CREODONTS were archaic carnivores and there were other enormous

animals with huge slicing teeth. TAE-
NIODONTS were examples of bearlike herbivores with huge gnawing teeth banded
with enamel. The herbivores browsed in
the tropical forests that developed as the
climate warmed. Modern sharks appeared
in the seas.

paleoecology The investigation of prehistoric ecology as revealed by studying
fossils and their artefacts, pollen samples,
and the rocks in which such structures
occur.

Paleogene *See* Tertiary.

Paleolithic The older Stone Age, when
stone tools can first be recognized as such,
extending from about 2 mya to about
10 000 years ago. *See also* Cro-Magnon
man; human evolution; Neolithic.

paleontology The scientific study of extinct organisms, including their fossil remains, and impressions left by them.
Sometimes the subject is divided into *paleobotany*, the study of fossil plants, and *paleozoology*, the study of fossil animals.

Paleozoic The first and oldest era in
which life became abundant, about
590–230 mya. It is divided into six main
periods: the Cambrian, Ordovician, Silurian, Devonian, Carboniferous, and Permian. Beginning with aquatic invertebrates
and algae, the era ended with the invasion
of land by tree ferns and reptiles. It is believed that at the beginning of the Paleozoic
the land mass was much less than that of
the present day and possibly formed a single supercontinent called *Rodinia* (similar
to the later PANGEA). This split throughout
the Paleozoic into several separate blocks
that occupied the southern hemisphere.
The enormous *Panthalassa Ocean* occupied the northern hemisphere. By the end
of the Paleozoic, the continental blocks
had drifted together again and collided to
form Pangea. The collisions caused the formation of huge mountain ranges, which
were gradually eroded causing large deposits of sandstones (red sandstones and

deserts, for example) and mudstones (*see*
Devonian; Permian).

In the seas of the Early Paleozoic, marine life flourished, depicted by the Cambrian Explosion and the Great Ordovician
radiation (*see* Cambrian; Ordovician). Any
continental life was represented on the
beaches by algae, crustacea, and worms.
By Silurian times, primitive land plants had
developed, but by late Devonian times,
forests developed on the sandbanks, followed by the characteristic coal forests and
swamps of the Carboniferous. The ancient
lobe-finned fishes (coelacanths) evolved
into ancestors of the earliest amphibians,
followed by the reptiles, thus establishing
life on the land. *See also* geological time
scale; Sedgwick.

paleozoology *See* paleontology.

palynology *See* pollen analysis.

Pangea The single early Mesozoic supercontinent that existed about 225 million years ago. It broke up on an east–west
axis, separating into the enormous land
masses to the north (LAURASIA) and GOND-
WANA to the south. *See* continental drift.

pangenesis The theory, no longer accepted, introduced by Darwin to explain
the inheritance of variation. He postulated
that the body fluids carry particles from all
over the body to the reproductive cells
where they affect the hereditary material
and thus the characters inherited by the
next generation. Pangenesis was used to
explain the erroneous theory of the inheritance of ACQUIRED CHARACTERISTICS. *See
also* Lamarckism; neoDarwinism; Weismannism.

panmixis Random mating throughout a
population.

Panthalassa Ocean *See* Paleozoic.

pantodonts *See* amblypods.

parallel evolution (parallelism; parallel
speciation) The evolution of similar features independently in closely related or-

ganisms as a result of strong selection in the same direction. An example of how this may have taken place is revealed by studies of sticklebacks inhabiting Canadian lakes. They contain two distinct stickleback species, one that feeds on plankton, the other species a bottom feeder. The analysis of mitochondrial DNA (mtDNA) (*see* mitochondrion) has shown that the species in the same lake are more closely related to one another (despite their different feeding habits) than to the species in other lakes, showing parallel evolution. However, gene sequencing reveals a different explanation – possibly unlike morphs may have got into the lake at different times, interbred, and exchanged mtDNA, in which case the species may appear to be more closely related than it actually is. *Compare* convergent evolution.

paralogous Describing HOMOLOGOUS genes that have highly conserved sequences and functions. *See* conserved sequence; conserved function. *Compare* analogous; orthologous.

Paranthropus boisei An extinct early robust AUSTRALOPITHECINE (between 1.2 and 1.4 million years old) first discovered by Mary LEAKEY in the Olduvai Gorge in 1959. *P. boisei* (first named *Zinjanthropus boisei*) was found to be a relative of *Paranthropus robustus*. *P. boisei* individuals were taller than *P. robustus* individuals, had longer faces, more prominent crests (sagittal crests) on their skulls, and showed more pronounced SEXUAL DIMORPHISM. *Compare Paranthropus robustus*.

Paranthropus robustus An extinct early AUSTRALOPITHECINE, the first of the robust australopithecines to be discovered in the 1930s by Robert Broom, working alongside Raymond DART in South Africa, first named *Australopithecus crassidens*. Many other remains of this australopithecine have been found at Swartkrans, Dreimulen, and Kromdraai. *P. robustus* individuals had a heavy build, prominent crests on the cranium, long broad flat faces with heavy jaws, and huge molars and premolars, indicating a vegetarian diet. The

species also exhibits SEXUAL DIMORPHISM. The specimens are dated 2 million and 1 mya and are 1.1–1.3 m tall. *Compare Paranthropus boisei.*

Parapatric speciation

parapatric speciation A controversial theory of speciation in which a new species is formed by a subpopulation of an ancestral species that is geographically continuous with the main population. It is possible in an area where two noticeably different forms of the same species (that were previously isolated) are in contact (a *hybrid zone* or belt) and requires REINFORCEMENT. *Compare* allopatric speciation; peripheral isolate speciation; sympatric speciation.

paraphyletic Describing a group of species that includes an ancestral species and some, but not all, of its descendants. The species included are those that have changed little. Paraphyletic groups are allowed in evolutionary and phenetic classification. *Compare* monophyletic; polyphyletic.

Parapsida (parapsids) *See* Reptilia.

parasite An organism that lives in or on another organism (the host) and is detrimental to its host. The intimate relationship between host and parasite means that they are likely to coevolve. Even if a host splits into two new species, the parasite in due course will do the same. The mirror-image phylogenies of hosts and parasites and the variation in parasite virulence over time can be attributed to COEVOLUTION.

Parasites are often described as being 'degenerate' because they no longer possess many of the structures present in their free-living ancestors, for example, a tapeworm has no digestive system. However, the loss of the digestive system in this animal represents the evolution of a specialized adaptation to a new environment – the tapeworm is an internal parasite of the gut of many mammals and obtains its food by absorption directly from its host's digestive system. It has no need for its own digestive system.

parasitic theory of sexual selection   A recent theory of female choice, similar to the HANDICAP THEORY, in which females choose mates that are resistant to parasitic infection. Bright plumage or fur and prominent secondary sexual characters are viewed as a sign of health and a female will preferentially choose a mate on these grounds. *See* sexual selection. *Compare* Fisher's theory.

Parazoa   A subkingdom of the kingdom Animalia containing the phylum PORIFERA (sponges). In some recent classifications it also contains the phylum Placozoa, comprising the tiny marine organism *Trichoplax*. *Compare* protozoa; Metazoa.

parietal eye   *See* pineal eye.

parsimony   A fundamental principle of phylogenetic reconstruction in which the most likely phylogeny is one that requires the least number of evolutionary changes. It is based on the accepted theory that evolutionary change is improbable.

parthenogenesis   Development of unfertilized eggs to form new individuals. It occurs regularly in certain plants (e.g. dandelion) and animals (e.g. aphids). Animals produced by parthenogenesis are always female and, if DIPLOID, look exactly like the parent. *Artificial parthenogenesis* can be induced by pinpricks or treatment with, for instance, cold or acid, especially in eggs shed in water.

Parthenogenesis produces HAPLOID or diploid individuals depending on the genetic state of the ovum when development of the embryo begins. Genetic recombination cannot occur in parthenogenesis and so sexual reproduction occurs occasionally. Aphids show regular alternation of parthenogenesis and heterogamy, whereas queen bees control parthenogenesis by allowing sperm to fertilize some eggs. *See also* apomixis.

partial dominance   *See* co-dominance.

passerines   (perching birds) Birds in which the feet are adapted for grasping branches, having three toes pointing forward and one pointing backward. They constitute the largest order (Passeriformes) of birds (class AVES), with over 5000 species, and include the larks, thrushes, warblers, finches, sparrows, and starlings.

pathogen   Any organism that is capable of causing disease or a toxic response in another organism. Many bacteria, viruses, fungi, and other microorganisms are pathogenic.

patristic   Describing similarity due to common ancestry. *Compare* homoplastic.

***Pax6* gene**   *See* eye.

PCR   *See* polymerase chain reaction.

Pearson, Karl   (1857–1936) British biometrician. Pearson's career was spent largely on applying statistics to biology. Between 1893 and 1906 he published over a hundred papers on statistics in which such now familiar concepts as the standard deviation and the chi-square test for statistical significance were introduced. Later work was published in *Biometrika*, the journal founded by Pearson, Francis Galton, and Walter Weldon in 1901 and edited by Pearson until his death.

Pearson and Weldon became involved in an important controversy with William BATESON on the nature of evolution and its possible measurement. The biometricians emphasized the importance of continuous variation (*see* quantitative inheritance) as the basic material of natural selection and proposed that it be analyzed statistically. Bateson and his supporters, whose views were reinforced by the rediscovery of the works of Gregor MENDEL in 1900, attached more importance to discontinuous variation (*see* qualitative variation) and argued that breeding studies are the best way to illuminate the mechanism of evolution.

The validity of MENDELISM eventually became generally accepted. At the same time, however, the immense value of biometrical techniques in analyzing continuously variable characters like height, which are controlled by many genes, was also recognized. Following Weldon's death in 1906 Pearson spent less time trying to prove the biometricians' case and devoted himself instead to developing statistics as an exact science. He prepared and published many volumes of mathematical tables for statisticians. He also devoted much of his time to the study of EUGENICS. In 1925 he founded and edited until his death the *Annals of Eugenics*.

Pearson is also known as the author of *Grammar of Science* (1892), in which he argued that science does not explain but rather summarizes our experience in a convenient language.

peat Partially decomposed plant material that accumulates in waterlogged anaerobic conditions in temperate humid climates, often forming a layer several meters deep. Peat varies from a light spongy material (sphagnum moss) to a dense brown humidified material in the lower layers. If mineral salts are present in the waterlogged vegetation, neutral or alkaline *fen* peat is formed (the salts neutralize the acid produced by decomposition). If there are no mineral salts in the water (as in rain), acid *bog* peat is formed. Peat is used as a fuel and is the first step in coal formation.

Peking man *See Homo erectus.*

pelagic Inhabiting the open upper waters rather than the bed of a sea or ocean. Pelagic animals and plants may be divided into the plankton and nekton. Life is found throughout the pelagic zone although the numbers of species and individuals decrease with increasing depth. *Compare* benthic. *See also* photic zone.

Pelecypoda (Bivalvia; lamellibranchs) A class of marine and freshwater mollusks, the bivalves, characterized by a laterally compressed body and a shell consisting of two dorsally-hinged valves. Some bivalves are anchored to the substratum by tough filaments (the *byssus*), e.g. *Mytilus* (mussel). Others burrow into sand, e.g. *Cardium* (cockle); rocks, e.g. *Pholas* (piddock); or wood, e.g. *Teredo* (shipworm). Some, e.g. *Pecten* (scallop), swim by clapping the shell valves together. Bivalves have a poorly developed head and large paired gills used for respiration and, in many, for filter feeding.

The pelecypods evolved in Ordovician times and became fairly widespread in the Paleozoic. By the Carboniferous period, the bivalves were very similar to those of the present day. They became increasingly common during the Triassic, replacing the brachiopods as the most important shellfish. Oysterlike forms were common in the Jurassic.

pelvic girdle (hip girdle) A rigid bony or cartilaginous skeletal structure in the posterior region of the vertebrate body, to which the hindlimbs or fins are attached. In tetrapods, it usually consists of two sides, each consisting of, ventrally, an anterior pubic bone and a posterior ischium and, dorsally, an ilium. They meet at the acetabulum – an articular surface for the hind limb. Each ilium is fused to the sacral vertebrae to permit the transmission of thrust from the hindlimbs to the body to produce movement, and also to allow the weight of the body to be supported by the girdle. The pelvic girdle of fish consists of simple bars of cartilage or bone.

Pelycosauria *See* Mammalia; Reptilia.

Pennsylvanian The US name for the Upper Carboniferous period in the geological time scale.

pentadactyl limb A limb having five

digits; its bone components have a basic arrangement characteristic of all tetrapod vertebrates. It evolved from modifications to the paired paddlelike fins of the ancestral lobe-finned fish in association with the transition from water to land (*see* Osteichthyes). Various alterations have been made to this basic limb type by reduction or fusion of elements as an adaptation for different functions and modes of progression, such as swimming, digging, flying, and running. *See also* digitigrade; plantigrade; unguligrade.

peppered moth *See* industrial melanism.

peptide A type of compound formed of a number of amino acid molecules linked together. The link between amino acids is called a *peptide bond*. According to the number of amino acids linked together they are called di-, tri-, oligo-, or polypeptides. Peptides can be produced by the partial hydrolysis of PROTEINS.

perching birds *See* passerines.

period *See* geological time scale.

peripatric speciation *See* allopatric speciation.

peripheral isolate speciation *See* allopatric speciation.

Perissodactyla The order of mammals that contains the odd-toed ungulates, including the horses and zebras (with one toe) and the rhinoceroses (with three toes). The middle digit bears the weight of the body. These herbivorous mammals typically have feet encased in a protective horny hoof, lips adapted for plucking, strong cropping incisor teeth, and molars and premolars adapted for chewing. The stomach is simple and bacterial digestion of cellulose occurs in the cecum.

The spread of grasslands and savanna in the Oligocene that continued into the Miocene encouraged the diversity of the herbivores, which replaced the archaic herbivores of earlier epochs. Herbivores' limbs became adapted for running long distances in the new environment and their teeth became adapted for feeding on the tough siliceous grasses.

The rhinoceroses were very abundant in the Oligocene and *Indricotherium* was the largest mammal of all time (8 m high). The woolly rhinoceros was a human contemporary and disappeared in the last Ice Age. The tapirs were also more widespread in the Eocene and Oligocene and like the other Perissodactyla, gradually declined, many becoming extinct in the Pleistocene. Two other extinct groups include the *titanotheres*, massive horned animals from the Oligocene of North America, and the horselike *chalicotheres*, with clawed toes for digging up roots. *Compare* Artiodactyla. *See* horse evolution.

permanent teeth The second set of teeth of most mammals, replacing the deciduous teeth (milk teeth). *See also* diphyodont.

Permian Named for the city of Perm, in Russia, the last period of the PALEOZOIC era, some 280–250 mya. The ancient continental blocks continued to move together to form PANGEA, resulting in widespread volcanic activity and mountain building. The rocks that formed by erosion and sedimentation of the newly formed mountains are mainly red sandstones (New Red Sandstone). The Permian began with the continuing glaciation in the southern hemisphere, followed by global warming, leading to very hot dry conditions, much too hot to support life in the interiors of the continents.

In the seas, marine animals consisted mainly of crinoids, brachiopods, bryozoans, rugose corals, gastropods, and bivalves. The trilobites were dying out and the ammonites evolved. Life flourished in tropical reefs at the edges of various Permian basins, e.g. the Delaware and Midland Basins of Texas.

On land, amphibians were greatly reduced in numbers, but reptiles became increasingly widespread, especially the pelecysaurs (mammal-like reptiles), which died out before the end of the Permian and were replaced by the therapsids. The plants included the seed ferns (e.g. *Glossopteris*), giant horsetails, and giant clubmosses. The gymnosperms largely replaced the pterido-phytes, for example, conifers, cycads, and ginkgoes evolved as they were better adapted to the dry conditions. Many coal seams were formed in the Permian. Many modern insect groups also evolved in the Permian.

The mass extinction at the end of the Permian wiped out all of the solitary corals, most of the bryozoans, bra-chiopods, and crinoids, and on land, most of the therapsids, although the few of the latter that survived produced all the subse-quent mammalian groups. Many huge coniferous forests completely disappeared. The reasons for the extinction may have been a combination of factors: increasing temperature; reduction of sea levels; an in-crease in carbon dioxide; intense volcanic eruptions – rather than a single cause. *See also* geological time scale; mass extinction.

pesticide-resistant insects   Insects that are able to survive and reproduce despite the presence of pesticides. These resistant variants increase in frequency over time if pesticides remain present in their environ-ment. For example, many insects, such as houseflies and certain species of mosqui-toes, have evolved resistance to the pesti-cide DDT. Four genes are involved in DDT resistance by the housefly. Two genes detoxify the poison, one delays absorption of DDT through the cuticle, and the fourth gene acts by an as yet undiscovered method.

Phaeophyta (brown algae)   A phylum of protoctists comprising mainly marine algae, notably the macroscopic thallose seaweeds that inhabit the intertidal zones. They contain the pigments chlorophyll *a* and *c*, β carotene, and the xanthophylls, which give the algae their characteristic brown color. Food is stored as mannitol or laminarin and the cell walls contain cellu-lose or hemicellulose. The classification of brown algae is contentious. Based on se-quence analysis and certain of their charac-teristics (especially those containing chlorophyll *c* as well as *a*), certain taxono-mists place them in the phylum Chromista, along with yellow-green algae, DIATOMS, and *pseudofungi* (which includes water molds and also *Phytophthera infestans*, the cause of the great potato blight famine in Ireland). These groups have other similari-ties that include: chloroplasts positioned inside the endoplasmic reticulum; chloro-plasts with three membranes; and the re-mains of nuclear material within the chloroplast. It is thought that these organ-isms appropriated chloroplasts by captur-ing a photosynthetic unicellular alga much later than the red and green algae of the plant kingdom and evolved much later (*see* endosymbiont theory). The Phaeophyta contains nine orders, including the Fucales, or wracks (e.g. *Fucus*), and the Laminari-ales, or kelps (e.g. *Laminaria*).

phage (bacteriophage)   A virus that in-fects bacteria. In GENETIC ENGINEERING, nonviral DNA can be inserted into a phage, which is then used as a cloning vector (*see* gene cloning; genetic engineering; phage).

phalanges   A series of small rod-shaped bones that form the skeleton of the fingers and toes (digits) of tetrapod limbs. In the typical PENTADACTYL LIMBS of five digits, there are two phalanges in the first digit and three in each of the others. In some species they may be greatly elongated or re-duced. They form hinge joints with each other and with the metacarpals or metatarsals. *See also* adaptation.

phanerogam   In early classifications, any plant that reproduces by seed. The phanerogams are thus equivalent to the spermatophytes of more recent taxonomic systems. *Compare* cryptogam.

Phanerozoic   *See* Precambrian.

pharynx   The part of the alimentary canal between the buccal cavity and the esophagus. In mammals, it has openings from the mouth and nasal passage at its an-terior end, and to the esophagus and tra-chea at the posterior end. The Eustachian tubes from the middle ears also open into the pharynx.

In *Branchiostoma*, fish, and amphibian tadpoles, the pharynx is perforated by gill slits, and water, passing out through these, supplies oxygen to the blood in the gill filaments.

In worms, the pharynx is often muscular and aids the ingestion of food.

phenetic Describing or relating to the observable similarities and differences between organisms. Phenetic classification systems are based on such characteristics, rather than evolutionary relationships between groups. *See* phenetic species concept. *Compare* phylogenetic.

phenetic discontinuity A gap in the range of phenotype variation in a population. *Compare* taxic discontinuity.

phenetic distance *See* distance.

phenetic species concept The definition of a SPECIES as a group of organisms that have similar observable characteristics, i.e. they are phonetically similar. *Compare* biological species concept; cladistic species concept; ecological species concept; recognition species concept.

phenocopy A change in the appearance of an organism caused by the environment, but which is similar in effect to a change caused by gene mutation. Such changes, which are not inherited, are generally caused by environmental factors (e.g. malnutrition, radiation) affecting the organism at an early stage of development.

phenotype The observable characteristics of an organism, which are determined by the interaction of the GENOTYPE with the environment. Many genes present in the genotype do not show their effects in the phenotype because they are masked by DOMINANT alleles. Genotypically identical organisms may have very different phenotypes in different environments, an effect particularly noticeable in plants grown in various habitats. *See* environmental effect; genotypic effect; quantitative genetics.

phenotypic differentiation The crea-

tion of two or more phenotypically different forms from a single ancestral PHENOTYPE during speciation.

phenotypic parallelism The situation in which two genetically different organisms have virtually indistinguishable morphological structures. The reverse can also be true in cases where the genome can produce several phenotypes, depending on the environmental conditions, e.g. in METAMORPHOSIS.

phenotypic plasticity The sensitivity of a phenotype to changes in the environment.

pheromone A volatile organic molecule excreted by certain animals that causes a physiological or behavioral response in other members of the same species. Pheromones are important in the social behavior of many animals (insects and mammals). They help to promote social order and coordination in colonies, they are used in sexual attraction, and are also involved in attack and escape responses of some animals.

philopatry The tendency of an individual to stay in, or return to, its home area.

phosphorites Rocks laid down in shallow seas, some of which have preserved soft-bodied fossils in fine detail. *See* Ediacara fauna.

photic zone The surface layer of an ocean or lake that is penetrated by sunlight and in which the phytoplankton flourish. Red and yellow wavelengths of light penetrate to about 50 m while blue and violet light may reach 200 m. The diatoms, which are the main components of phytoplankton, may be found down to 80 m. Beyond 200 m the water is perpetually dark.

photosynthesis The synthesis of organic compounds (carbohydrates) in the CHLOROPLASTS from carbon dioxide and water using light as the source of energy and releasing oxygen

$$6CO_2 + 6H_2O + \text{solar energy} \rightarrow$$
$$C_6H_{12}O_6 + 6O_2$$

In the reaction, hydrogen used for synthesizing carbohydrates is obtained by water splitting and gaseous oxygen is produced. In an alternative method of photosynthesis in bacteria that possess bacteriochlorophyll, water is not used as a hydrogen source and therefore oxygen is not produced. The sulfur bacteria, for example, use either hydrogen sulfide or molecular hydrogen as a hydrogen source rather than water. The CYANOBACTERIA generally photosynthesize using water as a hydrogen donor, but in certain circumstances they can use hydrogen sulfide rather than water. Photosynthesis is thought to be an ancient process as the oldest known Cyanobacteria fossils (STROMATOLITES, about 3500 million years old) were probably capable of photosynthesis. Around the time that eukaryotic cells were evolving there was a significant increase in atmospheric oxygen levels, indicating that photosynthesis was becoming widespread. Photosynthesis was probably instrumental in increasing the amount of gaseous oxygen in the atmosphere as well as increasing the supply of organic compounds in the ancient biosphere. The change in the composition of the atmosphere would probably have been very slow and gradual as the gaseous oxygen would be likely to have been very toxic to many of the existing organisms. It is likely that photosynthesis would have become the dominant process because water was a more accessible hydrogen donor than gaseous hydrogen. See chloroplast; endosymbiont theory. See also origin of life.

photosynthetic bacteria A group of bacteria able to photosynthesize through possession of a green pigment, bacteriochlorophyll, which is slightly different from the chlorophyll of plants. They do not use water as a hydrogen source, as do plants, and an oxidized by-product is produced rather than oxygen. Photosynthetic bacteria include the green sulfur bacteria, purple sulfur bacteria, and purple nonsulfur bacteria. See also Cyanobacteria.

phyletic See phylogenetic.

phyletic evolution See phylogenetic evolution.

phyletic gradualism (gradualism) The theory, in opposition to the theory of PUNCTUATED EQUILIBRIUM, that evolution occurs at a constant rate throughout time and new species arise from the gradual transformation of ancestral species. Darwinism and neoDarwinism predict that the evolution of adaptation is gradual but do not predict that evolution occurs solely in the pattern of phyletic gradualism. There is evidence in the fossil record for both gradual evolution and punctuated equilibrium.

phyletic lineage See phylogenetic lineage.

phylogenetic (phyletic) Relating to or reflecting the evolutionary history of an organism. Phylogenetic classifications are based on the assumed evolutionary relationships between organisms rather than their observable characteristics. Phylogenetic relationships are traditionally inferred from morphological character analysis but increasingly, molecular (DNA and RNA protein) sequences are used. Neither is always more reliable and they can indicate different relationships. See molecular phylogenetics; morphology; parsimony. Compare phenetic.

phylogenetic evolution (phyletic evolution) The evolutionary changes occurring in a phylogenetic lineage over time.

phylogenetic lineage (phyletic lineage) A branch of a phylogenetic tree containing all the linear descendants of an ancestral species.

phylogenetic trait analysis A comparative method in which the traits being compared are plotted on the branches of a previously constructed PHYLOGENY and the origin and history of the traits inferred from cladistic principles and the position of the traits. Compare comparative trend analysis.

phylogenetic tree See phylogeny.

phylogenomics *See* molecular phylogenetics.

phylogeny (phylogenetic tree; tree) The evolutionary history of a group of organisms, depicted as a branching diagram showing ancestral relationships. Rooted phylogenics specify the position of the oldest ancestor and have a time axis. Unrooted phylogenies do not specify the oldest ancestor and are therefore timeless. A *bifurcation* is a point in a phylogeny that connects three branches. *See* parsimony; phylogenetic.

phylum One of the major groups into which a KINGDOM of organisms is classified. Phyla may be divided into subphyla. In some plant classifications (especially older ones) the term DIVISION is used instead of phylum.

physiological race The existence of physiologically distinct but morphologically identical races within a species. Such *physiological races* are important in host–pathogen studies, particularly in planning programs to breed for crop resistance. The cereal rust fungus *Puccinia graminis*, for instance, has over 200 physiological races, which have developed in response to new cereal cultivars as they come on the market.

physiology The way in which organisms or parts of organisms function. *Compare* morphology.

phytogeography (plant geography) The study of the geographical distribution of plant species. Phytogeographical and zoogeographical areas do not necessarily coincide, since barriers and factors affecting growth and distribution are sometimes different for plants and animals. *See* biome. *See also* zoogeography.

phytoplankton *See* plankton.

Pilbeam, David Roger (1940–) British physical anthropologist. Anthropologists distinguish between HOMINIDS, which are human species and their extinct ancestors, and the HOMINOIDS, which comprise the superfamily containing humans and apes. Pilbeam has sought to identify the time in the Miocene (between 25 mya and 5 mya) at which the separation of the hominids from the hominoids occurred. In 1932 in the Siwalik Hills in India G. E. Lewis had discovered the fossil remains of a creature he named RAMAPITHECUS (Rama's ape) in rocks about 15 million years old. In 1961 Elwyn Simon, later to be a Yale colleague of Pilbeam, was struck by the small canines and the shape of the dental arch of *Ramapithecus*, seeing in them hominid characteristics.

Pilbeam began a general review of Miocene hominoid fossils. In *Ramapithecus* he thought he could see signs of bipedalism. With its reduced canines, he argued, food must have been prepared in some way, implying that the hands must have been free, possibly to use tools. The creature could well have been both bipedal and terrestrial. In 1968 Pilbeam argued that about 20 million years ago there had been three species of *Dryopithecus* (tree ape) and that these had been ancestral to the chimpanzee, gorilla, and orangutan (pongids). This left the 15 million year old *Ramapithecus* as a hominid and the possibility that hominid and pongid lines could have been separated for 30 million years and more.

Pilbeam's account received wide support and appeared to become increasingly confirmed with the discovery of further fossils. Yet by the late 1960s evidence of another kind that would seriously question the position of *Ramapithecus* was beginning to appear. Biologists such as Vincent SARICH had begun to use variations in protein structure to measure evolutionary divergence. Their evidence suggested that humans and African apes had been separated for no longer than five million years. Clearly, *Ramapithecus* could not have been a Miocene hominid.

Following Sarich's revelations and further fieldwork, Pilbeam has proposed a new evolutionary sequence. In 1980 in Turkey he discovered a partial skull of *Sivapithecus*, a hominoid fossil very similar to *Ramapithecus*. It also closely resembled the sole surviving Asian great ape, the orangutan, but showed little resemblance to any of the australopithecines. Thus the 15 million year old *Ramapithecus* represents not the hominid–hominoid split, but the hominoid divergence between the African and Asian great apes.

Pilbeam has since offered the opinion that he would "never again cling so firmly to one particular evolutionary scheme," and that "fossils themselves can solve only part of the puzzle, albeit an important part."

Piltdown man (*Eoanthropus dawsoni*) The most famous paleoanthropological hoax. In 1908 in Piltdown, England, a workman found part of a human skull in a gravel pit and gave it to an amateur geologist, Charles Dawson. Digging by eminent paleontologists revealed more skull fragments, a lower jaw with teeth, and fossil animal bones of elephant, rhinoceros, mastodon, hippopotamus, and deer. In 1953, 45 years later, Piltdown man fossils were found to be those of an orangutan. Someone had filed down the teeth and altered the lower jaw. The discovery of the AUSTRALOPITHECINES in the 1950s caused researchers to examine the Piltdown fossils more closely and revealed the evidence of tampering.

Nebraska man (*Hesperopithecus haroldcookii*) was believed to be the first anthropoid ape from North America based on a single worn fossil tooth of a peccary (pig) found in northwestern Nebraska in 1922. The discovery was published once in a respectable London magazine and disproved five years later.

pineal eye (parietal eye; 'third eye') A structure derived from the pineal gland and thought to have existed in fossil vertebrates. A well-known example is the TUATARA of New Zealand. The eye is situated on the top of the head and seems to be light-sensitive. It has a lens and retina and nerve fibers connected to the brain.

pineal gland A gland that arises from an outgrowth on the dorsal surface of the vertebrate forebrain and secretes the hor-

mone melatonin. It is thought to have given rise to the third eye in fossil vertebrates. *See* pineal eye.

pinnipeds *See* Carnivora.

Pisces A term sometimes used in classification to include the two classes of fishes – OSTEICHTHYES and CHONDRICHTHYES. Fishes are poikilothermic aquatic vertebrates with a streamlined body, a powerful muscular finned tail for propulsion, and paired pectoral and pelvic fins for stability and steering. There is usually a body covering of scales. The jaws and pharyngeal gill slits are enlarged to deal with the increased need for oxygen and nutrients brought about by rapid locomotion.

Pithecanthropus erectus *See Homo erectus.*

Placentalia *See* Eutheria.

Placodermi (ancient fishes) The placoderms (Silurian–Permian) were armored fish (*see* Agnatha; Cyclostomata) but evolved along with the CHONDRICHTHYES (cartilaginous fish) and OSTEICHTHYES (bony fish) from a common ancestor with hinged jaws and paired fins. The evolution of jaws is a landmark development in vertebrate evolution, enabling new methods of feeding and the ability to exploit new sources of food. The paired fins enabled successful movement to search for the new food sources. There were marine and freshwater placoderms, varying from small forms a few centimeters long to the enormous *Dinichthys*, more than 3 m long with a massive armored head and 'shoulders'. The jaws were primitive and the hyomandibular (the upper part of the first gill arch) was not included in their suspension.

placodonts A group of extinct marine euryapsid reptiles, some with armored turtlelike shells, which lived from the Triassic to the Cretaceous and fed on shellfish. *See also* Ichthyosauria; plesiosaurs; pliosaurs; Reptilia.

plankton A varied collection of aquatic

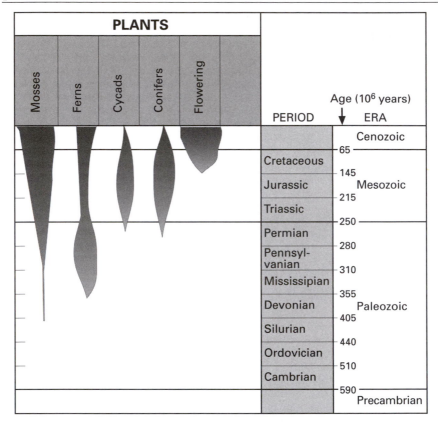

Plant: evolution of some of the main plant groups

organisms that drift freely, not being attached to any substrate and not possessing any organs for locomotion. The most important components of the plant plankton (*phytoplankton*) are the DIATOMS upon which the planktonic animals (*zooplankton*) (e.g. crustaceans) feed. The larvae of many species (e.g. cod) make up a large part of the plankton, especially in early summer. The plankton form the basis of the food chain in the sea. Microscopic plankton are termed *nanoplankton*. *See also* benthic; nekton.

plant An organism that can make its own food by taking in simple inorganic substances and building these into complex molecules by a process termed photosynthesis. This process uses light energy, absorbed by a green pigment called chloro-phyll, which is found in all plants but no animals. One major characteristic that distinguishes plants from other plantlike organisms, such as algae or fungi, is the possession of an embryo that is retained and nourished by maternal tissue. Fungi and algae lack embryos and develop from spores. Plants are also characterized by having cellulose cell walls, not found in animals, and by the inability to move around freely except for some mobile microscopic plants. Plants also differ from animals by generally responding to stimuli very slowly, the response often taking a matter of days and only occurring if the stimulus is prolonged. *Compare* algae; animal; Fungi.

plant geography *See* phytogeography.

plantigrade Describing the mode of progression in some mammals (e.g. bears, rabbits, and humans) in which the entire sole of the foot, i.e. digits and metatarsals (or metacarpals), is in contact with the ground. *Compare* digitigrade; unguligrade.

planula A small ciliated larva of a cnidarian. After swimming to a suitable site, it settles and develops into a polyp. *See* Cnidaria; Hydrozoa; planuloid hypothesis.

planuloid hypothesis The most widely accepted theory of the origin of the Eumetazoa (*see* Metazoa). It is envisaged that the PLANULA larva (planuloid stage) of the phylum CNIDARIA could be ancestors of all multicellular animals except for the PORIFERA (sponges). An ancestral unicellular organ is believed to have given rise to a creeping solid planula-type animal. Later, gastrulation evolved and a gastrovascular cavity developed within the new organism (called a *planuloid*). Planuloids then gave rise to the radially symmetrical cnidarians and later the bilaterally symmetrical forms that developed into the other eumetazoan phyla.

A second theory (the *plakula-bilaterogastrea hypothesis*) envisages a two-layered creeping flat organism (a *plakula*) that obtained food from the muddy or sandy sediments by digestion carried out by the ventral layer of cells. Possibly, the organism could raise part of its body to form a temporary digestive cavity (a *gastraea*) and even to assume a bilaterally symmetrical arrangement (a *bilaterogastraea*). The discovery that *Trichoplax adhaerens* (a flat creeping animal), the most primitive metazoan known, often raises its body in this way to form a temporary digestive cavity gave support to the theory, together with supporting molecular evidence. However, *T. adhaerens* has no bilateral symmetry and the planuloid hypothesis is favored at present.

plasmagene A GENE contained in a self-replicating cytoplasmic particle. Inheritance of the characters controlled by such genes is not Mendelian because appreciable amounts of cytoplasm are passed on only with the female gametes. Mitochondria (*see* mitochondrion) and plastids contain plasmagenes. *See* cytoplasmic inheritance.

plasmalemma *See* plasma membrane.

plasma membrane (cell membrane; plasmalemma) The membrane that surrounds all living cells. *See* membrane.

plasmid An extrachromosomal genetic element found within bacterial cells that replicates independently of the chromosomal DNA. Plasmids typically consist of circular double-stranded DNA molecules of molecular weight 10^6–10^8. They carry a variety of genes, including those for antibiotic resistance, toxin production, and enzyme formation, and may be advantageous to the cell. Plasmids are widely used as cloning vectors in GENETIC ENGINEERING.

plasmogamy Fusion of protoplasm, usually referring to the fusion of cytoplasm but not nuclei. Plasmogamy in the absence of karyogamy (fusion of nuclei) occurs between fungal mycelia of different strains to form a heterokaryon.

plastid *See* endosymbiont theory.

plastogene A gene present in a self-replicating plastid. Inheritance studies have shown that plastogenes control leaf color in some plants, e.g. yellow-leaved *Primula sinensis*.

plate tectonics The theory developed in the 1960s that the Earth's crust consists of moveable rigid plates (*tectonic plates*) that may separate or join in different geological periods. The plates, on which the continents are situated, move slowly and continuously on top of the molten mantle across the surface of the planet, resulting in CONTINENTAL DRIFT. Each plate extends into the sea and ocean from the continental shelf. Lateral movements result in tear faulting at plate margins (e.g. the San Andreas fault zone); plates moving apart create mid-oceanic ridges, with new crust forming at the join (Mid-Atlantic Ridge);

and plates moving down beneath others create ocean trenches. Plate movements result in earthquakes, volcanic activity, faulting, and mountain building. *See* continental drift.

Platyhelminthes (flatworms) A phylum of primitive wormlike invertebrates including the classes Turbellaria (aquatic free-living planarians), and the parasitic Trematoda (flukes) and Cestoda (tapeworms). Flatworms are triploblastic bilaterally symmetrical unsegmented animals lacking a coelom and blood system. The flat body provides a large surface area for gaseous exchange. The gut, when present, is often branched and has only one opening (the mouth) and a sucking pharynx. Protonephridia carry out excretion and reproduction is by a complex hermaphrodite system.

More primitive flatworms have a nerve net similar to the CNIDARIA, but others have a number of longitunal nerve cords, these reducing in number in the most advanced species. The latter also have a swollen anterior end, indicating the beginnings of a primitive 'brain' and the evolution of a definite 'head' end (*see* cephalization).

platyrrhine A member of the group of *New World monkeys* with narrow noses and usually a prehensile tail. Humans did not evolve from this group. *See* Primates. *Compare* catarrhine.

pleiomorphism The occurrence of different morphological stages during the life of an organism. Examples are the larval, pupal, and adult forms of an insect, and the different spore forms of the rust fungi.

pleiotropy The situation in which a single gene produces more than one phenotypic effect. For example, a single gene in tobacco plants is responsible for long petioles and also for longer calyces, anthers, and capsules. One gene affecting the development of more than one body part could cause a DEVELOPMENTAL CONSTRAINT. *See also* sickle-cell anemia.

Pleistocene The first epoch of the QUA-TERNARY period, from about two million years ago until the last glaciation ended about 10 000 years ago. Uniquely in the Pleistocene, there was a rapid reversal between each of the four ICE AGES and the interglacial periods. This resulted in many extinctions of terrestrial and marine organisms and major redistributions of organisms. The consequences, especially of the fourth Ice Age, resulted in many organisms being displaced toward the equator. The ice sheets covered North America and northwest Europe about 18 000 years ago. They had disappeared in Europe by about 8500 years ago and in North America by about 6500 years ago. The Bering land bridge connected Siberia with North Alaska.

The northern tundra of the Pleistocene, with cold-tolerant plants such as dwarf trees, mosses, sedges, and lichens, supported a range of animals, including the woolly mammoth (*Mammuthus primigenius*), and woolly rhinoceros (*Coelodonta antiquitatis*). However, these larger animals with hairy coats for extra insulation were probably confined to the boreal forests further south, leaving the Tundra for reindeer, elk, and oxen, etc., being better adapted to graze on the short vegetation. Saber-toothed cats (*Smilodon*) inhabited North America as major carnivores. Cave bears and North American bison evolved later in this period.

Toward the equator, hominid evolution continued and *Homo erectus* moved out of Africa into Europe and Asia, followed by *Homo sapiens* toward the end of the Pleistocene (*see Homo*; human evolution). Many present-day mammals of South America and Africa resemble the pre-Ice Age mammals of Europe. Most of the large spectacular terrestrial mammals, such as the woolly mammoth, died out in the Pleistocene, possibly due to hunting by humans and/or detrimental environmental factors.

plesiomorphy A shared character state in two species inherited from a distant ancestor. *Compare* apomorphy; homoplasy; synapomorphy.

plesiosaurs A group of extinct marine

euryapsid reptiles that lived from the Triassic to the Cretaceous. They had very long thin necks, turtlelike bodies with flippers or paddles, and short tails. *Elasmosaurus* had over 70 neck vertebrae. Plesiosaurs fed on fish and ammonites. *See also* Ichthyosauria; nothosaurs; placodonts; pliosaurs; Reptilia.

Pliocene The epoch of the TERTIARY period, about 7–2 mya, that followed the Miocene. The climate became increasingly cold as glaciation began in the northern hemisphere. The herbivores (e.g. the ungulates) continued to flourish in the savannas, the PERISSODACTYLA declining and the ARTIODACTYLA diversifying (e.g. in the savanna of North America). In South America, many mammals disappeared. The Panamanian land-bridge had formed linking North and South America, and animals from the north migrated south and vice versa (the *Great American Interchange*). It was formerly believed that the North American invaders had caused the extinction of certain unique mammals such as giant ground sloths (e.g. *Megatherium*, over 6 m long, and *notoungulates*, which looked like rodents and were the size of rhinoceroses). There was, in fact, only a small depression of the diversity of South American forms (from 26 to 21 genera) as the new genera occupied different ecological niches to those of the indigenous species. It is possible that the climate changed as the Andes formed, resulting in savanna replacing rainforest and woodland, causing major habitat destruction and a decline in the populations of these animals.

In the East African Rift Valley, the hominids (*see Australopithecus*; *Homo*) became clearly distinguishable from the apes, marking the start of human evolution. *See also* geological time scale.

pliosaurs A group of extinct marine euryapsid reptiles that lived from the Triassic to the Cretaceous. Unlike PLESIOSAURS, they had short necks and large long heads. They also had massive teeth, turtlelike bodies, and paddlelike limbs. They were ferocious carnivores. For example, *Liopleurodon* is

the largest and heaviest known carnivore, as much as 12 m long. *See also* Ichthyosauria; nothosaurs; plesiosaurs; placodonts; Reptilia.

pluteus A form of DIPLEURULA larva characteristic of brittle stars and sea urchins, in which the ciliated band is continuous, with a small pre-oral lobe and well-developed post-anal lobes, supported by calcareous ribs.

poikilothermy (exothermy) The condition of having a body temperature that varies approximately with that of the environment. Most animals other than birds and mammals are poikilothermic ('cold-blooded'). *Compare* homoiothermy.

point mutation *See* mutation.

pollen analysis (palynology) A means of obtaining information on the composition and extent of past floras by examining the remains of pollen grains in peat and sedimentary deposits. The outer wall (exine) of the pollen grain is very resistant to decay, and reliable quantitative information on the vegetative cover many thousands of years ago can be made. The size and shape of pollen and the patterns on the exine can be used to distinguish genera, and sometimes even species, so qualitative estimates may also be made.

pollex A first digit of the forelimbs of tetrapods; it forms the thumb in humans. In the typical PENTADACTYL LIMB it contains two phalanges; however, there are modifications and reductions to this general plan and in some mammals it is absent. In humans and other primates it has two phalanges and is in opposition to the fingers to allow grasping (the opposable thumb). *Compare* hallux.

pollution Any damaging or unpleasant change in the environment that results from the physical, chemical, or biological side-effects of human industrial or social activities. Humans, more than any other species, have contributed to the destruction of many habitats, and consequently of many other species as a result of their activities (*see* endangered species; extinction). Pollution can affect the atmosphere, rivers, seas, and the soil.

Air pollution is caused by the domestic and industrial burning of carbonaceous fuels, by industrial processes, and by vehicle exhausts. Among recent problems are industrial emissions of sulfur dioxide causing *acid rain*, and the release into the atmosphere of chlorofluorocarbons, used in refrigeration, aerosols, etc., is linked to the depletion of ozone in the stratosphere, causing destruction of the *ozone layer*. The latter acts as a protective shield, absorbing harmful ultraviolet radiation that could destroy living organisms on the planet. Carbon dioxide, produced by burning fuel and by motor vehicle exhausts, is slowly building up in the atmosphere and raising the temperature (*see* GREENHOUSE EFFECT). Vehicle exhausts also contain carbon monoxide and other hazardous substances, such as fine particulate dusts. Lead was formerly a major vehicle pollutant, but the widespread introduction of lead-free petrol has eliminated this problem in most countries. Photochemical smog, caused by the action of sunlight on hydrocarbons and nitrogen oxides from vehicle exhausts, is a problem in many major cities.

Water pollutants include those that are biodegradable, such as sewage effluent, which cause no permanent harm if adequately treated and dispersed, as well as those which are nonbiodegradable, such as certain chlorinated hydrocarbon pesticides (e.g. DDT) and heavy metals, such as lead, copper, and zinc in some industrial effluents. The latter accumulate in the environment and can become very concentrated in food chains. The pesticides DDT, aldrin, and dieldrin are now banned. Water supplies can become polluted by leaching of nitrates from agricultural land, or of a wide range of potentially toxic substances from domestic and industrial waste tips. The discharge of waste heat can cause thermal pollution of the environment, but this is reduced by the use of cooling towers. In the sea, oil spillage from tankers and the inad-

equate discharge of sewage effluent are the main problems.

Other forms of pollution are noise from airplanes, traffic, and industry and the disposal of radioactive waste.

See also conservation; CITES.

polyandrous species A species in which one female mates with several males and more males than females have offspring. *Compare* monogamous species; polygynous species.

Polychaeta (polychaetes) A class of marine annelid worms, the bristle worms. Many are carnivorous and active crawlers. Some, e.g. *Nereis* (ragworm), burrow in sand or mud while others build tubes of sand or mucus, which they rarely leave. Each body segment bears a pair of limblike locomotory *parapodia*, in which numerous stiff hairlike chaetae are embedded. The well-defined head bears sense organs. The sexes are usually separate and development is via a ciliated larva.

The TROCHOPHORE larva indicates the close evolutionary relationship between, for example, annelids and mollusks. Fossil worms are not well preserved because of their soft bodies, but usually are represented by fossil tracks, burrows, and tubes. The minute chitinous jaw components (known as *scolecodonts*) of fossil polychaetes have often been preserved. Polychaetes have been represented in the fossil record since Cambrian times and the BURGESS SHALE has yielded some excellent well-preserved fossils.

polygene A gene with an individually small effect on the phenotype that interacts with other polygenes controlling the same character to produce the continuous quantitative variation typical of such traits as height, weight, and skin color. *See* quantitative inheritance.

polygenic inheritance *See* quantitative inheritance.

polygynous species A species in which several females mate with one male and some males do not mate at all. *Compare* monogamous species; polyandrous species.

polymerase An enzyme that regulates the synthesis of a polymer. Examples include *RNA polymerases* and *DNA polymerases*. RNA polymerases synthesize RNA using the noncoding strand of DNA as a template. There is only one type of RNA polymerase in prokaryotes, but in eukaryotes there are three different types: type I makes ribosomal RNA, type II makes messenger RNA precursors, and type III makes transfer RNA and 5S ribosomal RNA. They are all large enzymes made of many subunits and require the presence of a number of additional proteins to function. *See* transcription.

DNA polymerases synthesize double-stranded DNA from single-stranded DNA either involved in REPLICATION or DNA REPAIR. *See also* reverse transcriptase.

polymerase chain reaction (PCR) A technique for amplifying small samples of DNA rapidly and conveniently. Developed in 1983, it is now used widely in research and forensic science, e.g. to produce a suitable quantity of DNA for genetic fingerprinting from the minute amounts present in traces of blood or other tissue. To amplify a particular segment of DNA it is necessary first to know the sequence of bases flanking it at either end. This enables the construction of short single DNA strands (primers) that are complementary to and will bind with these flanking regions. Then the sample is incubated with the primers, nucleotides, and enzymes, especially a DNA polymerase that is stable at high temperatures, in a water bath. By varying the temperature precisely and rapidly, amplification proceeds in cycles of DNA denaturation, annealing of primers, and replication of new DNA strands, each lasting about 20 seconds. After 30 cycles, some 10^9 copies of the original DNA are produced. The temperature cycles are controlled automatically. mRNA can also be amplified, but it must first be converted to DNA by a reverse transcriptase.

polymorphism (genetic polymorphism) A distinct type of VARIATION in which there is more than one discrete GENOTYPE in a population with a frequency that is too high to be due to recurrent MUTATION. The phenotypes often appear as distinct forms (*morphs*). A *balanced polymorphism* persists over many generations and is maintained by contending advantages and disadvantages. For example, if different conditions exist in the environment of a particular species, some morphs may be more successful in one locality, whilst others may be more suited in other locations where different conditions prevail. In SICKLE-CELL ANEMIA, for example, individuals heterozygous for the condition are often better adapted than the homozygotic individuals. A *transient polymorphism* occurs when one form is increasing at the expense of the other, so the latter is eventually reduced to the status of a rare mutant. The appearance of dark forms of the peppered moth in industrial areas is an example (*see* industrial melanism). They become rare when the pollution decreases. Polymorphism usually results from the occurrence of different allelic forms of a gene and balanced polymorphism arises when the heterozygote is at an advantage compared to the homozygotes. *See* heterozygous advantage; restriction fragment length polymorphism.

polypeptide A compound that contains many amino acids linked together by peptide bonds. *See* peptide. *See also* protein.

polyphyletic Describing a group of species descended from more than one ancestor. The ultimate common ancestor is not included. Polyphyletic groups are allowed in EVOLUTIONARY CLASSIFICATION and PHENETIC classification. *Compare* monophyletic; paraphyletic. *See also* Protista.

polyphyodont A type of dentition in which the teeth are replaced throughout the animal's lifetime if damaged or broken. It is found in frogs and lizards. *Compare* diphyodont; monophyodont.

polyploidy The condition in which a

cell or organism contains three or more times the haploid number of chromosomes. Polyploidy is far more common in plants than in animals and very high chromosome numbers may be found; for example in octaploids and decaploids (containing eight and ten times the haploid chromosome number). Polyploids are often larger and more vigorous than their diploid counterparts and the phenomenon is therefore exploited in plant breeding, in which the chemical colchicine can be used to induce polyploidy. Polyploids may contain multiples of the chromosomes of one species (autopolyploids) or combine the chromosomes of two or more species (allopolyploids). Polyploidy is rare in animals because the sex-determining mechanism is disturbed. For example a tetraploid XXXX would be sterile. *See* allopolyploidy; autopolyploidy.

polyribosome   *See* ribosome.

polysome   *See* ribosome.

polysomy   *See* aneuploidy.

polytene chromosomes   *See* puff.

population   A group of organisms of the same species (or other groups within which individuals may exchange genetic information) occupying a particular space. A population is continually modified by increases (birth and immigration) and losses (death and emigration), and is limited by the food supply and the effects of environmental factors such as disease. *See* Malthus.

population genetics   The study of the changes in frequency of GENES and HAPLOTYPES in a population and the processes that influence such changes. Models of population genetics are used when only a few genes are involved and their genetics are known. *See* one-locus model; multilocus model. *See also* Hardy–Weinberg equilibrium. *Compare* quantitative genetics.

Porifera (sponges)   A phylum of primitive multicellular animals, the sponges, that probably evolved a multicellular structure independently of the other multicellular animals. All are sessile and almost all are marine. The body of a sponge is a loose aggregation of cells, with minimal coordination between them, forming a vaselike structure. Flagellated cells (choanocytes) line the vase, and cause water currents to flow in through apertures (ostia) in the body wall and out through one or more openings (oscula) at the top. Sponges have an internal skeleton of chalk or silica spicules or protein fibers (as in the bath sponge). Sponges may be derived from flagellated PROTOZOA and may be related to the choanoflagellates, which have a single flagellum surrounded by a collar rather like the choanocytes of the sponges. Nucleotide sequence analysis places them about halfway between the choanoflagellates and the most primitive CNIDARIA (coelenterates). Certain authorities believe that their evolutionary relationship to the Animal Kingdom is so tenuous that they should be placed in a separate kingdom, the PARAZOA.

They have been represented in the fossil record since Precambrian times, mainly by siliceous spicules, and thus evolved very early on. Weblike skeletons (e.g. *Paleophragmodictya*) have been found in the EDIACARAN FAUNA of Australia from the late Precambrian. *Hydnoceros*, a Devonian fossil, is a glass sponge about 20 cm high similar to the present-day Venus' flower basket. Calcareous sponges (*see* stromatoporoid) were very abundant in the Paleozoic and Mesozoic and, along with corals and bryozoa, contributed to reef building in the ancient seas.

positive frequency-dependent selection   *See* frequency-dependent selection.

postorbital fenestrations   *See* temporal fossae.

postzygotic isolation   REPRODUCTIVE ISOLATION in which a zygote is formed that either fails to develop or produces a sterile adult. Mechanisms of postzygotic isolation include *hybrid inviability*, in which offspring are inviable or have drastically reduced viability, and *hybrid sterility*, in which offspring fail to produce functional gametes. *Compare* prezygotic isolation. *See also* Haldane's rule.

potassium–argon dating *See* radioactive dating.

Poulton, Sir Edward Bagnall (1856–1943) British zoologist. Influenced by the writings of Alfred Russel Wallace, Poulton made an intensive and detailed study of the adaptive importance of protective coloring and mimicry in nature. His results, published in *The Colours of Animals* (1890), were strictly Darwinian with an emphasis on the inheritance of factors arising from the continuous variation found in a population.

Poulton maintained this belief despite the rediscovery of the works of Gregor Mendel and the consequent insistence on the role of mutation in evolution. In such works as *Essays on Evolution* (1908) Poulton argued against the growing Mendelian orthodoxy, insisting that adaptations as complex as mimicry could not have been brought about by mutation.

preadaptation *See* exaptation.

prebiotic The time in the Earth's history before biological life evolved.

Precambrian The time in the earth's geological history that precedes the Cambrian period, i.e. from the origin of the earth, nearly 5 billion years ago, to the start of the Cambrian, around 570 mya. The term 'Precambrian' is now used mainly descriptively, and has been largely discarded as a geological term in the light of greater knowledge of the early evolution of life. Precambrian time is now divided into three eons: *Hadean*, from the Earth's origin to about 3900 mya: *Archean* ('ancient age'), 3900–2390 mya; and *Proterozoic* ('early life'), 2390–570 mya (the Cambrian marks the start of the *Phanerozoic* eon, which extends to the present day).

The oldest fossils discovered so far are remains of bacterialike organisms, dating from about 3500 mya. Indeed, there is abundant evidence of flourishing colonies of CYANOBACTERIA and other bacteria throughout the Archean and Proterozoic eons. This takes the form of STROMATOLITES, rock structures representing the remains of sediment trapped or precipitated by bacterial communities. However, the earliest remains of single-celled eukaryotes are much later, dating from about 1400 mya, while the first appearance of multicellular animals is in the EDIACARA FAUNA, in rocks dated to the last 100 million years of Precambrian time. *See also* black smokers.

preformation The theory that the embryonic development of animals and plants consists merely of growth or extension of a preformed germ or program. Early adherents of the theory postulated the presence of tiny human figures (*homunculi*) in the heads of the sperms, while modern biochemical preformationists assume that the complexity of organisms is only the complexity of nucleic acid extended.

premolar A mammalian tooth situated between the CANINE teeth or INCISORS in front and the molars behind. *See also* teeth.

prezygotic isolation REPRODUCTIVE ISOLATION in which no zygote is formed. Mechanisms of prezygotic isolation include *temporal* or *seasonal isolation*, where mating occurs at different times in different populations. For example, it is possible that two species of Californian pine, *Pinus radiata* and *Pinus muricata* could cross-pollinate, but *P. radiata* produces pollen in early February whereas *P. muricata* produces pollen in April. Another mechanism is *habitat isolation*, where populations occupy different habitats in the same geographical area. For example, the toads *Bufo americanus* and *Bufo woodhousei* are able to interbreed, but *B. americanus* usually breeds in shallow pools and ponds whereas *B. woodhousei* usually breeds in streams. *Compare* postzygotic isolation. *See also* reinforcement.

Primates The order of mammals that contains the lemurs, monkeys, great apes, and humans. Most primates are relatively unspecialized arboreal mammals with a very highly developed brain, quick reactions, and large forward-facing eyes allowing binocular vision. The shoulder joint has evolved to allow movement in all directions and the elbow joint also allows a certain amount of rotation. The opposable thumb and (usually) big toe are used for grasping and the digits have nails. There are five functional digits on each foot. The young undergo a long period of growth and development, during which they learn from their parents. Most of these characteristics are adaptations to an arboreal way of life. The limbs are adapted for swinging about in trees and for grasping and hanging on to branches. The flattened face and binocular vision are adaptations for hunting moving insects (early primates are believed to have been insectivores) and for judging distances (e.g. between branches) accurately.

Living primates are often classified into two suborders: the PROSIMIANS (lemurs, aye-ayes, etc.) and the ANTHROPOIDS (TARSIERS, New World Monkeys, Old World Monkeys, gibbons, apes, and humans). New World Monkeys have prehensile tails; the more advanced Old World monkeys lack prehensile tails, and the great apes are large tail-less primates that typically swing from trees by their long arms.

The primates probably evolved from an extinct group known as the *omomyids*. The oldest primate fossil *Altiatlasus* (late Paleocene) from Morocco consists of just ten molars and is believed to have been about the size of a mouse. *Aegyptopithecus*, a fossil monkey from the late Oligocene of Egypt, had some anthropoid apelike features, and *Proconsul* (now often assigned to the genus *Dryopithecus*) of East Africa (23–15 mya) was an ape, an ancestor of the African apes and humans. Most omomyids are found in the Eocene of Europe and North America and resemble present-day tarsiers. The most prolific fossil primates were the *adapiformes*, e.g. *Smilodectes*. It is unclear which of these early (prosimian) groups contained the common ancestor of the primates. It is believed that early prosimians split into two

groups. One evolved into the present-day prosimians (lemurs and lorises). The other evolved into a common ancestor of the tarsier/anthropoid line, which later split into the tarsiers and the anthropoids.

primordial soup   *See* origin of life; protein evolution.

Pringsheim, Nathanael (1823–94) German botanist. Pringsheim was among the first to demonstrate sexual reproduction in algae and observe ALTERNATION OF GENERATIONS. He further showed that sexual reproduction involves fusion of material of the two sex cells.

From studies (1873) on the complex morphological differentiation in a family of marine algae, the Sphacelariaceae, Pringsheim opposed the Darwinian theory of evolution by natural selection. Like the Swiss botanist, Karl Naegeli, he believed the increase in structural complexity to be a spontaneous morphological phenomenon, conferring no survival value.

Proboscidea   The order that contains the largest living terrestrial mammals – *Loxodonta* (African elephant) and *Elephas* (Indian elephant). Elephants are characterized by the trunk (*proboscis*), formed from the elongated nose and upper lip, which is used for bathing, drinking, and collecting vegetation. The single pair of upper incisor teeth grow into large ivory tusks. There are no lower incisors, canines, or premolars. The huge ridged molars are used for grinding vegetation. Only two pairs are used at a time and are replaced when worn down.

Elephants evolved in the Eocene, and in the Miocene and Pliocene, along with many other mammals, assumed their modern form. In these times, elephants were more widespread than any other time. In the Eocene, they resembled pigs and it is thought that they evolved from the common ancestors of African conies and the sea cows. The now extinct woolly mammoth was abundant during the last Ice Age, hunted by early humans, and depicted in cave paintings.

procaryote   *See* prokaryote.

Proconsul *See* human evolution; primates.

profundal The deepwater zone of a lake beyond a depth of ten meters. Little light penetrates this zone and thus the inhabitants are all heterotrophic, depending on the littoral and sublittoral organisms for basic food materials. *Compare* littoral; sublittoral.

progenesis *See* paedomorphosis.

Prokaryotae *See* Bacteria; Monera.

prokaryote (procaryote) An organism whose genetic material (DNA) is not enclosed by membranes to form a nucleus but lies free in the cytoplasm. Organisms can be divided into prokaryotes and eukaryotes, the latter having a true nucleus. This is a fundamental division because it is associated with other major differences. Prokaryotes comprise the kingdoms BACTERIA and ARCHAEA. All other organisms are eukaryotes (*see* Eukarya). Prokaryote cells were the first form of cellular life. The first half of life on earth was exclusively prokaryotic. *See* cell; origin of life; Cyanobacteria. *Compare* eukaryote.

promoter A specific DNA sequence at the start of a gene that initiates transcription by binding RNA polymerase. In *Escherichia coli* the RNA polymerase has a protein 'sigma factor' that recognizes the promoter; in the absence of this factor the enzyme binds to, and begins transcription at, random points on the DNA strand. In eukaryotic cells, binding of RNA polymerase to the promoter involves proteins called transcription factors. *See* transcription.

pronation The rotational movement of the lower forelimb (forearm) so that the forefoot (hand) is twisted through 90 degrees in either direction in relationship to the elbow. Pronation in humans occurs when the palm of the hand faces downwards or backwards and the radius and ulna are crossed. Movement so that the palm of the hand faces upwards or for-

wards and the radius and ulna are parallel is *supination*.

pronephros The first type of vertebrate kidney to develop; the functional kidney of larval fish and amphibians. It is comprised of a variable number of open-ended ducts, which are segmentally arranged, just behind the heart. They collect fluid waste from the coelom and are drained by a collecting tube (pronephric duct) leading to the cloaca. It is later replaced by the mesonephric or metanephric kidney (*see* mesonephros; metanephros).

prophase The first stage of cell division in MEIOSIS and MITOSIS. During prophase the chromosomes become visible and the nuclear membrane dissolves. Prophase may be divided into successive stages termed LEPTOTENE, ZYGOTENE, PACHYTENE, DIPLOTENE, and DIAKINESIS. The events occurring during these stages differ in meiosis and mitosis, notably in that bivalents (pairs of homologous chromosomes) are formed in meiosis, whereas homologous chromosomes remain separate in mitosis.

prosimians Literally meaning 'premonkeys', a suborder (Prosimii) of the PRIMATES. Prosimians are the most primitive primates and include the *lemurs* and aye-ayes (only found in Madagascar) and the galagos, pottos, and lorises of tropical Africa and southeastern Asia. The group also includes the two extinct fossil groups, the *omomyids* and *adapiformes*. Lemurs are small tree-dwelling animals with long snouts and bushy tails, but their hands and feet have opposable digits, mostly with nails except for the second toe, which has a claw. The early prosimian ancestral stock evolved into two lines early on to develop into present-day prosimians and the common ancestor of the tarsier/anthropoid line. *Compare* anthropoids.

protein One of a large number of substances that are important in the structure and function of all living organisms. Proteins consist of one or more polypeptides, which are made up of AMINO ACID molecules joined by PEPTIDE links. Their molecular weight may vary from a few thousand to several million. About 20 amino acids are present in proteins. Simple proteins contain only amino acids. More complex proteins have other chemical groups attached to the amino acids. The primary structure of a protein is the particular sequence of amino acids present. The secondary structure is the way in which the polypeptide chain is arranged, and the tertiary structure is the way in which the protein chain is folded.

protein evolution The structural and functional changes of proteins that occur during evolution. Such changes are caused by mutations in the coding sequences of genes, and are manifest as alterations in the amino acid sequence of the proteins concerned. Some mutant proteins will have altered functions, and hence the phenotype of the organism is significantly affected too; other changes in amino acid sequence may have only moderate or negligible impact on the protein's overall properties. There are two main routes of protein evolution, which reflect the course of evolution of the corresponding genes. Along one route, a single gene can be duplicated to produce PARALOGOUS, or sister, genes in the same species. Over time, these sister genes can acquire mutations that give their proteins new properties, enabling them to perform novel functions (i.e., they are paralogous proteins). Along the other route, as species evolve and diverge, descendants of the common ancestral genes acquire mutations, and hence the sequences of the corresponding proteins diverge. Such genes, and their proteins, are described as OR-THOLOGOUS. The extent of this divergence is assessed by aligning and comparing the sequences, which is performed by computerized methods (*see* genomics. Substitutions, deletions, or additions of amino acids that affect the crucial structural or functional features of a protein, such as the active site or polypeptide folding of an enzyme, are of greatest selective importance. Such amino acids tend to be highly conserved during evolution. However, proteins can accumulate numerous mutations in noncritical stretches of the primary sequence while maintaining the molecule's overall shape and functional sites. Mutations that do not alter protein structure can influence the evolution of a protein by affecting its expression.

In the *'primordial soup'* from which life evolved, it is generally accepted that RNA was the first replicating molecule and that catalytic activity was also carried out by RNA, in the form of RIBOZYMES. At some point, proteins took over catalysis and RNA became the coding molecule for protein synthesis. Proteins are much better catalysts than RNA, but to confer a selective advantage, protein production must be heritable. Hence a system evolved to replicate the RNA encoding useful proteins and to translate the code into the correct polypeptide. How this GENETIC CODE evolved is unknown, although it must have happened very early in the evolution of life. A crucial step in the evolution of the genetic code and TRANSLATION is the bonding of an amino acid to a small RNA molecule with a specific sequence. This primitive TRANSFER RNA (tRNA) could attach an amino acid to a ribozyme by complementary base pairing. If another primitive tRNA paired to the ribozyme, the two amino acids could bond together to form a peptide. With the addition of further amino acids, the peptides attached to ribozymes became longer and, through a series of intermediates, eventually took over catalytic activity. As enzymes became larger and more complex, the translation system evolved into the present system with a tRNA for each amino acid and RIBOSOMES for the synthesis of polypeptide chains.

It is probable that amino acids, which were abundant in the primordial soup, were initially used as cofactors to improve the efficiency of ribozyme catalysis. RNA chains are negatively charged so basic amino acids and short peptides would neutralize the repulsion between the different parts of a ribozyme, allowing better substrate binding and more efficient catalysis. Many enzymes today have nucleotide cofactors, which could be evidence of their RNA origin. Proteins also evolved and acquired functions by combining small ancestral proteins, which is reflected in the interrupted structure of eukaryotic genes.

protein sequencing The determination of the primary structure of proteins, i.e. the type, number, and sequence of amino acids in the polypeptide chain. This is done by progressive hydrolysis of the protein using specific proteases to split the polypeptides into shorter peptide chains. Terminal amino acids are labeled, broken off by a specific enzyme, and identified by chromatography.

protein synthesis The process whereby proteins are synthesized on the ribosomes of cells. The sequence of bases in MESSENGER RNA (mRNA), transcribed from DNA, determines the sequence of amino acids in the polypeptide chain: each codon in the mRNA specifies a particular amino acid. As the RIBOSOMES move along the mRNA in the process of TRANSLATION, each codon is 'read', and amino acids bound to different TRANSFER RNA molecules are brought to their correct positions along the mRNA molecule. These amino acids are polymerized to form the growing polypeptide chain. The polypeptide chain can be further modified and is then folded into its three-dimensional shape and transported to its destination.

proteome The complete set of proteins expressed in an organism; their structure, function, expression patterns and interactions. Investigation of the proteome is called *proteomics* and involves a wide range of techniques. Now that the goal of the Human Genome Project and other genome sequencing projects has been largely achieved, attention is being switched to the proteome of humans and other organisms and a Human Proteome Project was set up in 2001 to coordinate international research efforts.

proteomics *See* proteome.

Proterozoic *See* Precambrian.

prothallus A flattened disk of cells that forms the free-living haploid gametophyte generation of certain PTERIDOPHYTES, e.g. the fern *Dryopteris* (*see* Filicinophyta). In homosporous plants, there is only one type of prothallus with both male and female sex organs. In heterosporous plants, the microspores give rise to small male prothalli bearing male sex organs (*see* antheridium), and larger female prothalli bearing female sex organs (*see* archegonium). The prothallus is greatly reduced in spermatophytes. *See also* Angiospermophyta; gymnosperm.

Protista In some classifications, a kingdom of simple organisms including the bacteria, algae, fungi, and protozoans. It was introduced to overcome the difficulties of assigning such organisms, which may show both animal and plantlike characteristics, to the kingdoms Animalia or Plantae. Today the grouping is considered artificial (they are separate evolutionary lines), and many taxonomists support a system whereby the bacteria and fungi are both assigned to separate kingdoms, while algae and protozoans constitute various phyla of protoctists, i.e. the group is POLYPHYLETIC. If multicellular groups are also included, the kingdom is referred to as the PROTOCTISTA. *See* prokaryote.

Protochordata *See* acraniate.

Protoctista A kingdom of simple eukaryotic organisms that includes the algae, slime molds, funguslike oomycetes, and the organisms traditionally classified as protozoa, such as flagellates, ciliates, and sporozoans. Most are aerobic, some are capable of photosynthesis, and most possess flagella or cilia (undulipodia) at some stage of their life cycle. Protoctists are typically microscopic single-celled organisms, such as the amebas, but the group also has large multicellular members, for example the seaweeds and other conspicuous algae. *See* Apicomplexa; Chlorophyta; Ciliophora; Euglenophyta; Foraminifera; oomycete; Phaeophyta; Radiolaria; Rhizopoda; Rhodophyta; Zoomastigina.

protoplasm The living contents of a

cell, comprising the CYTOPLASM plus NUCLEUS.

protostomes The name comes from the Greek words '*protos*' meaning 'first' and '*stoma*' meaning 'mouth'. The term refers to an evolutionary line of bilaterally symmetrical animals based on certain embryonic features. The earliest embryo is a ball of cells. A pocket develops and some cells migrate inside to form an inner layer of cells. The outer layer is the ectoderm and the inner layer is the endoderm. A pore (*blastopore*) remains and develops into the mouth of the organism, hence the name, 'mouth first'. Protostomes include the nematodes, nemertines, mollusks, annelids, and arthropods. *Compare* deuterostomes. *See also* bilateral symmetry.

Prototheria *See* Mammalia; Monotremata.

protozoa A group of single-celled heterotrophic often motile eukaryotic organisms, traditionally classified as animals and constituting a phylum, or subkingdom, Protozoa. In more recent classifications they are placed with other single-celled or simple multicelled eukaryotes in the kingdom PROTOCTISTA. They range from plant-like forms (e.g. *Euglena, Chlamydomonas*) to members that feed and behave like animals (e.g. *Ameba, Paramecium*). There are over 30 000 species living universally in marine, freshwater, and damp terrestrial environments. Some form colonies (e.g. *Volvox*) and many are parasites (e.g. *Plasmodium*). Protozoa vary in body form but specialized organelles (e.g. cilia and flagella) are common. Reproduction is usually by binary fission although multiple fission and conjugation occur in some species. The main protozoan phyla are: RHIZOPODA (rhizopods); ZOOMASTIGINA (flagellates); APICOMPLEXA (sporozoans); and CILIOPHORA (ciliates). *See also* Foraminifera; Radiolaria.

provirus *See* latent virus.

proximate causation (mechanical causation) The biochemical and physical processes that cause traits within the lifetime of an organism. *Compare* ultimate causation.

pseudoallele A mutation in a gene that produces an effect identical to another mutation at a different site in the same gene locus. The two pseudoalleles thus act as a single gene but do not occupy the same position, as evidenced by the occasional rare recombinations between them that result in the CIS–TRANS EFFECT.

pseudocoelomate An animal with a body cavity that has similar functions to a COELOM, but is enclosed partly with endoderm and partly with ectoderm, rather than being completely enclosed with mesoderm as a true coelom would be. Examples are the acanthocephala (spiny-headed worms), the ROTIFERA, and the NEMATODA.

pseudoextinction The apparent disappearance of a species from the fossil record because evolved forms have been classified as new species.

pseudofungi *See* Phaeophyta.

pseudogene A DNA sequence that resembles a gene but is nonfunctional. Pseudogenes have high potential to form new genes by further mutation as they already have useful sequences, such as those signaling transcription.

Psilophyta A phylum of vascular seedless plants comprising the whisk ferns. It contains only two living subtropical genera (*Psilotum* and *Tmesipteris*). They lack shoots and roots; instead they have rhizoids on subterranean parts of the dichotomously branching axis, which bears tiny alternate scalelike or leaflike outgrowths. Whisk ferns may be descendants of *Rhynia* and similar leafless plants known from fossils of the late Silurian and early Devonian – some of the earliest of all plants. *Rhynia* and two other species (*Asteroxylon* and *Hornea*) are specimens found in the famous Rhynie chert beds of Scotland, UK, and *Psilophyton* from the Devonian of

Quebec. The fossil forms are placed in the order Psilophytales.

pteridophyte Any vascular non-seed-bearing plant. Pteriodophytes include the club mosses (phylum LYCOPODOPHYTA), horsetails (SPHENOPHYTA), whisk ferns (PSILOPHYTA), and ferns (FILICINOPHYTA). In older classifications these groups constitute classes of a single phylum (or division), the Pteridophyta. In all pteridophytes, as in seed-bearing plants but unlike the non-vascular plants, the diploid sporophyte is the more conspicuous phase of the life cycle.

Pteridospermales *See* Cycadofilicales.

pterodactyl *See* Pterosauria.

Pterosauria An extinct order of flying reptiles, the pterodactyls, that evolved from the ARCHOSAURS in the Triassic. They were particularly common in the Jurassic and survived until the Cretaceous. Fossils are always found in marine deposits. They had long forelimbs with a very elongated fourth finger, which supported the delicate leathery wing membrane. Although they had some structural adaptations to flight, they were probably incapable of the same sort of flight as birds. Their very weak hind legs suggest that they were unable to stand upright on land and their mode of life probably involved swooping or gliding over the sea to catch fish. They had beaked jaws and primitive forms, such as *Rhamphorhynchus*, had teeth, but teeth are absent in more advanced forms, such as *Pteranodon*.

puff (Balbiani ring) A swelling that is seen in certain areas of the giant (*polytene*) chromosomes found in the salivary glands and other tissues of certain dipterous insects, e.g. *Drosophila*. Puffs originate in different regions of the chromosome in a certain sequence and their occurrence can be correlated with specific developmental events. Others occur only in certain tissues. The puffs are sites of active TRANSCRIPTION

of probably just a single gene, albeit present as numerous copies.

punctuated equilibrium A theory of evolution proposed by two US paleontologists, Nils ELDREDGE and Stephen GOULD, that there have been long periods of geological time, lasting for several million years (i.e. in equilibrium), when there is little evolutionary change within a species, punctuated by short periods of rapid speciation of less than 100 000 years. Also, such a sudden evolution of a new species may arise within a marginal part of a population consisting of a small number of individuals. The opposing theory is that of PHYLETIC GRADUALISM, which is often thought to be more in line with Darwinism and neo-Darwinism.

punctuation A short period of rapid evolutionary change associated with SPECIATION. *Compare* stasis. *See* punctuated equilibrium.

pure line The succession of descendants of a homozygous individual that are identical to each other and continue to breed true, i.e. they produce genetically identical offspring. Pure lines cannot be improved by selection since all variation within them, barring the occasional mutation, is environmental. In plants pure lines are obtained by selfing, which halves the heterozygosity each generation, while in animals inbreeding tends to increase homozygosity.

purine A simple nitrogenous organic molecule with a double ring structure. Members of the purine group include the bases adenine and guanine, which are constituents of the nucleic acids, and certain plant alkaloids, e.g. caffeine and theobromine.

pyrimidine A simple nitrogenous organic molecule whose ring structure is contained in the pyrimidine bases cytosine, thymine, and uracil, which are constituents of the nucleic acids, and in thiamine (vitamin B_1).

Q

Qatzeh skull   *See Homo sapiens.*

QTL   *See* quantitative inheritance.

quadrate   One of a pair of bones of the upper jaw in bony fish (Osteichthyes), amphibians, reptiles, and birds that form the points of articulation with the lower jaw. They are homologous with the palato-pterygo-quadrate bar, a paired cartilage forming the upper jaw in cartilaginous fish (Chondrichthyes).

quadruped   *See* tetrapod.

qualitative variation   (discontinuous variation)   A form of variation in which a character has two or more distinct forms. Examples are human blood groups and Mendel's pea characters. It generally occurs when there are two or more allelic forms of a major gene in a population. The inheritance of the ABO system of human blood groups is controlled by three alleles of the same gene.

quantitative genetics   The study of changes in the frequency and distribution of quantitative phenotypic characters controlled by many genes, whose genetics is unknown. The value of a phenotypic character, P, is expressed as a deviation from the mean and is the sum of the genotypic effect, G, and the environmental effect, E, i.e. $P = G + E$.

quantitative inheritance   (continuous variation; polygenic inheritance; multifactorial inheritance)   The pattern of inheritance shown by traits, such as height in humans or grain yield in wheat, that show continuous variation within a certain range of values. Such traits are typically controlled by many different genes (polygenes) distributed among the genome. The identification and manipulation of genetic loci determining quantitative traits (*quantitative trait loci*, QTLs) is of great importance in plant and animal breeding, where the goal is often to improve such traits.

quantitative trait loci   *See* quantitative inheritance.

quartz   One of the most important rock-forming minerals, consisting of silicon dioxide (SiO_2). It is an important and widespread constituent of many rocks. For example, it is found in granite (an igneous rock); in quartzite (a metamorphic rock); and in sandstone (a sedimentary rock).

Quaternary   The most recent period of the Cenozoic era from about 2 mya to the present day and composed of the PLEISTOCENE and HOLOCENE epochs. Literally the 'fourth age', it is characterized by the emergence of humans. Interestingly, as this period has been chosen artificially and marks the beginning of human history and not the occurence of a catastrophe or major geological event, it continues to increase with our own continuing human presence.

The positions and distribution of the continents of the Earth by the beginning of the Quarternary were very similar to those of the present day. The Bering land bridge only diappeared comparatively recently and migrations of animals were possible between Eurasia and North America, and between North America and South America by the Isthmus of Panama. This caused the formation of the Gulf Stream, which isolated the Arctic Ocean from warm currents. Antarctica had also been cut off in the Tertiary and both events resulted in ice sheets expanding in both the northern and southern hemispheres. The periods of glaciation (*see* Ice Age) punctuated by rapid much warmer interglacial periods meant that many animals moved southward and northward as a direct response to the climate changes. For example, fossil lions and hippopotamuses normally associated with present-day tropical Africa have been found in Britain.

Human evolution probably began in East Africa (*see* out of Africa theory) and by the Holocene, permanent settlements had been established and agriculture had developed. Humans expanded all over the world, great ancient civilizations came and went and the world population continued to expand to its present 10 000 million. *See also* geological time scale; human evolution.

R

R *See* selection response.

race In classification, a taxon below the rank of SPECIES, sometimes being placed between SUBSPECIES and VARIETY. The term is sometimes used instead of ECOTYPE, for groups of individuals that have uniform ecological preferences or physiological requirements.

radial symmetry The arrangement of parts in an organism in such a way that cutting in any plane across the diameter splits the structure into similar halves (mirror images). Radial symmetry is characteristic of many sedentary animals, e.g. CNIDARIA and ECHINODERMATA. The term *actinomorphy* is generally used to describe radial symmetry in plants, particularly flowers. *See also* bilateral symmetry.

radioactive dating Any method of dating that uses the decay rates of naturally occurring radioactive isotopes to assess the age of rocks, fossils, and archeological remains. Organic matter less than 7000 years old can be dated using radiocarbon dating. This uses the fact that the isotope carbon-14 is found in the atmosphere and taken in by plants when they photosynthesize, and subsequently assimilated by the animals that feed on them. When plants and animals die, no more carbon is taken in and the existing ^{14}C decays to the nonradioactive isotope carbon-12. If the proportion of ^{14}C to ^{12}C in the atmosphere and the decay rate of ^{14}C to ^{12}C are both known, as they are, then the sample may be dated by finding the present proportion of ^{14}C to ^{12}C. Specimens over 7000 years old can be dated by other radioisotope methods, e.g. *potassium–argon dating* and *rubidium–*

strontium dating. Potassium–argon dating is based on the decay of potassium-40 to argon-40. It is very useful because potassium is found in many different types of rocks and the decay takes place very slowly making it possible to date rocks that are over 3 billion years old. Rubidium–strontium dating is useful for very large ages, such as 1×10^9 years to 4×10^9 years. These methods are used to establish absolute geological time.

Radiolaria (radiolarians) An order of the phylum RHIZOPODA that consists of marine single-celled organisms with a central capsule and a skeleton either of silica or strontium sulfate. Radiolarians are pelagic and when they die, cover the ocean bottom with their empty skeletons, forming a *radiolarian ooze* (*siliceous ooze*). Some cherts are formed from compression of radiolarian oozes, for example, the Rhynie Chert. Many rock formations contain fossil radiolarians. They range in age from Cambrian to Recent.

radiolarian ooze *See* Radiolaria.

radius One of the two long bones of the lower forelimb (forearm) in tetrapods. In humans, it forms the anterior (preaxial) border of the forearm, extending from the upper side of the elbow joint to the thumb side of the wrist (carpus). It is able to twist against the larger ulna bone in a pivot joint, to turn the palm of the hand upwards or downwards. The radius and ulna may be fused in some species. *See illustration at* pentadactyl limb.

Ramapithecus An extinct primate genus, dated 12–14 mya and once thought to be a possible ancestor of the *australo-pithecines*. Fossil jaw and teeth fragments were discovered in East Africa and India in 1932 and although seemingly apelike, were considered to be from a possible human ancestor. In 1976, the discovery of a complete jaw ruled out this possibility and certain authorities assign *Ramapithecus* to the genus *Sivapithecus*, believed to be ancestral to the orangutan (*see* Pilbeam). *Ramapithecus* and *Sivapithecus*, along with the genus *Proconsul*, are now usually assigned to the genus *Dryopithecus*. *See* primates.

random drift   *See* genetic drift.

rank   The hierarchical status of a taxon in a classification scheme. For example, the taxon Annelida has the rank of phylum, while the taxon Oligochaeta has the rank of class.

rate of evolution   The rate of evolution can be measured as the rate of change of a character (horse teeth being a classic example) over time and is often expressed in units called *darwins*. Rates of evolution measured in this way from the fossil record are slower than those produced by artificial selection experiments, showing that natural selection and random drift can comfortably account for the rate of evolution observed in fossils.

Larger changes in characters, e.g. the evolution of limb to wing, cannot be measured in darwins so the character is divided into discrete stages and the rate of change between the stages measured. Rates of evolution at higher taxonomic levels can be examined using taxonomic data to give general taxonomic rates of evolution. These can be measured as the number of taxa (at a given taxonomic level) per million years or as a *survivorship curve*, which plots the survival time of taxa in a lineage against time. Rapid taxonomic evolution is indicated by a high number of taxa per million years or a steep survivorship curve.

All measurements show that rates of evolution have varied throughout geological time, with faster rates occurring over short time periods. *See* molecular clock;

punctuated equilibrium; sexual reproduction.

ratites   A group (formerly considered a subclass or superorder) that contains the flightless birds, such as *Struthio* (ostrich) of Africa – the largest living bird, *Dromaius* (emu) of Australia, *Rhea* of South America, and the recently extinct *Diornis* (moa) of New Zealand. Ratites are large heavy fast-running birds with long powerful hind limbs and reduced wings. They are confined to open lands in the southern hemisphere, where carnivores are few and their approach is easily seen. They have no keel on the sternum. The soft curly feathers lack barbs and the palate differs from that of other birds. The feathers and palate are thought to have evolved by NEOTENY. Ratites are descended from flying birds by several different evolutionary lines and are probably not closely related to each other. *See also* Aves.

reaction norm   A property of a single genotype, which describes how development relates genotype to phenotype with respect to the environment. It is used in analyzing patterns of gene expression.

reading frame   A sequence of bases in messenger RNA coding for a polypeptide chain or protein. The grouping of bases into triplets (codons) is determined by the position of the start codon, and any addition or deletion of a base within the frame will alter the codons from that point onwards. *See* gene mutation.

recapitulation   The theory proposed by HAECKEL that the embryological development of an organism summarizes the evolutionary history of the species. The theory is now regarded as a gross oversimplification, though it is true that the embryos of related species resemble each other more closely than do the adults.

Recent   *See* Holocene.

recessive   An allele that is only expressed in the phenotype when it is in the homozygous condition. *Compare* dominant. *See also* double recessive.

reciprocal altruism   Altruistic behavior between two unrelated individuals. Most altruistic behavior occurs between related individuals and has an underlying genetic motive, but in a few species individuals behave altruistically toward genetically unrelated individuals. Such behavior could be an evolutionary advantage by increasing an individual's chance of survival. Reciprocal altruism is usually seen in species with large brains, e.g. chimpanzees and humans. *See* altruism; inclusive fitness.

recognition species concept   Species that recognize each other as potential mates, i.e., they have a shared mate recognition system. *Compare* biological species concept; cladistic species concept; ecological species concept; phenetic species concept.

recombinant DNA   1. Any DNA fragment or molecule that contains inserted foreign DNA, whether from another organism or artificially constructed. Recombinant DNA is fundamental to many aspects of genetic engineering, particularly the introduction of foreign genes to cells or organisms. There are now many techniques for creating recombinant DNA, depending on the nature of the host cell or organism receiving the foreign DNA. Particular genes or DNA sequences are cut from the parent molecule using specific type II RESTRICTION ENDONUCLEASES, or are assembled using a messenger RNA template and the enzyme REVERSE TRANSCRIPTASE. In GENE CLONING using cultures of bacterial or eukaryote tissue cells, the foreign gene is inserted into a *vector*, e.g. a bacterial PLASMID or virus particle, which then infects the host cell. Inside the host cell the recombinant vector replicates and the foreign gene is expressed. Plasmids are also used to insert foreign DNA into plants. One of the most common is the Ti (tumor-inducing) plasmid of the bacterium *Agrobacterium tumefaciens*. This causes crown gall tumors in plants, and its plasmid has been used on a range of crop

plants. Some cells, for example, mouse embryos can be injected with DNA. The embryos are then implanted into receptive mothers, which give birth to transgenic offspring. The same principle is used with other mammals, including sheep. Another technique, used in transfecting certain plant cells or cell organelles, for example, is to shoot DNA-coated microprojectiles, such as tungsten or gold particles, at the host cell target. This is termed *biolistics*. *See* genetic engineering.
2. DNA formed naturally by RECOMBINATION, e.g. by crossing over in MEIOSIS or by CONJUGATION (sexual reproduction involving the union of two individuals) in bacteria.

recombination   (genetic recombination) The random regrouping of genes that regularly occurs during meiosis as a result of the independent assortment of chromosomes into new sets, and the exchange of pieces of homologous chromosomes (crossing over). Recombination results in offspring that differ both phenotypically and genotypically from both parents and is thus an important means of producing variation.

There is no universally accepted theory as to why recombination exists. Experiments have shown that recombination does not exist in order to create genetic variation and it is an evolutionary disadvantage when it breaks up a favorable group of genes in linkage disequilibrium. An accepted theory is that recombination exists because of environmental change. Recombination can recreate multilocus genotypes that would otherwise be lost, which could be an advantage in a changing environment if a 'lost' genotype that was disadvantageous in one environment became advantageous in a new environment. *See* sexual reproduction.

red algae   *See* Rhodophyta.

Red Queen effect   (law of constant extinction)   A theory of COEVOLUTION in which natural selection continually operates on two competing species causing them to perpetually adapt and improve at a constant rate. For example, the limb sizes and brains of both carnivores and herbivores have increased considerably in the last 60 million years, resulting in both types of animals being able to run faster and becoming more intelligent. The predator (carnivore) is no more successful than it once was because the prey (herbivore) has also evolved. The theory is named after the Red Queen in *Through the Looking Glass* by Lewis Carroll, who remarked that in her country, you had to run very fast to remain in the same place.

reduction division   The first division of MEIOSIS, including prophase, metaphase I, and anaphase I. It results in a haploid number of chromosomes gathering at each end of the nuclear spindle.

reductionism   The scientific and philosophical belief that a complex system, such as a living organism, can be fully understood through knowledge of its component parts, e.g. its organs, tissues, cells, and molecular structure. An opposing scientific and philosophical idea is the *holistic* approach, in which the whole living organism is considered to be greater than the sum of its component parts, i.e. the whole organism has overriding special qualities.

regeneration   The regrowth by an organism of an organ or tissue that has been lost through injury, AUTOTOMY, etc. The powers of regeneration vary between different groups; they are best seen in plants and lower animals. In some cases a complete organism can sometimes be regenerated from a few cells. Regeneration in mammals is limited to wound-healing and regrowth of peripheral nerve fibers.

regulator gene   *See* gene; homeobox; operon.

reinforcement   The enhancement of PREZYGOTIC ISOLATION between two incompletely formed species by NATURAL SELECTION. Different forms of the same species preferentially mate with their own type. Reinforcement is controversial but would be required for SYMPATRIC SPECIATION and

PARAPATRIC SPECIATION, but not for ALLOPATRIC SPECIATION.

relative dating   *See* dating techniques.

Remanié fossils   An enormous group of fossils formed by the accumulation of skeletal material over a long time period that has been rolled together and mechanically worn before being buried in sediment. Remanié fossils occur in BONE BEDS, for example the sedimentary rock is usually very thin, either because there were rapid currents or because there was a poor supply of sediment at the time of its formation.

repair nuclease   *See* DNA repair.

repeated gene   Multiple copies of the same functional gene. Some repeated genes such as ribosomal RNA genes exist in TANDEM REPEATS while others are scattered around the genome. *See* repetitive DNA. *See also* gene cluster; gene family.

repetitive DNA   DNA that consists of multiple repeats of the same nucleotide sequences. Unlike prokaryotic cells, eukaryotic cells contain appreciable amounts of repetitive DNA; much of this is not transcribed and constitutes part of the so-called JUNK DNA. There are various types of repetitive DNA: MICROSATELLITE DNA, MINISATELLITE DNA, SATELLITE DNA, TRANSPOSONS, and REPEATED GENES. *See also* selfish DNA.

replication   The mechanism by which exact copies of the genetic material are formed. Replicas of DNA are made when the double helix unwinds and the separated strands serve as templates along which complementary nucleotides are assembled through the action of the enzyme DNA polymerase. The result is two new molecules of DNA each containing one strand of the original molecule, and the process is termed *semiconservative replication*. Because the two DNA strands are antiparallel and DNA polymerase only works in one direction, one DNA strand, the *leading strand*, is synthesized continuously and the other, the *lagging strand*, is synthesized in fragments. These fragments are called *Okazaki fragments* and are linked together by the enzyme DNA ligase. Most prokaryotes have three types of DNA polymerase and eukaryotic cells have at least four. It is important for survival that DNA replication does not introduce incorrect bases that would cause mutation so DNA polymerase 'proofreads' the newly synthesized DNA and mistakes are corrected by the mismatch repair system. In RNA viruses an RNA polymerase is involved in the replication of the viral RNA.

reproductive character displacement Displacement for a character that influences reproductive isolation. *See* character displacement.

reproductive investment The combined effort required to produce and care for each offspring multiplied by the number of offspring.

reproductive isolation The state in which two individuals (of the opposite sex) from different populations cannot produce fertile offspring. The main reason is usually a geographical one but as the populations evolve, other changes take place, which may be phenotypic, morphological, physiological, behavioral, or genetic. *See* cichlids; isolating mechanism; prezygotic isolation; postzygotic isolation; speciation.

reproductive success The number of offspring produced in a lifetime by a single individual.

reproductive value The expected contribution of an organism at a particular stage of life to its REPRODUCTIVE SUCCESS. Residual reproductive value is the contribution to reproductive success that an organism could potentially make over the rest of its life.

Reptilia The class of vertebrates that contains the first wholly terrestrial tetrapods, which are adapted to life on land by the possession of a dry skin with horny scales, which prevents water loss by evaporation. Fertilization is internal and

there is no larval stage. The young develop directly from an amniote egg that has a leathery shell and is laid on land, i.e. it is a CLEIDOIC EGG (*see* amniote). Respiration is by lungs only and the heart has four chambers, although oxygenated and deoxygenated blood usually mix. Other advanced features are the clawed digits and the metanephric kidney. Like amphibians, but unlike birds and mammals, reptiles are poikilothermic.

Modern forms include the predominantly terrestrial lizards and snakes (order SQUAMATA), as well as the aquatic crocodiles and alligators (order Crocodilia), and turtles (order Chelonia; Testudines in some classifications). The ancient order Rhyncocephalia is represented by a single modern form, the TUATARA (*Sphenodon*), which is found on a group of small islands off the coast of New Zealand. Unlike other modern reptiles, it has a PINEAL EYE, which was a feature of primitive reptiles.

The first reptiles evolved from the Amphibia in the late Carboniferous at a time when there were abundant forests and insects on which they could feed. The class expanded during the Permian and they became the dominant tetrapod group (notably the DINOSAURS) in the MESOZOIC era – often described as the 'Age of Reptiles'. The advanced features of the reptiles enabled them to replace the Amphibia on land.

The reptiles are divided into four subclasses based on their skull structure, in particlar, the arrangement of gaps or holes, known as TEMPORAL FOSSAE, that develop between the bones just behind the eyes on each side of the skull. Their function was probably to anchor jaw muscles, enabling a more powerful chewing action.

The *Anapsida* (e.g. *Hylonomus*) have no temporal fossae and are the most primitive group. They arose in the Pennsylvanian and include the COTYLOSAURS (stem reptiles) of the late Carboniferous. The present-day turtles and tortoises are the only surviving members of the anapsids.

The *Synapsida* (e.g. *Eothyris*) have one large temporal fossa on each side of the skull and include the *pelycosaurs*, the mammal-like reptiles (e.g. *Dimetrodon*), which gave rise to the *therapsids*, the immediate ancestors of mammals (*see* Mammalia).

The *Diapsida* (e.g. *Allosaurus*), have two temporal fossae on both sides of the skull and include two superorders: the ARCHOSAURS (thecodonts), also known as the 'Ruling reptiles' from which the *Pterosauria*, the crocodilians (represented by present-day order, Crocodilia), the dinosaurs, and the birds eventually evolved; and the *Lepidosaurs*, which gave rise to the two orders SQUAMATA (represented by present-day lizards and snakes) and Rhyncocephalia.

The *Eurapsida* (*Parapsida* in some classifications) (e.g. *Grippia*) have one temporal fossa high up on top of the skull on both sides. They evolved from the diapsids, one of the original two fossae having closed up, possibly to strengthen their skulls for life in water. This group includes the ICHTHYOSAURIA, PLESIOSAURS, and PLACODONTS, which were marine Mesozoic reptiles, all now extinct.

The first synapsids (pelycosaurs) appeared in the early Pennsylvanian and dominated the late Pennsylvanian and early Permian. In the late Permian the therapsids evolved from the pelycosaurs and flourished into the Triassic. The first diapsids appeared in the late Pennsylvanian and remained an obscure group throughout the Permian. By the end of the Triassic, the therapsids declined (many families becoming extinct) and the archosaurs began their domination, occupying the ecological niches of the therapsids. Primitive synapsid reptiles were massive animals with thick-boned heavy skeletons, the pelycosaurs were less so, but the Triassic therapsids that survived were again cumbersome, with weighty skeletons.

Many of the archosaurs and lepidosaurs of the Triassic had much more slender skeletons, with a reduction of bone mass and hollow bones. This was accompanied by a trend toward walking on two legs (bipedalism) and enlargement of the ischium of the pelvic girdle that enabled an erect posture. The legs also increased in size to bear the weight of the body. The dinosaurs became the dominant group in the Jurassic and Cretaceous, many of the larger ones again becoming quadrupedal to support their massive bodies. The pterosaurs, some with wingspans of up to 13 m, dominated the skies in the Jurassic and Cretaceous. ARCHAEOPTERYX provides evidence of birdlike reptiles during this period. The euryapsids evolved from the diapsids in the Triassic and the ichthyosaurs, plesiosaurs, and placodonts became the most successful marine reptiles of the Mesozoic. By the end of the Mesozoic, the plesiosaurs, ichthyosaurs, placodonts, and dinosaurs had disappeared, leaving only the groups that evolved into modern reptiles as the sole representatives of this enormous and diverse class. *See also* Alvarez theory; K–T event; mass extinction.

residual reproductive value   *See* reproductive value.

respiration   The oxidation of organic molecules to provide energy in living organisms. In animals, food molecules are respired, but autotrophic plants respire molecules that they have themselves synthesized by photosynthesis. The energy from respiration is used to attach a high-energy phosphate group to ADP to form the short-term energy carrier ATP, which can then be used to power energy-requiring processes within the cell. The actual chemical reactions of respiration are known as *internal* (*cell* or *tissue*) *respiration* and they normally require oxygen from the environment (*aerobic respiration*). Some organisms are able to respire, at least for a short period, without the use of oxygen (*anaerobic respiration*), although this process produces far less energy than aerobic respiration. Respiration usually involves an exchange of gases with the environment; this is known as *external respiration*. In small animals and all plants exchange by diffusion is adequate, but larger animals generally have special respiratory organs with large moist and ventilated surfaces (e.g. lungs, gills) and there is often a circulatory system to transport gases internally to and from the respiratory organs.

restriction endonuclease (restriction enzyme) A type of enzyme, found mainly in bacteria, that can cleave and fragment DNA internally. They are so named as they restrict their activity to foreign DNA, such as the DNA of an invading virus; thus their function is protection of the cell. Some restriction endonucleases cleave DNA at random, but a particular group of enzymes, known as *class II restriction endonucleases*, cleave DNA at specific sites. Most recognize a sequence of six nucleotides, but some only five or four. The specific sites on the cell's own DNA are protected from this enzyme activity by methylation, which is controlled by another type of site-specific enzyme.

The resulting fragments of DNA may be blunt-ended, i.e. the two strands finish at the same point, or may have a cohesive or 'sticky' end with a single strand extending. Both types of fragment can be inserted into a cloning vector using a DNA ligase enzyme. The discovery of these enzymes formed the basis for the development of GENETIC ENGINEERING, since they enable the isolation of particular gene sequences and the DNA fragments can be easily replicated. About 2500 type II restriction endonucleases have been discovered, with some 200 different cleavage site specificities. They have been named according to the organism in which they occur. For example, *EcoR1* is obtained from *Escherichia coli*, strain R, and was the first enzyme to be isolated in this bacterium.

restriction fragment length polymorphism (RFLP) Variation among the members of a population in the sites at which restriction enzymes cleave the DNA, and hence in the size of the resulting DNA fragments. It results from differences between individuals in nucleotide sequences at the cleavage sites (*restriction sites*). The presence or absence of particular restriction sites can be ascertained using DNA probes in the technique called Southern blotting. Restriction sites vary enormously, and this variation is exploited in analyzing and comparing the genomes of different individuals, e.g. to establish how closely related they may be. Restriction sites are also invaluable as genetic markers in chromo-some mapping, and can be used to track particular genes. *See* chromosome map.

restriction map A map of a segment of DNA showing the cleavage sites of RESTRICTION ENDONUCLEASES and their physical distance apart, usually measured in base pairs. It can be used to reveal variations in restriction sites between individuals of the same species or between different species (*see* restriction fragment length polymorphism). This variation serves as a key to the organism's genes, since the restriction sites can be used as markers to identify closely linked genetic loci and allow investigation of deletions, insertions, or other mutations. They are an essential tool in chromosome mapping.

The first step in constructing a restriction map is to label the ends of the DNA with a radioisotope. Then the DNA is subjected to a series of total and partial digests with one or more restriction enzymes. The fragments resulting from each digest are separated according to size by gel electrophoresis, and the order of fragments, and hence restriction sites, deduced from the various fragment sizes and the labeled ends. *See also* genetic fingerprinting.

restriction site *See* restriction fragment length polymorphism.

retrotransposon A TRANSPOSON that uses a REVERSE TRANSCRIPTASE as part of its transposition mechanism.

retrovirus An RNA-containing VIRUS whose genome becomes integrated into the host DNA (by means of the enzyme reverse transcriptase) and then replicates with it. These viruses can cause cancerous changes in their host cells i.e. they are oncogenic by means of the activity of one or more of their genes. HIV is a nononcogenic retrovirus. *See* AIDS.

reverse transcriptase An enzyme that catalyzes the synthesis of DNA from RNA (i.e. the reverse of transcription, in which mRNA is synthesized from a DNA template). The enzyme occurs in certain RNA viruses known as RETROVIRUSES, e.g. HIV (*see* AIDS) and enables the viral RNA to be 'transcribed' into DNA, which is then integrated into the host DNA and replicates with it. Reverse transcriptase does not have the proof-reading ability of DNA polymerase and causes a high mutation rate in the viral genome. Retroviruses therefore mutate and evolve into different strains rapidly, even within a single infection. Reverse transcriptases are used in GENETIC ENGINEERING and nucleic acid sequencing to make complementary DNA (cDNA) from an RNA template.

RFLP *See* restriction fragment length polymorphism.

Rhaetic series *See* bone beds.

Rhizopoda (Sarcodina) A phylum of ameboid protozoan protoctists that lack cilia and flagella (undulipodia). They have an irregular shape due to the formation of pseudopodia, used for locomotion and food capture. Most are solitary, occurring in marine and fresh waters, but a few are parasites (e.g. *Entamoeba*). Many (e.g. *Ameba*) have no internal skeleton, but some (e.g. *Difflugia*) have a protective outer test or shell. *See also* Foraminifera; Radiolaria.

Rhodesian man *See Homo sapiens.*

Rhodophyta (red algae) A phylum of the PROTOCTISTA (in some classifications assigned to a division of the kingdom Plantae) of mostly multicellular, mainly marine, seaweeds. They are found worldwide on beaches, rocky shores, and sometimes in quite deep water. Their characteristic red color results from their unique photosynthetic pigments: allophycocyanin, phycocyanin, and phycoerythrin (the prefix 'phyco' is derived from the Greek word 'phykos', meaning 'seaweed'). They also contain chlorophyll *a*, which produces starch. The main food product is 'floridean' starch (stored in the cytoplasm rather than in the plastids). The red pigments allow red algae to live at greater depths than other algae because they reflect red light and absorb blue light, which penetrates deeper water. The cell walls contain cellulose, hemicellulose, and large quantities of mucopolysaccharides (mucilages). The colloid agar, obtained from the red alga *Gelidium*, is used in the culture of bacteria.

The life cycles usually involve an alternation of generations, but the sperm cells lack flagella, relying on water currents for fertilization, which is a primitive feature of these algae.

The fossil record is sketchy initially, because of their soft bodies, but calcareous red algae (*coralline algae*) have been discovered in the late Cambrian. Red algae are very important in the formation of tropical reefs, which they have been involved in for millions of years. The coralline algae secrete a shell of calcium carbonate around themselves in the same way as corals.

Rhyncocephalia *See* Reptilia; tuatara.

rhyncosaurs *See* Triassic.

Rhynia *See* Psilophyta.

Rhynie Chert *See* Fungi; Insecta; Psilophyta; Radiolaria; Silurian.

ribonuclease (RNase) Any nuclease enzyme that cleaves the phosphodiester bonds between adjacent nucleotides in RNA. *Exoribonucleases* cleave nucleotides from one or both ends of the RNA molecule, while *endoribonucleases* cleave bonds within the molecule.

ribonucleic acid *See* RNA.

ribosomal RNA (rRNA) The RNA found in the RIBOSOMES. The base sequences of particular ribosomal subunits are highly conserved and are used to work out evolutionary events that occurred 500–1500 mya, such as the acquisition of chloroplasts and mitochondria by eukaryotes.

ribosome A small ORGANELLE found in large numbers in all cells that acts as a site for PROTEIN SYNTHESIS. In most species ribosomes are composed of roughly equal amounts of protein and RNA. The ribosome consists of two unequally sized rounded subunits arranged on top of each other like a cottage loaf. Eukaryotic cells have larger ribosomes than prokaryotic cells but the ribosomes in mitochondria and chloroplasts are about the same size as prokaryotic ribosomes. During TRANSLATION the ribosome moves along the messenger RNA (mRNA), enabling the peptide linkage of amino acids delivered to the site by transfer RNA molecules according to the code in mRNA. Several ribosomes may be actively engaged in protein synthesis along the same mRNA molecule, forming a *polyribosome* or *polysome*. See origin of life; ribozyme.

ribozyme   Any RNA molecule that has catalytic activity. It is now known that INTRONS (noncoding messenger RNA sequences) often catalyze their own removal from the primary messenger RNA transcript and the splicing together of the cleaved ends, in a process called *self-splicing*. Following its removal, the intron ribozyme may catalyze further reactions, including splitting of RNA molecules and even peptide bond formation. Such ribozymes have remarkable similarities with viroids, the minute plant pathogens consisting simply of RNA circles, and it has been proposed that *viroids* are escaped introns.

ring species   Two geographically isolated species that continue to be distinct species (reproductively isolated) when they are put in the same location but are connected by a continuous population of intermediates that can interbreed, for example, the circumpolar gull species. This well-documented ring species of gull begins as a gray-mantled pink-legged herring gull in the North Seas, but in Canada some appear to be similar, whereas others have a quite different appearance and are known as vega gulls. Circumventing the North Pole to Siberia, across Asia, and across Europe, the gulls become even more different (black-backed with yellow legs) and they live alongside the original herring gulls of the North Sea, with whom they cannot interbreed. The interesting point about ring species is that within the 'ring' or circle, adjoining intermediate populations can and do interbreed.

RNA   (ribonucleic acid)   A nucleic acid found mainly in the cytoplasm and involved in protein synthesis. It is a single polynucleotide chain similar in composition to a single strand of DNA except that the sugar ribose replaces deoxyribose and the pyrimidine base uracil replaces thymine. RNA is synthesized on DNA in the nucleus and exists in three forms: MESSENGER RNA, TRANSFER RNA, and RIBOSOMAL RNA. In certain viruses, RNA is the genetic material. It is generally accepted that RNA was the ancestral replicator because it is simpler than DNA (being single stranded); uracil is made more easily than thymine and ribose sugars are made more easily than deoxyribose sugars in experiments on the proposed prebiotic chemical soup. Moreover, some RNA molecules (RIBOZYMES) have catalytic activity and assist in their own replication. RNA undergoes spontaneous damage easily and could not sustain complex living systems. It is possible that double-stranded RNA genomes evolved before DNA became the genetic material. See also origin of life.

RNA polymerase   See polymerase.

robust australopithecines   See australopithecines.

Rodentia   The largest and most successful order of mammals, including *Rattus* (rat), *Mus* (mouse), *Sciurus* (squirrel), and *Castor* (beaver). Rodents are herbivorous or omnivorous mammmals with one pair of chisel-like incisor teeth projecting from each jaw at the front of the mouth and specialized for continuous gnawing. The incisors, which grow throughout life, have enamel only on the front. The wearing down of the softer dentine behind produces a sharp cutting edge. Skin folds can be inserted into the gap (diastema) between the incisors and ridged grinding molars so that inedible material (such as wood) need not be swallowed. Rodents are found universally and are mostly nocturnal and terrestrial. They are noted for their rapid breeding.

Rodents evolved in the late Paleocene from a group of small fossil mammals, the *anagalids*, and diversified in the Eocene into a number of groups. At the same time many ancient and primitive mammalian groups such as the rodentlike MULTITUBERCULATES, became extinct. The first rodents resembled modern squirrels. Most fossil beavers, e.g. *Daemonelis*, lived in burrows beneath the ground. The mouselike forms (*murids*) evolved in the Eocene, along with the guinea pigs, that evolved in the Asian or African Eocene. The extinct giant beaver (*Castoroides*) of the Pleistocene grew to the size of a bear. Rodent fossils have been very important in paleoclimatology studies and studying evolutionary patterns as they are often found in cave deposits.

Rodinia   *See* Paleozoic.

Romer, Alfred Sherwood (1894–1973) American paleontologist. One of the major figures in paleontology since the 1930s, Romer spent the greater part of his career researching the evolution of vertebrates, based on evidence from comparative anatomy, embryology, and paleontology (*see* craniates). His work has had considerable influence on evolutionary thinking, especially with regard to the lower vertebrates. He paid particular attention to the relationship between animal form and physical function and environment, tracing, for example, the physical changes that occurred during the evolutionary transition of fishes to primitive terrestrial vertebrates. He made extensive collections of fossils of fishes, amphibians, and reptiles from South Africa and Ar-

gentina and from the Permian deposits in Texas. His best-known publication is *Man and the Vertebrates* (1933), subsequently revised as *The Vertebrate Story* (1959).

rooted tree   *See* phylogeny.

root reptiles   *See* cotylosaurs.

Rotifera   A phylum of microscopic aquatic invertebrates that are widely distributed, usually in fresh waters. Rotifers (the name is from Latin: 'wheel bearer') are bilaterally symmetrical and unsegmented with a body divided into head, trunk, and tail regions. They are characterized by a ciliated crown on the head (*corona*), used in feeding and locomotion, which appears like a rotating wheel when beating. The muscular pharynx has well-developed jaws. Excretion is carried out by protonephridia. Males are often degenerate and parthenogenesis is common.

Rotifers are rare as fossils, the oldest having been found in the Dominican AMBER of the Eocene. Nucleotide sequencing has confirmed their alliance with the parasitic phylum Acanthocephala (spiny-headed worms), and with the Annelid/Molluscan lineage.

roundworms   *See* Nematoda.

rRNA   *See* ribosomal RNA.

rubidium–strontium dating   *See* radioactive dating.

rudimentary character   *See* vestigial character.

'Ruling reptiles'   *See* archosaurs.

ruminants   *See* Artiodactyla.

s   *See* selection coefficient.

S   *See* selection differential.

saltation   A sudden event resulting in a jump in evolution, for example, new mutations that give rise to immediate speciation. *See* transmutation.

saltationism   The belief that evolutionary change is the result of the sudden appearance of a new individual that is the progenitor of a new type of organism. *See also* phyletic gradualism; punctuated equilibrium.

Sarcodina   *See* Rhizopoda.

Sarich, Vincent   (1934–) American biochemist. Sarich was struck by the range of dates, from 4 mya to 30 mya, within which anthropologists of the early 1960s placed the origin of the split between the HOMINIDS and the great apes. He began work, in collaboration with his Berkeley colleague Allan WILSON, to see if there was a more precise method of dating using the genetic relationship between humans and apes. They chose to work with proteins, which closely reflect genes, choosing the blood-serum protein albumin. As humans and apes diverged further from their common ancestor, their albumins would also have diverged and would now be recognizably different.

Serum samples from apes, monkeys, and humans were purified and then injected into rabbits to produce antiserums. A rabbit immunized against a human sample (antigen) will also react to other anthropoid antigens, only not as strongly. Because antigenic differences are geneti-

cally based, response differences will therefore measure genetic differences between species. Sarich chose to work with a group of proteins found in blood serum known collectively as the complement system. Antigens tend to attract and fix some of the complement. The amount of complement fixed could be measured precisely. Thus differences in complement-fixation rates produced by the albumin of a human and a gorilla when injected into immunized rabbits would measure their immunological distance.

If it could be assumed that protein differences between species have evolved at a constant rate, immunological distance would also be a measure of evolutionary separation. Sarich and Wilson took as their base line the date 30 mya marking the separation between the hominoids and the old-world monkeys. Thereafter it was a relatively easy matter to turn immunological distance into dates.

The results were clear but surprising. *Homo*, on this scheme, separated from the chimpanzees and gorillas only 5 mya. This was a bold claim to make in 1967 when orthodox opinion, argued for example by David PILBEAM, placed the split between hominids and hominoids closer to 15 million years. What is more they had the skull of *Ramapithecus*, dating from this period, to prove their point. Initially, Sarich's views were rejected out of hand by paleontologists. Slowly, however, Sarich made converts. He argued, "I know my molecules have ancestors, you must prove your fossils had descendants." They found it more and more difficult to do so. Consequently, when it became clear that *Ramapithecus* was the ancestor not of humans but the orangutan, opposition to Sarich largely disappeared.

satellite DNA   A type of repetitive DNA that can be separated by centrifugation from the main DNA fraction because it has a base composition unlike that of most DNA. Satellite DNA is made of thousands of TANDEM REPEATS of up to hundreds of base pairs and is found at the middle (centromere) or end (telomere) of chromosomes.   *Compare*   microsatellite; minisatellite. *See also* junk DNA; selfish DNA.

Saurischia   *See* dinosaur.

sauropod   *See* dinosaur.

scala naturae   *See* Great Chain of Being.

scolecodonts   *See* Polychaeta.

Scopes Monkey trial   A famous trial that took place in Dayton, Tennessee, in 1925 concerning the teaching of evolution in schools. Tennessee had made it unlawful "to teach any theory that denies the story of divine creation as taught by the Bible and to teach instead that man was descended from a lower order of animals." A group of people in Dayton set up a test case to challenge the law by prosecuting John Scopes, a general-science teacher who had taught some biology in the local school. They were mainly motivated by gaining publicity for Dayton and expected that Scopes would lose the case. The defense hoped that a higher court would subsequently declare laws against teaching evolution to be unconstitutional.

The trial generated enormous interest. The case was prosecuted by William Jennings Bryan, a prominent politician who was leading a campaign to abolish the teaching of evolution in American schools. The defence was led by Clarence Darrow, a leading lawyer, who used the trial to attack fundamentalist views. The press, including the journalist H. L. Mencken, were mostly sympathetic to the defense. Toward the end of the trial Darrow asked the court to return a verdict of guilty, so that he could appeal to the Tennessee Supreme Court. Scopes was fined 100 dollars. A year later the Supreme Court reversed the decision but on a technicality, not on constitutional grounds. The trial was the subject of a play and later a film, *Inherit the Wind*, made in 1960.

scorpions   *See* Arachnida.

Scott, Dukinfield Henry   (1854–1934) British paleobotanist. In 1889 Scott met William Williamson who awoke in him a passion for PALEOBOTANY. He worked mainly on the plants of the Carboniferous but also published such general works as his *Extinct Plants and Problems of Evolution* (1924). With Williamson and Albert Seward, Scott was one of the founders of the scientific study of fossil plants, a task as crucial to the study of evolution as better-known searches for fossil vertebrates.

Scyphozoa   A class of the CNIDARIA, the jellyfish, in which the medusa is the only or dominant form and the polyp is absent or restricted to a small larval stage. The medusae are highly organized with the mouth at the end of a tube (manubrium) hanging down underneath and leading to the coelenteron, which is divided into four pouches and contains a canal system (gastrovascular cavity) for food distribution. The tentacles around the rim bear stinging cnidocytes. Jellyfish are found universally and range in diameter from about 70 mm (e.g. *Aurelia*) to 2 m (e.g. *Cyanea*). They are known from the fauna of ancient Cambrian times and are the first representatives of the cnidarians to be discovered. Scant impressions of jellyfish have also been discovered in Permian and Jurassic rocks and their structure has changed little since ancient times.

seasonal isolation   *See* prezygotic isolation.

sea urchins   *See* Echinoidea.

secondary sexual characteristic   *See* sexual character.

Sedgwick, Adam (1785–1873) British geologist and mathematician. In 1831 he began a study of the PALEOZOIC rocks of Wales, choosing an older region than the Silurian recently discovered by Roderick Murchison. In 1835 he named the oldest fossiliferous strata the CAMBRIAN (after Cambria, an ancient name for Wales). This immediately caused a problem for there was no reliable way to distinguish the Upper Cambrian from the Lower SILURIAN.

Sedgwick formed a close friendship with Murchison. The two made their most significant joint investigation with their identification of the Devonian System from studies in southwest England in 1839. The partnership between Sedgwick and Murchison was broken when Murchison annexed what Sedgwick considered to be his Upper Cambrian into the Silurian. The bitter dispute between the two over these Lower Paleozoic strata was not resolved until after Sedgwick's death, when Charles Lapworth proposed that the strata should form a new system – the ORDOVICIAN.

Sedgwick's works included *A Synopsis of the Classification of the British Paleozoic Rocks* (1855). Sedgwick was, throughout his life, a committed opponent of Darwin's theory of evolution.

sedimentary rocks Rocks composed of sediments, usually with a layered appearance. The sediments are composed of particles that come mostly from the weathering and deposition of preexisting rocks, but often include material of organic origin. Sedimentary rocks are deposited mainly under water, usually in approximately horizontal layers (beds) and are classified according to the size of the particles, for example, sandstones, mudstones, conglomerates, and breccia. Organically formed sedimentary rocks are derived from the remains of plants and animals, for example limestone and coal. Chemically formed sedimentary rocks result from natural chemical processes and include sedimentary iron ores. Many sedimentary rocks contain FOSSILS.

seed ferns *See* Cycadofilicales.

seed plants *See* spermatophyte.

segment One of a series of repeated parts of the body. *See* metameric segmentation.

segmentation *See* metameric segmentation.

segregation The separation of the two alleles of a gene into different gametes, brought about by the separation of homologous chromosomes during meiosis. *See* Mendel's laws.

segregational load A type of GENETIC LOAD caused by Mendelian inheritance. For a polymorphism maintained by heterozygous advantage, the segregation of chromosomes at meiosis means the population inevitably produces homozygotes in every generation so the average fitness of the population is less than that of a population containing only heterozygotes. *See* independent assortment; recombination.

segregation distortion *See* meiotic drive.

Selachii The order of CHONDRICHTHYES that contains the sharks, which have been known since Devonian times. Sharks are fast aggressive predators with a widely gaping mouth and numerous sharp teeth that are continuously replaced. The streamlined torpedo-shaped body tapers into a well-developed heterocercal tail and the paired fins have narrow bases, making them mobile and effective in controlling motion through the water. The spiracle and gill slits are situated laterally. They are so well adapted to their habitat that they have changed very little in their evolutionary history.

Skates and rays are sometimes included in this order. They are specialized for living on the sea bed, having a dorsoventrally flattened body, dorsal eyes and spiracle, ventral gill openings, and winglike pectoral fins.

Selaginella A genus of club mosses (*see* LYCOPODOPHYTA) comprising the spike mosses. A typical representative of the genus is *S. kraussiana*, which is a creeping regularly branched plant with four rows of leaves arranged along the horizontal stem in opposite pairs. The roots develop from a unique structure (the rhizophore) and the strobili arise as vertical branches. Often described as a LIVING FOSSIL, the genus *Selaginella* may be an ancestral form of the other lycopods, first appearing in the Carboniferous.

selection   A synonym for NATURAL SELECTION. *See also* artificial selection; canalizing selection; density-dependent selection; density-independent selection; directional selection; disruptive selection: frequency-dependent selection; group selection; individual selection; kin selection; sexual selection; species selection; stabilizing selection.

selection coefficient   (*s*) A quantitative expression of the reduction in FITNESS of a genotype relative to the ideal genotype. It can be calculated from the HARDY–WEINBERG EQUATION.

selection differential (*S*)   The difference between the population mean and the mean phenotype of the parents that produce the next generation. It can be calculated from TRUNCATION SELECTION experiments and used in estimating NARROW SENSE HERITABILITY. *See also* selection response.

selectionism   A theory that some types of evolutionary event such as molecular changes are mainly caused by NATURAL SELECTION.

selection pressure   The strength with which the environment eliminates a particular phenotype, so causing the gene responsible for this to decrease in the population. It is thus a loose indication of the force of natural selection.

selection response (*R*)   The difference between the mean value of a given trait in the parental population and the offspring mean. It can be calculated from TRUNCA-

TION SELECTION experiments and used in estimating NARROW SENSE HERITABILITY. *See also* selection differential.

selenodont   *See* molar.

selfish DNA   JUNK DNA that can move around within the genome of an organism or insert copies of itself at various random sites in the genome like a molecular parasite. It can sometimes cause harm by giving rise to genetic diseases. Natural selection would only act to remove selfish DNA if it interfered with a cellular function or if there was so much that replicating it slowed the cell cycle and was an energetic burden. Selfish DNA has therefore been put forward as a solution to the C-FACTOR PARADOX as it can account for the varying amounts of noncoding DNA seen in different species. The prime examples of selfish DNA are the mobile genetic elements called TRANSPOSONS. Some authorities also regard INTRONS as selfish DNA.

selfish gene   The generally accepted concept that NATURAL SELECTION directly adjusts the frequency of genes, specifically the mutations that produce changes in characters. Ultimately, adaptations exist because they increase the reproduction of the genes encoding them. The argument for the theory is that organisms (phenotypes) die and genomes (genotypes) are disrupted by recombination so only the gene is permanent enough for its frequency to be altered over successive generations. The term was introduced by Richard DAWKINS in 1976. *See also* gene; unit of selection.

self-splicing   *See* ribozyme.

semiconservative replication   *See* replication.

sequence alignment   The critical part of MOLECULAR PHYLOGENETICS in which multiple sequences of DNA, RNA, or proteins are aligned by computer algorithms and HOMOLOGOUS residues (bases or amino acids) lined up in columns. In order to do this, gaps are inserted into the sequences to account for insertions and deletions that are assumed to have occurred over time. An alignment is therefore a hypothetical model of mutations and the best alignment is the one that represents the most probable evolutionary scenario. It is not usually possible to unarguably establish the best alignment because of the complexity of the algorithms. There are a number of algorithms available, none of which are ideal, and the choice of algorithms is usually checked and edited by hand. HOMOPLASY is a signifcant danger in aligned sequences and can be reduced by statistically weighting certain sequence positions, but it cannot be completely eliminated.

sequence homology   *See* homologous.

sequencing   *See* gene sequencing; protein sequencing.

series   *See* geological time scale.

Sewall Wright effect   *See* genetic drift.

sex chromosomes   The chromosomes that determine sex in most animals. There are two types: in mammals these are called the *X chromosome* and the *Y chromosome*. In the heterogametic sex (XY) they can usually be distinguished from the other chromosomes, because the Y chromosome is much shorter than the X chromosome with which it is paired (unlike the remaining chromosomes, which are in similar homologous pairs). *See* sex determination; sex linkage.

sex determination   In species having almost equal numbers of males and females sex determination is genetic. Very occasionally a single pair of alleles determine sex but usually whole chromosomes, the sex chromosomes, are responsible. The 1:1 ratio of males to females is obtained by crossing of the homogametic sex (e.g. XX) with the heterogametic sex (e.g. XY). In most animals, including humans, the female is homogametic and the male heterogametic, but in birds, butterflies and some fishes this situation is reversed. In some species sex is determined more by the number of X chromosomes than by the pres-

ence of the Y chromosome, but in humans the Y chromosome is important in determining maleness. Many genes are involved in determining all aspects of maleness or femaleness, but it is thought that in humans one particular gene on the Y chromosome acts as sex switch to initiate male development. In the absence of this male switch gene (i.e. in XX individuals) the fetus develops as a female. Rarely, sex is subject to environmental control, in which case unequal numbers of males and females develop. In bees and some other members of the Hymenoptera, females develop from fertilized eggs and are diploid while males develop from unfertilized eggs and are haploid, the numbers of each sex being controlled by the queen bee.

sex linkage   The coupling of certain genes (and therefore the characters they control) to the sex of an organism because they happen to occur on the X sex chromosome or its equivalent. The heterogametic sex (XY), which in humans is the male, has only one X chromosome and thus any recessive genes carried on it are not masked by their dominant alleles (as they would be in the homogametic sex). Thus in humans recessive forms of the sex-linked genes appear in the male phenotype far more frequently than in the female (in which they would have to be double recessives). Color blindness and hemophilia are sex linked.

sex ratio   The ratio of males to females (at the zygote stage) in a population, which is 50:50 in most species. If the sex ratio deviates from 50:50, for example by *local mate competition* in which an individual only competes with a limited portion of the population, then natural selection will drive it back.

sexual character (secondary sexual characteristic)   A character associated with sexual reproduction that develops in male and female animals at the onset of sexual maturity in association with masculinity and femininity. Primary sexual characters are sex organs required for breeding. Secondary sexual characters are not needed for breeding but function during reproduction and are apparently advantageous for survival. Secondary sexual characters develop in males and females at the onset of sexual maturity, usually as a result of the effects of hormones (e.g. androgens or estrogens), secreted by the sex organs at this time. In humans, males grow hair on the face and the voice deepens, females develop breasts and the hip girdle enlarges. Secondary sexual characters are used by many animals in courtship rituals, which are preliminary to mating and reproduction, e.g. a male peacock displays its enormous colorful tail. In a number of species, males develop unusual and seemingly deleterious secondary characters that can be explained by SEXUAL SELECTION. See Fisher's theory; handicap theory.

sexual dimorphism The difference in phenotypes between males and females of the same species.

sexual reproduction The formation of a new organism by the fusion of two gametes to form a zygote. The majority of species reproduce sexually and in unicellular organisms, whole individuals unite, but in multicellular organisms, only gametes combine. Male gametes and female gametes are produced in sex organs (e.g. ovary and testis in animals; carpel and anther in plants), which, with associated structures, form a reproductive system and aid in the reproductive process. Individuals containing both male and female systems are described as monoecious in plants or hermaphrodite in animals. Generally, MEIOSIS occurs before gamete formation resulting in HAPLOID gametes. At fertilization when gametes fuse, the DIPLOID number of chromosomes is restored.

One of the fundamental, and as yet unanswered, problems of evolutionary biology is why sexual reproduction exists. Sex has an in-built 50% reduction in fitness so it must have a selective advantage large enough to make up for this cost. RECOMBINATION at meiosis is a direct consequence of sexual reproduction and modern theories of why sex exists are concentrated on recombination. Three popular theories

are: 1. Sexual reproduction speeds up the rate of adaptive evolution by increasing the rate at which beneficial mutations are combined in an individual. The higher the rate at which beneficial mutations arise, the higher the rate of evolution. 2. Sexual reproduction removes more disadvantageous mutations than asexual reproduction 3. Sexual reproduction is advantageous in the coevolutionary struggle between hosts and parasites.

sexual selection A theory developed by Darwin to explain the evolution of bizarre male secondary sexual characteristics in which individuals are chosen as mates because of their fitness relative to other members of the same sex. Sexual selection can be divided into male competition (competition among males for access to females) and *female choice* (the preference of females for males with certain characteristics). Darwin's demonstration that POLYGYNOUS SPECIES show greater SEXUAL DIMORPHISM than monogamous species suggests that sexual selection is important. *See* cichlids; Fisher's theory; handicap theory; parasitic theory of sexual selection.

shotgun cloning *See* gene cloning.

siblings (sibs) Two or more offspring from the same cross. In animals, brothers and sisters are siblings. In plants, the products of a self-pollination are termed sibs.

sibling species Reproductively isolated species with very similar phenotypes that can only be distinguished with difficulty.

sibs *See* siblings.

sickle-cell anemia A frequently lethal inherited blood disorder in humans caused by a point mutation (*see* gene mutation) in the hemoglobin beta gene (*HBB*). The mutation results in normal hemoglobin being replaced by an abnormal type known as hemoglobin S. In a homozygous individual the hemoglobin S crystallizes under acid conditions (i.e. when carbon dioxide levels increase after exercise, for example). This causes the red blood cells, usually disk-shaped, to distort and become sickle-shaped (crescent-shaped). They thus carry less oxygen and also impair circulation by blocking capillaries, resulting in severe pain, and eventually causing damage to the heart and brain. About 80% of homozygous individuals die before child-bearing age.

Individuals heterozygous for the allele are carriers, showing some symptoms, but not very serious ones. Lethal genes are usually held at low frequency in the population, but in Africa, the allele is (surprisingly) carried by up to 20% of the population. The carriers have an unusually high resistance to malaria, a killer disease in Africa, and so there is a HETEROZYGOUS ADVANTAGE. Selection operates for the allele in heterozygous individuals. In the United States, however, the frequency of the sickle-cell allele in the descendants of African black people is declining, because malaria is infrequent, a clear example of evolution in action.

Hemoglobin S differs from normal hemoglobin at just one position in each of the two beta polypeptide chains, the amino acid glutamine being replaced by valine.

Sickle-cell anemia is also an excellent example of a pleiotropic allele with more than one effect (see pleiotropy).

sigma factor   See transcription.

silent mutation   See gene mutation.

Silurian   The period, some 440–405 mya, between the Ordovician and the Devonian periods of the Paleozoic. The Caledonian OROGENY continued throughout this period. An early period of glaciation reversed and the climate continued to warm throughout the period.

GRAPTOLITES continued to flourish, and many free-living planktonic types evolved and thrived in oxygen-poor nitrogen-rich water where upwelling causes sea water to rise from the ocean depth (see black smokers). They are important zone fossils for this period. The warm seas enabled corals and sponges (see Porifera) to produce enormous reefs (coral–STROMATOPOROID reefs). Calcified CYANOBACTERIA and siliceous

sponges also contributed to the reef building. Many other organisms flourished around the reefs, including the jawless fishes (the ostracoderms), some of which were armored, with head shields (see Cyclostomata; Agnatha). Fishes with jaws also appeared (see Chondrichthyes; Osteichthyes; Placodermi).

The first vascular land plants appeared ,for example *Rhynia* from the Rhynie Chert of Scotland. They were small branching plants bearing sporangia and grew in moist lowland conditions. Land plants had a marked effect on the environment, reducing carbon dioxide concentrations in the atmosphere, creating leaf litter, and enhancing the flow of nutrients. In Australia, the Silurian plants were more advanced than the *Rhynia*-like forms of the northern hemisphere. *Baragwanathia* had leaves and roots; *Sawdonia* had kidney-shaped sporangia. The earliest (wingless) insects resembled springtails, and evolved at the very end of the Silurian, continuing into the Devonian (see Insecta). *See also* geological time scale.

Simpson, George Gaylord   (1902–84) American paleontologist. Simpson worked extensively on the taxonomy and paleontology of mammals. His main contribution was his elucidation of the history of the early mammals (see Mammalia) in the late Mesozoic and the Paleocene and Eocene. To this end, beginning with field trips to Patagonia and Mongolia in the 1930s, he traveled to most areas of the world. In addition to a number of monographs he produced, in 1945, *Principles of Classification and the Classification of Mammals,* a major reference work on the subject. In such works as *The Meaning of Evolution* (1949) and *The Major Features of Evolution* (1949) he also did much to establish a neoDarwinian orthodoxy, as did similar works by Theodosius Dobzhansky and Ernst Mayr. Such works brought together population genetics, paleontology, and chromosomal studies to establish for the first time a broad consensus concerning the nature and mechanism of evolution.

Sinanthropus pekinensis See *Homo erectus*.

single-factor inheritance The control of one character by one gene. This gives rise to discontinuous variation in such characters, and intermediates between the dominant and recessive forms of the gene do not usually occur; for example, a person either is or is not red-green color blind. *Compare* quantitative inheritance.

Siphonaptera The order of the INSECTA that contains the fleas (small wingless insects), which are all ectoparasites of mammals and birds, e.g. *Pulex irritans* (human flea). Although rare as fossils, they have been found in the Oligocene in Baltic AMBER. Some questionable fossils of the Siphonaptera have been discovered in the Cretaceous, but it is possible that they evolved in the Jurassic, along with the first mammals.

Sivapithecus See Pilbeam; *Ramapithecus*.

skeleton A hard structure that supports, protects, and maintains the shape of an animal. It may be external to the body (EXOSKELETON) or within the body (ENDOSKELETON). Skeletal material is well preserved as FOSSILS and has provided a wealth of information about animals throughout geological time.
    The first animals with skeletons existed in the early Cambrian when the main multicellular phyla had already evolved. Animals with skeletons included sponges with spicules, brachiopods and mollusks with shells, echinoderms with spicules, annelids with cuticles, and arthropods with exoskeletons. Calcified CYANOBACTERIA and ancient siliceous sponges (*archaeocyaths* or 'ancient cups') were early reef builders, forming habitats for many groups of marine animals. Skeletons allowed animals to move in search of food and away from predators (e.g. TRILOBITES); they raised sedentary animals above the substrate, which benefited filter feeders; they were used to chop up food (teeth, jaws, and claws); and they protected animals in

stormy weather; they protected soft bodies from harmful ultraviolet radiation. It is possible that they evolved when limestones consisting of calcium carbonate replaced dolomites, which comprised magnesium carbonates. It has been suggested that skeletons may even have developed as storage organs for excess calcium and phosphates. Probably various different events in the Cambrian contributed to the evolution.

skin The outer layer of the body of an animal. In vertebrates it protects the animal from excessive loss of water, from the entry of disease-causing organisms, from damage by ultraviolet radiation, and from mechanical injury. Conservation of water has been an important factor in the evolution of animals on land. Skin contains numerous nerve endings and therefore also acts as a peripheral sense organ. In warm-blooded animals it plays a part in the regulation of body temperature.

slime bacteria See myxobacteria.

slime molds (slime fungi) Simple unicellular or multicellular eukaryotic organisms that display distinct changes in form during their life cycle. They have an ameboid stage, which lacks cell walls and feeds by engulfing bacteria by phagocytosis; and they can form multicellular differentiated reproductive structures that resemble the fruiting bodies of fungi or primitive plants. The ameboid stages aggregate in masses, often visible as slimy masses on rotting logs, vegetation, etc. 'True' slime molds, or *plasmodial slime molds*, form a large mass of multinucleate cytoplasm (*plasmodium*), which pulsates internally and moves only as it grows. *Cellular slime molds* form a mass of cells, or slug (*pseudoplasmodium*), that moves around leaving a slime trail. Both produce a stalked fruiting body (*sporophore*) that produces spores, which give rise to individual amebas.
    The classification of the slime molds has always been contentious. They exhibit features of animals, fungi, and plants, and at some time have been classified as all three. For example, in one scheme they are placed in the phylum Myxomycota as part

of the kingdom Fungi. This phylum contains two classes: Myxomycetes (plasmodial slime molds) and Acrasiomycetes (cellular slime molds). However, certain recent classifications place them respectively in the phyla Myxomycota and Rhizopoda in the kingdom Protoctista.

snails *See* Gastropoda.

snakes *See* Squamata.

Snowball Earth The theory that instabilities in the Earth's climate system caused a series of prolonged glacial periods around 600–700 mya, in which the entire planet was covered by ice. It depends on the fact that ice has a higher albedo than water (i.e. reflects more radiation). As ice forms, less absorption of solar radiation occurs, and even greater cooling occurs. Under certain conditions, it is claimed, there could be runaway glaciation, with a complete covering of ice. These periods could be ended because of build-up of carbon dioxide in the atmosphere from volcanic activity (i.e. by an extreme greenhouse effect). The theory is supported by computer modelling and by certain geomagnetic and geological anomalies. Following this period the Earth warmed and it has been claimed that these conditions resulted in an explosion of multicellular life forms evolving from the primitive organisms that had survived the Snowball Earth period.

social Darwinism The application of the principles of natural selection to society, asserting that social structure is determined by how well people are suited to living conditions.

somatic Describing the cells of an organism other than germline cells. Somatic cells divide by mitosis producing daughter cells identical to the parent cell. A *somatic mutation* is a mutation in any cell not destined to become a germ cell; such mutations are therefore not heritable.

somatic mutation *See* somatic.

somite Any of the blocks of tissue into which the MESODERM of vertebrate embryos is divided lateral to the NOTOCHORD and neural tube. The segmentation into somites usually starts in the region of the hindbrain and continues anteriorly into the head and posteriorly into the trunk. Each somite later forms: the *myotome* (muscle block), *nephrotome* (a portion of the kidney), and contributions to the axial skeleton (*sclerotome*) and dermis (*dermatome*).

southern ape *See* australopithecines.

specialization 1. *See* adaptation. 2. *See* physiological specialization.

speciation The formation of one or more new species from an existing species. Central to this is the splitting of a single interbreeding population into two populations that do not breed with each other; i.e. each becomes reproductively isolated from the other. There are several theoretical models of speciation, which differ in the amount of GEOGRAPHIC ISOLATION required. Many modern studies involve investigations of the CICHLID fishes, especially those of the African Great Lakes, because many species have evolved in a comparatively short period of time. *See* allopatric speciation; parapatric speciation; sympatric speciation.

species A taxonomic unit comprising one or more populations of similar organisms, all the members of which are able to breed amongst themselves and produce fertile offspring. They usually have recognizably distinct morphological characteristics and are normally isolated reproductively from all other organisms, i.e. they cannot breed with any other organisms. Several theoretical concepts can be defined (*see* biological species concept; cladistic species concept; ecological species concept; phenetic species concept; recognition species concept).

Two or more related species that are unable to breed because of geographical separation are called allopatric species (*see* allopatric speciation). Related species that are able to interbreed and are not geographically isolated but do not do so because of differences in behavior, breeding season, etc. are called *sympatric species*.

Sometimes there is an almost complete continuum between closely related species, and even between genera, and interbreeding will occur, resulting in *hybrid swarms*. This may happen in disturbed regions. Where species form apomictic clones (*see* apomixis), which are difficult to distinguish from one another, they are termed aggregate species, e.g. the bramble (*Rubus fructicosus* agg.).

Subgroups with distinct morphological or (especially in microorganisms) physiological characteristics are termed SUBSPECIES or RACES. Groups of similar species are classified together in genera. *See also* binomial nomenclature; speciation.

species selection Selection at the species level, acting on those characters that affect their chances of extinction. Species selection does not produce adaptations, but affects large-scale evolutionary patterns. *See also* group selection; kin selection. *Compare* individual selection.

Spencer, Herbert (1820–1903) British philosopher. Some years before the publication of Charles DARWIN's *The Origin of Species*, Spencer had formulated his own theory of evolution and applied it to the development of human societies. A generation earlier, Karl von Baer had demonstrated that heterogeneous organs develop from homogeneous germ layers in the embryo. Spencer adopted this observation, applying it to the development of animal species, industry, and culture, defining evolution as the progression from "an indefinite incoherent homogeneity to a definite coherent heterogeneity." He believed in the inheritance of acquired characteristics, but adapted his views when *The Origin* was published, integrating the theory of natural selection into his scheme and popularizing the term "survival of the fittest."

Even though it was quite inappropriate to apply Darwin's theory to social development, Spencer's 'social Darwinism' was very influential outside scientific circles and was used to justify many industrial and social malpractices. Darwin himself remarked that Spencer's habit was to think very much and observe very little. The same criticism may be seen in T. H. HUXLEY's comment that Spencer's idea of a tragedy was a "deduction killed by a fact."

spermatocyte *See* spermatogenesis.

spermatogenesis The formation of spermatozoa within the testis in male animals. Precursor cells in the germinal epithelium lining the seminiferous tubules begin to multiply by MITOSIS and form *spermatogonia*, even before the animal is born. However, the production of spermatogonia is most significant from the onset of sexual maturity when they give rise to huge numbers of spermatozoa.

A spermatogonium destined to form spermatozoa migrates inward towards the lumen of the tubule and enters a growth phase, which results in the formation of a primary *spermatocyte*. The primary spermatocyte then undergoes MEIOSIS and the first meiotic (or reduction) division results in the formation of two secondary spermatocytes, containing the haploid number of chromosomes. Each secondary spermatocyte undergoes the second meiotic division and produces two spermatids. By a series of changes the spermatids then become transformed into spermatozoa, during which time they are attached to Sertoli cells. When mature, the spermatozoa pass from the seminiferous tubules into the epididymis for temporary storage.

spermatogonium *See* spermatogenesis.

spermatophyte (seed plant) Any seedbearing plant. In many older classifications they constituted the division (phylum) Spermatophyta, subdivided into the classes Angiospermae and Gymnospermae. *See* Angiospermophyta; Gymnosperm. *See also* tracheophyte.

spermatozoon (*pl.* spermatozoa; sperms) The small motile mature male reproductive cell (gamete) formed in the testis of an animal. It differs in form and size between species; in humans it is about 52–62 μm long and comprises a head region containing a haploid nucleus, a middle region containing mitochondria, and a long tail region containing an undulipodium (flagellum). It is covered by a small amount of cytoplasm and a plasma membrane. Spermatozoa remain inactive until they pass from the testis during coitus, when secretions from the prostate gland and seminal vesicles stimulate undulating movements to pass along the tail and effect locomotion. About 200–300 million spermatozoa may be released in a single ejaculation, although only one may fertilize each ovum.

Sphenodon punctatum *See* tuatara.

Sphenophyta A phylum of vascular non-seed-bearing plants that contains one living order, the Equisetales, comprising one genus, *Equisetum* (horsetails), and three extinct orders, the Calamitales, Sphenophyllales, and Pseudoborniales. Horsetails have jointed grooved stems and leaves arranged in whorls. They were particularly abundant in the Carboniferous when the genus *Calamites* formed a large proportion of the forest vegetation, some treelike species reaching heights of 30 m.

spiders *See* Arachnida.

spinal column *See* vertebral column.

spindle The structure formed during MI-TOSIS and MEIOSIS that is responsible for moving the chromatids and chromosomes to opposite poles of the cell. The spindle consists of a longitudinally orientated system of protein microtubules whose synthesis starts late in interphase under the control of a microtubule-organizing center. In plants and animals this is the centrosome. A special region of the centromeres of each pair of sister chromatids, the *kinetochore*, becomes attached to one or a bundle of spindle microtubules. During anaphase, the kinetochore itself acts as the motor, dissassembling the attached microtubules and hauling the chromatid towards the spindle pole. Later in anaphase, the unattached interpolar microtubules actively

slide past each other, elongating the entire spindle.

spliceosome *See* splicing.

splicing 1. The joining of DNA fragments by the action of the enzyme *DNA ligase*.
2. The enzymatic removal of INTRONS from heterogeneous nuclear RNA (hnRNA) and the subsequent joining of the cut ends of the EXONS to form a continuous messenger RNA (mRNA). Some mitochondrial RNA (mtRNA) catalyzes its own splicing. hnRNA produced by transcription of DNA in the nucleus is spliced in the nucleus by a complex assembly of RNA and protein called a *spliceosome*. Alternative splicing can produce different mRNAs by splicing different exons together. *See* ribozyme.

sponges *See* Porifera.

spontaneous generation The erroneous belief that modern living organisms can be formed from inorganic material, given the right conditions. This belief should not be confused with the concept of gradual inorganic evolution and ABIOGENE-SIS.

The theory was examined experimentally in 1668 by the Italian physician, Francesco Redi. He believed that maggots on decaying meat were produced by some outside agent and did not arise spontaneously. When he covered meat with a fine gauze, no maggots formed because the gauze prevented female flies from laying their eggs on the meat. However, despite this discovery, the debate about spontaneous generation continued for the next two hundred years until it was finally disproved by the famous French chemist and microbiologist, Louis Pasteur, in 1862.

Pasteur placed nutrient solutions in identical flasks, which he then boiled, leaving some open to the air, and sealing the others. He found that no microorganisms developed in the sealed flasks, but that microorganisms in the air had entered the unsealed ones. He also used special flasks, each with the neck drawn out into an S shape, which were unsealed, and showed that the boiled nutrient solution did not show evidence of microorganisms unless the neck was broken off close to the flask, allowing the microorganisms present in the air to get in. *See also* evolution; origin of life.

sporogonium The sporophyte generation in mosses and liverworts. It develops from the zygote and comprises the foot, seta, and capsule. The sporogonium is parasitic on the gametophyte generation.

sporophyte The diploid generation giving rise asexually to haploid spores. In vascular plants, the sporophyte is the dominant generation, while in bryophytes it is parasitic on the GAMETOPHYTE. *See* alternation of generations.

sporozoan Any of various parasitic protoctists with a complicated life cycle involving the alternation of sexual and asexual reproduction and the production of spores to insure dispersal to another host. In older classifications they constituted a class of PROTOZOA, the Sporozoa, but in more recent schemes they are distributed among several phyla, especially the APICOMPLEXA.

Squamata The order that contains the most successful living reptiles, the lizards and their descendants, the snakes, characterized by a body covering of overlapping horny scales. In some classifications the order is known as *Lepidosauria*. Lizards typically have a long tail, four limbs – although some, e.g. *Anguis* (slowworm), are limbless – an eardrum, and movable eyelids. Snakes lack an eardrum and their eyes are covered by transparent spectacle eyelids. They have an elongated body lacking limbs and girdles, a deeply forked protrusible sensory tongue, and an extremely wide jaw gape made possible by the loose articulations of the skull bones. The prey is swallowed whole. Primitive snakes (e.g. *Python*) suffocate their prey; the more advanced types use their fanglike teeth. Some, e.g. *Vipera* (viper), inject fast-acting poisons through their fangs to kill large animals. *See* Reptilia.

squamosal One of a pair of bones on the side of the skull of most vertebrates. In mammals, each has a process anterior to the ear, which curves forward and fuses in an arch with the jugal bone to form the cheek bones. The process also articulates at its posterior end with the dentary of the lower jaw.

stabilizing selection NATURAL SELECTION that favours individuals with the mean value for a character and acts to eliminate extremes. It reduces the amount of genetic variability in a population. *See* mutation. *Compare* directional selection; disruptive selection.

stage *See* geological time scale.

stapes (stirrup) The stirrup-shaped bone attached to the oval window (fenestra ovalis) of the ear, which forms the innermost ear ossicle in mammals. It is homologous with the hyomandibular of fishes.

starfish *See* Asteroidea.

stasis A period in the history of a TAXON in which there is apparently no evolutionary change. Certain authors believe that it is possible that the GENOTYPE is very well-adapted to any fluctuations in the environment (sometimes termed *cohesion of the genotype*) resulting in a stable phenotype. *See also* living fossil.

stationary evolution A mode of coevolution in which the competing species evolve to an optimally adapted state and stay there, forming a stable equilibrium. If the equilibrium is disturbed by environmental changes, the species will evolve to a new equilibrium. *Compare* Red Queen effect.

Stebbins, George Ledyard (1906–) American geneticist. In his *Variation and Evolution in Plants* (1950) Stebbins was the first to apply the modern synthesis of evolution, as expounded by Julian Huxley, Ernst MAYR, and others, to plants. In collaboration with Ernest Babcock, Stebbins also studied POLYPLOIDY – the occurrence of three or more times the basic (haploid) number of chromosomes. When an artificial means of inducing polyploidy was developed Stebbins applied it to wild grasses and in 1944 managed to establish an artificially created species in a natural environment. Polyploids have proved extremely useful in plant-breeding work (*see* allopolyploidy; autopolyploidy). Knowledge of naturally occurring polyploid systems has also helped greatly in understanding the relationships and consequently in classifying difficult genera such as *Taraxacum* (the dandelions).

Stebbins also studied gene action and proposed that mutations that result in a change in morphology act by regulating the rate of cell division in specific areas of the plant.

stegosaur *See* dinosaur.

stem reptiles *See* cotylosaurs.

stepped cline A CLINE with a sudden change in gene or character frequency, for example, a hybrid zone. *See* parapatric speciation.

stirrup *See* stapes.

Stone Age *See* Lubbock; Neolithic; Paleolithic.

stoneworts *See* Chlorophyta.

strand slippage *See* tandem repeats.

stromatolite A layered cushionlike mass of chalk formed by the actions of certain bacteria, notably blue-green bacteria. Communities of these organisms trap and bind lime-rich sediments. Modern stromatolite-building communities are confined to salt flats or shallow salty lagoons where bacterial predators cannot survive, but the fossil record demonstrates a much more widespread distribution in the PRECAMBRIAN period. Some stromatolites date back nearly 3500 million years, making them the oldest known fossils. *See* cyanobacteria.

stromatoporoid Extinct calcareous sponges (*see* Porifera) whose fossils can be massive, chocolate-drop in shape, tabular, encrusting, cylindrical, or even arm-shaped ('ramose'). There are two main groups of fossil stromatoporoids that lived in different eras, the Paleozoic and the Mesozoic. After their appearance in the Ordovician, the Paleozoic stromatoporoids were dominant reef builders for over 100 million years. The second group of stromatoporoids, from the Mesozoic, may represent a distinct group with a similar growth form. They were also important contributors to reef formation, especially during the Cretaceous. Sponges similar to fossil stromatoporoids are found in today's oceans.

structural gene *See* operon.

struggle for existence The number and variety of obstacles that an individual has to overcome in order to survive, grow, and reproduce. *See* Darwinism.

subduction zone A zone where rocks of an oceanic plate are forced to plunge below a much thicker continental crust, along margins between adjoining plates. As the plate descends it melts and is released into the MAGMA below the earth's crust. Such a zone is marked by volcanic eruptions and earthquakes. *See also* plate tectonics.

sublittoral 1. The marine zone extending from low tide to a depth of about 200 m. Large algae (e.g. kelps) are found in shallower waters while certain red algae may be found in deeper water. Numerous animals are found in this zone, including mollusks, echinoderms, arthropods, cnidarians, etc. *Compare* littoral; benthic. 2. The zone in a lake or pond between the littoral and profundal zones, extending from a depth of about 6–10 m. Its depth is limited by the *compensation level* – the depth at which the rate of photosynthesis is equalled by the rate of respiration, and below which plants cannot live. The sublittoral zone contains plankton, a large mollusk population, and freshwater crustaceans. *Compare* littoral; profundal.

subspecies   The taxonomic group below the species level. Crosses can generally be made between subspecies of a given species but this may be prevented in the wild by various isolating mechanisms, e.g. geographical isolation or different flowering times.

substitution   1. The replacement of one allele by another in a population.
2. *See* gene mutation.

sulfur bacteria   Filamentous autotrophic chemosynthetic bacteria that derive energy by oxidizing sulfides to elemental sulfur and build up carbohydrates from carbon dioxide. An example is *Beggiatoa*. *See* black smokers; origin of life. *See also* photosynthetic bacteria.

superdense theory   *See* big-bang theory.

supination   *See* pronation.

survival of the fittest   *See* Darwinism; fitness.

survivorship curve   *See* rate of evolution.

swim bladder (air bladder)   A large thin-walled cavity found in bony fishes (*see* Osteichthyes; Teleostei), by which the fish is able to adjust its buoyancy as it swims at different depths. It contains oxygen and nitrogen. It is surrounded by a network of blood vessels and oxygen can be extracted from the blood to adjust the volume of gas in the bladder. Certain authorities believe that the swim bladder evolved from a primitive lung such as that of the ancient lungfish (*see* Dipnoi). The lung of a lungfish is situated dorsally and is connected to the ventral part of the esophagus by a tube. The tube may then in the course of evolution have become connected to the side and eventually to the dorsal surface of the esophagus, as is the case with most swim bladders of present-day fish. The swim bladders of some modern fish are not connected to the esophagus and fish that dwell on the bottom of the seas and oceans do not posses a swim bladder.

Interestingly, the swim bladder is also responsible for the detection of sounds, which cause high-frequency changes in the tension of the bladder walls, and in some teleost fish it acts as a resonator or sound producer. *See also* Weberian ossicles.

symbiosis   A beneficial interaction between two or more individuals from different species as seen in MUTUALISM and COMMENSALISM. It is now used more narrowly to mean mutualism. *See also* endosymbiont theory; eukaryote; mitochondrial Eve; parasite.

Sympatric speciation

sympatric speciation   Speciation in which a new species is formed from a subpopulation that overlaps the geographical area of the ancestral species. It is possible in a polymorphic population that shows assortative mating within each polymorphic group and requires reinforcement. The existence of sympatric speciation is controversial in animals but is well-known in plants (*hybrid speciation*). *Compare* allopatric speciation; parapatric speciation. *See also* polyploidy.

sympatric species   *See* species.

sympatry   Living in the same geographic region. *Compare* allopatry.

synapomorphy   A shared character state in two species inherited from their immediate common ancestor. *Compare* apomorphy; homoplasy.

Synapsida (synapsids)   *See* Reptilia.

synapsis (pairing)   The association of homologous chromosomes during the prophase stage of MEIOSIS that leads to the production of a haploid number of bivalents. Homologous chromosomes pair point to point so that corresponding regions lie in contact (*see* bivalent).

synonomous codon   *See* codon bias.

synthetic theory of evolution   *See* neo-Darwinism.

system   *See* geological time scale.

systematics   The area of biology that deals with the diversity of living organisms, their relationships to each other, and their CLASSIFICATION. The term may be used synonymously with *taxonomy*.

systemic arch   A blood vessel found in adult TETRAPODS that carries usually oxygenated blood from the heart to the dorsal aorta, which serves the body. It has evolved from the fourth aortic arch. Amphibians and reptiles retain both arches, birds only the right arch, and mammals only the left arch.

T

T *See* thymine.

taeniodonts An extinct order of herbivorous mammals that evolved in the early Paleocene in North America, probably from insectivores (*see* Insectivora) resembling *Cimolestes*. The earliest and best-known example (from New Mexico) is *Onychodectes*, which was about the size of a large domestic cat, with sharp enamel-covered incisors and canines, cheek teeth adapted for grinding, muscular limbs ending in five digits with claws, and a long muscular tail. Early taeniodonts had short snouts and probably fed on roots and vegetables, digging them up with their powerful claws. Although they were widespread and successfully occupied ecological niches vacated by the extinct dinosaurs, these earlier taeniodonts had died out by the middle of the Paleocene. They were replaced by larger forms (e.g. the 20 kg *Wortmania* and about 2 million years later by the 50 kg *Psittacotherium* (the 'parrot beast'), and finally by the pig-sized *Stylinodon* of the Eocene epoch. The later taeniodonts had characteristically large chisel-shaped canines. Taeniodonts probably competed with a similar group, the TILLODONTS, but became extinct later in the Eocene with increasing competition from the ARTIODACTYLA, particularly the piglike forms. *See also* Mammalia.

tandem repeat A series of two or more identical nucleotide sequences situated immediately one after the other in a nucleic acid. They are common in noncoding repetitive DNA. Very short tandem repeats are probably formed by *strand slippage* during replication and longer tandem repeats are probably formed by unequal CROSSING OVER. Both of these occurrences are more likely to happen on repeated sequences. *See* chromosome; microsatellite; minisatellite; satellite DNA. *See also* noncoding DNA.

tapeworms *See* Cestoda.

taphonomy The study of the processes that occur in dead animals and plants that result in the formation of a FOSSIL.

tarsal bones Bones in the distal region of the hind limb of tetrapods; in humans they form the ankle and heel bones. In the typical pentadactyl limb there are 12 tarsal bones arranged in three rows. However, there are various modifications and reductions to this pattern; in humans there are only seven. They articulate with each other and with the metatarsal bones distally. One tarsal bone, the *talus*, forms the hinge joint of the ankle with the tibia and fibula. *Compare* carpal bones.

tarsiers A suborder (Tarsidae) of the PRIMATES, resembling monkeys. They are nocturnal and mostly arboreal, characterized by very large eyes, long limbs, long hairless tails, and large hairless ears. Tarsiers use their hands to grasp insects and lizards on which they feed. They are found in the Philippines, Borneo, and Sumatra.

Taung skull (Taung child) *See* Australopithecus africanus; Dart.

taxic discontinuity A gap in the range of variation among related taxa, e.g. among the species of a genus. *Compare* phenetic discontinuity.

taxometrics *See* numerical taxonomy.

taxon A named group of any rank in taxonomy. Ranunculaceae (a family) and *Triticum* (a genus) are examples.

taxonomy The area of SYSTEMATICS that covers the principles and procedures of CLASSIFICATION.

T-cell *See* AIDS.

tectonic plates *See* plate tectonics.

teeth Hard dense structures growing on the jaws of vertebrates and used for seizing, biting, and chewing. In mammals each tooth consists of dentine, covered by enamel, enclosing a pulp cavity. It has a crown above the gum (gingiva) and a root embedded in a socket of the jaw bone (*see* heterodont). Fish, amphibians, and many reptiles have teeth that are modified denticles distributed over the palate (*see* homodont).

Mammals have four types of teeth: INCISOR; CANINES; PREMOLARS; and MOLARS. *See also* carnassial teeth; diphyodont; monophyodont; polyphyodont.

teleology The explanation of phenomena by their purpose (rather than their cause) and belief in the existence of driving forces.

Teleostei The largest order of bony fishes and the most numerous group of living vertebrates. Toward the end of the CRETACEOUS, the teleosts evolved into many diverse forms. They are found in most types of aquatic environment and show great variety of form. Teleosts have thin rounded bony scales, a symmetrical (homocercal) tail, and shortened jaws with reduced cheek bones, which allow the mouth to gape widely. In most the fins are supported by a few strong movable spines, and the pectoral fins, at the anterior end of the body, assist the pelvic fins. Internally there is a SWIM BLADDER, which is hydrostatic in function and confers buoyancy and thus great maneuverability and is a major contribution to their success. Fertilization is external and the eggs are unprotected. *See also* Osteichthyes.

telomerase *See* telomere.

telomere The structure found at the ends of linear CHROMOSOMES. It consists of simple tandemly repeated sequences with one strand being G rich and the other C rich. The repeated sequences are added by the enzyme *telomerase* and exist to maintain chromosome length during replication and so prevent the loss of coding sequences.

temporal fenestra *See* temporal fossae.

temporal fossae Gaps or holes that develop between the bones just behind the eyes, usually positioned on each side of reptilian skulls in the temporal region. The arrangement is used by taxonomists to divide the class REPTILIA into four subclasses: Anapsida, Synapsida, Diapsida, and Eurapsida. The holes are also termed *temporal fenestra*, *postorbital fenestrations*, and *apses* (meaning 'arches'). The gaps are believed to have evolved in order to anchor more powerful jaw muscles.

temporal isolation *See* prezygotic isolation.

terminal addition A mode of evolution in which evolutionary changes in characters occur only in the adult form, i.e. not during development. There is a tendency for evolution to proceed via terminal addition, which has been explained in two ways. The first explanation is that mutations during development, especially embryonic development, are more likely to be macromutations and have large deleterious phenotypic effects. The second explanation is that selection pressure from the external environment will be greater on independent adults than on a protected embryo or juvenile. The two explanations are not mutually exclusive. There are examples of evolution not proceeding via terminal addition; e.g. heterochronic evolution (*see* heterochrony) and the evolution of new developmental stages. *See* homeotic mutation; paedomorphosis; Von Baer's law.

termination codon   *See* translation.

terrestrial   Living on land.

territory   An area occupied and defended by an animal for such purposes as mating, nesting, and feeding. The type and size of territory depends on its function – a nesting territory may be small but a feeding territory may be very large – and on the size and nature of the animal and its requirements. Territories are common among vertebrates, particularly birds, and also occur occasionally in certain invertebrates.

Tertiary   The larger and older period of the CENOZOIC, being composed of the Paleocene, Eocene, Oligocene, Miocene, and Pliocene epochs (65–2 mya). Literally the 'third age', it is characterized by the emergence of mammals. The Tertiary may also be divided into two subperiods: the *Paleogene*, which comprises the Paleocene, Eocene, and Oligocene epochs, followed by the *Neogene*, which comprises the Miocene and Pliocene epochs.

Following the K–T EVENT at the end of the Cretaceous, the climate had begun to warm up, resulting in the growth of tropical forests in the Eocene epoch. This was followed by a gradual cooling, and the development of the open savanna of the Oligocene. The Tertiary ended with the Pliocene glaciation. The main geological events included the continuation of the Laramide OROGENY, which gave rise to the Rocky Mountains in North America. This was followed by the Alpine orogeny. Australia then separated from Antarctica, India drifted northward to collide with Asia, causing the formation of the Himalayas. At the end of the Tertiary, North America and South America joined up at the Isthmus of Panama, and rift valleys formed in East Africa.

The mammals diversified immediately to occupy the niches left by the extinction of the dinosaurs and other reptile groups. Many strange and bizarre groups of ar-

chaic mammals appeared, e.g. AMBLYPODS, TAENIODONTS, TILLODONTS and MULTITUBERCULATES. These were replaced by the familiar modern mammalian groups. The herbivores diversified in conjunction with the evolution of grasses in the Miocene epoch. They were, in turn, preyed upon by the diversifying carnivores. In the seas, whales appeared as well as modern sharks. The PRIMATES evolved in the Tertiary and the period ended with the appearance of the AUSTRALOPITHECINES, the earliest HOMINIDS, which evolved in the environs of the newly formed East African rift valley. *See also* geological time scale.

test cross   *See* double recessive.

Tethys Sea   *See* Triassic.

tetraploid   A cell or organism containing four times the haploid number of chromosomes. Tetraploid organisms may arise by the fusion of two diploid gametes that have resulted from the NONDISJUNCTION of chromosomes at meiosis. Tetraploids may also arise through nondisjunction of the chromatids during the mitotic division of a zygote. *See also* polyploid; allopolyploid; allotetraploid; autotetraploid.

tetrapod   A vertebrate with four limbs; i.e. an amphibian, bird, mammal, or reptile.

tetrasomy   *See* nondisjunction.

thecodont   A former name for ARCHOSAUR.

thecodont theory   *See* Aves.

therapod   *See* dinosaur.

Therapsida (therapsids)   Primitive mammal-like synapsid reptiles that evolved in the Permian. *See* Mammalia; Reptilia.

Theria   *See* Eutheria; Mammalia; Metatheria.

'third eye'   *See* pineal eye.

Thompson, Sir D'Arcy Wentworth (1860–1948) British biologist. In 1917 Thompson published *On Growth and Form*, in which he developed the notion of evolutionary changes in animal form in terms of physical forces acting upon the individual during its lifetime, rather than as the sum total of modifications made over successive generations – the latter being the traditional credo postulated by Darwinists. In a later edition (1942), however, Thompson admitted the difficulty of explaining away the cumulative effect of physical and mental adaptations, which can scarcely be accounted for in the experience of one generation. In addition to such theoretical work, Thompson was much involved in oceanographic studies, as well as fisheries and fur-seal conservation in northern Europe.

threatened species *See* endangered species.

Thymidine

thymidine The NUCLEOSIDE formed when thymine is linked to D-ribose by a β-glycosidic bond.

Thymine

thymine Symbol: T. A nitrogenous base found in DNA. It has a pyrimidine ring structure.

tillodonts An extinct order of herbivorous mammals that probably evolved from ancient insectivorelike mammals (*see* Insectivora). Once thought to have evolved in the late Paleocene of North America, with the discovery of *Esthonyx*, even older tillodont fossils have been discovered in the earlier Paleocene of China, e.g. *Interogale* and *Meiostylodon*. Thus they probably evolved in Asia and their sudden appearance in North America indicates a migration (probably across the Bering land bridge). Unlike the TAENIODONTS, which they were thought to resemble, it is the second incisor that enlarged and was ever growing, whereas the other teeth became more reduced. Later tillodonts (*Trogosus* and *Tillodon*) had longer snouts than the taeniodonts. The early tillodonts were about the size of a small dog, but later ones reached bearlike proportions, probably weighing about 150 kg. They had well-developed forelimbs for digging and tearing roots and vegetables and their teeth were adapted for pulling and grinding. They became extinct in the middle Eocene in America and the late Eocene in Asia, and like the taeniodonts, experienced increasing competition from the evolving ARTIODACTYLA. *See also* Mammalia.

titanotheres *See* Perissodactyla.

T lymphocyte *See* AIDS.

tornaria The free-swimming larva of the HEMICHORDATA, such as the acorn worms. Tornaria larvae, which have folded bands of cilia for swimming, resemble the BIPINNARIA and PLUTEUS larvae of ECHINODERMATA. This suggests a close evolutionary relationship between the echinoderms and the chordate group through the hemichordates (*see* dipleurula).

trace fossil *See* fossil.

tracheid An elongated XYLEM conducting element with oblique end walls. The walls are heavily lignified. Tracheids are the sole xylem conducting tissue of pteridophytes and most gymnosperms.

tracheophyte   Any plant with a differentiated vascular system; i.e. all plants except the bryophytes (liverworts and mosses). In some classifications they constitute the division (phylum) Tracheophyta, comprising the various subdivisions of vascular plants. *Compare* pteridophyte; spermatophyte.

trade-off   A cause of apparently imperfect ADAPTATIONS where a single character performs more than one function. The adaptations of that character are therefore a compromise between the adaptations required for each function. For example, in the tropical plant *Begonia involucrata*, there are separate male and female flowers on the same plant. Bees gather pollen from the male flowers and sometimes visit the female flowers. The pollen represents a reward for the bees, which therefore visit male flowers more frequently. The male and female flowers look very similar, but the female flowers are often smaller. Larger female flowers, however, 'trick' the bees into visiting them. The trade-off is that fewer larger female flowers are produced, but the result is that the larger flowers are pollinated by the bees.

trait   A characteristic or condition.

transcription   The process in living cells whereby RNA is synthesized according to the template embodied in the base sequence of DNA, thereby converting the cell's genetic information into a coded message (MESSENGER RNA, mRNA) for the assembly of proteins, or into the RNA components required for protein synthesis (RIBOSOMAL RNA and TRANSFER RNA). The term is also applied to the formation of single-stranded DNA from an RNA template, as performed by the enzyme REVERSE TRANSCRIPTASE, for example in RETROVIRUS infections (*see* AIDS). Details of DNA transcription differ between prokaryote and eukaryote cells, but essentially it involves the following steps. Firstly, the double helix of the DNA molecule is unwound in the region of the site marking the start of transcription for a particular gene. Then the enzyme RNA polymerase moves along one of the DNA strands, the transcribed strand (or noncoding strand, since the code is carried by the complementary base sequence of the RNA), and nucleotides are assembled to form a complementary RNA molecule. The POLYMERASE enzyme proceeds until reaching a stop signal, when formation of the RNA strand is terminated. Behind the enzyme, the DNA double helix re-forms, stripping off the newly synthesized RNA strand. In eukaryotes, transcription is initiated and regulated by a host of proteins called *transcription factors*; in prokaryotes an accessory *sigma factor* is essential for transcription.

In many eukaryotic genes the functional message is contained within discontinuous segments of the DNA strand (EXONS), interrupted by nonfunctional segments (INTRONS). Initially, both exons and introns are transcribed to form so-called *heterogeneous nuclear RNA* (hnRNA). Subsequently the noncoding intron sequences are spliced out to form the fully functional mature mRNA transcript, which then leaves the nucleus to direct protein assembly in the cytoplasm, in the process called TRANSLATION. *See also* splicing.

transcription factor   *See* transcription.

transfer RNA (tRNA)   A type of RNA that participates in protein synthesis in living cells. It attaches to a particular amino acid and imports this to the site of polypeptide assembly at the RIBOSOME when the appropriate codon on the messenger RNA is reached. Each tRNA contains an anticodon, whose base triplet pairs with the complementary codon in the mRNA molecule. Hence, because there are 64 possible codons in the genetic code, of which about 60 or so code for amino acids, there may be up to 60 or so different tRNAs in a cell, each with a different anticodon, although most cells apparently have only about 40 which indicates there is some flexibility (or 'wobble') in the base pairing between the codon and anticodon (*see* wobble hypothesis). In experiments it is the third base of the codon that shows imprecise binding, which fits in with the degeneracy of the genetic code.

The correct amino acid is attached to a tRNA molecule by an enzyme called an *aminoacyl–tRNA transferase*. There are 20 of these, one for each type of amino acid. This attachment also involves the transfer of a high-energy bond from ATP to the amino acid, which provides the energy for peptide bond formation during TRANSLATION.

transformation   1. A permanent genetic recombination in a cell, in which a DNA fragment is incorporated into the chromosome of the cell. This may be demonstrated by growing bacteria in the presence of dead cells, culture filtrates, or extracts of related strains. The bacteria acquire genetic characters of these strains.
2. The conversion of normal cells in tissue culture to cells having properties of tumor cells. The change is permanent and transformed cells are often malignant. It may be induced by certain viruses or occur spontaneously.

transformism   *See* Lamarckism.

transient polymorphism   *See* polymorphism.

transition   *See* gene mutation.

transitional fossil   A FOSSIL or group of fossils representing a series of similar species, genera, or families, that link an older group of organisms to a younger group. Transitional fossils often combine some traits of older, ancestral species with traits of more recent species, for example, a series of transitional fossils documents the evolution of fully aquatic whales from terrestrial ancestors (*see* Cetacea). Transitional fossils are rare, which promotes the view that major groups evolve rapidly from small populations. *See also Archaeopteryx*; horse evolution; missing link.

translation   The process whereby the genetic code of messenger RNA (mRNA) is deciphered by the machinery of a cell to make proteins. Molecules of mRNA are in effect coded messages based on information in the cell's genes and created by the process of transcription. They relay this information to the sites of protein synthesis, the RIBOSOMES. In eukaryotes these are located in the cytoplasm, so the mRNA must migrate from the nucleus. The first stage in translation is *initiation*, in which the two subunits of the ribosome assemble and attach to the mRNA molecule near the *initiation codon* (AUG), which signals the beginning of the message. This also involves various proteins called *initiation factors*, and the initiator TRANSFER RNA (tRNA), which always carries the amino acid N–formyl methionine (in prokaryotes and mitochondria) or methionine (in eukaryotes).
The next stage is *elongation*, in which the peptide chain is built up from its component amino acids. tRNA molecules successively occupy two sites on the larger ribosome subunit in a sequence determined by consecutive codons on the mRNA. As each pair of tRNAs occupies the ribosomal sites, their amino acids are joined together by a peptide bond. As the ribosome moves along the mRNA to the next codon, the next tRNA enters the first ribosomal site, and so on, leading to elongation of the peptide chain. Having delivered its amino acid, the depleted tRNA is released from the second ribosomal site, which is then occupied by the tRNA with the growing chain. This process continues until the ribosome encounters a *termination codon*. Then the polypeptide chain is released and the ribosome complex dissociates, marking the *termination* of translation.
Following its release, the polypeptide may undergo various changes, such as the removal or addition of chemical groups, or even cleavage into two. This *post-translational modification* produces the fully functional protein. Folding of the protein is assisted by a class of molecules called *chaperones*. *See also* transcription.

translocation   *See* chromosome mutation.

transmutation   The idea, held by Erasmus Darwin (Charles Darwin's grandfather), that one species could change into another. The theory of transmutationism states that evolutionary change is caused by sudden new mutations (SALTATIONS) that immediately give rise to new species. *See* Darwinism.

transposable genetic element *See* transposon.

transposon (transposable genetic element; jumping gene) A segment of an organism's DNA that can insert at various sites in the genome, either by physically moving from place to place, or by producing a copy that inserts elsewhere. The simplest types are called *insertion sequences*; these comprise about 700–1500 base pairs. More complex ones, called *composite transposons*, have a central portion, which may contain functional genes, flanked by insertion sequences. Transposons can affect both the genotype and phenotype of the organism, e.g. by disrupting gene expression, or causing deletions or inversions. In eukaryotes, transposons account for much of the repetitive DNA in the genome. *See* repetitive DNA; selfish DNA.

transversion *See* gene mutation.

tree *See* phylogeny.

tree of life The phylogeny describing the relationships between all living organisms. As with all phylogenies it is not fixed, but the best fit for the available data, and has been redrawn many times. Comparative anatomy is not useful when trying to establish relationships between diverse organisms (e.g. plants do not have limbs; animals do not have leaves), but DNA sequencing can be used to compare all life because all living things contain DNA. A major alteration to the tree of life was the division of life into three cellular kingdoms, ARCHAEA, BACTERIA, and EUKARYA, from the previous two kingdoms. Recent evidence indicates that life may not have originated from a single common ancestor, but that early organisms freely and continually swapped genetic material, forming a genetic matrix from which the three cellular kingdoms eventually emerged. There is also evidence from the ENDOSYMBIONT THEORY that genetic material was transferred millions of years after the kingdoms split. *See also* origin of life.

Trematoda *See* Platyhelminthes.

Triassic The oldest period of the Mesozoic, 250–215 mya. It is marked by a decrease in the number and variety of cartilaginous fishes and an increase in primitive amphibians and reptiles. The supercontinent of PANGEA, which had formed during the PERMIAN, dominated all conditions. Erosion of the mountains formed in the Paleozoic continued from the Permian into the Triassic, giving enormous sandstone deposits (New Red Sandstone) as in the Permian. Many of these sandstones were formed from sand dunes and wind erosion was a feature of this period. Pangea was bisected by the *Tethys Sea* along an east–west axis. The climate was very hot and dry and the desert conditions of inland areas were uninhabitable for most living organisms. However, around the margins of the Tethys Sea, living organisms that had survived the end-Permian extinction (mainly bivalves and gastropods) began to thrive. On the land, the LYCOPODOPHYTA were dominant. *Glossopteris*, the seed fern that had provided food for the herbivorous mammal-like reptiles (the dicynodonts), was replaced by another type of seed fern, *Dicroidium*. In turn, the dicynodonts were replaced by another group of herbivorous mammal-like reptiles, the *rhyncosaurs*. The broad-leaved seed ferns were no longer dominant and replaced by narrow-leaved conifers, which were better adapted to the hot dry climate toward the end of the Triassic. Both *Dicroidium* and the rhyncosaurs that fed on them became extinct by the end of this period. The carnivorous mammal-like reptiles (the cynodonts) persisted during the Triassic, and had evolved into the earliest mammals, e.g. *Megazostrodon*, by the end of the Triassic.

The ARCHOSAURS ('ruling reptiles') began to flourish, and the first DINOSAURS evolved. The reptiles dominated the land and by the end of the period, the pterosaurs (*see* Pterosauria) dominated the air. Many types of marine reptiles evolved in the seas

– the shellfish-eating PLACODONTS, the long-necked fish-eating NOTHOSAURS (which may have evolved into PLESIOSAURS), and finally, the magnificently adapted ICHTHYOSAURIA. Also in the seas, fish flourished and the AMMONITES gradually replaced the NAUTILOIDS. The first corals, resembling present-day forms, also evolved.

At the end of the Triassic, another MASS EXTINCTION wiped out 90% of the plant species on land and about one-third of the marine and land animals. The reasons for this are controversial. There may have been a GREENHOUSE EFFECT causing temperatures to rise considerably. Also, about 10 million years before the end of the Triassic period, a meteorite struck the Earth (the *Manicouagan event*), the evidence from its impact having been found by the discovery of an enormous crater in Quebec, Canada. Some authorities argue that the Manicouagan event is too early to have impacted on such a large extinction, and may have caused an earlier smaller extinction. *See also* geological time scale.

tribe In plant classification, the rank subordinate to family, but superior to genus in the taxonomic hierarchy. The tribe is only introduced in classifications of very large families such as the grasses in which the tribes Oryzeae, Triticeae, and Aveneae are examples in the subfamily Pooideae. Tribe names generally end in -eae.

trilobites (Trilobita) A class of extinct marine bottom-dwelling arthropods abundant in the Paleozoic and thought to be closely related to the ancestors of other arthropods, particularly the Crustacea. Trilobites had an oval flattened body divided longitudinally into three lobes and transversely into a head (*cephalon*), body (*thorax*), and tail (*pygidium*). The head bore compound eyes, antennae, and four pairs of jointed forked appendages with an inner projection used as an aid in feeding. There were numerous paired appendages on the body.

Trilobites probably evolved in Precambrian times, reaching their peak in the Cambrian and Ordovician, and finally becoming extinct in the Permian, when only a single species remained. They spread worldwide and certain species are used as ZONE FOSSILS. *Triarthus becki* from the Ordovician shale near Rome, Italy, is one of a number of fossils that are so well preserved that details of their structure and growth have been studied by sectioning the specimens. Some trilobites were BENTHIC, crawling over the ocean floor (e.g. *Triarthus* and *Isotelus* from the Ordovician), others were PELAGIC, feeding on zooplankton (e.g. *Carolinites*). Three features contributed to their success. They had remarkably well-developed bulging compound eyes with up to 15 000 lenses, allowing them to more easily escape from predators and to hunt for food. Secondly, they molted seasonally (shown by fossil evidence of large groups, together with their discarded exoskeletons). Their remarkable eyesight was probably a great advantage at such a vulnerable time in their lives. Thirdly, certain trilobites had rolled-up bodies (e.g. *Acaste*), which probably protected them from predators. The latter included the cephalopods of the Silurian and the jawed fish of the Devonian.

triploblastic Describing an animal whose body is made from three embryonic germ layers: ectoderm on the outside, endoderm lining the gut and allied structures, and mesoderm between these two layers. Each of the three layers gives rise to a particular set of tissues and organs. Most animals are triploblastic; exceptions are the sponges and cnidarians.

triploid A cell or organism containing three times the HAPLOID number of chromosomes. Triploid organisms arise by the fusion of a haploid gamete with a DIPLOID gamete that has resulted from the nondisjunction of chromosomes at MEIOSIS. They are usually sterile because one set of chromosomes remains unpaired at meiosis, which disrupts gamete formation. In flowering plants, the nutritive endosperm tissue is usually triploid, resulting from the fusion of one of the pollen nuclei with the two polar nuclei.

trisomy *See* aneuploidy; nondisjunction.

tRNA *See* transfer RNA.

trochophore The free-swimming ciliated larva of mollusks, annelid worms, and several minor groups of invertebrates. Its rounded body is encircled by a band of cilia and it has other bands and tufts of long cilia on its surface. It has a digestive canal opening by a mouth and anus. The presence of this larva indicates a close evolutionary relationship between the groups that possess it. Since it is unlike the DIPLEU-RULA larva, it is believed that mollusks, annelids, and related groups are only distantly related to the echinoderms.

truncation point *See* truncation selection.

truncation selection A form of ARTIFI-CIAL SELECTION where only individuals with values of a certain trait more extreme than a particular value (the *truncation point*) are selected for breeding.

tuatara (*Sphenodon punctatum*) The only surviving member of the ancient order *Rhyncocephalia* of the class REPTILIA, found on a few islands off the coast of New Zealand. Its superficial appearance is lizardlike, but it has various primitive characteristics, including a median PINEAL EYE, three temporal bridges in the skull, persistent abdominal ribs, a widely roofed mouth, a firmly attached quadrate bone, and the absence of a male copulatory organ. Tuataras grow to about 1 m in length and are covered with granular scales. They live on land and in water and

in burrows, feeding on fishes, insects and worms. Their eggs are enclosed in hard white shells and are laid in holes in the ground, taking about 13 months to hatch.

Rhyncocephalians evolved in the Permian and most became extinct by the Eocene epoch.

Tunicata *See* Urochordata.

Turbellaria *See* platyhelminthes.

Turkana Boy *See Homo ergaster*; *Homo erectus*.

type The material used to define a species. It is usually a dried specimen stored in a herbarium but may also be a drawing. The term 'type' is also used to describe the representative species of a genus, the representative genus of a family, etc. For example the genus *Solanum* is the type genus of the family Solanaceae.

typological species concept *See* morphological species concept.

typology *See* essentialism.

tyrannosaurs (tyrant lizards) A family of saurischian theropod DINOSAURS that lived in the Cretaceous of North America and Asia. They were the largest carnivores ever to have lived on land and had powerful clawed hind limbs, reduced forelimbs, an enormous skull with huge jaws, and daggerlike teeth. *Tyrannosaurus rex* ('king of the tyrant lizards') had sharp curved teeth up to 15 cm in length and a skull over a meter long and almost as high. The body was about 17 m long and over 6 m high.

U

U *See* uracil.

uintatheres *See* amblypods.

ulna One of the two long bones of the lower forelimb (forearm) in tetrapods. In humans, it forms the posterior (postaxial) border of the forearm, extending from the back of the elbow to the wrist and lying parallel to the smaller radius bone. Its hooklike upper end forms the point of the elbow and its inner curved surface articulates over the lower end of the humerus.

ultimate causation (evolutionary causation) The processes (natural selection, chance, and constraints) that cause traits within a population or species over many generations. *Compare* proximate causation.

undulipodium *See* flagellum.

unequal crossing over *See* crossing over.

ungulate A hoofed grazing mammal belonging either to the order PERISSODACTYLA or to the ARTIODACTYLA. *See also* condylarths.

unguligrade The mode of progression in some mammals in which only the very tips of the fingers or toes are in contact with the ground. It is typical of hoofed mammals (ungulates), such as the horse. *Compare* digitigrade; plantigrade. *See also* horse evolution.

unicellular Consisting of a single cell. The oldest known unicellular fossils are approximately 3500 million years old,

some 3000 million years older than the oldest known MULTICELLULAR fossils. Life on earth began about 4000 million years ago so over 80% of the history of life on earth belongs solely to unicellular organisms. *See* Cyanobacteria; origin of life.

uniformitarianism The theory, now generally accepted, that all geological changes have occurred by the gradual effect of processes that have been operating over a long period of time and are still going on today. *Compare* catastrophism. *See also* Hutton; Lyell.

unique mutation model *See* infinite allele model.

unit of selection 1. The entity in the biological hierarchy whose frequency is directly adjusted by natural selection. It is generally accepted that it is the replicating gene. *See* selfish gene.
2. The (higher) level in the biological hierarchy that benefits from and possesses adaptations. Accepting that selection acts on replicating genes, adaptations will benefit the biological level that shows heritability, which is usually the individual organism.

unity of type The fundamental similarity in structures seen in organisms of the same class irrespective of their habitat and lifestyle.

unrooted tree *See* phylogeny.

Upper Paleolithic tools Stone tools (mostly from the range 40 000–12 000 years ago) whose use seems to have evolved independently in Africa and Asia. The range of tools (both stone and bone) had proliferated and the techniques to make them had become more complicated. Fish hooks had appeared, along with needles. These tools are associated with NEAN-DERTHAL MAN and HOMO SAPIENS. During the early PALEOLITHIC, CRO-MAGNON MAN and the Neanderthals existed simultaneously, and about 40 000–34 000 years ago the latter declined and became extinct. *See also* Acheulian tools; Oldowan industrial complex.

Upright man   *See Homo erectus.*

Uracil

uracil   Symbol: U. A nitrogenous base that is found in RNA, replacing the thymine of DNA. It has a pyrimidine ring structure.

ureotelic   Excreting nitrogen in the form of urea. Amphibians and mammals are ureotelic. *Compare* uricotelic.

uricotelic   Excreting nitrogen in the form of uric acid. Reptiles and birds are uricotelic. *Compare* ureotelic.

Urochordata (Tunicata)   A marine subphylum of chordates (*see* Chordata) including the sessile sea squirts (e.g. *Ciona*) and pelagic forms (e.g. *Oikopleura*). The chordate characters of notochord, dorsal nerve cord, and gill slits are clearly seen in the tadpolelike free-swimming larva. In the adult the gill slits are modified for filter feeding, the notochord is absent, and the nerve cord reduced (except in *Oikopleura*, in which the notochord and nerve cord are retained). The unsegmented globular body is enclosed in a protective tunic with two openings, an inhalant mouth and an exhalant atriopore.

One theory of their origin is that tunicates and the higher chordates evolved from a common ancestor similar to the present-day free-swimming larva and the adult form is a specialization. A second theory is that the common ancestor was a sessile form and that the higher vertebrates evolved from the larval form. *Compare* Cephalochordata.

Uridine

uridine   The nucleoside formed when uracil is linked to D-ribose by a β-glycosidic bond.

V

V *See* variance.

variable number tandem repeats *See* genetic fingerprinting.

variance (V) A statistical measure of the variability in a population relating to a particular factor such as the environment or genetics. The higher the variance, the more variation there is. Genetic variance (VG) and environmental variance (VE) are calculated from the genetic effect (G) and environmental effect (E). Phenotypic variance (VP) is calculated from the phenotypic character value (P). *See* quantitative genetics.

variation The extent to which the characteristics of a species can vary. Variation can be caused by environmental and genetic factors. Environmental variation (phenotypic plasticity) results in differences in the appearance of individuals of a species because of differences in nutrition, disease, population density, etc. Genetic variation (variation in chromosome number, gene number, alleles, or DNA sequence) is generated by recombination and MUTATION. The level of genetic variation seen in polygenic characters appears to be too high to be explained by a balance between the mutation rate and the rate of STABILIZING SELECTION – the *mutation-selection balance*. It is probable that NATURAL SELECTION is acting in ways that favor variation, e.g. HETEROZYGOUS ADVANTAGE. *See* natural selection. *See also* quantitative inheritance.

variety The taxonomic group below the subspecies level. The term is often loosely used to describe breeds of livestock or various cultivated forms of agricultural and horticultural species.

varve *See* varve dating.

varve dating A method of dating events in the PLEISTOCENE based on counting and correlating seasonally deposited thin layers of sediment (*varves*) in glacial lakes. Glacial melting in spring and summer result in a sudden introduction and deposition of coarse sediment, followed by finer sediments in autumn and winter. Investigations of the annual rhythms has resulted in a detailed chronology for the Pleistocene.

vascular plants Plants containing differentiated cells forming vascular tissue, which comprises the xylem and phloem. Vascular tissue transports water and nutrients through the plant and also provides strength and support. It is characteristic of the tracheophytes (pteridophytes and spermatophytes). Vascular plants are able to achieve considerable vertical growth upwards and into the soil. They have thus been able to colonize the drier habitats that are inaccessible to the more primitive nonvascular bryophytes.

vector 1. *See* gene cloning.
2. An animal, often an insect or tick, that carries a disease-causing organism from an infected to a healthy animal or plant, causing the latter to become infected. For example, the mosquito transmits malaria and other diseases to humans.

veliger The second larval stage of aquatic mollusks (except members of the Cephalopoda), which develops from the TROCHOPHORE. During this stage, the shell and foot develop and the viscera become rotated so as to produce the asymmetry characteristic of the adult mollusk. *See* Mollusca.

ventral aorta   The blood vessel in fish and embryonic tetrapods that carries deoxygenated blood from the anterior end of the heart and divides to form the six paired aortic arches. It is equivalent to the ascending limb of the aorta in adult tetrapods.

vermiform appendix   *See* appendix.

vernalization   *See* Lysenko.

vertebral column (backbone; spinal column)   A series of bones or cartilages (vertebrae) that run along the dorsal side of the vertebrate body from the head to the tail region. The whole column provides a flexible axial support to the body and forms a protective channel (neural canal) for the spinal cord. The vertebrae become larger and stronger toward the major weight-bearing region, i.e. where the pelvic or the pectoral girdles are attached.

vertebrate   *See* craniate.

vessel   An advanced form of xylem conducting tissue composed of vertically arranged cells known as vessel elements. They are found in the ANGIOSPERMOPHYTA and the gymnosperm order GNETALES and are an advanced evolutionary feature of land plants.

vestigial character   A character that is functionless and generally reduced in size but bears some resemblance to the corresponding fully functioning organs found in related organisms. Examples include the wings of flightless birds, the limb girdles of snakes, the appendix and the ear muscles of humans, and the scale leaves of parasitic flowering plants. The presence of vestigial organs is thought to indicate that the ancestors of the organism possessed fully functioning organs, which, because of gradual changes in the environment or their lifestyle, became of less use and so did not develop fully in modern forms.

vicariance biogeography   *See* biogeography.

viroid   *See* ribozyme.

virulence   The relative pathogenicity of an organism. Virulence depends on the invasiveness and toxicity of the pathogen and may vary between strains of the same organism.

virus   An extremely small infectious agent that causes a variety of diseases in plants and animals, such as smallpox, the common cold, and tobacco mosaic disease. Viruses can only reproduce in living tissues and outside the living cell they exist as inactive particles (*virions*) consisting of a core of DNA or RNA surrounded by a protein coat (*capsid*). The virion penetrates the host membrane and liberates the viral nucleic acid into the cell. Usually, the nucleic acid is translated by the host cell ribosomes to produce enzymes necessary for the reproduction of the virus and the formation of daughter virions. The virions are released by lysis of the host cell. Other viruses remain dormant in the host cell before reproduction and lysis, their nucleic acid becoming integrated with that of the host. Some viruses are associated with the formation of tumors. As RNA is thought to be the first replicating molecule, it is possible that viruses with RNA genomes are *molecular fossils. See also* retrovirus.

viverravine   *See* Carnivora; Oligocene.

viviparity   1. (*Zoology*) A type of sexual reproduction in animals in which the embryo develops within the mother's body and derives continuous nourishment by close contact with maternal tissues, usually through a placenta. It results in the birth of live young and occurs in most mammals. *Compare* oviparity; ovoviviparity.
2. (*Botany*) The production of young plants instead of flowers, as in some grasses.
3. (*Botany*) The germination of seeds or spores that are still attached to the parent plant.

VNTR   *See* genetic fingerprinting.

volcano   A vent or fissure on the Earth's surface connected by a conduit to the Earth's interior, from which MAGMA (which becomes lava), gas, dust, and fine particles are erupted. Igneous rocks, e.g. basalt, are formed as a result of volcanic action. Hot water and steam can also escape through vents and are produced by ground water coming into contact with hot molten magma beneath the surface.

Von Baer's law   The early developmental stages of a group of related species are more similar than the later stages because ancestral characters appear earlier in development than derived characters.

vulpavine   *See* Carnivora; Oligocene.

W

Waddington, Conrad Hal (1905–75) British embryologist and geneticist. As a geneticist and a Darwinian, Waddington introduced two important concepts into the discussion of evolutionary theory. The first dealt with developmental reactions that occur in organisms exposed to natural selection and proposed that such reactions are generally canalized. In other words, they adjust to bring about one definite end result notwithstanding small changes in conditions over the course of the reaction.

The second idea was introduced in his 1953 paper *Genetic Assimilation of an Acquired Character*, in which he tried to show that the inheritance of acquired characteristics, the 'heresy' of Jean LAMARCK, could in fact be incorporated into orthodox genetics and evolutionary theory (*see* genetic assimilation). As an example Waddington quoted the calluses formed on the embryonic rump of an ostrich. If the Lamarckian explanation of the inheritance of an earlier acquired characteristic is rejected then what remains is the convenient but implausible appearance of a random mutation.

Waddington claimed to have demonstrated experimentally the process of genetic assimilation in normal fruit flies (*Drosophila*). He subjected the pupae of the flies to heat shock and noted that a small proportion developed lacking the posterior cross-vein in their wings. Careful breeding increased the proportion of such flies and eventually Waddington built up a stock of flies without cross-veins that had never been subjected to heat shock. The experiment has been criticized as dealing with nonadaptive traits. It also appears to be the case that other genetic mechanisms are available to explain the data without assuming genetic assimilation.

wahlund effect The higher proportion of homozygotes found in a divided POPULATION compared with a single population of the same size.

Wallace, Alfred Russel (1823–1913) British naturalist. Wallace received only an elementary schooling before joining an elder brother in the surveying business. In 1844 he met the entomologist Henry BATES. Wallace persuaded Bates to accompany him on a trip to the Amazon, and they joined a scientific expedition as naturalists in 1848.

Wallace published an account of his expedition in his *A Narrative of Travels on the Amazon and River Negro* (1853). In 1854 he traveled to the Malay Archipelago, where he spent eight years and collected over 125,000 specimens, a journey described in his *Malay Archipelago* (1869). In this region he noted the marked differences between the Asian and Australian faunas, the former being more advanced than the latter, and proposed a line, still referred to as WALLACE'S LINE, separating the two distinct ecological regions. He suggested that Australian animals are more primitive because the Australian continent broke away from Asia before the more advanced Asian animals evolved and thus the marsupials were not overrun and driven to extinction. This observation, together with a reconsideration of Thomas MALTHUS's essay on population, led him to propose the theory of evolution by natural selection. He wrote an essay entitled *On the Tendency of Varieties to Depart Indefinitely from the Original Type*, which he sent to DARWIN for his opinion. On receipt, Darwin realized this was a summary of his own views and the two papers were jointly presented at a meeting of the Linnaean Society in July 1858.

Wallace continued to collect evidence for this evolutionary theory, making an important study of mimicry in the swallow-tail butterfly and writing pioneering works on the geographical distribution of animals, including his *Geographical Distribution of Animals* (2 vols., 1876) and *Island Life* (1880).

In addition to his scientific and political pursuits, Wallace also participated in many of the more dubious intellectual movements of the 19th century. He supported spiritualism, phrenology, and mesmerism. His views on these matters led Wallace to disagree with Darwin on the evolution of humans. Man's spiritual essence, Wallace insisted, could not have been produced by natural selection. Darwin commented, "I hope you have not murdered our child."

Wallace's line   A hypothetical boundary in Indonesia between the islands of Bali and Lombok. It separates the AUSTRALASIAN and ORIENTAL zoogeographical regions and was drawn by A. R. WALLACE, co-founder with DARWIN of the theory of evolution.

warm-blooded   *See* homoiothermy.

warning coloration (aposematic coloration)   A conspicuous coloring or marking by which a noxious or dangerous animal can be recognized by potential attackers. Since these animals have developed their foul taste or dangerous nature to protect themselves from predation, it is important for them to warn potential predators of this. Warning coloration is common in insects, for example, the bright black-and-yellow stripes of many wasps. Venomous snakes often advertise their dangerous nature by their conspicuous markings.

Weberian ossicles   A paired chain of three or four small bones in certain fish (e.g. carps and catfishes) that connect the swim bladder with the auditory capsule. They are modified from the first four vertebrae and are comparable in function with the EAR OSSICLES in higher vertebrates in that they conduct pressure changes from the swim bladder to the inner ear.

Weismann, August Friedrich Leopold (1834–1914) German biologist. In his early work Weismann made much use of the microscope, but failing eyesight forced him to abandon microscopy for theoretical biology. His microscopic observations, especially those on the origin of the germ cells of hydrozoans, were nevertheless put to good use in the formulation of his theory of the continuity of the germ plasm, which he published in 1886 (English translation, 1893; *The Germ-Plasm: A Theory of Heredity*). Weismann had noted that germ cells can be distinguished from somatic cells early in embryonic development, and from this he visualized the protoplasm of the germ cell (germ plasm) as being passed on unchanged through the generations and therefore responsible for inheritance. Although the body might be modified by environmental effects, the germ plasm – well protected within it – could not be. This insulation of the germ plasm from environmental influences – the so-called *Weismann barrier* – is one of the fundamental tenets of modern Darwinian theory (*see* Darwinism). Weismann himself argued strongly against the Lamarckian theory of the inheritance of acquired characteristics (*see* Lamarckism). His publication *Studies in the Theory of Descent* (1882) contained a preface by Darwin.

Weismann barrier   *See* Weismann.

Weismannism   The ideas put forward by WEISMANN criticizing the theory of the inheritance of acquired bodily characteristics implicit in Lamarckism and certain aspects of Darwinism. Weismann synthesized his ideas into the 'Theory of the Continuity of the Germ Plasm', which emphasized the distinction between the somatic cells and the germ cells and stated that inheritance was effected only by the germ cells.

whales   *See* Cetacea; missing link.

whisk ferns   *See* Psilophyta.

wild type   The GENOTYPE or PHENOTYPE that occurs naturally in most members of a species.

Wilson, Allan Charles   (1934–91) New Zealand biochemist. In 1967, in collaboration with Vincent SARICH, Wilson argued that MOLECULAR CLOCKS could reveal much about the early history of humans. Against the opposition of paleontologists they claimed that the divergence between humans and the great apes began only 5 mya. Their view seems to have prevailed.

In the 1980s Wilson sought to challenge the paleontologists once more, this time on the issue of the emergence of modern humans. While anthropologists favored a date of 1 million years, Wilson's work suggested a time no later than 200 000 years ago.

He chose to work with mitochondria, the cellular organelles that convert food into energy (*see* mitochondrion). Like a cell nucleus, mitochondria also contain DNA. It encodes, however, only 37 genes as opposed to the 100 000 of nuclear DNA. Further, MITOCHONDRIAL DNA evolved rapidly and regularly and, surprisingly, it is inherited from the mother alone. It follows, Wilson pointed out, that "all human mitochondrial DNA must have had an ultimate common female ancestor." Where and when, he went on to ask, could she be found?

Wilson adopted the parsimony principle that subjects are connected in the simplest possible way. That is, the fewer differences found in mitochondrial DNA, the closer they were connected. Mitochondria from 241 individuals from all continents and races were collected and analyzed. The tree constructed had two branches, both of which led back to Africa.

What was the date of this MITOCHONDRIAL EVE? Wilson measured the ratio of mitochondrial DNA divergence between humans to the divergence between humans and chimpanzees. The ratio was found to be 1:25 and, because human and chimpanzee lineages diverged 5 mya, human maternal lineages must have separated by 1/25 of this time, namely, 200 000 years ago (*see* out of Africa theory).

Wilson's hypothesis, first presented in 1987, has provoked considerable opposition. Those who prefer a multiregional explanation of human evolution (*see* multiregional theory) have questioned most of Wilson's assumptions and have argued that until it is backed up by unequivocal fossil evidence it must remain speculative.

wings   *See* Aves; Insecta.

wobble hypothesis   The hypothesis that the base pairing of the third base of a tRNA ANTICODON is not specific. It is consistent with the degeneracy of the GENETIC CODE.

Wolffian duct   One of a pair of ducts in fish and amphibians that transports urine from the kidney to the cloaca. In the male it is a urinogenital duct, also transporting spermatozoa from the testes. In reptiles, birds, and mammals, it is functionally replaced by the ureter and persists only in the male, forming the epididymis and vas deferens. *See also* mesonephros.

World Continent   *See* zoogeography.

Wright, Sewall   (1889–1988) American statistician and geneticist. He began his researches into the population genetics of guinea pigs. His first work aimed to find the best combination of inbreeding and crossbreeding to improve stock, this having practical application in livestock breeding. From this he also developed a mathematical theory of evolution.

His name is best known in connection with the process of GENETIC DRIFT, the *Sewall Wright effect*.

X chromosome The larger of the two types of SEX CHROMOSOME in mammals and certain other animals. It is similar in appearance to the other chromosomes and carries many sex-linked genes. *See* sex determination.

xenungulates *See* amblypods.

xylem The water-conducting tissue in vascular plants. It consists of dead hollow cells (*tracheids* and *vessels*), which are the conducting elements, together with additional supporting tissue.

Y

Y chromosome The smaller of the two types of SEX CHROMOSOME in mammals and certain other animals. It is found only in the heterogametic sex. *See* sex determination.

Yucatán crater *See* Alvarez theory.

Z

Zinjanthropus boisei See *Paranthropus boisei.*

zircons Crystals of zirconium silicate that trap uranium and can be used in dating some ancient rocks, e.g. the ACASTA ROCKS.

zone fossil (indicator fossil; index fossil) A species that is characteristic of a particular sedimentary rock and restricted to it in time, for example, certain AMMONITES in the Cretaceous.

zoogeographical region *See* zoogeography.

zoogeography The study of the geographical distribution of animal species. Such studies show that the Earth can be divided into distinct *zoogeographical regions*, each having its own unique collection of animal species. For example, the continents of the Southern hemisphere – Australia, subSaharan Africa, and South America – each have a characteristic fauna not found elsewhere. Anteaters, sloths, and armadillos are native to South America; marsupial and monotreme mammals are characteristic of Australia; while Africa shows a greater diversity of fauna than any other region.

The *island continents* consist of the AUSTRALASIAN region (Australia, New Zealand, and the surrounding islands, and the NEOTROPICAL region (South America). The other regions are grouped into the *World Continent* (Europe, Asia, Africa, and North America), which have comprised a more or less continuous land mass throughout geological time. This group consists of the following four regions (that

may also be grouped with one another as *Arctogea*): NEARCTIC (most of North America), PALEARCTIC (Europe, northern Asia, and North Africa), ORIENTAL (southern Asia), and ETHIOPIAN (subSaharan Africa). *See also* phytogeography; Wallace's line.

zoology The scientific study of animals.

Zoomastigina A phylum of heterotrophic protoctists that possess one or more undulipodia (flagella) for locomotion. It includes both free-living forms (e.g. *Naegleria*) and parasites (e.g. *Trypanosoma*, which is responsible for sleeping sickness), and aerobic and anaerobic forms. In some recent classifications this phylum has been disbanded and its members dispersed to other taxa according to whether or not they possess mitochondria.

zooplankton *See* plankton.

zooxanthellae *See* dinoflagellate.

Zuckerandl, Emile (1922–) Austrian molecular evolutionary biologist. Zuckerandl has examined the hemoglobin (red blood pigment) from a number of animal species. Human hemoglobin is composed of four chains. The beta-chain consists of 146 amino acids. When compared with the beta-chain of a gorilla it differs at just one point, containing arginine where the gorilla has lysine. In contrast horse-beta differs at 26 sites and fish hemoglobin has a total lack of overlap.

Zuckerandl argued that comparison of hemoglobin chains offered a way to measure the rate at which evolution works. Thus variations between the alpha and beta hemoglobin chains of humans with those of horses, pigs, cattle, and rabbits produced a mean number of differences of 22. If the estimated time of their common ancestor is 80 million years then it can be estimated that there should be a change of one amino acid per seven million years.

Zuckerandl's approach has been adapted by other workers. Vincent SARICH in 1967 used the protein albumin to establish a MOLECULAR CLOCK and Allan WILSON has used MITOCHONDRIAL DNA.

zygomorphy   *See* bilateral symmetry.

Zygomycota (zygomycetes)   A phylum of FUNGI whose members have haploid, nonseptate hyphae (i.e. hyphae without crosswalls). Asexual reproduction is by spores produced in sporangia or by coni-dia. They are mostly saprophytic, absorbing nutrients from decaying vegetation or other organic matter. Examples are the bread molds *Rhizopus* and *Mucor*. They evolved later than the Ascomycota and Basidiomycota (*see* Fungi).

zygote   The diploid cell resulting from the fusion of two haploid GAMETES. A zygote usually undergoes cleavage immediately. *See also* embryo.

zygotene   In MEIOSIS, the stage in mid-prophase I that is characterized by the active and specific pairing (synapsis) of homologous chromosomes leading to the formation of a haploid number of bivalents.

APPENDIXES

Appendix I

The Animal Kingdom

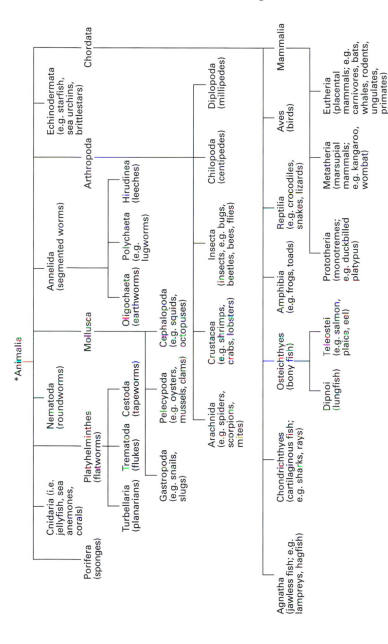

*Only major phyla and classes are shown

Appendix II

The Plant Kingdom

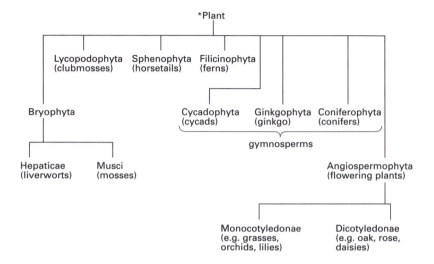

*Extinct and mostly extinct groups are excluded

Appendix III

Webpages

The following are university department websites:

University of California, Irvine, Department of Ecology and Evolutionary Biology
ecoevo.bio.uci.edu/
University of Connecticut, Department of Ecology and Evolutionary Biology
www.eeb.uconn.edu/
Harvard University, Department of Organismic and Evolutionary Biology
www.oeb.harvard.edu/
Princeton University, Department of Ecology and Evolutionary Biology
www.eeb.princeton.edu/
University of Tennessee, Department of Ecology and Evolutionary Biology
eeb.bio.utk.edu/
Yale University, Department of Ecology and Evolutionary Biology
www.eeb.yale.edu/

There are many museum sites on the Web:

American Museum of Natural History   www.amnh.org/
Harvard Museum of Natural History   www.hmnh.harvard.edu/
Smithsonian Institution National Museum of Natural History
                                            www.mnh.si.edu/
The Natural History Museum, London   www.nhm.ac.uk/
Yale Peabody Museum of Natural History   www.peabody.yale.edu/

A list of annotated evolution links can be found at:

Nearctica   www.nearctica.com/evolve/evolve.htm

Links for Palaeontology can be found at:

UK Palaeontological Association   www.palass.org/

Bibliography

Alberts, Bruce; Johnson, Alexander; Lewis, Julian; Raff, Martin; Roberts, Keith; & Walter, Peter *Molecular Biology of the Cell*. 4th ed. New York: Garland Science, 2002

Dawkins, Richard *The Selfish Gene*. 2nd ed. Oxford, U.K.: Oxford University Press, 1989

Dawkins, Richard *The Blind Watchmaker*. Harlow, U.K.: Longman, 1996

Dawkins, Richard *Climbing Mount Improbable*. Harmondsworth, U.K.: Penguin, 1997

Dixon, Dougal; Jenkins, Ian; Moody, Richard; & Zhuralev, Andrey *Cassell's Atlas of Evolution*. London, U.K.: Cassell, 2001

Gould, Steven Jay *The Panda's Thumb*. New York: W. W. Norton, 1992

Gould, Steven Jay *The Structure of Evolutionary Theory*. Cambridge, Mass.: Harvard University Press, 2002

Jones, Steve *Darwin's Ghost*. New York: Random House, 2000

Maynard Smith, John *Evolutionary Genetics*. 2nd ed. Oxford, U.K.: Oxford University Press, 1998

Maynard Smith, John *The Theory of Evolution*. 2nd ed. Cambridge, U.K.: Cambridge University Press, 2000

Mayr, Ernst *What Evolution is*. London, U.K.: Wiedenfeld & Nicholson, 2002

Ridley, Mark *Evolution*. Oxford, U.K.: Blackwell Science, 2003

Zimmer, Carl *Evolution*. London, U.K.: Arrow Books, 2003